i-Net+™ Certification Study System

i-Net+™ Certification Study System

Joseph J. Byrne

® IDG Books Worldwide, Inc
An International Data Group Company
Foster City, CA • Chicago, IL • Indianapolis, IN • Dallas, TX

IDG
BOOKS
WORLDWIDE

i-Net+™ Certification Study System

Published by
IDG Books Worldwide, Inc.
An International Data Group Company
919 E. Hillsdale Blvd., Suite 400
Foster City, CA 94404
www.idgbooks.com (IDG Books Worldwide Web site)

Library of Congress Card Number: 00-100825

ISBN: 0-7645-4655-4

Printed in the United States of America

10 9 8 7 6 5 4 3 2 1

1B/RV/QT/QQ/FC

Distributed in the United States by IDG Books Worldwide, Inc.

Distributed by CDG Books Canada Inc. for Canada; by Transworld Publishers Limited in the United Kingdom; by IDG Norge Books for Norway; by IDG Sweden Books for Sweden; by IDG Books Australia Publishing Corporation Pty. Ltd. for Australia and New Zealand; by TransQuest Publishers Pte Ltd. for Singapore, Malaysia, Thailand, Indonesia, and Hong Kong; by Gotop Information Inc. for Taiwan; by ICG Muse, Inc. for Japan; by Intersoft for South Africa; by Eyrolles for France; by International Thomson Publishing for Germany, Austria and Switzerland; by Distribuidora Cuspide for Argentina; by LR International for Brazil; by Galileo Libros for Chile; by Ediciones ZETA S.C.R. Ltda. for Peru; by WS Computer Publishing Corporation, Inc., for the Philippines; by Contemporanea de Ediciones for Venezuela; by Express Computer Distributors for the Caribbean and West Indies; by Micronesia Media Distributor, Inc. for Micronesia; by Chips Computadoras S.A. de C.V. for Mexico; by Editorial Norma de Panama S.A. for Panama; by American Bookshops for Finland.

For general information on IDG Books Worldwide's books in the U.S., please call our Consumer Customer Service department at 800-762-2974. For reseller information, including discounts and premium sales, please call our Reseller Customer Service department at 800-434-3422.

For information on where to purchase IDG Books Worldwide's books outside the U.S., please contact our International Sales department at 317-572-3337 or fax 317-572-4002.

For consumer information on foreign language translations, please contact our Customer Service department at 800-434-3422, fax 317-596-5692, or e-mail rights@idgbooks.com.

For information on licensing foreign or domestic rights, please phone +1-650-653-7098.

For sales inquiries and special prices for bulk quantities, please contact our Order Services department at 800-434-3422 or write to the address above.

For information on using IDG Books Worldwide's books in the classroom or for ordering examination copies, please contact our Educational Sales department at 800-434-2086 or fax 317-572-4005.

For press review copies, author interviews, or other publicity information, please contact our Public Relations department at 650-653-7000 or fax 650-653-7500.

For authorization to photocopy items for corporate, personal, or educational use, please contact Copyright Clearance Center, 222 Rosewood Drive, Danvers, MA 01923, or fax 978-750-4470.

ABOUT IDG BOOKS WORLDWIDE

Welcome to the world of IDG Books Worldwide.

IDG Books Worldwide, Inc., is a subsidiary of International Data Group, the world's largest publisher of computer-related information and the leading global provider of information services on information technology. IDG was founded more than 30 years ago by Patrick J. McGovern and now employs more than 9,000 people worldwide. IDG publishes more than 290 computer publications in over 75 countries. More than 90 million people read one or more IDG publications each month.

Launched in 1990, IDG Books Worldwide is today the #1 publisher of best-selling computer books in the United States. We are proud to have received eight awards from the Computer Press Association in recognition of editorial excellence and three from Computer Currents' First Annual Readers' Choice Awards. Our best-selling ...For Dummies® series has more than 50 million copies in print with translations in 31 languages. IDG Books Worldwide, through a joint venture with IDG's Hi-Tech Beijing, became the first U.S. publisher to publish a computer book in the People's Republic of China. In record time, IDG Books Worldwide has become the first choice for millions of readers around the world who want to learn how to better manage their businesses.

Our mission is simple: Every one of our books is designed to bring extra value and skill-building instructions to the reader. Our books are written by experts who understand and care about our readers. The knowledge base of our editorial staff comes from years of experience in publishing, education, and journalism — experience we use to produce books to carry us into the new millennium. In short, we care about books, so we attract the best people. We devote special attention to details such as audience, interior design, use of icons, and illustrations. And because we use an efficient process of authoring, editing, and desktop publishing our books electronically, we can spend more time ensuring superior content and less time on the technicalities of making books.

You can count on our commitment to deliver high-quality books at competitive prices on topics you want to read about. At IDG Books Worldwide, we continue in the IDG tradition of delivering quality for more than 30 years. You'll find no better book on a subject than one from IDG Books Worldwide.

John J. Kilcullen

John Kilcullen
Chairman and CEO
IDG Books Worldwide, Inc.

Eighth Annual Computer Press Awards ≥1992

Ninth Annual Computer Press Awards ≥1993

Tenth Annual Computer Press Awards ≥1994

Eleventh Annual Computer Press Awards ≥1995

IDG is the world's leading IT media, research and exposition company. Founded in 1964, IDG had 1997 revenues of $2.05 billion and has more than 9,000 employees worldwide. IDG offers the widest range of media options that reach IT buyers in 75 countries representing 95% of worldwide IT spending. IDG's diverse product and services portfolio spans six key areas including print publishing, online publishing, expositions and conferences, market research, education and training, and global marketing services. More than 90 million people read one or more of IDG's 290 magazines and newspapers, including IDG's leading global brands — Computerworld, PC World, Network World, Macworld and the Channel World family of publications. IDG Books Worldwide is one of the fastest-growing computer book publishers in the world, with more than 700 titles in 36 languages. The "...For Dummies®" series alone has more than 50 million copies in print. IDG offers online users the largest network of technology-specific Web sites around the world through IDG.net (http://www.idg.net), which comprises more than 225 targeted Web sites in 55 countries worldwide. International Data Corporation (IDC) is the world's largest provider of information technology data, analysis and consulting, with research centers in over 41 countries and more than 400 research analysts worldwide. IDG World Expo is a leading producer of more than 168 globally branded conferences and expositions in 35 countries including E3 (Electronic Entertainment Expo), Macworld Expo, ComNet, Windows World Expo, ICE (Internet Commerce Expo), Agenda, DEMO, and Spotlight. IDG's training subsidiary, ExecuTrain, is the world's largest computer training company, with more than 230 locations worldwide and 785 training courses. IDG Marketing Services helps industry-leading IT companies build international brand recognition by developing global integrated marketing programs via IDG's print, online and exposition products worldwide. Further information about the company can be found at www.idg.com.   1/26/00

CREDITS

ACQUISITIONS EDITORS
Jennifer Humphreyville-Fusilero
Jim Sumser

PROJECT EDITOR
Brian MacDonald

TECHNICAL EDITORS
David Schueller, A+, MCP
Brian Schwarz

COPY EDITORS
Eric Ritter
Julie M. Smith

BOOK DESIGNER
Kurt Krames

QUALITY CONTROL SPECIALISTS
Laura Taflinger
Chris Weisbart

GRAPHICS AND PRODUCTION SPECIALISTS
Jude Levinson
Michael Lewis
Ramses Ramirez
Victor Pérez-Varela
Dina F. Quan

ILLUSTRATORS
Shelley Norris
Mary Jo Richards

PROOFREADING AND INDEXING
York Production Services

PROJECT COORDINATORS
Linda Marousek
Joe Shines
Louigene A. Santos

ABOUT THE AUTHOR

Joseph J. Byrne lives in St. Cloud, Minnesota, with his wife, Debra; daughter, Danielle; and son, Steven. Mr. Byrne was born in Chicago in 1958 and became fascinated with computers at the time of the personal computer's genesis. In 1979, soon after starting his career as a software developer, Mr. Byrne realized the importance of the personal computer and began learning about computer networking. In 1985, he founded his first company, which provided PC-based network services and support. In 1995, he sold the business and took a position as a senior systems engineer with Marco Business Products, Inc. During his 21 years in the information technology field, Mr. Byrne has achieved many industry-respected certifications. He is an MCSE, Master CNE, Compaq ASE, and CNP. He is a member of the Institute of Electricians and Electrical Engineers (IEEE), the Institute of Networking Professionals (INP), and the Association of Internet Professionals (AIP).

To my father who taught me, by example, the true meaning of fatherhood. And to my mother, whose encouragement and unending faith help me achieve my dreams. And to my wife, Debbie, whose love and friendship have been essential to my life in more ways than imaginable.

FOREWORD

The Internet is defining the future of Information Technology. You don't have to be a business analyst to understand the impact the Internet will have on the workplace in the global economy. We have already seen the pioneers of e-commerce redefine the playing field in the market. In many organizations, charting the strategic direction for e-commerce is somebody else's job, certainly someone with a better understanding of technology than you. Well, I've got news for you. As the owner, leader, executive, or manager of the organization, it is *your* job to define the strategic direction of your company. I assure you, your competitors, suppliers, and customers are developing theirs. If you're technologically challenged or simply lack confidence, do something about it. Network certification is not just for techies anymore; it's for business leaders who want to leverage technology to thrive in the new millennium.

The *i-Net+ Certification Study System* is an excellent first step in understanding the concepts of the World Wide Web and applying them to your organization. Joe Byrne is not only "book smart" but "street smart." He has taken his 20 years of practical real-life technical experiences and presented them in this easy to understand i-Net+ certification study guide. It is often quoted "if you want to be successful, associate with successful people." Joe surrounds himself with talented technical engineers, co-workers, customers, and friends who all have influenced his passion for this book.

Don't rely on just a few technical persons within your organization to shape the future of your company. Start by committing to a structured approach to understanding the Internet opportunity. Don't delegate it — get certified yourself. Joe has helped many companies define their Internet strategies. Let him help you by applying *i-Net+ Certification Study System* to your personal development plan as you go forward into the future of Information Technology.

Jeff Gau
Director, Marco Business Products

PREFACE

The *i-Net+ Certification Study System* is designed to teach critical Internet concepts to everyone interested in starting or enhancing a career that requires Internet skills. People new to the information technology field will gain valuable insights into the workings and function of the Internet while experienced Network professionals will gain the additional Internet experience needed to take their career to the next level. The demand for Internet-related professionals is at an all-time high in the business world and is projected to at least double in the next decade. Possessing the i-Net+ Certification is an industry-recognized sign that you have mastered the basic skills many companies need to take them into the future.

The i-Net+ Certification Study System takes the reader through the entire i-Net+ objectives blueprint with exceptional clarity, encompassing not only the core requirements, but also providing real-world examples to ensure the reader has complete mastery of the material. The author is a member of the i-Net+ objectives development team and presents material entirely relevant to the subject matter. The i-Net+ Certification program has been well received by the industry and will surely set the benchmark for entry-level Internet technicians moving into all areas of the field.

HOW THIS BOOK IS ORGANIZED

This book is organized in five parts, followed by a Resources section that contains appendixes, supplemental materials, and a CD-ROM. Within these major parts, each chapter begins with an overview of the topics that will be covered in that chapter. Then, pertinent information on each topic is presented. An Exam Preparation Summary, summarizing the preparation strategies for the exam, and a Key Point Summary, summarizing the chapter highlights and reviewing important material, follow. At the end of each chapter are Instant Assessment questions to make sure you understand and can apply what you've read.

Throughout many of the chapters, I present some hands-on exercises for you to work through that are designed to provide practical experience with the concepts in the exam objectives. These exercises cover software installation, configuration, and Web document creation. In order to get the most benefits from these exercises you will need access to a computer and an Internet connection. Please refer to the following "Hardware and Software You'll Need" section in the Preface, or in Appendix D if you're not sure you have the necessary equipment for these exercises.

Part I: Internet Basics

Part I lays the foundation for the rest of the book by explaining key concepts and components of the Internet and Internet careers. This section begins by explaining what things the Internet can be used for, progresses on to how the Internet is constructed, and finishes up by describing the many methods used to connect to the Internet.

Part II: Internet Clients

In Part II we'll see that each of the primary Internet services, e-mail, Web browsing, etc, requires its own special software and explain how to configure these pieces to connect both stand-alone and network computers to the Internet. Also in part II we'll look at potential problems related to the client software and how to handle these problems when they occur.

Part III: Web Site Development

In Part III we'll turn our attention to the World Wide Web. The section begins with the concepts of Web page development and the components used to make a Web site useful and attractive. After the basics are covered, we'll look at more advanced technologies used to make Web sites interactive including an overview of database integration and basic programming techniques. This section will conclude with a discussion of the requirements necessary before a Web site goes "live."

Part IV: Networking, Infrastructure, and Security

Part IV covers the hardware used to provide the platform for Internet connectivity in a business environment. Specifically this section deals with necessary network and server components and how these pieces are used to provide Internet connectivity and security to users with the enterprise. Along with the tremendous resources the Internet brings, there are also many security concerns that will be addressed in Part IV, as well as a number of troubleshooting techniques and tools used to assist in problem resolution.

Part V: Understanding the Business Side of the Internet

Part V will conclude our study with a close look at how the Internet is used by businesses to provide services and products to other businesses and to consumers. We'll look at the new paradigms of conducting business over the Internet, sometimes called *e-commerce* or *e-business*. This new business model not only provides tremendous advantages over traditional methods, but brings with it new problems such as delivery, supply, and government regulations that many companies may never have had to deal with before. We'll also look at copyright issues in this section and see how to protect the work done to create our global stores. We end the section, and the book, with a look into the future of the Internet and examine some of the changes planned to make this communication tool as commonplace around the world as the telephone is today.

Resources

The appendixes in the back of the book contain a wealth of information. In addition to a detailed glossary and thorough index, you'll find exam preparation tips, answers to chapter Instant Assessment questions and labs, and a description of the CD-ROM contents. Appendix A contains the exam objectives for the i-Net+ exam, and a cross-reference chart that maps the Exam Objectives to the book contents for study purposes.

CD-ROM

The accompanying CD-ROM contains the following materials: an electronic version of this book in Adobe Acrobat (PDF) format, Adobe Acrobat Reader, Microsoft Internet Explorer 5.0, Netscape Communicator 4.7, FTP-ServU (FTP server), MDaemon (e-mail server), Wingate (Internet Proxy/Firewall), WebExpress

(WYSIWYG HTML editor), HTMLNotes (HTML editor), JWeb and Xitami (Web servers), SimpleDNS (DNS server), and popular copyright forms in Adobe Acrobat format. In addition, to help ensure that you are ready for the exam, a copy of BeachFront Quizzer's i-Net+ test prep practice test is included.

How to Use This Book

This book can be used either by individuals working independently or by groups in a formal classroom setting. For best results I recommend the following plan of attack as you use this book: First, read the chapter and the Exam Preparation Summary at the end. Use the summary to test your mastery of the key concepts for that chapter. If you're unclear about any point in the summary, go back and reread those section(s). Then do *all* of the Instant Assessment questions at the end of the chapter.

Don't be afraid to go beyond the confines of the examples and hands-on exercises presented. Remember, the important thing is to master the tasks that will be tested on the exam. Your testing experience will be much more pleasant if you have the confidence that comes from working with the Internet and seeing first hand how all the various services work. If at all possible, I highly recommend building an Internet server with the programs on the CD, registering your own domain name, and connecting this server to the Internet. You will be amazed at how much you can learn from making mistakes, and how rewarding it is to see your own creation participating in the global community of the Internet.

The flow of the book was carefully designed to take you from simple concepts in the beginning to advanced concepts and techniques at the end. Your study time will be much less complicated if you work through each of the chapters in sequential order.

After you've completed your study and reviewed the questions in the book, use the BeachFront Quizzer product on the CD-ROM to take the practice tests. This will help familiarize you with the type of exam questions you'll face when you take the real exams. They will also help you identify weak areas that need more work.

The important thing to remember about practice tests is that they *resemble* the exam, but they are not exact copies of it. I have found from my own studies that it is more important to know *why* the answer is correct than to know the answer itself, especially on practice exams. That means that if you can answer all the questions in the Instant Assessment and the practice exams without even a single guess, you are probably ready to take the test.

If you are the least bit unsure about an answer, go back and study the related sections. Appendix A contains a table that maps the objectives on the exam to the chapters and sections in this book. Use that table to correlate the objectives listed in the practice exam with the appropriate part of the book, then read the entire section before you try to take the practice exam again.

Prerequisites

The i-Net+ exam is geared to people with little or no previous experience with the Internet, although previous experience with computers and computer networking is important to get the most out of this book.

Determining What You Should Study

Your individual certification goals ultimately determine which parts of this book you should study. Whether you want to pass the i-Net+ exam or you just want to develop a comprehensive working knowledge of the Internet, I recommend you study, in sequential order, the entire book.

Minimum System Computer Requirements for the Exercises and Examples

- Intel-based computer with Pentium processor, 32 MB RAM, 500MB or greater available hard disk space
- CD-ROM drive
- Mouse
- VGA monitor and graphics card
- Network adapter and cabling for some examples

Software Requirements

- Microsoft Windows 95/98 or NT (released version, not beta)
- The software included on the CD-ROM

ICONS USED IN THIS BOOK

Several different icons used throughout this book draw your attention to matters that deserve a closer look:

 **This icon points you to another place in this book (or to another resource) for more coverage on a given topic. It may point you back to a previous chapter where important material has already been covered, or it may point you ahead to let you know that a concept will be covered in more detail later.**

 Be careful here! This icon points out information that can save you a lot of grief. It's often easier to prevent tragedy than to fix it afterwards.

 This icon identifies important advice for those studying to pass the i-Net+ exam.

 This icon points out an interesting or helpful fact, or some other comment that deserves emphasis.

 Here's a little piece of friendly advice, or a shortcut, or a bit of personal experience that might be of use to you.

That should be enough to get you started. With a lot of study, some adventurous exploration of the Internet, and some prematurely gray hairs, you should be ready for the exam. Good luck on your way to becoming an i-Net+ professional!

ACKNOWLEDGMENTS

Putting together a book is a huge undertaking that requires many individuals, working many long and hard hours. Several very important people were essential to the completion of this book. I'd like to take a minute and recognize some of these people personally for their help.

I own a deep level of gratitude to Dave Schueller for his diligence and dedication as my technical editor to ensure the material is presented clearly and accurately. Dave added many fine insights and suggestions that greatly increased the value of the final product.

I also wish to recognize the many fine and talented co-workers at Marco who contribute to my knowledge and success on a daily basis. Special thanks to Wayne Gamradt, Terri Gill, Mike Welling, Dick Deal-Hanson, and Steve Knutson for consistently demonstrating the real meaning of professionalism and teamwork.

The IDG Books Worldwide team has been super to work with, especially acquisitions editors Jim Sumser and Jennifer Humphreyville-Fusilero, development editor Brian MacDonald, copy editors Julie M. Smith and Eric Ritter, and the graphics and production teams. I thank you for the countless hours spent reviewing chapters and helping me through the publishing process. All of these people helped make the final product a well-polished one.

Contents at a Glance

CONTENTS

Internet Basics

I n Part I, you'll look at the basic concepts that form the building blocks of the Internet. I'll begin with a short history of this technology and a look at some of the career opportunities popular today. In subsequent chapters you'll look at the various options available and requirements necessary to connect computers to the Internet, as well as the services that are available once you're connected. You'll also cover the basic concepts of Internet domain names, protocol standards, and finish up with an introduction to the World Wide Web.

i-NET+™

An Introduction to the Internet

About Chapter 1

What's your address? Just a few years ago, the logical answer would have included a street name and number, and possibly a city name or other location to uniquely identify where you physically lived. Today, however, that may not be the answer to the question being asked. It wasn't long ago that terms like *web* referred to things spiders built, *Archie* and *Veronica* were mere cartoon characters, and the word *gopher* described nothing more than a small animal whose entire existence seemed to revolve around digging millions of holes in your yard. The times have changed, however, and all of these terms have different meanings in the Internet world.

In this chapter, we'll take a look at the very basic concepts of the Internet as a communications tool. We'll make some analogies to other well-known technologies to help us understand how the Internet works, and what types of functions it provides. The primary goal of this chapter is to take a brief tour of the Internet and to introduce the building blocks that form the foundation of this sometimes-complex technology. I'll point out several components that are commonly used on the Internet and outline where in the book we'll go to see more details. It is not necessary for you to put all of these basic pieces together right away. Rather, I want you to be able to visualize and imagine what the Internet can do for you.

The Internet is changing the world—the way we gather information, exchange ideas, and find out what's new in our neighborhoods or around the world. The Internet is having a huge impact on all of these things and more, even if we're not directly aware of it. Your doctor might use the Internet to collaborate with specialists around the world on matters vital to your health. Your local weather report was probably purchased though a service on the Internet that provides constant weather patterns and predictions to meteorologists worldwide. Journalists are reporting on stories around the world that happened just moments before, all from sources on the Internet. You or your children may have already used the Internet to do research for school or work. These uses are becoming commonplace around the globe. So let your imagination go, and let's get started!

WHAT IS THE INTERNET, AND WHERE DID IT COME FROM?

The bottom line is quite simple: The Internet is a communications tool. Under all of the hype and acronyms, its primary purpose is to facilitate the sharing of information between two or more people. Keep this in mind as we go forward: the real goal of the Internet is to provide new ways to communicate.

Throughout the ages, mankind has searched for and developed faster and easier methods of communicating over longer and longer distances. In the 1800s, when people started moving into the Western territories of the United States, the Pony Express was created to hand deliver letters and packages over great distances. People longed for a faster way to send simple messages that did not necessarily require a printed page, so the telegraph system was expanded. This communication tool used an electromagnetic system to tap out Morse code across copper lines connecting different parts of the country. After the telegraph, the telephone became the standard method of long distance "real-time" communication. The basic telephone technology has not really changed all that much, although advances in its application have created even faster communication tools. In the 1970s and 1980s, the fax machine became a near necessity for most businesses. For the first time in history, paper-based messages could be transmitted between people in seconds. In the 1990s the fax machine has become standard equipment for both commercial and personal paper communications.

All of these technologies dramatically changed the way people lived and communicated. Just as the telegraph, telephone, and fax systems simplified and expedited communications, so does the Internet. As a new century begins, the Internet is becoming the next major leap in personal communications. Interestingly enough, Internet jargon adopts as metaphors many terms familiar from everyday life. As we'll see shortly, electronic mail, or *e-mail* works, sounds, and operates much like our standard postal systems. *Chat rooms* are places on the Internet where people gather to discuss topics of interest, much like you might do at a dinner party. The health of your computer equipment can be compromised by *viruses,* electronic illnesses very analogous to human viruses.

In simple terms, the Internet is nothing more than the collection of computers located all around the globe connected to one another for the purpose of sharing information. Recent estimates show that one in every three people living in a developed country has a personal computer that is connected to the Internet. Of the two-thirds who do not have their own Internet connection, one-third still use the Internet either at work or on a public access computer, such as might be found at a local library. Within the next decade, Internet-connected devices will likely be as common as the telephone, television, and radio. Most middle-class families will have more than one device to connect to the Internet with, and most people will have additional access from work or school. The Internet has already reached down to very young school-age children who will never look upon the Internet as a new technology, but as a tool that is as indispensable as any communication device ever known, much like many who grew up with the telephone.

To understand how the Internet is connected, let's compare it to the modern telephone system that we all use daily. The handset that you use to communicate with others is connected in much the same way that computers are connected on the Internet. Most telephones are connected globally through a series of wires centralized in buildings that control the flow of the voice signals. Sometimes there is no easy place to run wires, or the cost of running wire is prohibitive. In these situations satellites and other radio-transmitted signals fill the gap. The Internet is connected together in much the same way. A primary group of large computers and other devices centrally located help to direct the flow of communications. We'll learn about this infrastructure in greater detail in Chapter 2.

In the computer world, two or more devices connected together for the purpose of communications are called a *network*. Since the telephone fits this definition, we call this a telephone network, or *voice network*. When computers are placed at the end of the connections, we call it a computer network, or *data network*. Normally when computers are connected within a single building, or in very close proximity, the network is named local, or *LAN*, for Local Area Network. When the computers are located farther away, whether between buildings, across oceans, or anywhere in between, we call it a Wide Area Network, or *WAN*. Figure 1-1 shows these relationships. Since the Internet is composed of connected computers worldwide, it is considered a WAN. However, the Internet is a Wide Area Network with a number of unique characteristics.

Perhaps the defining characteristic of the Internet is that it is not "owned" by any one person or group. Anyone who wants to access it can, for free. (We'll look at the catch to this in just a minute.) Most networks, local or wide area, are owned, operated, and maintained by a private company, an educational institution, a government, or perhaps an individual. The Internet, however, does not have a central ownership. Anyone who has the right equipment and a little time to invest can become part of the Internet. Another unique aspect of the Internet is that it is not tied to a specific type of computer. You can connect to the Internet from an IBM compatible personal computer (a PC), an Apple Macintosh, a large mainframe computer, a small hand-held computer, or even your television set! Very soon, affordable Internet-specific devices will become commonplace. These devices might take the form of wristwatches, cellular telephones, or other devices not even thought of today. At the heart of this equipment will be a tiny computer. However, it will not likely resemble what we think of as a computer today. Throughout this book, I'll give you glimpses of what future Internet components are likely. However, since the Internet seems to be redeveloping itself every few months, nobody knows for certain what products and services will be offered next.

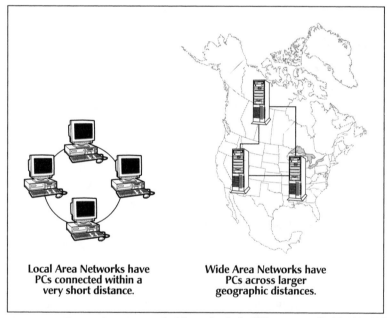

Local Area Networks have
PCs connected within a
very short distance.

Wide Area Networks have
PCs across larger
geographic distances.

FIGURE 1-1 Computers connected in a single building are called LANs. When the connections cross long distances, they're called WANs.

Although there are some prerequisites and standards that must be followed, if you have a computer or any Internet device, you can be part of the Net. The "catch" to connecting to the Internet, which I mentioned earlier, is this: Although there is no central authority who charges for access to the Internet, almost everyone who connects to the Internet does so through an *Internet Service Provider*, or ISP, which usually charges for its services. Many European citizens get free Internet access and other governments are looking into similar policies, but private ISPs provide the bulk of all Internet connections, especially in North America. Typically, people connect to the Internet using their existing telephone lines, and pay a monthly fee that ranges from US$14.95 to US$25.95. Prices vary, however, depending on the speed of the connection and what optional services are added on. Although the Internet has been around for over three decades, this network is still very young, and new methods for accessing it are created almost daily. By the end of the 1990s, the bulk of all connections are *analog dial-up*. This simply means that most people use inexpensive devices called *modems* to connect their computers to an ISP over a regular telephone line. However, faster *digital* connections are being developed at such a fast rate that many people will soon be able to afford to connect to the Internet at speeds hundreds of times faster than the analog method. A digital connection means that the data does not need to be converted to voice-quality signals to be sent across a standard telephone line. The communication takes place directly between computers, which is much faster. In addition, many digital connections are *always on*. This technology does not require you to dial into another computer. Rather, your Internet connection is always instantly available. Figure 1-2 shows the difference between dial-up connections and digital connections.

Using Internet Technology

Let's take a look at how an average person might use the Internet. Suppose I have some free time, and I'd like to hear what's been going on in your life lately. I could pick up the telephone and call you, but we live 2,000 miles apart and in different time zones. Instead, I'll go to my computer and type in your Internet address. Within seconds, I'm able to read all about the great vacation you just took. You've written all about the places you've been, the sights you've seen, and the people you've met. In addition to your stories you've added some great photos and even a few short video clips. One of your sunset photos is absolutely breathtaking. Since I have a collection of sunset photos, I'd like to add a copy of your picture to my collection. With a few simple clicks of the mouse, my computer sends a request to your computer to send me a copy of the desired photograph. Being an amateur photographer myself, I'm really interested in what camera equipment you used, and I'd love to know all of the technical details of how the photo was taken. Rather than writing you a conventional letter and possibly waiting weeks for a reply, I simply call up my *e-mail* program and zip off a quick note to ask you for this information. Within seconds my electronic letter is waiting for you in your Internet mailbox.

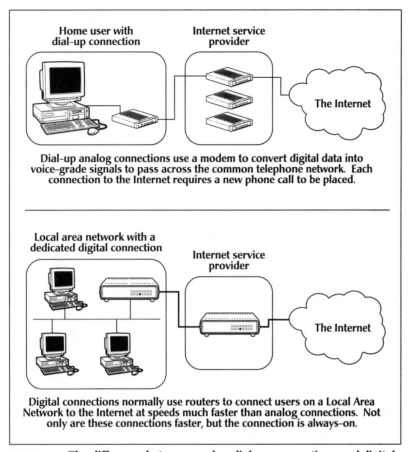

FIGURE 1-2 The difference between analog dial-up connections and digital connections

This scenario utilized three of the primary Internet services: Web browsing, file transfer, and e-mail. Let's take a brief look at these to introduce us to some of the more popular Internet uses.

Web Browsing

A primary Internet service for displaying and sharing information is the World Wide Web, or *Web* for short. Many people mistakenly refer to the World Wide Web as the Internet, when in fact it is only one of many Internet services. The Web gets its name from the concept of a spider web. If you draw a map of the world with all the wires that connect together all of the computers on the Internet, the picture would resemble that of a large spider web. You have probably seen an advertisement that directs you to a Web page. The address often begins with www, which stands for the World Wide Web. In Chapter 2, we'll look at real web addresses and you'll see how this nomenclature fits into the larger picture.

The Web allows people to share information quickly and easily. The Web, and most Internet services, is based around a computer concept called *client/server.* One computer acts as a *server* to provide information, and another computer, the *client,* requests information from the server. The client computer uses a computer program called a *browser* to retrieve and display the information provided by the server. There are many Web-browsing programs available, but by far, the two most popular are Microsoft Internet Explorer and Netscape Communicator. We'll examine the use and features of browser programs in Chapter 2.

To provide information on the Web, you first need a computer to act as a Web server. There are lots of Web server software packages available that run on any number of different computer platforms. Some of the most popular are Microsoft's Internet Information Server (IIS), Netscape's FastTrack server, and the Apache server. We'll look at these servers in more detail in Chapter 4. Once the server is operational, it must be connected to the Internet. So people can reach the Web pages whenever they want to, the Internet connection must be available all the time. Most people who connect to the Internet from their homes use a dial-up system, where their computer software uses a standard telephone line to call into the Internet. When they no longer need access, the telephone call, and their access, is closed. This type of connection is fine for the casual user, but is not well suited for server-based connections. We'll discuss Internet servers and connection options in greater detail in Chapters 4 and 5.

With the server connected to the Internet, the next step is to create the actual *Web site.* A Web site is a collection of one or more pages of text and/or pictures that is accessible across the Internet. A *Web page* is very similar to a printed page you'd find in a book. The length varies depending on the author's needs, and it may contain just text, just pictures, or a combination of both. The page might be simple black and white, or it may contain thousands of colors. Animation is popular, so it's not uncommon to also find moving pictures on many Web pages. Music is another object that can be shared via a Web page. Imagination is about the only limiting factor when it comes to this medium. In Chapter 6 we'll discuss the elements that make up Web pages, including some of the more technical programming aspects. Although many Web sites use special programming techniques to make their content more interesting, the underlying component of a Web page is plain and simple text, much like this printed page.

The File Transfer Protocol

The second service used in our scenario was the downloading of a picture from a Web page. The term *download* simply describes the process of copying data from a remote computer to a local one. The data can be a picture on a page, as we just discussed, or it might be a computer program that you want to try for a while before deciding to purchase. It can also be a complete music CD. Just about anything that can be displayed on a Web page, or packaged into a computer file can be made available for download. The principle method of transferring files between computers across the Internet is called *File Transfer Protocol*, or FTP. There are servers on the Internet that exist solely to send files to requesting computers. These servers are aptly named FTP servers. Like the Web, FTP services are based on the client/server model. A client computer requests a file and a server computer provides it, as illustrated in Figure 1-3. To make this process easier for people new to the Internet, modern Web browsers incorporate FTP functions right into the Web-browsing program. The Web page contains an area that can be clicked to initiate an FTP process. The end user (or client) does not need to know anything about FTP or have a separate FTP program to download useful information via this built-in function.

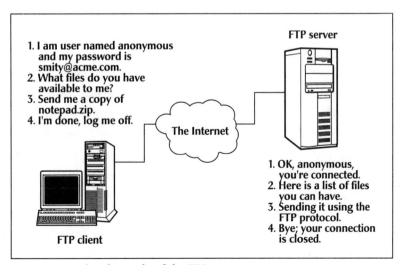

FIGURE 1-3 A visual sample of the FTP process

Electronic Mail

The third item we looked at was e-mail. Simply stated, electronic mail, or e-mail, is a computerized version of the common postal system. You compose a letter on your computer, then send it to a particular person, or to groups of people. Rather than placing the letter in an envelope, stamping it, and dropping it into a local mailbox, the process is carried out electronically on your computer over the Internet. Although standard postal mail may take days to reach its destination, electronic mail can be transmitted and received in seconds - anywhere around the world. Although you can't send packages electronically (at least not so far), you can send just about anything your computer can create and store. For example, if you've taken a great set of vacation pictures, you can have them developed onto a CD that is readable by your computer. You can then create an e-mail message and *attach* the photos to it. When your message is received, the person on the other end will also get a copy of the pictures attached to the message. Attachments can be picture files, document files, even music files. It really doesn't matter.

You probably have at least one telephone number that can be dialed from anywhere around the world. This number is yours and yours alone. Just like your telephone number uniquely identifies you (or the place you receive telephone calls), an e-mail address identifies you. More precisely, it identifies your mailbox on the server that holds your incoming electronic mail. These electronic mailboxes and your personal e-mail address are normally provided by your ISP. The e-mail process is similar in concept to the standard postal system. Once you have created the electronic message, you indicate whom you are sending it to, and what your return address is. Both of these are called *e-mail addresses*. The post office (another server on the Internet) sends the message through a series of additional servers until it reaches the server that specifically knows the person you are sending the message to. From there, the message is placed into his or her personal mailbox, where it awaits retrieval by an e-mail program. You receive e-mail from others in the same way. Once you download your messages from your e-mail server you can reply to the sender, file the message away for future reference, delete it, print it, or do whatever you feel like doing with the information. The same options exist if there is an attachment to the message.

It is possible, common in fact, for people to have more than one e-mail address. Many people have business addresses and separate personal addresses. Some people even have multiple business addresses or multiple personal addresses. There are even services that exist simply to provide easy-to-remember e-mail addresses. For example, your e-mail address might be something like `vtimperley@mail.acmecorp.west.com`. An e-mail alias service might provide you with an easier to remember address such as `vtimperley@usmail.net`. In this case, all electronic messages sent to `vtimperley@usmail.net` are automatically forwarded to the mailbox at `vtimperley@mail.acmecorp.west.net`. This makes it easier for people to remember and use your e-mail address. In addition, if your primary mailbox at acmecorp west should ever change, you only need to have the company which is using the alias change the e-mail address they forward your e-mail to. Nobody else ever has to change address books, or even know that your primary mailbox has moved.

THE HISTORY OF THE INTERNET

Before we can really understand the Internet, it is helpful to know some of its history. Although the i-Net+ exam will not test you on Internet history, it is worth spending a few minutes learning.

concept link

If you're interested in learning the real facts of the Internet's history, I highly recommend that you read the book *Where Wizards Stay Up Late: the Origins of the Internet*, by Katie Haffner. This book was written by and about the people who first envisioned the Internet and how they made those visions a reality.

There is a common, yet mistaken, belief that the United States military began the Internet. This folklore story describes a military strategy to develop an intricate network of communication lines so that no single failure would cut off vital communications. Since the Internet could indeed attain this communications goal, the United States military did support and help fund some of the preliminary Internet research. However, the real purpose behind the Internet was to develop a method for scientists and university students to share information regardless of the distance between them or the kinds of computers being used. Back in the 1950s and 1960s, when all of these ideas were being formulated, there were no standards for computer communications. Computers manufactured by different companies, even different computers manufactured by the same company, did not necessarily "talk" to each other. If information was needed on computer A that already existed on computer B, that information more than likely would have to be re-entered into computer A. This was not only time consuming, but was prone to errors and greatly hindered the sharing of educational and scientific information.

In 1958, shortly after the Russians launched the very first satellite, President Eisenhower established the Advanced Research Projects Agency (ARPA) for the purpose of identifying scientific advances that might be used within the Government structure. With the world's fascination with the new explorations in space this agency was granted a large (in its time) budget of US$13 billion for various research and development projects. The core members of ARPA were not government officials, but managers, scientists, and researchers from the business community. Roy Johnson became the first director of ARPA, recruited for this position from General Electric. The largest body of support for ARPA came from the scientific community in the nation's universities. With these scientists' support, the agency began sponsoring many new research and development projects. Almost from the very beginning, it was clear that the network of universities was greatly hindered because it lacked efficient methods of sharing research information quickly and easily. To overcome this situation, ARPA provided funding for a handful of universities to develop a means to interconnect their computer systems. Since the Advanced Research Projects Agency funded the original investment for this development, the "network" took on the name *ARPANET*. The ARPANET would eventually become today's Internet.

A LOOK AT INTERNET STANDARDS

The first step toward interconnectivity was to establish a common "language" that all computers could understand. These standards define a set of rules known as *protocols*. Hardware manufacturers and programmers agreed to adhere to the rules defined by a particular protocol so data communications could take place between different computers.

The early Internet developers adopted and refined the *Transmission Control Protocol / Internet Protocol*, or TCP/IP, for use across the Internet. TCP/IP provides the common framework for transmitting data between any two computers, regardless of where they are located. In Chapter 4 we will take a detailed look at the TCP/IP protocol suite, as it is a cornerstone of Internet communications.

Once the method of data transmission was agreed upon, other protocols had to be established so that all computer types accessing the network could use the information. As we discussed earlier, Web pages share a common protocol, or set of rules, so that any browser run on any type of computer can request and display the information on the Web site. The protocol chosen for this service is called *Hypertext Markup Language*, or HTML. We will get into the details of this protocol in Chapter 6.

We've already discussed FTP, which is the protocol for transferring files between two computers. E-mail services use a number of different protocols depending on where in the process the messages are being handled. When one server is sending the e-mail to another server (server to server), a protocol such as the *Simple Mail Transport Protocol*, or SMTP, is used. Once the final server has identified the recipient as existing within its area of service, it places the message in a personal mailbox. When an e-mail client program is fired up to retrieve that mail, it typically uses the *Post Office Protocol 3*, or POP3 protocol.

None of these protocols are stagnant. In other words, just because the "rules" have been established doesn't mean that they don't change or aren't improved. In fact, quite the opposite is true. Many protocols are revised and updated rather frequently, if for no other reason than to accommodate the incredible explosion in Internet use. So if any one person or organization doesn't own the Internet, how on earth can standards be adopted? That is a very good question, and the methods used throughout the Internet community may be an excellent model for any large organization. Basically, a number of committees have been formed to "oversee" the process of Internet standards. Since there is no governing body, anyone can make suggestions to create or modify a standard. These suggestions are called *Request for Comments*, or RFCs. When someone has an idea that they feel would make the Internet run more smoothly, or perhaps has developed a new service and want the Internet community to accept it, they submit an RFC to a volunteer committee known as the *Internet Engineering Task Force*, or IETF. (You can visit their Web page at `www.ietf.org`.) All RFCs submitted to the IETF are made available for review by anyone interested. Each RFC is reviewed by a technical expert, a task force, or the RFC editor and is then assigned a classification, or state. There are five states of RFCs as outlined in Table 1-1.

TABLE 1-1 RFC CLASSIFICATION STATES	
CLASSIFICATION STATE	*DESCRIPTION OF THE CLASSIFICATION STATE*
Required	These are the agreed upon standards referring to items that *must* be implemented on all TCP/IP based hosts.
Recommended	Implementation of specifications in this classification is recommended, but not required.
Elective	Implementation of these policies is optional. Most items in this class are applications that have been agreed upon, but never became widely used.
Limited use	Items not intended for general use. May be proprietary.
Not recommended	Concepts that are not recommended for implementation in any form.

It is easy to see that cooperation must exist for the Internet to work. Every vendor who manufactures an Internet component must abide by these standards or communication simply won't be possible. This cooperation must exist between the hardware manufacturers that make the computers and other devices that move the data across the cables, the software developers that write the programs that access and serve the data, and all other people in between. When you look at the whole picture, the Internet is really an amazing piece of technology.

WHAT ARE SOME PRACTICAL USES OF THE INTERNET?

As we discussed earlier, the Internet was originally developed as a means for scientists and university students to share information electronically. This purpose is still a large part of the Internet, but many businesses and entrepreneurs saw the enormous potential to commercialize this new medium. You are probably already aware of this commercialization simply from seeing the www.*something*.com listed in so many advertisements.

These entrepreneurs understood that the Internet offers access to millions of potential customers. Not only is there a huge audience at your fingertips, but reaching them with creative marketing techniques is fast and very inexpensive.

For example, consider the possible cost of a standard direct mailing campaign by breaking out the minimum expenses listed below.

1. Designing the sales brochure or document

2. Printing the brochure in multiple colors

3. Obtaining a mailing list large enough to provide positive results on a 10% return

4. Postage- and mailing-related costs

5. Labor required to process the returns for additional information or for purchasing the product or service

The expense to this advertising method is considerable, possibly exceeding $10,000 for a single three-color brochure mailed to a mere 15,000 households or businesses. Over the Internet, this same process could be accomplished for no more than a few hundred dollars, perhaps much less! The brochure can be created by any number of off-the-shelf graphic programs — in brilliant multicolored fashion. And, a million e-mail addresses can cost as little as $50; there are *zero* postage costs, and the ordering and information-gathering can be automated via a Web page! So using the Internet for mass marketing is not only cheaper, but allows you to use far better eye-catching advertisements and reach millions rather than thousands of potential customers. If you own a business, regardless of what product or service you provide, the Internet surely offers you an excellent method of marketing your wares.

There are hundreds of non-business reasons for the Internet as well. Just about any type information you may need is easily and quickly available. The following list is just a small sample of items you can locate on the Net.

- Find out what movies are playing at your local theater
- Check the nightly TV listings
- Find the current news, weather, and sports
- Play games by yourself, or against many different opponents around the world
- Research medical information
- Plan a trip, get driving directions, or purchase airline tickets
- Download a selection from a new music CD to see if you want to purchase it
- Take a class on just about any subject you can think of

- Get a complete college degree

- Download hundreds of software programs to evaluate before purchasing

- Research and build your family tree

- Locate an old friend, and send him or her e-mail

- Do your banking or track financial investments

I could continue this list ad infinitum, but I think you get the point. There are so many things available on the Internet, just about anyone can use it to improve their quality of life. Of course, there are many areas of the Internet that are not suitable for everyone. Since there is no regulating body for this technology, many people use it for "services" you probably don't want children to see.

INTERNET-RELATED CAREERS

It is logical to assume that people with skills related to the Internet will be in high demand. This assumption is not only accurate but is almost an understatement. The phenomenon known as the Internet has happened so quickly, and has already become such an important part of everyday life, that nearly every business sector needs people with skills related to Internet activity. I believe it would be a safe bet to say that you are reading this book for precisely that reason. You already know, or are at least aware, that careers for Internet professionals abound. It is for this very reason that CompTIA has developed the i-Net+ Certification program. This certificate program will provide you, the Internet professional, a measuring stick that will show employers and customers that you have mastered the baseline skills required to live and work in an Internet-connected world.

Where Does i-Net+ Certification Fit In?

CompTIA and IT industry leaders researched and developed a vendor-neutral, entry-level Internet certification program that tests baseline technical knowledge of Internet, intranet, and extranet topics, independent of specific Internet-related career roles. If you have no experience with these topics, this book and the i-Net+ certification exam will give you provable job skills. If you're a networking pro with little or no Internet expertise, this program is for you too! The objectives examined with i-Net+ include Internet basics, Internet clients, development, networking, security, and business concepts. The exam is designed to test Internet technicians who are hands-on specialists responsible for implementing and maintaining the infrastructure and services and developing related applications. i-Net+ certification is a natural fit for any individual interested in demonstrating baseline technical knowledge that will enable them to pursue or enhance a variety of Internet-related careers. The exam covers a broad range of technical Internet skills that are not tied to any particular product.

Although this book is designed to give you the information you need to pass the i-Net+ certification exam, my goal is also to provide you with a deeper understanding of how the Internet operates, and what specific skills you must master to give yourself the competitive edge. Whether you're a novice computer user or a seasoned professional, the Internet has leveled the playing field in many respects. There are literally thousands of new businesses that have capitalized on the Internet's unique ability to bring products to consumers. Some have even grabbed large market shares away from traditional big businesses. It has also created new opportunities that require skill sets and knowledge that computer veterans may never have developed. Therefore, my goal in writing this book is not simply to see you pass the i-Net+ certification exam, but also to give you a resource of real-world information that will help you find your perfect niche in this exciting new field.

In reality, the Internet story is just being written. There are so many aspects to the Internet that new job descriptions are being created every day. However, there will always be some basic skills that people will need to possess to be employed in this field. Like the Information Technology field as a whole, there are many different avenues that you might wish to pursue. The i-Net+ exam focuses mainly on the hardware/networking and Web-design segments, but these are just two of the largest career possibilities you might choose. Hardware folks deal with the physical products that make computers and computer networks operate, while the software people spend most of their time creating programs that make these computers capable of sharing the information people want. For the remainder of this chapter I will discuss some of the primary Internet-related job functions available today and give you a general description of what responsibilities these positions require.

Telecommunications Engineer

The underlying framework of the Internet is built on the typical telecommunication equipment that the phone system has used for years. Although new products and faster access methods are being developed, many telecommunications engineers have their roots in the telephone network systems. These folks usually monitor vendors' installation of equipment, and perform system testing and evaluation activities. They are responsible for inspecting and reviewing hardware installation, wiring, power, grounding, system database validation, and other activities to ensure quality installation of services for their clients. In addition, telecommunications engineers often prepare sites for new installations, replacing cabling and wiring systems and terminal equipment.

Systems Engineer

Moving out from the telecommunication aspect of the hardware side you'll usually find the systems engineers. These are the people responsible for bringing Internet communication services together: sort of the "plumbers" of the Internet. For the millions of computers on the Internet to communicate, many hardware components need to be connected and configured. Systems engineers need to understand (and stay on top of) current hardware solutions and have a detailed understanding of network and Internet protocols. Typically, a systems engineer begins his or her career as a network engineer or network administrator responsible for a single private computer network. Many network vendors such as Microsoft, Novell, and Santa Cruz Operation offer training and advanced certification programs for their particular network operating system. A systems engineer normally has ten or more years of experience in the computer field.

Network Engineer

The network engineer is normally a consumer of Internet services. These people are mostly concerned with the operations of a private network. The network engineer is responsible for identifying the access options and designing and configuring the best method for the given network. The network engineer may also design methods of providing remote access for off-site employees to gain access to the Internet through the corporate network.

PC Infrastructure Engineer

PC infrastructure engineers normally carry out the real hands-on types of work within a private network. These people are responsible for taking the designs of the Systems Engineers and installing client hardware (usually personal computers). This may entail installing the Internet software, such as the browsers and e-mail programs, as well as configuring the TCP/IP settings on each device.

Help Desk Engineer

The help desk engineer is often involved with training and assisting the end-users in standard desktop software such as Internet browsers, word processing programs, spreadsheets, and other applications. Most problems are handled first at the help desk, then if need be, escalated to the next level support group.

Business Analyst

The Internet business analyst is responsible for finding new solutions for helping clients or employees communicate on the Internet. Some responsibilities include researching assignments, interactive strategy development, and working with producers to make sure the ideas come to life. Qualifications for these positions usually include strong problem-solving skills and the ability to document user requirements for use by software developers.

Project Manager

When the Internet is introduced into a company, many teams are often required to pull all of the pieces together smoothly. Each of these teams normally has a person designated as the project manager. The project manager interacts with the staff to analyze existing operational procedures and interpret how client or employee needs can be better met. These professionals usually serve as liaisons between the clients or employees and the Internet implementation team with regard to technology issues.

Security Analyst

The Internet creates a whole new security problem where corporate information is maintained. Once you connect a private network to the Internet, you have created a connection to the outside world. The security analyst's job is to maintain the integrity and safety of the corporate network. To perform this job effectively, the security analyst must have a detailed understanding of network and Internet protocols and know how to analyze server and firewall logs. A *firewall* is a hardware device, sometimes a specialized computer, placed between the private network and the Internet connection. The firewall's job is to watch all of the traffic between the network and the Internet and block certain communications based on the needs of the organization. These devices, as well as Internet servers, produce detailed reports of all the traffic passing through to assist the security analyst in identifying potential threats these devices might not detect as harmful. While this career path requires a great deal of advanced training and experience, it is perhaps the fastest-growing job responsibility in the Internet field.

Graphic Artist

If you've ever seen a Web page, you probably know that it takes some pretty creative people to make the site attractive. The Internet has created a whole new world of opportunities for people with artistic flair! Most computer graphics are created with the use of special graphics software. The graphic artist will usually have an in-depth knowledge of such programs as Photoshop, Flash, QuarkXpress, Shockwave, QuickTime, and other related applications. Experience designing Web sites, in addition to an understanding of Web navigation techniques and user interface design skills, is usually required or highly desirable.

Web Designer

While the Web is only one aspect of the Internet, it is without a doubt a very important part. Almost every organization looking at the Internet begins with a Web site. It is logical, therefore, that Web designers are in high demand. This position normally involves managing Web page development and performing basic Web programming tasks to connect corporate databases to the Web site. Additionally, the Web designer is required to ensure that pertinent information is kept up-to-date for the areas of product marketing, engineering, regulatory business analysis, and project management. Desired skills also include the ability to take raw information and present it in a way that is easy to understand.

Programmer

Although simple Web pages do not need a great deal of custom programming, programmers make Web sites truly come to life. Desired experiences in Web programming include CGI programming, Perl, and Java development (all of which we'll discuss in Part III). Programmers are not only in high demand for Web development but for just about all aspects of the Internet and corporate networks. Without programmers, the computer would be a pretty useless tool.

Database Developer and Administrator

A great deal of corporate data is stored, maintained, and accessed from a *database*. In its simplest form, a database is a structured set of rules for logically storing related items of information. Most corporate databases store millions of items of information, and keeping it optimized and well managed is a full-time job. Often, the data contained within these databases needs to be available, securely, over the Internet. Database developers and database administrators are responsible for ensuring reliability, functionality, and accessibility of these databases for end users, over either the private network or the public Internet.

EXAM PREPARATION SUMMARY

This chapter presented an introduction to the Internet. The main point of this chapter is that the Internet, with all of its hype and sometimes confusing terms, is really nothing more than a new communication tool. Much like the postal and telephone systems, the Internet provides us with a new medium to share information faster and easier. We discussed the three most common services of the Internet: Web browsing, file transfer, and e-mail. We took a brief look at the history of the Internet, and discussed the importance of standards throughout the system. I presented a few examples of typical Internet applications, and finished up the chapter by reviewing a number of the most common careers available within this industry.

Now review the key concepts for this chapter to make sure you understand the material you just read.

- The Internet is a communication tool that uses computers to facilitate communications.

- A collection of computers within a small area such as a single room, floor, or building, is called a *Local Area Network,* or LAN. Computers connected across greater distances are referred to as a *Wide Area Network* or WAN. The Internet is a special version of a WAN.

- The Internet is not owned by any one person or group. Anyone with a computer or other Internet-enabled device can participate in all the Internet has to offer.

- Hardware and software producers generally agree on Internet *standards* that are overseen by the *Internet Engineering Task Force,* or IETF. These standards are called *Request for Comments,* or RFCs. Although anyone can submit an RFC, not all RFCs are adopted as standards.

- The Internet can be used by businesses to greatly reduce the cost of marketing their services and products while reaching a much larger audience.

- The number of Internet-related jobs is exceptional. There are positions for technically orientated computer people, graphic artists, business specialists, and marketing experts.

APPLYING WHAT YOU HAVE LEARNED

The following review questions give you an opportunity to test your knowledge of the information presented in this chapter. The answers to these assessment questions can be found in Appendix B. If you missed some, review those sections in this chapter before going further.

Instant Assessment Questions

1. What two methods are used to connect computers together on the Internet?

2. What term is used when describing two or more computers connected for the purpose of sharing information?

3. What type of company do most people subscribe to in order to access the Internet?

4. What two methods are most commonly used when connecting to the Internet?

5. Most Internet services require two computers to communicate. One computer fills requests made to it by another. What term is used to describe this type of computer relationship?

6. What is the primary protocol, or "common language," of the Internet?

7. What protocol is used to copy files between computers?

8. What protocol is used between servers to transport e-mail messages?

9. How many classification states are there in the RFC process?

10. What type of organized storage method do many businesses use to maintain their information, which increasingly is required to be accessible on the Internet?

Components of the Internet

About Chapter 2

Now that we've seen some of the services available on the Internet, let's jump right into the fun stuff. It's all fine and dandy to read about what you can do once connected, but to fully appreciate the Internet, you simply must experience it!

In Chapter 2 we're going to take a look at the components required to connect to the Internet, both as an individual and as an organization. We'll look at some tips on selecting an appropriate Internet Service Provider and some things to look out for. If you don't already have an Internet connection, you may want to read this chapter first, find a provider in your area, get connected, and then review this chapter. If you are unable to get an Internet connection, you may want to check with your local library. Most public libraries offer free use of Internet computers. In addition, you might check your local yellow pages to see if there is an "Internet Café" nearby. Over the past few years many entrepreneurs have opened these small coffee shops that include Internet access rented by the hour.

Once you have a connection, we'll learn about Internet addressing and how to identify and locate various services on the World Wide Web. We'll also look at how Internet standards are created and whose job it is to maintain them.

Finally, we'll take the plunge and actually go online. I'll show you how to set up and configure your computer's modem, Internet access software, and the Internet browser that will take us to the World Wide Web. We'll connect to the Web and look at a few interesting sites and learn a little bit about navigating our way around this new frontier.

So take a deep breath and read on.

CONNECTION REQUIREMENTS AND OPTIONS

We've discussed the fact that the Internet is a fully connected communications tool. In other words, the Internet is really one big collection of computers that are all connected together. It is logical therefore, that there must be some fundamental *connection point* for all of these computers to connect to, and in fact there is. In the United States, there are four *Network Access Points*, or NAPs, that form the high-speed *backbone* of the Internet. These sites, as pictured in Figure 2-1, are located in New York, Washington D.C., Chicago, and San Francisco. These four NAPs are operated by Ameritech in Chicago, Pacific Bell in San Francisco, Sprint in New York, and Metropolitan Fiber Systems in Washington, D.C. The NAPs are a key component of the Internet backbone because the connections between them determine how traffic is routed. The term *backbone* is used to describe the main network connections that compose the Internet. These NAPs can be loosely equated with major airport hubs that serve many different, privately owned airlines. The individual customer selects a smaller access provider known as an *Internet Service Provider,* or ISP, which in turn is connected to one or more of these NAPs. Internet access is provided in tiers. The top is composed of major ISPs directly connected to the NAPs, who connect with one another in a *peering* arrangement. These ISPs then offer access to smaller, local ISPs, who are often better equipped to service businesses and individuals.

ISPs are basically divided into these three service scopes:

1. Local ISPs that provide dial-up or digital Internet access directly to the consumer.

2. ISPs that provide high-speed intermediary access between local ISPs and the primary Internet backbone.

3. Value-added ISPs that offer specialty servers like Web-site hosting, e-mail, and security (firewalls).

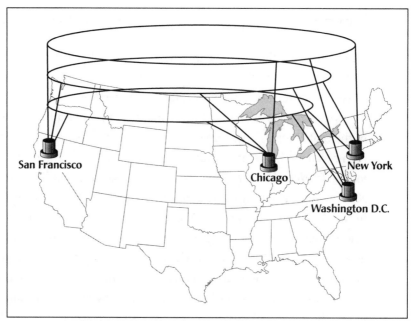

FIGURE 2-1 Map of the Major Network Access Points in the United States.

Dial-Up Access Providers

Consumers are usually charged a flat monthly fee for Internet access from a local provider. This connection is usually made through a computer *modem*. A modem is a small device that converts digital computer information into an analog signal that can be carried across normal telephone wires, and converts analog signals back to digital for the computer to read. If your computer was purchased new since 1998, it probably has a modem built in. The fastest modem speed available as of January 1, 2000 is 56Kbps. This means that the maximum speed at which the device can send and receive data is 56 kilobytes per second (a kilobyte equals 1,024 bytes). The main limiting factor to analog modems is the fact that the signals need to be converted between digital (the computer source) and analog (the telephone service) and back again at both ends. Many smaller ISPs maintain modem *pools* that may be local to the customer base, or they may connect to a *Local Exchange Carrier,* which is part of the public switched network (the telephone company). The ISP needs the ability to offer local telephone numbers to its subscribers so the subscribers don't end up paying expensive long-distance telephone charges. The local access point is known as the local *Point of Presence,* or POP. From here, the data traffic is routed either to a larger regional POP, or to a NAP connection directly. A device called a *router* is used to direct traffic to its proper destinations. Figure 2-2 shows how this data flow from a consumer to the Internet might be accomplished.

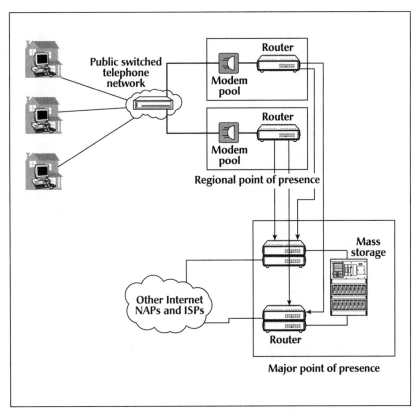

FIGURE 2-2 Example of a dial-up access route

Oversubscription Concerns

Because the ISP has larger and faster connections to the Internet backbone, it is able to resell many smaller pieces to its subscribers. To maximize their invest-ments, most ISPs oversubscribe their service, counting on the fact that not all subscribers will be connected at the same time. This is similar to how airlines sell more seats on a particular flight than they actually have. The airlines make money by selling seats from one point to another. They certainly don't want a plane in the air with an empty seat, so they count on a certain percentage of people not show-ing up. Most of the time this works. Other times, the airlines must offer "inconvenience incentives" to other travelers who can afford to leave later. In the ISP market, this is not a big issue most of the time. There have been a few cases, however, when oversubscribing has caused many problems. A few years ago, America Online (AOL), a leading provider of Internet access, charged its members a flat monthly fee for a fixed number of hours. This payment plan helped to ensure that members only connected to the service for the actual time they wanted to be online. Members who used more than their allotted hours within a given month had to pay additional charges. To compete with independent ISPs who offered unlimited Internet access, AOL changed its policy and removed the fixed-hour restrictions. Unfortunately, the company underestimated the popularity of this change and was quickly overwhelmed with member connections. AOL members started accessing the system for hours at a time, and tended to leave their connections on even if they weren't actually using the service. This led to numerous busy signals and very angry members. Eventually a class-action lawsuit was filed against America Online for not providing the promised service. To America Online's credit, it invested an enormous amount of time and money into its network and soon eliminated the saturation problems. Most ISPs learned the lessons of AOL and therefore are very accurate when assessing how many subscribers they can support before oversubscribing becomes a problem.

High-Speed Consumer Alternatives

Through the end of the 1990s, most home users connected to the Internet via this standard modem scenario. There are, however, faster types of connections on the horizon, depending on where you live, and how much money you are willing to pay. Two high-speed access methods that are becoming more widely available are cable and DSL.

Many of the same companies that provide cable TV service today are providing Internet connections as well. The cable company provides an additional jack that connects to a special cable modem. The computer is then attached to the modem by means of a network card installed in the computer. This service provides direct, all-digital service at speeds up to 10Mbps per second. A dedicated connection means that the Internet service is "always-on," so there is no need to dial in to the ISP before connecting to the Internet. In addition, since these connections are all digital, there is no speed penalty for converting the data from digital to analog and back to digital as with a regular modem.

Digital Subscriber Line, or DSL, is another high-speed option that might be available where you live. Digital service is provided on top of an existing telephone line without interrupting normal voice communications. Like cable, a special DSL modem is used to separate the digital signal from the analog signal. A standard telephone line is connected to the DSL modem from the wall jack, and then to the telephone. The computer is connected to the DSL modem via a network card in the computer. DSL service offers speeds up to 7Mbps per second, but is typically sold at 256Kbps or 512Kbps speeds to keep costs lower. The down side to DSL is its distance limitations. Currently, DSL cannot reach distances farther than about three miles from the central switching office of the telephone company. This limitation is slowly being removed as new hardware is developed, but whether it will eclipse cable as the high-speed access of choice is yet to be seen. In either event, when selecting an Internet Service Provider, you should look carefully at what high-speed options are available in your area.

Other High-Speed Options for Businesses

Because DSL and cable are relatively new services, many businesses, schools, libraries, and other institutional users who have required faster connection speeds have turned to other digital alternatives. The more popular of these options have been provided by the telephone companies. At the lower end is the *Integrated Services Digital Network*, or ISDN. ISDN is an international telecommunications standard for transmitting voice, video, and data over digital lines running at 64Kbps. The telephone companies commonly use a 64Kbps channel for digitized, two-way voice conversations.

On the other end of the spectrum is a *T carrier line*, which is a point-to-point dedicated, digital circuit. The monthly cost is typically based on distance. T carrier lines are widely used for private networks as well as interconnections between an organization's local area network and the telephone company. A T1 line uses two wire pairs (one for transmit, one for receive) and *Time Division Multiplexing* (TDM) to interleave 24 64Kbps voice or data channels. Channels may be combined and the total 1.544Mbps capacity can be broken up as required. T2s provide speeds of 6.312Mbps while T3s offer 44.736Mbps.

A pair of communications devices called *Digital (or data) Service Unit/Channel Service Unit*, or DSU/CSU, connects an in-house line to the external digital T1 circuit. It is similar to a modem, but connects a digital circuit rather than an analog one. The CSU terminates the external line at the customer's premises. If the customer's communications devices are T1 ready and have the proper interface, then the CSU is not required, only the DSU is. The DSU does the actual transmitting and receiving of the signal and provides buffering and flow control. The DSU and CSU are often in the same unit. The DSU may also be built into a *multiplexor*, a device commonly used to combine the digital signals of high-speed lines. The DSU/CSU is then connected via a serial connection to a router, which is a device that connects two separate networks together. When the router is connected to the company's private network, all users on that network can access Internet services.

CONSIDERATIONS IN SELECTING AN ISP

OK, so exactly which option should you select? That's a good question, but I'm afraid there are no simple answers. You need to assess for yourself what speeds you're willing to live with and how much you're willing to pay. For a standard analog dial-up account, you can have reasonable speeds for most Internet activities at a monthly cost usually between $15 and $25. If you have cable, DSL, or other higher-speed options in your geographic area, you might want to examine those options as well. Most of these connections cost between $35 and $65 per month. Of course, businesses should look at the digital options first and perhaps at the T carrier options offered by their telephone service providers. Pricing for these situations vary greatly from under $100 to over $1,000 per month. Although there are many considerations when choosing an Internet Service Provider, the following list should provide you with some guidelines that will help you select the ISP that's right for you.

Analog Dial-Up Accounts

So you're considering using a dial-up account, because of price or because that's all that's available in your area. Depending on where you live, you may have a choice of a number of local ISPs, as well as several national services. Here are some factors to consider when making a choice.

1. The location that an ISP services should be the first item you check. You'll want to ask the ISP for the phone number of their nearest POP. This is the number your modem will dial (potentially for long periods of time). Once you find out the phone number(s), check with your local phone company to determine if calls to that number are within your local calling area. The cost of "non-local" phone calls will easily surpass the slight differences in monthly fees the ISPs charge.

2. What connection type does the ISP use to connect with the rest of the Internet? Since access speeds are defined by the slowest link, and many people will be sharing the same primary line the ISP has to the Internet itself, your selected ISP should have *at least* a T1 connection from one (or more) of the major access providers.

3. Is the ISP oversubscribing so much that you're likely to hear many busy signals? To see for yourself, simply pick up your phone and dial their POP phone number several times a day during the times when you hope to get online. A low monthly fee means nothing if you can't get through.

4. Does the ISP offer additional services that you might need such as Web hosting or additional e-mail accounts? Most ISPs include a small amount of disk space on their Web site for you to store your own Web pages. In this case, your Web address (see below) will often contain the ISP's address followed by your account name. For example, `http://www.theispname.com/yourname`. You may or may not need Web space, but it's nice to know if space is included in the price. More likely, you may want additional e-mail addresses. Many ISPs offer one e-mail address with your base account, but it's likely that you will want addresses for other family members, or to separate business from personal e-mail. The ISP should have the ability to offer multiple addresses, but they will probably levy an additional monthly charge for each additional address.

5. Finally, consider price. As I mentioned previously, monthly rates can range from $15 to $35 per month for unlimited access time and a few megabytes Web storage space. I would highly advise against committing to a year or more worth of service until you've used the service for a while. Even then, you may find that faster access methods will become available before your

long-term contract expires, leaving you little choice but to continue using the slower service until your contract is fulfilled.

Commercial and Other High-Speed Accounts

As mentioned above, companies with more than a few PCs on a LAN will be interested in a dedicated connection. For price and performance, most organizations will opt for a T1 connection that provides up to 1.5Mbps of throughput. ISPs charge a flat monthly rate for a T1 which includes their fee and the cost of a dedicated line from your location to their nearest POP. When evaluating these ISP services, keep in mind the following points:

1. Consider only those ISPs who have significant backbone capacities and who are directly connected to the Internet's Network Access Points. Only a few ISPs operate extensive high-speed backbone networks; most derive their connectivity from the larger ISPs.

2. Examine the backbone of the ISP's network. Buying a T1 from an ISP is worthless if it doesn't have the capacity to handle the aggregate traffic of all its users. Many ISPs have high-speed connections to and from the Network Access Points, but not to the local points-of-presence. If your business is located in an area that is only served by a single T1 connection to the main backbone, you will likely suffer from poor Internet performance. The ISP should gladly show you a map of their connections. A good example of this is found in Figure 2-3.

3. Evaluate the other services the ISP offers which you may need, including

   o Router configuration for your dedicated connection

   o Firewall products for enhanced security

   o Web hosting services (so you don't have to maintain your own server)

4. Look for alternatives to T connections. ISDN, DSL, and cable may offer acceptable speeds at greatly lower costs.

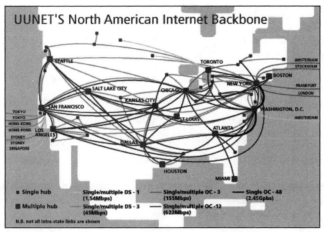

FIGURE 2-3 **A sample of an Internet Service Provider's coverage area**

INTERNET ADDRESSING

Much like a mailing address or a personal telephone number, every device connected to the Internet must have a unique address. These devices include all of the computers, routers, and other pieces of hardware that make the Internet work. Since computers deal strictly with numbers, Internet addresses are all numerical. Each Internet connected device is assigned a unique *Internet Protocol* or IP address. In the computer world, a protocol simply describes the set of rules that govern the transmitting and receiving of data. We'll discuss the IP protocol in more detail later on. For now, it's only important to know that an IP address comprises four sets of three digits each, such as 192.168.100.105. You can see that it would be rather difficult trying to remember a specific Internet site using only its IP

address. (Some of us have a hard enough time remembering our own telephone numbers, without hundreds of IP addresses to boot!) Since humans prefer working with names rather than numbers, the people who developed the Internet standards and procedures recognized that some method to convert names to IP addresses was critically important. Since the Internet is supposed to be a friendly and easy-to-use-tool, some method was required to give people the ability to use familiar names when locating services across the Net. Enter the *Uniform Resource Locator,* or URL.

URL Protocol Identifier

The URL defines a path to a particular Internet Service using a predefined format. The URL is prefixed with the type of protocol used by a particular service. For example, the World Wide Web (WWW) uses a protocol known as *Hypertext Transport Protocol,* or HTTP. Therefore, a URL pointing to a Web server will start with HTTP. The characters :// immediately follow the protocol type. Other common protocol prefixes used in URLs are listed in Table 2-1.

TABLE 2-1 COMMON PROTOCOL PREFIXES	
PROTOCOL PREFIX	**MEANING**
ftp://	FTP server (file transfer)
news://	Usenet newsgroups
mailto://	e-mail
wais://	Wide Area Information Server
gopher://	Gopher server
file://	file on local system
telnet://	applications on network server
rlogin://	applications on network server
tn3270://	applications on mainframe

exam preparation pointer

The i-Net+ exam will expect you to know the parts that make up a URL and in what order they occur. Pay specific attention to the prefix and memorize the nine common prefixes in Table 2-1.

URL Domain Name Identifier

The next portion of the URL is the *domain name.* A domain name is an organization's unique Internet identifier. More specifically, a domain name represents one or more specific IP addresses. For example, the Microsoft Corporation owns the unique Internet domain name microsoft.com. Microsoft owns more than one IP address, but this domain name references them all. In order to identify a specific IP address with Microsoft, a complete URL is required, as we'll see in a moment. The .com portion of the domain name is called a *Top Level Domain* identifier, or TLD. The TLD is used to refine and organize domain names into smaller categories. Currently, there are only a limited number of TLDs. The most popular of these are listed in Table 2-2.

TABLE 2-2 TOP LEVEL DOMAIN IDENTIFIERS	
TOP LEVEL DOMAIN IDENTIFIER	**MEANING**
.gov	Government agencies
.edu	Educational institutions
.org	Organizations (nonprofit)
.mil	Military
.com	commercial business
.net	Network organizations (usually ISPs)

exam preparation pointer

Like the URL prefixes, the exam will ask you to identify the top level domains listed in Table 2-2. You should memorize this list and understand what types of organizations they identify.

URL Country Level Identifier (CLD)

Although rarely used in the United States, a *Country Level Domain name* might also be added to the TLD. The Country Level Domain identifier is a two character code that identifies a specific country such as .uk for the United Kingdom, or .ca for Canada.

Therefore, the proper URL to describe or locate the primary Web server owned by the Microsoft Corporation would look like this:

```
http://www.microsoft.com.us
```

If we were to type this address into a Web browser program, we would reach the default Web page stored on a Web server belonging to Microsoft, which is registered as a company in the United States. Most modern Web browsers assume the protocol type and Country Level Domain identifier for us, meaning that we could shorten this address to:

```
www.microsoft.com
```

and our browser program would take us to the same location. It's also worth noting that case is not important in a URL. For example:

```
WWW.MICROSOFT.COM
www.Microsoft.com
www.MicroSoft.Com
```

all refer to the exact same Internet location.

It's also helpful to understand that computers read addresses from right to left. Thus, if you send an e-mail message to the address `Jacque@univ.net.fr`, the message would first be sent to France since `fr` is the country code for France. The French routers would then send the message to `univ.net` where Jacque can use his e-mail program to retrieve the message the next time he signs on.

Port Numbers

The last item of a URL is called the *Port* number. Port numbers are assigned to applications running on a server. The number is used to link the incoming data to the correct service. Most of the time, the port number is omitted from the URL because standard, or *well known* port numbers are assumed by the application. For example, the port number for HTTP (Web) servers is 80, so when looking up a Web page based on the URL, the browser assumes port 80 unless you specify otherwise. Suppose you have a Web server that you don't want widely accessed. You could configure the server to use port 49810 for example, instead of the default port 80. (Private use port numbers range from 49152 to 65535.) The only way a Web browser would be able to connect to this server would be to construct the URL with the proper port number like this: `www.myserver.com:49810` Notice that the port number is the last item of the URL and is preceded with a colon (:). Some well-known port numbers are listed in Table 2-3.

PORT NUMBER	SERVICE
TABLE 2-3 WELL-KNOWN PORT NUMBERS	
20/21	FTP
23	Telnet
25	SMTP (Simple Mail Transport Protocol)
53	DNS (Domain Name Services)

PORT NUMBER	SERVICE
69	TFTP (Trivial File Transfer Protocol)
80	HTTP (Web)
110	POP3 (Post Office Protocol 3)
123	NTP (Network Time Protocol)

The complete list of defined port number can be found at `www.isi.edu/in-notes/iana/assignments/port-numbers`.

exam preparation pointer
You should understand what a well-known port number is used for, and know the common port numbers defined in Table 2-3.

Registering Your Own Domain Name

Domain names are being registered at a blinding rate. If you think you would like to own your own Web site, or if you'd like to have an e-mail address that is unique and personal to you, you may want to register your own domain name. As of January 1999, the cost for registering a domain name in the United States is $35 per year, with the first two years paid in advance.

The first step to owning your own Internet domain is to decide on a name and see if it is still available. Since many common domain names have already been registered, you should consider a few alternatives. When selecting a name, keep the following rules in mind:

- A domain name can be up to 26 characters long -- *including* the characters used to identify the Top Level Domain (`.net`, `.com`, `.org`).
- Domain names are not case sensitive.
- When entering the domain name you want, do not include "www" or "http." You should, however, put .com, .org, .net, or whichever top-level domain you want to use at the end of the domain name.
- If your first choice is not available, consider looking up the same name with a slight variation, or a different top-level domain. For example if *yourname.com* is not available, try *yourname.net*
- The only valid characters for a domain name are letters, numbers, and a hyphen "-". Other special characters like the underscore "_" or an exclamation mark "!" are NOT permitted.

Once you've selected a few variations, you'll need to check with an Internet name registration organization to see if your selection is available, and then complete the registration. Until recently, the only company authorized to register domain names was Network Solutions, Inc. Their Web page can be found at `http://www.networksolutions.com`. Although Network Solutions still registers domain names, we now have other choices. The organization that oversees domain name registrars is called The Internet Corporation for Assigned Names and Numbers, or ICANN. From their Web page at `http://www.icann.org/` you can find a list of all authorized domain name registrars. Although the process is quite easy, each of these companies has its own forms and procedures. You should visit one of these Web sites and follow the online instructions.

To complete the registration process, you will need to provide the IP addresses of two DNS servers (we'll discuss DNS services later on). It's unlikely that you will provide these servers yourself, so you will need a hosting company. The first place to look is your own ISP. Almost every ISP (and other special Web hosting companies) will host your site and handle all of the paperwork for you. If you're not quite ready to create your own Internet site, but you want to be sure that you don't lose your selected name to someone else, you can select a company who will register your name, then *park* it until you're ready to use it. Although a number of companies will do this, I have found one company that particularly stands out. They are located on the World Wide Web at `www.DomainsAreFree.com`. This company will register your domain name, park it free, and give you an unlimited e-mail forwarding address. This last feature enables you to start using your personalized domain name for all your e-mail. For example, suppose you register the domain name `Warzecha.com`. Your current ISP has provided you the e-mail address of `ScottW@MyISP.net`. The DomainsAreFree company will automatically forward all e-mail sent to *anything*`@Warzecha.com` to your existing `ScottW@MyISP.net` address. This auto-forwarding process is commonly used to create e-mail *aliases*. Since *all* e-mail sent to the `Warzecha.com` domain is forwarded to your existing e-mail account, regardless of who is identified to the left of the @ sign, you have an unlimited number of personalized e-mail addresses! So all messages sent to `ScottW@Warzecha.com`, `Scott@Warzecha.com`, or even `HeyYou@Warzecha.com` will be forwarded to your existing e-mail box at `ScottW@MyISP.net`. An additional benefit of owning your own domain name, and having the auto-forwarding option, is that your e-mail address (and all aliases) is yours for as long as you own the domain name. This is especially useful when you change ISPs. Since people will be sending mail to your personal domain account, Warzecha.com, you only need to change the address where your messages are being forwarded to and you'll never miss a single message.

HOW INTERNET STANDARDS ARE ADOPTED

I've explained that the Internet is not owned by any one person, group, organization, or government. It is truly a unique situation in today's competitive marketplace. Even though there is no commercial governing body, the Internet members voluntarily adhere to open protocols and procedures. At the technical and developmental level, the Internet is made possible through volunteer creation, testing, and implementation of Internet standards. These standards are developed by the *Internet Engineering Task Force,* or IETF. The standards are then reviewed and considered by the *Internet Engineering Steering Group* (IESG), with appeal to the *Internet Architecture Board* (IAB), and promulgated by the Internet Society as international standards. Standards and procedures are created and submitted by a process known as *Request For Comment,* or RFC. The RFC Editor is responsible for preparing and organizing the standards in their final form. At the applications level, the World Wide Web Consortium (W3C) plays the leading role in developing and promulgating Web standards.

What is the IETF?

The Internet Engineering Task Force is a loosely self-organized group of people who make technical and other contributions to the engineering and evolution of the Internet and its technologies. It is the principal body engaged in the development of new Internet standard specifications. Its mission includes

- Identifying, and proposing solutions to, pressing operational and technical problems in the Internet
- Specifying the development or usage of protocols and the near-term architecture to solve such technical problems for the Internet

- Making recommendations to the Internet Engineering Steering Group regarding the standardization of protocols and protocol usage in the Internet

- Facilitating technology transfer from the Internet Research Task Force to the wider Internet community

- Providing a forum for the exchange of information within the Internet community between vendors, users, researchers, agency contractors, and network managers

The IETF is not a traditional standards organization, although many specifications are produced that become standards. The IETF is made up of volunteers who meet three times a year to fulfill the IETF mission. There is no membership in the IETF. Anyone may register for and attend any meeting.

The actual technical work of the IETF is done in its working groups, which are organized by topic into several areas (such as routing, transport, or security). Much of the work is handled via mailing lists located on the Web at `http://www.ietf.org/maillist.html`. The IETF holds meetings three times per year.

The IETF working groups are grouped into areas, and managed by Area Directors, or ADs. The ADs are members of the Internet Engineering Steering Group. Providing architectural oversight is the Internet Architecture Board, (IAB). The IAB also adjudicates appeals when someone complains that the IESG has failed.

The Internet Assigned Numbers Authority (IANA) is the central coordinator for the assignment of unique parameter values for Internet protocols such as domain names and IP addresses. The IANA is chartered by the Internet Society (ISOC) to act as the clearinghouse to assign and coordinate the use of numerous Internet protocol parameters.

The RFC Process

The Requests For Comments (RFCs) are a series of notes, started in 1969, about the Internet. The notes discuss many aspects of computing and computer communication focusing on networking protocols, procedures, programs, and concepts, but also including meeting notes, opinion, and sometimes humor. The RFC Editor is the publisher of the RFCs and is responsible for the final editorial review of the documents. Suggestions about RFC publication, or submission of material to be considered for publication as an RFC should be sent via e-mail to `rfc-editor@ rfc-editor.org.`

Anyone can write an RFC. However, before a document can become an RFC it must be submitted first as an Internet Draft (ID). The first step for a potential RFC is for the document to become an Internet Draft so that it may be distributed, read, and commented on. The RFC Editor will request the IESG to review the document and give comments/suggestions. After a document is approved, it is edited and published. If the document is suggested as *Do Not Publish,* the author(s) will be notified by e-mail so they may know the reasons why. Sometimes documents sent in as individual submissions are remanded to an IETF Working Group because the subject is already being worked on. In these cases the author is usually asked to work with the IETF to develop the document. When an RFC has been classified as a suggested or recommended standard, most vendors and other Internet providers will implement these changes.

WEB BROWSER BASICS

Ok, I've talked a lot about connection methods, domain names, ISPs, and standards, but what does all of this do for you anyway? You've probably heard the Internet described as the *Information Superhighway,* so let's strap on our seatbelts and take a little trip down the autobahn of the World Wide Web.

The Web (as it's commonly referred to) and e-mail are undeniably the most popular Internet services available. In 1990, Tim Berners-Lee introduced the first program for sharing information in which any network-accessible information could be referred to by a single "Universal Document Identifier," which became the basis of today's Web. Mr. Berners-Lee describes his "Web" this way:

"The dream behind the Web is of a common information space in which we communicate by sharing information. Its universality is essential: the fact that a hypertext link can point to anything, be it personal, local or global, be it draft or highly polished. There was a second part of the dream, too, dependent on the Web being so generally used that it became a realistic mirror (or in fact the primary embodiment) of the ways in which we work and play and socialize. That was that once the state of our interactions was on line, we could then use computers to help us analyze it, make sense of what we are doing, where we individually fit in, and how we can better work together."

Mr. Berners-Lee's home page, which includes a complete history lesson on the World Wide Web, can be found at `http://www.w3.org/People/Berners-Lee`.

The dream has become a reality. The Web has created an electronic community whose members are located all around the world. Using Web technology, people are able to share ideas using many different media such as text, graphics, video, sounds, music, and more. There are no limits on what the Web can serve up, and new offerings are being added all the time. Not only has the Web changed the paradigms we've had about sharing information and communicating, but it's transformed how we invest, shop, and keep ourselves entertained.

In the following sections we'll explore the basic components of the Web browser application and then we'll jump right into connecting to the World Wide Web.

Netscape Navigator

As the Internet began to take shape as a viable commercial venture, a small group of program specialists formed a new company to produce the hottest browser software available in its time. Netscape Navigator clearly changed the face of the World Wide Web by bringing a powerful, yet easy to use Web browser program to the average user. Prior to the "browser war" that ensued when Microsoft began giving its Internet Explorer away free, Navigator supplied over 80% of the browser market. Navigator is still extremely popular, and like IE, is available for free at `http://www.netscape.com`. Many ISPs supply Navigator to their customers as their default browser. Figure 2-4 is version 4.61 of the Netscape Navigator main screen.

Microsoft's Internet Explorer

As the Internet became an increasingly necessary part of the computing experience, Microsoft introduced its own program for accessing the information on the World Wide Web that they called Internet Explorer, or IE. This free program quickly became a favorite of many Web users and is included as part of the Windows 95/98 operating system, the Microsoft Office Suite programs, and as a free download from the Internet. If you have Internet Explorer already installed on your computer, you will see its icon on your Windows desktop. If the program is not already installed, you can install it from your original Windows 95/98 CD or floppy disk set. Figure 2-5 shows the basic Internet Explorer version 5.0 screen.

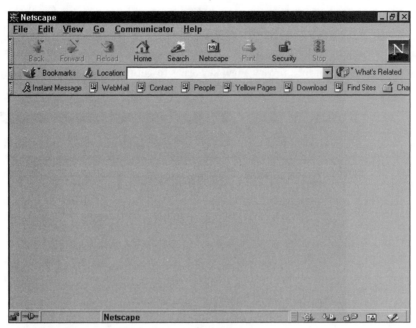

FIGURE 2-4 Netscape Navigator version 4.61

Common Browser Features

Like many software applications that perform the same task, there really isn't a compelling reason to select one of these programs over the other. Both do an excellent job of maximizing the features of the World Wide Web and both browsers are updated with new features and functionalities on a regular basis. Rather than discussing the minor differences between these two programs, we'll focus in on the basic uses of any browser, which are common to both of these applications.

Although there are some obvious differences, the programs have roughly similar user interfaces. For example, the title bar (the topmost line of the program window) shows the name and location of the Web site you are currently viewing. Below the title bar, both programs have a drop-down menu bar that provides access to the standard Windows application functions (Open, Save, Print, and so on). Although different in appearance, both programs have a tool bar that provides quick access to commonly used features. In addition, both programs have an *address box* where you can type in an URL for the browser to display. And finally, at the bottom of the screen, both programs have a *status bar* that provides quick visual indicators of what the program is doing. Like most applications, the best way to really learn all of the features and functions of these programs is to use them, but let's review a few key areas to get us on our (browsing) way.

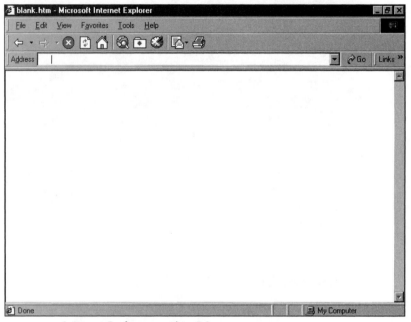

FIGURE 2-5 Internet Explorer version 5.0

We'll focus our attention on the *Navigation Toolbar* as this is rather unique to a browser program. Figure 2-6 shows the navigation bar in Navigator, and Figure 2-7 is IE's counterpart. Let's take a look at these buttons one at a time.

FIGURE 2-6 Navigator's Navigation Toolbar (version 4.61)

FIGURE 2-7 Internet Explorer's Navigation Toolbar (version 5.0)

o **Back:** As you travel from Web site to Web site, it's not hard to get lost. Quite often you will find yourself reading a Web page only to find a *hyperlink* that interests you. A hyperlink is a special linkage between two objects. The link is displayed either as text or as an icon. A text hyperlink displays as underlined text typically in blue. The mouse pointer will change shapes when it crosses over a Web hyperlink. When you click on the link, its associated page is displayed. This link might be on the same site, but it could just as easily be located on a Web site across the globe. If you've followed one or more hyperlinks to other Web pages, the back button will reconnect you with the previous page. In fact, this button keeps a list of the sites you've visited, so you can click it numerous times to return to all of the pages you've visited. Please note, however, that this list is only good for the active session. When you close the browser, this list is forgotten.

o **Forward:** This button functions similarly to the Back button described above, except that it returns you to a page you've viewed and returned from. For example, if we're looking at Page 1, then hyperlink to Page 2, and then click the Back button to return to Page 1, we could simply click the Forward button to again jump to Page 2. Like the Back button, this list is only maintained during the active session.

o **Reload/Refresh:** These two buttons perform the same function. If you want the browser to update the current page, this is the button to use. There are a number of reasons why we'd use this function. Perhaps the whole page was not successfully displayed. This can happen for a variety of reasons, but by pressing Reload/Refresh you are telling the browser to fetch a new copy of the page and display it. It is also possible that the first page displayed to you has been *cached*. We'll describe the concept of caching later on, but simply stated, Web pages can be kept in your computer's memory to improve performance. If this happens, it is possible that the page you're viewing is outdated. By pressing the Reload/Refresh button you can be assured the displayed page is current.

○ **Home:** Of all the buttons on the list, this is one you'll probably use quite a bit. When the browser starts, it wants to have something to display for you. This first page is called your *Home Page*, hence the name of the button. No matter where you are on the Web, clicking the Home button will always return you to this page. OK, so what exactly *is* the home page? Well, it's any Web page you'd like your browser to display first when it starts up. If you, your company, or school has a Web site, you can set your home page to be the starting page on that site. If you find an Internet Site that really interests you, you can make that your home page. In addition, you can create a Hypertext Markup Language (HTML) page of your own and set that as your home page. The point here is that the choice is yours. This is simply a tool that enables you to quickly return to a known point, usually a Web page that is meaningful to you. If you don't change this page, both Microsoft and Netscape will send you to their Web site.

○ **Search:** Although Explorer and Navigator use different programs, this button will invoke another application to allow you to quickly search the Internet for a specific word, phrase, or topic.

○ **Stop:** Even with the fastest Internet connection, some pages just seem to take forever to display. You can click this button anytime a page is being loaded into the browser to stop the process. Any hyperlinks that loaded before you pressed stop will still be active, but most of the time graphics will not be shown. Sometimes, if you press Reload/Refresh after you've stopped a page you will receive a faster connection.

○ **Print:** As you can probably guess, this button will send the currently displayed page to your printer.

Both Explorer and Navigator allow you to customize this button bar to add the features you use most often, or to remove buttons you rarely need. Since the process for customizing the programs is likely to change, please consult the online help for current directions.

HANDS-ON EXERCISES

In the following labs, we will install a new modem in a Windows 95/98 computer and configure it for *Dial Up Networking* (DUN). Once the modem is configured and working, we will configure both Microsoft's Internet Explorer and Netscape's Navigator Web-browsing software. Once we have completed these exercises, we will have full access to all of the services of the Word Wide Web that we've discussed in this chapter.

 Prerequisites for the following exercise: If you don't already have an Internet connection, use the criteria mentioned earlier to get your account set up. Select a service provider and decide what type of connection to use. Since analog dial-up running on Windows 95/98 is still the most common, I'll be using that for our examples throughout these exercises.

Installing the Modem

This Lab assumes that you do not have a modem installed in your computer yet. Even if you do, it is important to know how the process of adding new hardware is accomplished. Most new hardware such as modems, video cards, and network cards are developed to take advantage of Windows' *Plug-and-Play* capabilities. Plug-and-Play hardware is designed so that the Windows software can detect it and reconfigure the operating system as necessary. If your modem is plug-and-play capable, follow the installation guidelines of the manufacturer. Otherwise, the following procedure should be used.

1. Select Start ⇨ Settings ⇨ Control Panel. Then double-click Modems.

2. In the Install New Modem dialog box, uncheck the "Don't detect my modem; I will select it from a list check box," (it is unchecked by default) then click Next.

3. The Add New Modem process will begin searching your computer for a modem. If the process successfully detected your modem, skip to Step 7.

4. The next dialog box will inform you that no new modems were detected. Click Next.

5. Figure 2-8 shows the manual modem selection dialog box. Use the vertical scroll bar on the left-hand windowpane to locate the manufacturer of your

modem. If the modem came with a special installation disk, you can insert the diskette (or CD) into your computer and click on the Have Disk button.

6. Select the modem model displayed on the manufacturer list, and then click Next.

7. The software for your modem will now be installed.

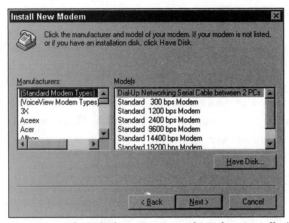

FIGURE 2-8   The Windows 9x Manual Modem Installation Dialog Box

The next step is to make sure that the modem responds to basic commands.

1. If the Modem Configuration window is not already displayed, click on the Modems icon in the Control Panel Window.

2. Click on the Diagnostic tab in the Modem Properties window.

3. Click on the modem you want to test (there can be more than one).

4. Click the More Info button.

If the modem responds properly, you will see test results similar to the output shown in Figure 2-9.

Installing and Configuring Dial–Up Networking (DUN)

Windows 95/98/NT makes connecting to the Internet via a dial-up connection very easy with the *Dial-Up Networking* utility. During the initial installation of

Windows you had the option of installing the DUN services. If your computer does not have these services already installed, follow the steps below.

1. Click Start ⇨ Settings ⇨ Control Panel. Then double-click Add/Remove Programs.

2. Click the Windows Startup tab.

3. Click Communications.

4. Check the Dial-Up Networking option box, and then click Ok.

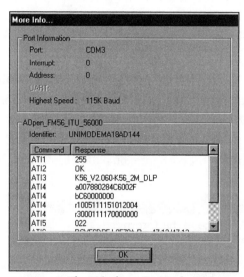

FIGURE 2-9 The Windows 9x Modem Diagnostics Dialog Box

   The last step in configuring the dial-up connection is to configure a dial-up service account to call your ISP. Windows 98 (and Explorer version 5 and higher) include a new Wizard program to walk you through each step of this process. You can launch the Wizard program by clicking the Connect to the Internet icon on your desktop, or it will be launched the first time you start Internet Explorer. Figure 2-10 shows the opening screen of the Wizard. Simply follow the program's dialog boxes to finish the connection.

   There are times when you may need to manually create the DUN services, or make changes to the settings. For example, this might be necessary if your ISP changes their phone numbers or other server settings, or if you have more than one ISP account. The following steps will show you how to add or reconfigure your dial-up settings.

1. Double click My Computer and then double-click Dial-Up Networking: The welcome screen appears.

2. Click Next. The Make New Connection dialog box is displayed, as shown in Figure 2-11.

   Type in a name for the computer you are dialing. This is for descriptive purposes only. If you have more than one ISP dial-up account, this is the description you will see to differentiate between the accounts. You may want to enter your ISP's name here, or simply call it something like "Internet Dial-Up."

   The other option on this screen is to select a modem and optionally to configure it. If you have more than one modem, you can click the drop-down selection box next to the modem's description to select a different modem. Likewise, if you want to make any changes to the way the selected modem is configured, you can click the configuration button before moving on.

FIGURE 2-10 Dial-Up Networking Installation Wizard in Windows *9x*

3. Click Next. The Telephone number box is displayed, as shown in Figure 2-12.

The telephone number in this dialog box refers to the telephone number of your ISP's local POP (Point of Presence). The ISP will provide you with this number when you sign up for service.

4. Click Next and the final screen will confirm that you have configured the Dial-Up Networking account. When you look at the Dial-Up Networking window now, you will have at least two icons similar to Figure 2-13. From here, you simply click the DUN icon for the ISP account you wish to call, and the Internet is just moments away!

FIGURE 2-11 Naming the Dial-Up account and selecting a modem

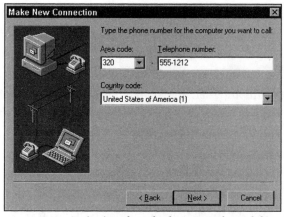

FIGURE 2-12 Assigning the telephone number of the Dial-Up account

FIGURE 2-13   Dial-Up Networking icons

Exploring the World Wide Web

In this section, we'll finally experience the Internet by dialing into our ISP, connecting to the Internet, and "surfing" the Web. If your browser and Dial-Up Networking services are configured properly, you should be able to simply double-click your browser icon on the Windows desktop to begin your journey. Since the browser application is requesting a resource (our home page) that is not located within our own network, or is not stored on our own PC, the DUN service will intercept this request and automatically start the dial-up process. If for some reason your dial-up window does not start automatically, simply follow these steps:

1. Double-click My Computer, then double-click Dial-Up Networking.

2. Double-click the ISP account you created in Lab 2-2.

The first time you start this service (whether automatically or manually) the DUN service will pause to ask for your user name and password. These items are supplied to you by your ISP when your account is created. This is how you tell the ISP who you are so their computers will grant you access to the Internet. If you want to further automate this process, simply check the option to Save Password before you select the Connect button.

At this point, the DUN service will inform you that it is dialing into the ISP and connecting to the Internet. You should also hear the sound of the modem, which is a series of high-pitched squeals. If you haven't started your browser yet, do so by clicking on the Browser's icon on your desktop as soon as the DUN service has established a connection.

While your home page is loading in the browser, you can see its progress in the status bar, which is located at the very lower left-hand corner of the screen. There is another easy way to tell that the browser is in the process of downloading items on the Web page. In both browsers, there is an animated icon in the upper right-hand corner of the browser window. For IE, this is a globe with the Windows logo in front, while Netscape uses its logo of the letter "N" against a sky background. When these icons are in motion, it tells you that the browser is busy downloading more information. When these icons are still, the page has been fully retrieved, or you've pressed the Stop button.

Now your browser should be up and displaying your default home page. Let's start our journey by going to a page with a known URL. In IE you'll notice the *Address* box just below the tool bar. In Netscape, this area is titled *Location*.

Click in the Address/Location box to highlight the current location.

1. Type in **http://www.netscape.com**
2. Press Enter.

(If you receive an error message, double-check your spelling, and make sure you are connected to your ISP.)

This is Netscape's home page. If you're using IE and you'd like to download a copy of Netscape, you'll find the download option at the top of this page.

Click in the Address/Location box to highlight the current location.

1. Type in **www.microsoft.com**
2. Press Enter.

Now you should see Microsoft's home page. Notice that this time, we excluded the `http://` portion. This is to demonstrate that the browser is "smart" enough to understand that since we're looking at Web pages, we will probably using the http protocol. Therefore, if we omit this part of the URL, the browser will assume that is what we want and fill that part in for us.

Click in the Address/Location box to highlight the current text.

1. Type in: **www.weather.com**
2. Press Enter.

You should now be looking at the front page of the Weather Channel's site. In a matter of moments, we've jumped through cyberspace to three different locations. For all intents and purposes, these three sites could be located at opposite ends of the earth, but the speed at which they are brought to us would remain relatively the same!

We should still be looking now at the front page of the Weather Channel's home page. If you move your mouse around on this page, you'll notice that the mouse icon changes to a pointing finger, and some of the text on the page changes too. These areas are the hyperlinks we discussed previously. Look over this page, and click on any one of these hyperlinks... go ahead, we'll wait for you.

Wow... there sure are a lot of choices! You'll notice when you jump to another page, it is full of even more hyperlinks. Let's select another link on the page you're looking at now and see where that takes us. It should be clear why the Web protocol is named *Hypertext Markup Language*: nearly every page we visit has more and more hyperlinks. Let's get back to the main weather page. To go back the way you came, you have two options: either re-enter the URL in the Address/Location box, or click the *Back* button. Since we've jumped two from the main Web page, we'll need to click the Back button twice to get back.

Let's assume that you'd like to visit this Web site often. You can simply remember the URL and enter it in every time you want to return, but as you find more and more interesting sites, you'll probably have a hard time organizing all of those URLs. Both IE. and Navigator provide a better way to remember and organize your favorite sites. In IE. this feature is called *Favorites* and in Navigator its called *Bookmarks*. To add this page to your list, follow one of the following steps:

Adding Favorites in Internet Explorer:

1. Select Favorites on the menu bar.
2. Select Add to Favorites from the drop-down menu.
3. Click Ok.

Adding Bookmarks in Netscape Navigator:

1. Select Bookmarks on the Location Tool bar.
2. Select Add Bookmark.

If you examine these options a bit closer, you will see that both programs also allow you to place your favorites/bookmarks in organized categories. We simply added the Weather Channel URL to the main list, but we could just as easily have entered it into a category list instead. When you do your own exploring, create a few customized folders for your saved favorites/bookmarks. Depending on your needs and temperament, you can organize these sites quite effectively.

Next, we'll see how these favorites/bookmarks make our life easier by leaving this site and using this feature to return to the Weather Channel with minimal effort.

1. Select the Home button. This should take you to whatever site you selected as your home page.

2. In IE. click on Favorites. In Navigator, click Bookmarks.

3. Scroll down the list and select The Weather Channel home page.

You should now be looking at the Weather Channel's page again. Pretty cool, eh? As you can see, this is a great way to keep your URLs organized. Remember, we've just touched on the basics of the Favorites/Bookmark functions. This feature is much more powerful and deserves some time on your own to explore further.

Finally let's review the concept of our home page. Remember that the browser program has to begin someplace. This home page is a site that you'll see often, and is the starting point of all your Web browsing. For this exercise, we'll use the Weather Channel page as our starting point, but more specifically, we'll set up the home page to show us our *local* weather page.

If you're not currently viewing the Weather Channel home page, return there using your stored Favorite/Bookmark. On the main page, you'll see a text box on the left-hand side where you can type in your zip code or city name. If you live in the United States, go ahead and type in your zip code, then click on *Go*.

If you live outside of the United States

1. Leave this box empty, then click on *Go*.

2. Scroll down the next page and click on View all international countries.

3. Select your city/area from the displayed world maps.

Next, we'll make this page our Home Page. Follow the steps for your browser.
Internet Explorer:

1. Select Tools ⇨ Internet Options. (For versions prior to 4, Select View ⇨ Options.)

2. Click the Use Current button.

Netscape Navigator:

1. Select Edit ⇨ Preferences.

2. Click Use Current button.

Now close your browser (click the X button on the top-right corner of the browser window). If the DUN service asks you to disconnect, click the *Stay Connected* button. From the desktop, restart your browser (either IE. or Navigator). You now see that your local weather page is displayed first. From here, you can continue exploring the Internet and always return to this page simply by clicking the Home button.

EXAM PREPARATION SUMMARY

In this chapter we looked at how the Internet is connected, starting with the main Network Access Points and working our way down to the local Internet Service Providers. Along the way we discussed what items to look for when selecting an ISP and what connection types might be available to you (dial-up or dedicated). We learned how Internet Services are addressed and how Internet Standards are adopted. We finished up the chapter with a hands-on lab to set up the hardware and software necessary to actually get on the World Wide Web and do a little exploring.

Now review the key concepts for this chapter to make sure you understand the material you just read:

- Internet access is provided in tiers, starting with the primary Network Access Points, or NAPs. Some ISPs provide high-speed intermediary access between local ISPs and the primary Internet backbone. Other ISPs who are better able to serve the individual consumer provide access at the local level.

- Access to the Internet is obtained either by dial-up or dedicated connections. Dial-up methods are the most popular for individuals and small business, while dedicated lines are often used for businesses and organizations with a large number of computers. Dial-up is usually analog with a maximum speed of 56Kbps. Dedicated digital lines offer speeds from 128Kbps (ISDN) to 44.736Mbps for "T" services.

- There are a number of options to consider when selecting an ISP, especially the location of its local Point of Presence (the telephone number you dial), the speed of its upstream connection, and its oversubscription percentage.

- The primary addressing method used to identify Internet Services is the Uniform Resource Locator, or URL. The URL is composed of particular identifiers such as the service protocol type, the domain name, and an optional country code.

- There is a specific process for registering a domain name. Some advantages of registering a domain include the ability to create customized e-mail addresses and aliases.

- Standards for the Internet are not defined by a governing body, but rather a number of volunteer groups. Most Internet users adhere to these standards so consistencies are maintained. The primary group to review and recommend standards is the Internet Engineering Task Force, or IETF. Standards are proposed using a Request For Comment, or RFC.

- Although there are a number of Internet browsers, Microsoft's Internet Explorer and Netscape's Navigator clearly are the most popular. Both of these programs perform the basic function of interpreting Hypertext Markup Language (HTML) documents and presenting them as text, graphics, video, and sound. The browser programs offer a number of navigation tools to make exploring the World Wide Web easy.

- Dial-up Internet connections through Windows 95/98/NT are aided by the Dial-Up Networking service, or DUN. This service requires a modem, which is usually installed automatically in Windows via the Plug-and-Play services or by manual configuration through the Windows control panel. DUN is then configured with the telephone access number, user name, and password of the ISP.

- Both IE. and Navigator provide an easy method of saving and organizing visited Web pages. IE. uses *Favorites*, while Navigator uses *Bookmarks*.

- When a Web browser starts, it first displays a predetermined HTML page known as the Home Page. This page can be located on the Internet, or locally on a personal computer or a private network.

APPLYING WHAT YOU HAVE LEARNED

The following review questions give you an opportunity to test your knowledge of the information presented in this chapter. The answers to these assessment questions can be found in Appendix B. If you missed some, review those sections in this chapter before going further.

Instant Assessment Questions

1. A high-speed backbone of the Internet is connected throughout the United States at four primary locations. Select three of the cities connected by this backbone.

A. Chicago

B. Detroit

C. San Francisco

D. Washington, D.C

2. Companies that offer Internet services to business and individuals are called

A. Network Access Points (NAP)

B. Points of Presence (POP)

C. Internet Service Providers (ISP)

D. Internet Access Providers (IAP)

3. What device is required to access the Internet over analog telephone lines?

A. CSU/DSU

B. Modem

C. DSL

D. Hub

4. All devices on the Internet have unique numeric addresses called

A. Internet Protocol numbers

B. Uniform Resource Locators

C. Home Pages

D. E-Mail Addresses

5. Internet addresses are composed of specific components. The first of these identifies

A. The Top Level Domain

B. The Country Level Domain

C. The Web Server Name

D. The Service Protocol Type

6. The prefix `http://` refers to this type of Internet Service

   A. A file download site

   B. A Dial-Up Networking Service (DUN)

   C. A non-profit organization Web page (`.org`)

   D. A World Wide Web site

7. The Top Level Domain name used by *most* service providers is

   A. `.com`

   B. `.net`

   C. `.mil`

   D. `.isp`

8. When typing an Internet Address into a browser, all letters must be in uppercase.

   A. True

   B. False

9. Domain names can have a maximum of _____ characters including the Top Level Domain identifier.

   A. 26

   B. 255

   C. 8

   D. 24

10. Internet subscribers must follow standards issued and maintained by what organization?

   A. The Internet Engineering Task Force

   B. The RFC Editor

   C. None, adherence is strictly voluntary

   D. The United Nations Committee on Internet Standards and Procedures

11. New Internet Standards are submitted by means of

   A. Request for Comments

   B. Work Group Documents

C. Do Not Publish Documents

D. E-mail

12. Connecting to the Internet using Windows 95/98, what service makes
    defining the connection easy?

    A. IE. Wizard

    B. Dial-Up Networking

    C. Netscape Navigator

    D. The Control Panel

13. Where do you test a modem's proper configuration in Windows 95/98?

    A. Start ⇨ Control Panel ⇨ Modems ⇨ New

    B. Start ⇨ Control Panel ⇨ Devices

    C. My Computer ⇨ Dial-Up Networking ⇨ Diagnostics

    D. Start ⇨ Control Panel ⇨ Modems ⇨ Properties ⇨ More Info

14. Which two tool bar buttons are common to both Internet Explorer
    and Navigator?

    A. Back and Favorites

    B. Bookmarks and Addresses

    C. Location and Address

    D. Forward and Home

15. The Refresh/Restart buttons

    A. Start the browser program from the desktop

    B. Update the hyperlinks on a Web page

    C. Download files from an FTP site

    D. Fetch a new copy of a Web page from the Web site

Internet Performance and Indexing

About Chapter 3

One of the eternal verities of the Internet is that it's never fast enough. No matter what connection speed you use, there will come a time when you'll long for a faster connection. When the 56K modem standards were finalized and vendors started pushing this faster technology, the marketers coined the phrase "World Wide Wait." Never mind that even at "slower" speeds, you can communicate with others in minutes rather than days or weeks. Can you think of any other technology, including the telephone, which allows you to jump around the world in seconds? Regardless of this amazing feat, I would venture to guess everyone who uses the Internet would prefer a faster connection.

Whether you're developing content, building infrastructure, or simply using the service, as an Internet professional you will be charged with helping to make the Internet connection faster. In this chapter you will learn how to work around some of the most common Internet bottlenecks. Some of these bottlenecks are hardware related; others are configuration or organizational issues.

As you've seen, the route of data across the Internet is a complex one. Many players are involved in transporting data from one server to another. Any of these access points is a potential performance obstacle. It's not possible to control each of these access points, so this chapter will focus on ones you can control. One thing to keep in mind, however, is that no matter how well you fine-tune your connection, someone, somewhere, is going to complain that the connection is too slow!

Analyzing the Local Situation

Let's examine a perfect scenario of connecting to a Web site through a local ISP. Looking at the process in steps, you can identify the areas within your control where performance tuning might help. First, we'll take an example of using a dial-up connection from a single computer as depicted in Figure 3-1. Afterward, we'll analyze the Return On Investment, or ROI, using a local area network

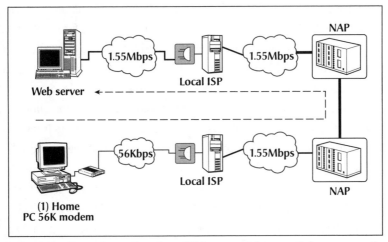

FIGURE 3-1   **Example routing for a Web request from a dial-up connection**

1. Your browser contacts the local ISP using a 56K modem.

2. The ISP authenticates your login, then routes your request to its upstream provider over a T1 line (1.55Mbps).

3. The tier-two ISP routes your request through its Network Access Point (NAP) to the high-speed backbone.

4. The next tier-two ISP who has authority for the domain of the server you want routes your request to the Web owner's local ISP across an OC3 connection (155Mbps).

5. The local ISP sends your request to the domain Web server connected by a T1.

6. The process is reversed to return the data to your browser.

In keeping with the old adage that a chain is only as strong as its weakest link, an Internet hookup is often only as fast as its slowest connection. Although the speed of your request increases once it leaves your local PC, you will never be able to send and receive data *from* your ISP any faster than your modem allows. When people complain about Internet performance, the local connection point usually is the biggest culprit. Therefore, this is usually the first area you'll want to optimize.

Comparing Dial-Up and Digital Connections from a Performance Viewpoint

Imagine everything in the preceding scenario worked as well as possible. First understand that a 56K modem is somewhat of a misnomer. 56K modems use the V.90 standard (finalized in 1998) that defines the transfer speed of data at 56Kbps downstream, but only 33Kbps upstream. Right off, you can see that you're not getting a true 56K link. Your requests sent *to* the Internet are only carried at 33Kbps.

Second, because the data signal is *modulated* (blending the digital signal into an analog signal carrier for transmission over the phone lines) a performance penalty is incurred during this process. The data sent to the Internet may not even achieve 33Kbps, and data coming back in will typically never exceed 45Kbps due to this modulation overhead.

Third, in the United States, the Federal Communications Commission regulated the maximum speed of V.90 technology at 53Kbps. So even if you could achieve the full speed of the modem back from the Internet, you're still only at 53Kbps.

It should be clear, then, that if performance is a real issue, the single best improvement you can implement is to replace the local analog connection with a digital one. I discussed the various options for digital connections in Chapter 2. For single users and small LANs (2 to 25 computers), cable or xDSL is probably the best choice. If neither of these is available, ISDN would probably be the next least expensive option. For larger organizations, these options are still better than an analog connection, but probably won't satisfy all Internet needs. In these situations, T-carrier lines are almost a necessity. Remember, however, that connection methods are improving almost monthly. Although cable is still relatively new, and xDSL has some distance and speed limitations today, it is *very* possible that these, or other similar technologies, will mature to the point of being better options than more expensive T lines. Additionally, as newer high-speed digital connection options become more common, the telephone companies are going to have no choice but to start lowering the cost of standard T carriers to be competitive. Make sure you do your homework and investigate all possible options available in your area before making a decision.

Building a Case for Digital Internet Connectivity

Often, it is difficult to convince upper management that a higher monthly cost digital solution is necessary. The argument usually centers around the *need* employees have for the Internet. Many business already worry that people will waste time surfing the Internet instead of getting their jobs done. But the same argument could be made for the telephones on employees' desks. What prevents an employee from wasting valuable company time chatting with friends or other associates during business hours? The answer to both is relatively clear. If workers are not completing their tasks, for whatever reason, then some form of reprimand is needed. The Internet, like the telephone, is subject to misuse. But most employers find that the Internet's productivity benefits far outweigh its costs.

However, in justifying the difference between a $25 monthly fee and a $250 fee, you'll probably need to make a stronger case. One easy method for showing the ROI (Return On Investment) for better Internet connectivity is to compare e-mail and faxing. Every business uses a fax machine these days. However, at the end of 1999, e-mail is quickly becoming the new standard. Just as a fax machine is useful only if there is a fax machine on the other end, e-mail is only useful if the person you need to communicate with has e-mail access. As your customers and vendors increase their use of e-mail, so must your company or you'll be left behind. In today's competitive market, that's a risky proposition.

To strengthen the case for e-mail, first analyze the amount of time people spend sending multiple-page faxes. Also, look at the cost of sending these faxes. At best, even a one-page fax sent to a toll number (especially if it's an interstate number) during peak business hours will probably cost about 40 cents. Multiply this by the number of pages sent during the day and you'll probably find your daily fax costs are fairly high. Multiply this by 20 or more business days and see where the numbers stack up compared to your flat monthly ISP rate.

Additionally, suppose your faxes consist of many spreadsheet documents. That spreadsheet may contain many small type fonts to fit neatly on a page, which will not duplicate as cleanly as the original. In addition, if your employees *receive* spreadsheets or other computer generated documents, the data cannot be easily transported into their computers. E-mailed attachments, on the other hand, produce an exact, clean duplicate. The attachment can easily be opened in the proper computer application without going through hoops to convert the paper copy to editable data. Given the benefits of all the other Internet services as well, it should be easy to build a case for creating a solid, all digital, Internet infrastructure.

Eliminating Non-Internet Performance Issues

When dealing with a LAN connected to the Internet, it is critically important to make sure the network is tuned for performance first. For example, if your network is running multiple protocols, such as IPX, IP, and NetBEUI, first try to standardize on one protocol, preferably TCP/IP. If your primary Network Operating System (NOS) is Novell's NetWare, upgrading to Version 5 will allow you to run pure IP and still maintain backwards compatibility for IPX applications and devices without having to bind IPX specifically on the LAN. If your NOS is Windows NT, Linux, or UNIX, you can run entirely on IP. If you have mixed environments with older NetWare servers, you may need both IP and IPX, but NetBEUI can probably be eliminated.

The cost of a professional network analysis by a trained engineer often pays for itself. A detailed packet analysis and infrastructure examination often uncovers oversaturated network segments or identifies network cards that are causing excessive traffic and decreasing overall performance. Properly upgrading a shared-media network to a switched network often increases performance more than any other single option. The important thing to remember is that when you add an Internet connection, you also add considerable traffic to the existing LAN. You want to be absolutely sure that your network will be able to handle this additional traffic without causing more problems. Often, this type of prediction cannot be accurately assessed without performing a detailed analysis with a dedicated network analyzer such as the Sniffer products. If you do not have access to these products, or are not trained to use them, seriously consider contracting out this service before proceeding.

CONCEPTS AND DEPLOYMENT OF CACHING TECHNOLOGIES

The term *cache* (pronounced "cash") describes the process of copying frequently accessed data from its source location to some other media closer to the user. The concept of data caching has been used for years on file servers and CPUs, but it is equally effective for Internet data. Caching can be utilized in many different locations on the Internet path to increase overall performance. Again, some of these service points are under your control and others are not. The easiest cache to control is built right into the browser.

When a cache is implemented, the system takes a copy of the data requested by the user and stores it in memory. Some implementations use volatile storage such as active RAM and other systems use non-volatile storage such as hard drives, Jaz drives, or optical disks. When a user requests information from the Internet (usually a Web page) the application first queries the cache. If the requested data is in the cache, the data is sent directly to the user, avoiding the long process of connecting to the Internet and retrieving the information all over again. If the information is not in cache, the application continues as normal, but places a copy of the retrieved data into the cache after delivering it to the user. It's easy to see that caching can greatly increase performance, *if* the same information is frequently queried. Figure 3-2 depicts two common areas where cache technology can be implemented and controlled on your local PCs and networks.

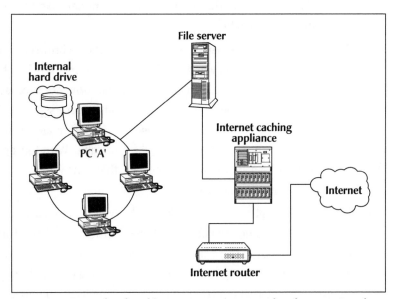

FIGURE 3-2 Example of caching access points on a local area network

Web-Browser Caching

The Web browser has caching capabilities built into the software. These pages are called *browser cache*. As you view Web pages and download files, the data is copied to RAM or the local hard drive up to the amount defined in the browser's preference settings. The browser also has a setting for controlling how often it checks the source for new revisions. This is important, as you don't want to view outdated (called *stale*) pages. Setting a larger cache size improves performance, at the cost of RAM or disk space. If your computer is limited on either of these, be careful how you allocate resources. Additionally, there are adjustable settings to control how often the browser checks for updates to a page taken from the cache. These options include

○ **When the page is requested.** This option instructs the browser to compare the page at the Internet site with the one stored in the cache. If the one at the site is newer, the browser reloads the page from the Internet site and copies the new page to cache. If not, the cached page is sent to the browser. This option assures that you always have the most current page, but is a bit slower than other options because the Internet site has to be queried before the page is presented to the user. On the other hand, this option can be faster than not using cache at all, because if a page has not changed, the data can be fetched from the faster local storage rather than across the slower Internet connection.

○ **When you start the browser.** This option instructs the browser to check all of the cached information when you first start your browser. This takes a little longer up front, but can increase overall performance because each page is not verified as you view them. With a large cache setting of 1MB or higher, the startup penalty may not be worth the performance penalty, but with a smaller cache size, it may hardly be noticeable. With this option, you run the risk that a page will be updated after the cache was checked, thereby giving you a stale page.

○ **Never.** With this option, you are telling the browser to always display the information stored in cache and not to check the Internet for updates. This may seem a bit useless, but there are a number of reasons you may use this. The primary reason is if you have a dial-up connection and you want the ability to perform some Internet browsing off-line. For example, if you frequently view a particular site that contains fairly static (non-changing) data, you could set the browser up so that the connection to the Internet is not automatically established while you're looking at this site. Because no requests are made to an outside network, the DUN service is never called upon to establish the dial-up connection. This would allow you to retrieve your information from the Web site very quickly without having to make the jump out to the Internet.

If you remember the discussions of the browsers from Chapter 2, the Refresh or Reload button forces the browser to download the requested Internet page whether it's in the cache or not. If you suspect that a page is stale, you can simply click the Refresh or Reload button to get the current version.

To adjust the settings of the cache in Internet Explorer v5.0 and above, follow these steps with the browser open. (The following options are located under the "View" menu option on browsers older than version 5.)

1. Select Tools ⇨ Internet Options. Click the Settings button.

2. The Settings dialog box as shown in Figure 3-3 is displayed.

FIGURE 3-3 Cache settings dialog box in Internet Explorer version 5

To adjust the settings of the cache in Netscape Navigator, follow these steps with the browser open.

1. Select Edit ⇨ Preferences. Then, in the Category tree on the left of the dialog box, select Advanced and Cache.

2. The Settings dialog box as shown in Figure 3-4 is displayed.

Depending on how often you visit the Web, and how many different sites you go to, it may be advisable to force the browser's cache to clear from time to time.

To clear the cache in Internet Explorer, refer to Figure 3-5 and follow these steps:

1. Select Tools ⇨ Internet Options.

2. The main dialog box contains a section labeled Temporary Internet Files. From here, you can delete the current contents (which is the cache) or change the cache settings.

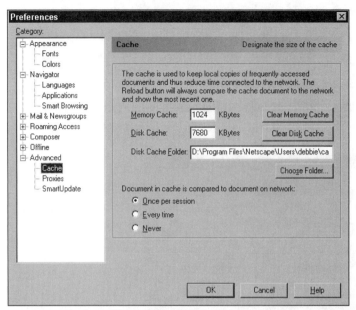

FIGURE 3-4   Cache settings dialog box in Netscape Navigator version 4.6

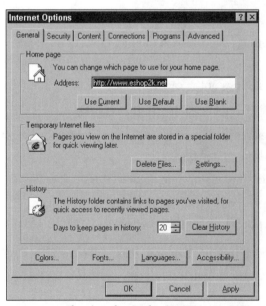

FIGURE 3-5   Clearing the Cache (Temporary Internet Files) in Internet Explorer
version 5

Referring back to Figure 3-4, the following steps clear the cache contents in Netscape Navigator:

1. Select Edit ⇨ Preferences. Then, in the Category tree on the left of the dialog box, select Advanced and Cache.

2. By selecting the two buttons on the right side of the dialog box, you can clear the cache in RAM, or the cache on the disk.

exam preparation pointer

The i-Net+ exam will expect you to understand the concept of the browser cache, where the settings are maintained, and how to clear the cache. Be sure you understand these concepts and know where the configuration tools are located for both types of browser.

Internet Caching Appliances

When the Internet was being designed, the concept of caching never entered the big picture. I doubt the originators ever imagined that the Net would reach the point that it has, and performance would become such an important issue. However, as businesses rush to get their private networks connected, they soon face performance problems.

At the close of 1998, there were roughly 140 million users on the Internet worldwide. The number of World Wide Web pages increases by an estimated 300,000 per week. Traffic over the Internet's infrastructure is doubling every year, and some Internet Service Providers see traffic growth of 1,000 percent a year. Recent estimates indicate that by 2001, the number of Web users will increase to over 175 million. No other technology has become so pervasive in such a short time. With the growing use of the Internet, issues such as network bandwidth, reliability, and performance are not just technical considerations, they are mission-critical concerns—especially for corporations who have emerging dependencies on successful e-commerce.

Browser caching helps reduce download times, but corporate networks need better answers and better solutions. Enter the *Internet Caching Appliance*, or ICA. These devices are designed simply to cache large amounts of information from the Internet for a specific group of people. Most of the time, one ICA is sufficient to boost performance for an entire LAN, but you can use multiple appliances to target specific applications, users, or selected areas of the Internet itself. By storing often-requested objects locally, in a cache, the ICA helps protect the network from traffic surges. In fact, the more users request the same Internet data, the more effective the cache is. The data is increasingly served locally, decreasing and often eliminating the traffic that would have otherwise demanded precious bandwidth. As a rule of thumb, a cache has a "hit" rate of 35 percent, which means that 35 percent of content requested through them can be successfully cached, and they therefore reduce upstream traffic on the network by that same percentage.

The ICA is typically a combined hardware-software solution designed as a self-contained "black box" that requires minimal installation and administration. Caching appliances are simply attached to the network like any other hardware resource, such as a printer or a router. Looking again at Figure 3-2: The ICA is centrally located on the local area network where it can cache requested data for all users. Regardless of who visits the Web page, others who ask for the same page later will benefit from the cache performance. Many of these appliances can be preconfigured to automatically download a specific list of Web pages and keep them current. Because these devices are designed specifically for this task, they are able to store and maintain large amounts of cached data, often in the hundreds of gigabytes range. In addition, the ICA can support gigabytes of RAM that increase cache retrieval exponentially.

With the increasing volume of Internet traffic and the resulting degradation in overall backbone performance, many ICA vendors are rallying for a new caching standard for the major Internet Access Points. This proposal places Internet Caching Appliances at strategic locations along the Internet backbone, and ISPs at every level. These ICAs then communicate with each other when requests for Internet information is generated. Because the very nature of cache technology has the caching capabilities increasing with the number of users accessing the cache, it only makes sense that Internet-wide caching has the potential to increase overall performance tremendously.

Forward Caching Technologies

ICAs are not only an effective way to increase Web browsing and file downloading, but they also offer attractive solutions to businesses that publish Web and file content to the Internet. Many businesses are rushing to put up electronic storefronts, or *e-commerce* sites. Poor performance can rapidly translate into lost sales and bad reputations. The ICA can be placed *in front* of the serving computers to provide *forward caching* for Web publishing acceleration. A sample diagram of this solution is depicted in Figure 3-6.

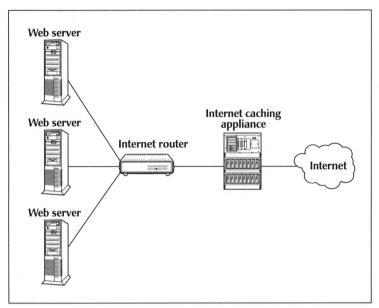

FIGURE 3-6   A Forward Cache design to increase Web server performance

To implement this caching technology, you simply place the ICA as the front end to one or more Web servers. This appliance then pretends to be the Web server, and browsers connect to it instead of directly to the Web server. The bulk of the Web service workload is thus off-loaded to the cache. The ICA stores the most frequently requested Web objects in RAM, enabling it to respond extremely quickly. Non-cacheable requests are passed through to the Web server, most of the time as fast or faster than if the browser were directly connected.

Internet Proxies

The previous two cache options have shown the two extreme ends of cache technology. Both methods deal specifically with increasing Internet performance. In the middle of these extremes is the Internet *proxy server.* A proxy server is placed between the Internet and the local area network and offers services in addition to caching. While similar in nature to the ICA, in that a proxy usually performs LAN-wide caching, a proxy is not strictly dedicated to caching. A proxy can be used as a very cost effective way to provide Internet access to many computers and offer a significant security measure as well. Proxy servers contain two network connections, one directly to the Internet, and the other to the local area network. All requests for

Internet services from the LAN are routed to the proxy that performs the actual retrieval of the information. Figure 3-7 shows an example of how this might look.

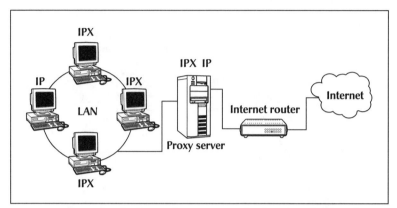

FIGURE 3-7   **Example of a Proxy Server on a mixed protocol network**

Notice that many of the PCs on the local area network are configured with IPX only. The Internet does not "speak" IPX, so normally these computers would either need an IP stack bound to them, or they would not be able to access Internet services at all. However, because the proxy server is connected to the LAN and the Internet with both the IPX and IP protocol, the proxy can assist the IPX-only computers to interact with the Internet. The proxy server can be, and usually is, configured as an Internet cache server as well. This is logical, because all Internet traffic is routed through this computer in the first place. This solution is considered an in-between solution, because caching is only one part of what the proxy server accomplishes.

Proxy device considerations

Proxy servers usually take two forms. Either the proxy is a black box dedicated only to proxy services, or it consists of a standard computer running special proxy software. Both of these technologies have advantages and disadvantages. The next section will examine the issues raised by both solutions.

Dedicated proxy devices

The dedicated proxy black box has become very popular in the past two years due to the high demand for increased Internet performance, and because of its normally low cost. One of the leaders in this technology is a company called Ramp

Networks (`www.rampnet.com`) whose WebRamp product was one of the first to market. Originally shipped as an analog proxy/router, this product has matured into providing all sorts of Internet connectivity solutions. Solutions such as these contain one or more analog, ISDN, or xDSL modems and connect directly to the LAN. Using this Internet connection point, users then have common access to the Internet. When analog modems are used, these devices are typically capable of *bonding* the connections together to create a single, larger connection to the ISP. For example, if the proxy box contains three 56Kbps modems, the device can connect to the ISP on all three lines simultaneously and bond these connections together to provide a single 168Kbps connection for all LAN users to share. Remember, however, that the best speed you are likely to achieve on analog lines is 45Kbps, so realistically these devices will bond together to at best a 135Kbps connection. However, this is still much better than a single, dedicated modem. Because the connection type is dial-up, the proxy device automatically initiates the dial-up connection when the first request for an Internet service is received.

If other users request access when a connection is already in progress, they simply "camp" on the existing connection. They are not required to wait while the dial-up process takes place, because the connection is already established. The line is not terminated until the last Internet user stops requesting Internet services. The cost savings here are obvious. The company only requires a single dial-up account with the ISP (around $25 per month) and this device, which sells for between $300 and $800 depending on options. This is a practical solution for light-duty Internet access requirements on LANs from 2 to 15 users. If the dedicated box is equipped with a digital connection type, such as ISDN or xDSL, the number of users adequately supported can extend up to 50.

A downside to the dedicated proxy "black-box" is that you are locked into the purchased connection type. If you purchase an analog dial-up box, then later decide to switch to xDSL, you will need to completely replace the device.

Software proxy solutions

Because the software proxy solution requires the addition of a dedicated computer, it usually carries a higher price tag. However, the additional flexibility of this option makes it more attractive to many. Like the dedicated proxy device, proxy software has proliferated in recent months. Prices for these applications range from free to thousands of dollars, mostly depending on how many users are supported and what additional features are included. On the hardware side, because the proxy is not performing "number crunching" type services, the CPU does not have to be the latest and greatest. Under normal conditions, a Pentium II-233, a 300MHz Celeron, or any equivalent processor will do nicely. The speed of the Network Interface Card (NIC), RAM, and disk space are more important. If possible, you should use a 100Mbps or higher NIC connected directly into a switched Ethernet port. While most proxy software runs on Windows 95/98/NT or Linux, the rest of the hardware should be configured to match the operating system's recommended components. Because the proxy does the caching for you, faster hard drives produce the best overall performance.

For a small number of users, perhaps a home office or small LAN, many free and inexpensive proxy servers are available. One of the finest free applications is simply called *Proxy* and is available for download at www.analogx.com. This extremely small (under 300K!) program offers a host of features and is perfect for sharing Internet access among a small (2 to 10) group of computers. This proxy does not offer Web caching but nonetheless is an excellent program for the purpose it serves.

For a very reasonable price, between $20 and $1,000 depending on the number of users, Wingate proxy server (wingate.deerfield.com) is probably the industry's best. This product offers a full range of services including proxy, firewall (security), and caching and can handle just about any size LAN. Wingate was among the very first low-cost alternatives for Internet proxy and caching and has undergone many improvements over its lifetime.

If your network is based on Microsoft's NT BackOffice product, you have a copy of Microsoft Proxy Server. This high-end proxy application seamlessly integrates into the NT operating system and provides a high degree of security via NT's user manager utility.

Although the software solution offers the same basic functions of the hardware only device, the major advantage of this method is its flexibility. The software operates with whatever Internet connection you select. The computer can be equipped with analog modems so the proxy software dials the ISP exactly as the hardware device does. In addition, the computer can be configured with a Network Interface Card to directly connect to the ISP, or it can connect through a router on the LAN. All of these options can be installed without the need to change or upgrade the proxy software. This greatly reduces reconfiguration costs and eliminates the need to purchase new hardware to take advantage of better connection methods.

Configuring Internet applications to use a proxy server

Almost all Internet applications allow the use of a proxy server. Both Internet Explorer and Navigator provide this feature, as do the major e-mail and FTP programs. Although many different Internet applications are in use today, we'll take a look at some of the more popular programs and see how they're configured for proxy use.

Web browsers

The connection method for Microsoft's Internet applications, including Internet Explorer and Outlook/Outlook Express (e-mail and Newsgroups) are defined from the Windows Control Panel. To define the proxy settings, follow these steps:

1. Select Start ⇨ Settings ⇨ Control Panel. When the Control Panel window opens, double-click Internet Options.
2. Select the Connections Tab, and click LAN Settings.
3. In the Proxy Server section, check the Use a Proxy Server check box.
4. Enter in the IP address of the proxy server computer or device.
5. Enter in the *Port* number for the Web services. As we learned in Chapter 2, the default port for the HTTP (Web) protocol is 80. If you've modified this setting on your proxy server, enter that value in this field instead.

Proxy settings for the Navigator browser are set from within the browser window as shown in Figures 3-8 and 3-9. The necessary configuration steps are as follows:

1. Select Edit ⇨ Preferences.
2. Select Advanced Settings.
3. Select Proxies.
4. Select Manual Proxy Configuration, and then click View.
5. In the Manual Proxy Configuration dialog box that appears, enter in the IP address of your proxy server and the corresponding port number.

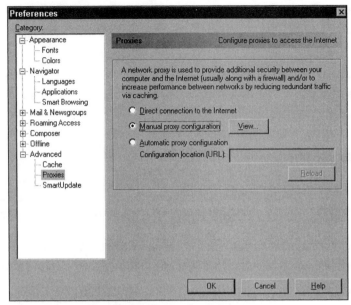

FIGURE 3-8 Configuring Navigator for Proxy use

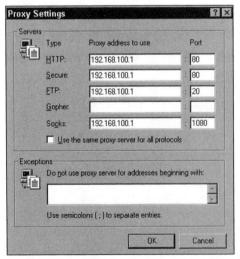

FIGURE 3-9 Configuring Server and Port numbers for Proxy use in Navigator

Qualcomm's Eudora is another very popular e-mail program. To configure it to use a proxy, start the application and follow these steps:

1. Select Tools ➪ Options.

2. In the Category section, select Getting Started.

3. Select Mail Server (Incoming), and enter the name or IP address of the proxy computer/device.

4. In the Login Name field, enter your POP3 account including your username and password.

5. Again in the Category section, Select Sending Mail.

6. In the Return Address field, enter your return email address as normal.

7. In the SMTP server field, enter the name or IP address of the proxy computer/device.

Other e-mail clients and Internet applications are configured in the same way. Consult the program's documentation for additional information.

PERFORMANCE ISSUES FOR WEB SERVERS

So far, this chapter has concentrated on improving performance strictly from the client side, but for companies who have Web sites, outbound performance issues are equally critical. Many of the issues we've dealt with already, such as connection types, ISP selection, and LAN performance tuning, should be followed for server performance as well. A very important item not to overlook in Internet serving performance is the physical hardware and software you use. Just as desktop applications perform better when run from a high-end computer designed to act as a server, so will your Internet content be served faster from a better server. Various operating systems can impact performance, as can the Internet server software itself. In addition, the way a Web site is designed, built, and maintained affects the performance end users deal with. I will discuss Internet servers and Web site development in detail in Chapter 6, but it's prudent to examine some performance issues now.

Web Site Creation Considerations

Let's examine a fictitious Web site for IDG Books. The basic construction of the www.idgbooks.com Web site is shown in Figure 3-10. Within each of these Web pages, various graphics, text, sound, and video will be used.

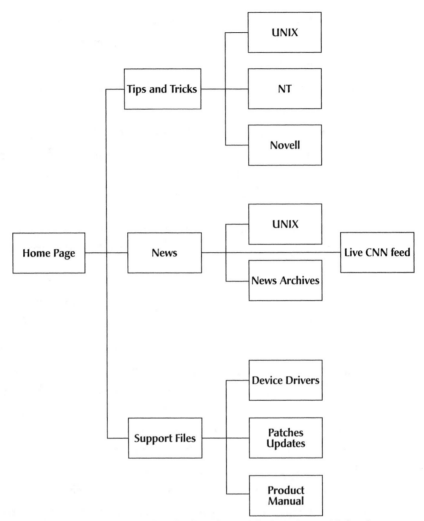

FIGURE 3-10 Tree structure for the fictitious Web site of www.idgbooks.com

Many Web authors are tempted to put their flashiest content right on the first page. This may be a great attention-getter, but if the opening page takes too long to load, most visitors won't wait and your content will never be seen. The first page of the Web site should be simple but informative, with links to other pages within the site that can contain more flair. Using a site map such as that used by idgbooks.com makes it much easier to visualize the overall flow of the site and provides a roadmap to plan when and where certain objects should be used.

Even on simple pages, certain multimedia components can cause the page to load too slowly. Among the biggest culprits are music and video files, high-resolution graphics, animated GIF files (discussed later), and links to objects on other Web sites. The use of music is (fortunately) losing favor among most Web programmers, but these other objects can still be found on many sites. The best index Web pages contain just enough simple graphics to look good and sufficient text to describe the purpose of the site and to help visitors navigate the rest of the pages. When designing Web pages, especially the "front door," keep these principles in mind:

o Use graphics sparingly, and use color reduction when possible. Many free and shareware programs exist that will reduce the color depth of your graphics. Although most good graphics programs do this, a lower-cost alternative is the GIF Cruncher program, available for about $50.00 (`www.spinwave.com`).

o Use Interlaced GIF images (we'll discuss image types in a later chapter) when possible. An interlaced GIF "fades in" from a blocky low-resolution image to higher resolutions as it is downloaded. Many users find this less frustrating than watching an image download line by line.

o If you have a lot of images to present on one page, use *thumbnails* (small versions) and link the larger images to them. This allows readers to choose the images they're willing to spend the extra time downloading.

o Always indicate the HEIGHT and WIDTH of your images in your HTML. Many browsers cannot display any part of a page until they know all of the dimensions of the objects that the page consists of.

o Do not include the `http://` directive when linking to pages and images located on your server. This prevents most browsers from caching them and causes the information to be reloaded as your readers navigate around your site.

Many home pages also utilize free "counter" services. These services keep track of the number of *hits* or visitors the site has had. To use these services, the graphic logo of the service must usually be included on the page. This creates a link to the serving site, so your page cannot complete until it has made an additional Internet connection to the service provider's site, which adds additional performance overhead.

Let's briefly examine the sample pages shown in Figures 3-11 and 3-12.

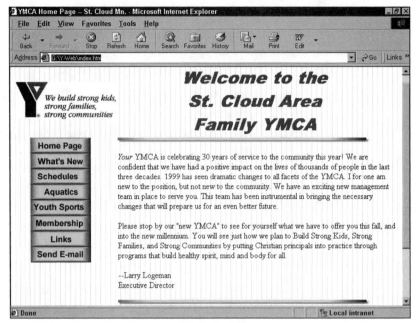

FIGURE 3-11   Example of a simple Web site home page

As you can see in Figure 3-11, this page is pretty basic. Graphics are limited to the organization's logo and a few navigation buttons. The bulk of the page is informative text. Visitors to this page will quickly know what they can find there without having to wait 30 to 60 seconds for the page to load. As a rule of thumb, you should assume that most Internet users will not wait longer than 45 seconds before either stopping a page from loading, or leaving a page altogether.

The page shown in Figure 3-12 makes much more use of graphics and other multimedia components. The calendar is created dynamically (the dates are calculated from the current day, and then each piece of the calendar is displayed). In addition, each day contains a hyperlink to another page that shows scheduled items for the selected day. To add a little pizzazz, the *Announcement* graphic initiates the playing of a 200K WAV file. The visitor requested the page and knows that there is information of particular interest to him or her (the schedule of events). So, it's much more likely that they will wait while the components of this page load.

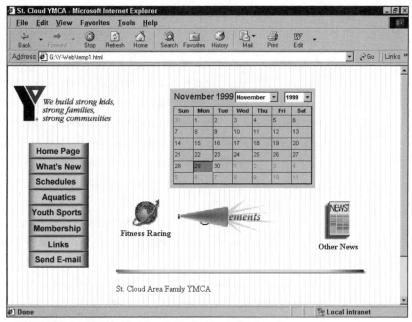

FIGURE 3-12 Example of a simple Web site home page

Using Effective Indexing and Site Maps

As people explore your Web site, they will be either looking for specific information, or just browsing. For e-commerce sites, most people are potential customers looking to make a purchase. It is extremely important that you don't lose a sale simply because the customer was unsuccessful in locating the item they wished to see or weren't aware it existed on your site. As products, services, and other items of interest (product reports, user manuals, reviews, or other documentation) are added they should be categorized and indexed.

In addition, the site map allows the viewer to visualize what categories are contained within your Web site and quickly jump to the appropriate page. The site map therefore is like a roadmap for the viewer to easily find what information you have placed on the site. The site map can be part of the main page, or self-contained within a page of its own.

Internet Search Engines

Creating index and search tags to be picked up by the major Internet search engines is very important. In Chapters 6 and 7 we'll look at how to add these keywords into your Web pages, and how commercial search engines index your site based on keywords and other text items contained within your pages. Most people will find your site either by following a link from another site (such as a banner ad) or by locating you through a major search engine or directory service such as *Yahoo!, Excite,* or *Lycos.* The search engines of these companies contain keyword references to the content of your site and provide methods for users to search for Internet sites based on phrases or keywords. For example, using Yahoo! to search Internet sites with the phrase "Coffee Makers" locates 51 separate Web pages. If your business sells, rents, or repairs coffee makers, you want to be included on that list.

Many of these search engines allow you to create your own record on their sites. You submit a form that includes a description of your site, along with keywords that you've predetermined. However, most of the larger search engines use a *spider* application. These special programs automatically review your site on the Internet and build a list of keywords based on various text algorithms. The most common method is to look for specific words within the text portion of your pages. This eliminates some work on your side, if you're willing to let these automated programs make assumptions of what your site is trying to convey. For example, your company might produce the best coffee maker in the world, but if these spider applications fail to recognize that fact, you may very well not be listed on a Yahoo! Search.

Most of the major spider applications allow you to place special *meta-tags* in your HTML documents to tell the program what specific keywords they should record.

The spider application must be programmed to understand this particular meta-tag, or the line is ignored. Most of the major search engines tell you what meta-tags they support, and what format must be followed for the spider to recognize the tags. When submitting your site to specific search providers, make sure you understand which meta-tags their spider uses.

Web searching techniques

The more information available on the Internet, the harder it is to locate. Fine-tuning your skills at searching the Internet will save you many hours of time and frustration and help you understand how your site is listed with the major search engines. Although each site uses different search methods, some basic techniques are usually common to all. Keyword searches, using words relating to what you're seeking, is the primary search method. Many of these utilities use special characters to designate how keywords are utilized, such as the plus (+) or minus (-) signs. Also, the use of quotation marks makes a difference. For example, if you performed a search at Yahoo with the keywords *NetWare Printing* you would find all sites with the words NetWare *or* Printing contained in them. However, if you were looking only for sites that contain *both* words as in "Printing with NetWare," you would place the phrase between quotation marks, like *"NetWare Printing."* Using the plus sign specifies that the keywords must all appear in the results, and a minus sign tells the search engine that the specified word must not appear in the results. For example, a search with keywords *NetWare + Printing* will locate sites pertaining to NetWare that *also* contain the words *Printing*. Likewise, a search with *NetWare – Printing* results in a list of NetWare sites that *do not* contain the phrase Printing

HANDS-ON EXERCISES

In the following lab you will test the caching capabilities of your browser software to see first hand how caching improves Web-browsing performance. Additionally, you'll install a proxy server to share a single Internet connection between two computers and examine the caching features of the proxy.

note ▼ **Prerequisites for the following exercise: To use the proxy for this lab, you will need two computers connected together. Both computers will need a functioning Network Interface Card. A network hub or switch is recommended between the computers, but a crossover Ethernet cable can be used directly between the PCs as well. If you don't already have a network setup, you can use the peer-to-peer networking built into Windows 95/98/NT. Additional information about setting up a home network, including directions for creating a crossover cable, can be found at** www.homepclan.com.

Web-Browser Caching

To experience the full impact of Web caching, start your browser of choice and turn the caching features off. The setup is slightly different for each browser.

To turn off caching in Internet Explorer 5, follow these steps:

1. Select Tools ⇨ Internet Options.
2. In the Temporary Internet Files section, click Delete Files, then select Settings.
3. In the Settings dialog box, check Never.
4. Write down the current amount of disk space reserved for temporary files.
5. Change the amount of disk space for temporary files to 1MB (the lowest amount allowed).

To turn off caching in Netscape Navigator 4.6, follow these steps:

1. Select Edit ⇨ Preferences.
2. Click Advanced, then click Cache.
3. Write down the current settings for Memory and Disk cache sizes.
4. Enter 0 as the cache size for the Memory and Disk settings.
5. Clear both the Memory and Disk cache by clicking their associated control buttons.
6. Select Never in the Advanced/Cache dialog box.

Now, to test how a page loads without a cache, follow these steps:

1. Close and restart your browser.
2. In the Address/location box, type `www.idgbooks.com`.
3. Visually note the length of time it takes the page to load.
4. Close and restart the browser.
5. In the Address/location box, type in `www.idgbooks.com`.
6. Note the length of time it takes the page to load.

Both times this page is loaded, all of the graphics and other elements must be read from the Internet server directly. Depending on your connection speed, you should be able to see each graphic as it's being displayed.

Now reset the cache settings in your browser and do the exercise again.

For Internet Explorer 5, follow these steps:

1. Select Tools ⇨ Internet Options.

2. In the Temporary Internet Files section, select Settings.

3. In the Settings dialog box, check the Every Time You Start Internet Explorer check box.

4. Change the amount of disk space for temporary files back to its original value.

For Netscape Navigator 4.6, follow these steps:

1. Select Edit ⇨ Preferences.

2. Click Advanced, and then click Cache.

3. Enter the original values for the cache sizes of the Memory and Disk settings.

4. Select Every Time in the Advanced/Cache dialog box.

Now see how the page loads with caching turned on.

1. Close and restart your browser.

2. In the Address/location box, type `www.idgbooks.com`.

3. Visually note the length of time it takes the page to load.

4. Close and restart the browser.

5. In the Address/location box, type `www.idgbooks.com`.

6. Note the length of time it takes the page to load.

This time, the browser cached the Web page after your first visit in Step 2, so the second time you visited the page (Step 5) should be noticeably faster.

Network Caching Through a Proxy Server

In this section you'll take a look at the caching capabilities of the network proxy server. You'll need two connected PCs to perform this exercise. If you don't already have TCP/IP configured on your computers, follow the online help for your Windows operating system to properly configure IP before beginning this section. For this exercise, we'll use the following IP addresses.

The Proxy Server's IP address is 192.168.100.1, with a subnet mask of 255.255.255.0. The Second PC's IP address is 192.168.100.2, with a subnet mask of 255.255.255.0.

If you already have static IP addresses assigned to your computers, simply replace your addresses with these where appropriate.

1. Follow the installation instructions in the back of this book to install the proxy software supplied on the included CD.

2. In the network settings dialog box of the second PC, change the default gateway address to 192.168.100.1, your proxy server.

3. On both computers, change the browser's connection settings to use the proxy server. This is different for Internet Explorer and Netscape Navigator.

   For Internet Explorer 5

   a. Start the browser and select Tools ➪ Internet Options. Click the Connections tab.

   b. Click the LAN Settings button.

   c. Click the Use a Proxy Server check box.

   d. Enter 192.168.100.1 as the IP address of the proxy server (or substitute your actual IP address).

   e. Enter 80 as the Port.

   f. Select OK.

   For Netscape Navigator 4.6

   a. Select Edit ➪ Preferences.

   b. Click Advanced.

   c. Select Proxies.

   d. Select Manual Proxy Configuration and click the View button.

   e. Enter 192.168.100.1 as the IP address of the proxy server (or substitute your actual IP address).

   f. Enter 80 as the Port.

   g. Click OK.

4. On the computer running the Proxy server, start your browser. The proxy software should initiate a connection with the ISP and your default home page will be displayed.

5. From the second PC, start your browser. On this computer, the home page should load without the normal wait for the dial-up networking process to call the ISP. In addition, your home page will already be in the proxy's cache so the page display should be very quick.

6. From the Proxy PC, go to `www.idgbooks.com`.

7. Now from the second PC, go to `www.idgbooks.com` and notice the difference in speed between the two displays. The proxy PC needed to download the page from the Internet site, while the second PC simply displayed the page from the proxy cache.

8. Alternating between the two computers, visit other Web sites and note the performance of the browser when you visit a page the other computer has already visited. If you have more than two computers on your LAN, try going to Web sites that you've visited and see how fast the pages are displayed.

9. Follow the steps from the last exercise to remove Internet caching from one of the browsers. Now revisit a Web page while connected through the proxy. Was the performance faster than without the proxy? Does the cache on the browser make a noticeable difference when connecting through the proxy?

EXAM PREPARATION SUMMARY

This chapter looked at a number of internal and external factors that affect the performance of Internet access. There are a number of access points and fine-tuning measures you can do to maximize the performance of your Internet service.

Now review the key concepts for this chapter to make sure you understand the material you just read.

- For businesses, a strong case can be made for deploying dedicated digital connections. The *Return On Investment* (ROI) is usually easy to calculate by simply analyzing the monthly cost of current fax usage.

- Typically, the speed of Internet access is only as fast as its slowest link. There are many factors that you have no control over, but by fine-tuning the components and implementing other performance techniques, you can greatly compensate for the areas out of your control. Of these techniques, caching technologies from the browser to the LAN can provide tremendous performance increases even with slow connections.

○ When designing and building Web pages and other Internet services, special attention must be paid to ensure that visitors are able to download information quickly and easily. Limiting the use of graphics and eliminating unnecessary multimedia components, especially on the front page, can increase the chances that visitors will continue past the first page to view other, possibly more artistic pages on the site. Providing the proper search tools and keywords is also very important so visitors will know how to find the site and be able to easily find specific information quickly. When designing a Web page, make a site map to make it easy to visualize the entire site in a single glance.

APPLYING WHAT YOU HAVE LEARNED

The following review questions give you an opportunity to test your knowledge of the information presented in this chapter. The answers to these assessment questions can be found in Appendix B. If you missed some, review those sections in this chapter before going further. Be aware, there may be more than one correct answer to each question.

Instant Assessment Questions

1. The fastest upload speed possible from a dial-up modem is

   A. 56Kbps

   B. 33Kbps

   C. 45Kbps

   D. 53Kbps

2. The specification of 56K modems is

   A. V.90

   B. V.35

   C. NAP

   D. DUN

3. Which of these connection types is generally the fastest?

   A. T1

   B. ISDN

   C. xDSL

   D. OC3

4. Running multiple protocols on a LAN, such as TCP/IP, IPX, and NetBEUI can increase overall performance because applications don't need to worry about what protocol to use; the network will provide this function.

   A. True

   B. False

5. Cache technology can be implemented

   A. In the browser

   B. By the desktop operating system

   C. By a special appliance connected to the network

   D. Only on Internet Explorer and Netscape Navigator

6. Caching technology works best when

   A. Implemented by a browser for only one person

   B. Many people use a Web browser

   C. Many Internet sites are visited infrequently

   D. Placed between the LAN and the Internet for all users

7. Cached files in Internet Explorer are called

   A. Seldom Used Files

   B. Temporary Internet Files

   C. Downloaded Files

   D. Cache Pages

8. When cost is more of a factor than performance gains, which proxy type is the best selection for a LAN with less than 20 computers?

   A. An ICA (Internet Caching Appliance)

   B. A dedicated "black box" proxy than bonds multiple dial-up lines

   C. A Pentium III computer with proxy software

   D. A dedicated ISDN, xDSL, or cable connection to the ISP

9. Indexing your site for publication on the World Wide Web should contain

   A. Keywords that help search engines such as that used by Yahoo! properly categorize your site

   B. A keyword "parsing" routine that allows searching on each word in a phrase

   C. Links to other sites of similar interest

   D. A keyword mechanism that searches on words and/or complete phrases

10. Placing predefined keywords in an HTML page is done through the use of

   A. Quotation marks

   B. Meta tags

   C. Square brackets

   D. Preceding the list with "Keywords="

Internet Clients

I n Part II, you'll look at the client side of the Internet circle. In order to use the services offered on the Internet, you need the proper software and infrastructure to support those services. You'll take a close look at the TCP/IP protocol suite, which is the "language" spoken by Internet computers. A firm understanding of this protocol suite is essential in every aspect of the Internet, and the i-Net+ exam will focus on this area greatly. As part of my discussion on TCP/IP, you'll see how people can use more familiar names to access different parts of the Internet instead of using the cryptic numbering systems computers need. You'll also see how to automate and organize the client settings to make our lives easier when large numbers of computers need to be maintained.

No matter which career path you take within the Internet industry, you'll probably have to deal with problem resolution and troubleshooting. In Part II we will examine many of the potential problems you're likely to face and see how to solve these issues with a systematic approach. You'll also see what common tools are available to help us identify, isolate, and resolve common Internet problems.

Another critical issue that needs to be addressed from the client prospective is security. Although you'll see later on that many security tools exist at the network and server levels, there are also many important client-sided security components that will help prevent accidental and intentional misuse of the Internet.

i-NET+™

The Building Blocks

About Chapter 4

Ihave alluded to all Internet devices having a unique address. In this chapter, you'll take a detailed look at these addressing protocols. Although entire books have been written about Internet addressing protocols, you will only examine the basic concepts required to get things started. After you have passed the i-Net+ exam, I highly encourage you to continue your studies, starting with Internet addressing. Although not terribly difficult to master, addresses are critical in all aspects of Internet services.

We're going to take a deep look into the various protocols that make communications across the Internet possible. No matter what area of the Internet you find yourself in, the protocols responsible for keeping data moving are important. From Web development to network design, understanding and following the rules of the protocol is a necessity.

We've discussed the client-server concept on which most Internet services are based, and in this chapter we'll look closer at the various Internet clients. For the i-Net+ exam you are expected to know what clients are used for which service and to have a basic idea of how they are configured.

So hang up the ISP connection for a short while and let's get started by seeing how Internet addressing works.

UNDERSTANDING PROTOCOLS

Imagine you are traveling to another country, a country whose native language is not your own. It's not hard to understand that communicating with the people you meet along the way is going to present a few problems. Perhaps you've picked up a translation dictionary, or have arranged for an interpreter. But even with these tools, your conversations will be somewhat limited. In Chapter 3, we saw how a proxy server can enable your private network to "talk" one language (such as IPX) and still communicate on the Internet using IP. The proxy translated our "language" to be compatible with the Internet. However, the Internet as an entity only speaks one language, so it's important to understand how to configure and use this language of the Internet.

The computer industry has been notorious for using proprietary hardware and software. To provide new features, or to improve on existing ones, companies have had to develop their own ways of implementing these changes. Despite being ubiquitous now, the computer is a relatively new device. Forty years ago, when large corporations began to implement computer technology, a single vendor (IBM, Data General) normally provided all of the hardware and software, so a proprietary architecture was not a concern. As computers became cheaper, smaller, and more powerful, small businesses and individuals demanded systems that could communicate with one other. If they owned an IBM PC, they expected it to work with a Hewlett Packard printer.

To ensure that all computers connected to the Internet could communicate, a standard language was defined. This standard language is the *Transmission Control Protocol / Internet Protocol,* often shortened to *TCP/IP.* TCP/IP is not actually a language, but a set of rules that define how data is transported around the Internet. In fact, TCP/IP is not a single protocol, but refers to a *suite,* or collection of protocols. As long as all devices connected to the Internet adhere to the rules of TCP/IP, data can be efficiently passed from one point to another. Numerous other protocols are used throughout the Internet, but the basic transportation of data, regardless of these other protocols or services, is based on TCP/IP.

Because TCP/IP is the protocol responsible for addressing and transporting the data, other protocols define the rules that specify how services are provided on the Internet. For example, in Chapter 2 we briefly looked at the HTTP protocol which is the rule set for Web-server communications across the Internet, and FTP, which defines how files are transferred between computers. Hundreds of other protocols are in use today, and new ones are being developed and accepted on a regular basis. As new methods of Internet communications are refined, new protocols must be created so that all Internet devices can take advantage of the services. Although many protocols exist, we will only take an in-depth look at the major protocols in use today. These are the protocols covered on the i-Net+ exam.

TRANSMISSION CONTROL PROTOCOL / INTERNET PROTOCOL

If there were no standard method of transporting data across the Internet, all of the other protocols and services would be worthless. Therefore, we'll begin with, and spend most of this chapter examining, TCP/IP. Please understand that complete books have been written on TCP/IP, so our discussions are not going to be exhaustive by any means. But we will learn the basics, including what TCP/IP is, what it does, and how it's configured.

The Internet Protocol

Let's look first at IP, the Internet Protocol. Formally, IP is implemented at the network layer that contains network addresses and is used to route a message to a different network. IP accepts *packets* — specifically formatted data — from the transport protocol (TCP or UDP, discussed in the next section), and creates a *datagram* for delivery. A datagram is the term given to the specific format that IP uses to package the data. A datagram includes the source address, the destination address, and the actual data. Think of the datagram as a letter that you might send to a friend through the normal postal system. The envelope (datagram) contains the letter (data) on the inside, and the outside has your friend's address (destination), and your return address (source). For IP to perform its duty, each device on the network must have a unique address.

A good analogy for the function IP provides is to look at how normal mail delivery works. Every home, apartment, and business has a unique address. A unique address is created by combining a building number, a street name, and a city name. While it's very likely that the number 14 is assigned to many houses within a given city, there is only one house number 14 on any particular street. Likewise, there may be many addresses of 123 Main Street in the world, but only one exists in any given city. Certainly, if your address were exactly the same as another in your town, you'd spend a great deal of time traveling across town exchanging mail!

Likewise, each device on an IP network, including the Internet, must have a unique IP address. As I mentioned, an IP address is a 32-bit number, shown in decimal format as four sets of three digits. These sets are called *octets*, each representing eight bits, or one byte. Each octet contains numbers between 0 and 255 (for a total of 256 possible values). For example, 192.168.100.105 represents a valid IP address. It would be seem logical, then, to assume there are a maximum of 4,294,967,296 possible Internet addresses available. The problem is, an IP address doesn't represent only the address of the end device (your house, for example) but also the network (your street) where the device exists. The network portion is identified in the first part of the address, and the end device, called the *host,* is identified in the second part of the address. In Internet lingo, everything connected to the network — client computers, servers, routers, and so forth — is called a host.

IP address classifications

So how can we identify which part of our IP address defines the network portion and which defines the host? First, IP addresses are divided up into *classes* as shown in Figure 4-1.

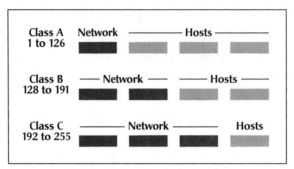

FIGURE 4-1 Matrix of IP address classifications

In Figure 4-1, we see that all IP address that begin with numbers between 1 and 126 are class A addresses. Likewise, IP addresses beginning with numbers between 128 and 191 are class B, and IP addresses equal to or greater than 192 are class C addresses. The class of the address helps us determine which part of the number represents the network portion, and which part is the host portion. Class A addresses tell us that only the *first* octet is used to define the network address and the last three octets define the host. Likewise, a class B address tells us that both the *first and second* octets define the network portion, while class C addresses use the first *three* octets to denote the network.

Knowing these classes, we can see that a class A IP address would allow for 126 separate networks, with each network containing a maximum of 16,777,216 hosts. If you were a city planner, you probably wouldn't want to base your street design on a class A IP scheme. If you did, you would be forced to use a maximum of 126 streets, even though each street could have over 16 million homes! A class B address might be more reasonable, with 16,384 streets each containing a maximum of 65,536 buildings. Yet, a class C formula might provide the best growth benefits. Using a class C system, your city could have many streets, 2,097,154 to be exact, but each street could have no more than 256 homes.

You may have noticed what looks like an omission in Figure 4-1. What happened to address 127? Class A runs from 1 to 126, but class B starts at 128, not 127. What gives? The IP address beginning with 127 is reserved for the local device.

This number always refers to the device where the IP protocol has been assigned. For example, if a computer is assigned the IP address of 192.168.100.110, it can also be referenced *locally* with the IP address of 127.0.0.1. The 127.0.0.1 address is primarily used for testing purposes to see if the IP has been properly configured.

There are additional exceptions to the address ranges defined within the IP classes. Suppose you want to send a message to everyone on a network. You could address the same message to each person separately. This takes time and is not very efficient. Therefore, IP provides an easier method, called a *broadcast*. When a device sees a broadcast message, it responds as if the message had been addressed specifically to that device. To accomplish this, broadcasts are transmitted using a zero. For example, the IP address 192.168.100.0 refers to the entire network defined as network number 192.168.100. In some instances, you might want to send a message to a selected *group* of people within a network. IP uses the number 255 for this purpose. Therefore, when assigning IP addresses, neither the network nor the host portion can be 0 or 255. To accommodate these special cases, the number of networks and hosts available for each IP class is reduced by two, as shown in Table 4-1

TABLE 4-1 NUMBER OF NETWORKS AND HOSTS PER IP CLASS

	CLASS RANGE	NUMBER OF NETWORKS	NUMBER OF HOSTS PER NETWORK
Class A	1 – 126	126	16,777,214
Class B	128 – 191	16,384	65,534
Class C	192 – 223	2,097,152	254

Defining a network

If we look at the number of hosts IP provides, it is easy to see that the Internet must be composed of multiple networks, or we would have run out of valid host addresses a long time ago. But what exactly defines a network? Generally, a network is created when a routing device is used to interconnect two or more groups of computers that share the same network number. Examine Figure 4-2. This figure shows two separate networks (with unique network numbers) connected by routers.

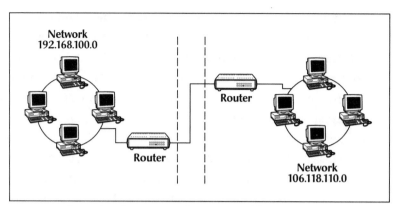

FIGURE 4-2 Example of two networks connected by routers

Most of the time, routing is performed by dedicated hardware appropriately called a *router*. Although not as common, a computer with two or more network interface cards (NICs) can also perform the routing functions. In Figure 4-2, each network has a router connected to its cable system. An additional port on the router is connected to some other medium that matches the router on the other end. For example, the two routers can be connected by a T1 or ISDN line. Although less likely, this connection could be made with analog dial-up modems as well.

Routers are matched in sets. If a company is connecting two (or more) of their own private networks, they maintain the routers connected to each network. If the business is connecting to the Internet, the company maintains the router attached to its network while the Internet Service Provider (ISP) maintains the router attached to their network. In all cases, routers are attached to each other and to a local network.

For private networks (networks not connected to the Internet), any IP address scheme can be used. However, when a network is connected to the Internet, it must use only registered addresses. For example, if the owner of the network 192.168.100.0 in our example wanted to add a router to connect to the Internet, all devices on that network would have to be readdressed with registered IP numbers. Simple math shows that IP addresses are in short supply. In fact, if every device that currently has Internet access used a registered IP address, there wouldn't be enough address to go around. This is one reason why many companies implement an Internet *proxy server*. The proxy computer is the only device on the private network that requires a registered IP address. Thus, an entire company can access the Internet with a single public address. Even with proxy servers, if Internet growth estimates are accurate, the network will run out of available IP address by the year 2003 or 2004. There simply aren't any alternatives to using the existing IP structure, so the Internet community is busy implementing the next step, IPv6. Briefly, IPv6 works much the same way as the current version, except that it increases the IP address size from 32 bits to 64 bits.

Subnets and subnetting

With the limited number of IP addresses available, a good address design would strive to achieve the best use of the available hosts on a particular IP address class. Often, however, the standard addressing methods create more networks, or more hosts, than are needed, wasting valuable IP addresses.

For example, suppose you are charged with connecting your company's 25 computers to the Internet, and you elect to assign each computer a valid IP address. If your ISP gives you a full class C address, 2,097,151 network addresses and 229 host address will go completely unused. With the shortage of registered Internet addresses, these situations simply cannot be allowed.

Therefore, the IP protocol provides a way to modify the basic addressing structure to make better use of a single IP address block. This method is known as *subnetting*. While the whole topic of subnets and subnet addressing can get quite complicated, it is important for us to understand the principles behind the process.

Every IP address is assigned a *subnet mask*. This is simply a numerical value that enables the IP process to determine precisely which part of the IP address is the network portion, and which is the host portion. Although the class structure provides this information for standard addressing, you must use the subnet mask when you're modifying the default address structure. Since there is no method other than the subnet mask to determine if a standard or modified addressing scheme is intended, all IP devices must include a subnet mask. Table 4-2 lists the default masks for the three IP classifications.

TABLE 4-2 DEFAULT SUBNET MASKS BY IP CLASS	
CLASS	*DEFAULT SUBNET MASK*
Class A	255.0.0.0
Class B	255.255.0.0
Class C	255.255.255.0

To understand how the subnet mask is applied for identifying the network from the host portion, we need to look at the IP address in binary form instead of decimal form. If you're not familiar with binary mathematics, the fundamental idea is that the only available numbers are zero (0) and one (1), and all possible values can be formed with combinations of 0 and 1.

Fundamentals of decimal-to-binary arithmetic

Please don't let this section intimidate you. Even if math isn't your strong point, I'm not going to lead you into a nuclear physics lesson, just a different way of looking at numbers. Binary is base 2, where decimal is base 10. For example, when counting in decimal you should start with 0, then 1, then 2, and so on, up to 9. For ten, you use a second digit in the tens place, and repeat the pattern: 10, 11, 12, 13,. Binary, or base 2, is exactly the same. However, you only have two numbers (0 and 1) to work with, not ten (0 through 9). Examine the series in Table 4-3.

TABLE 4-3 THE FIRST 10 NUMBERS IN DECIMAL AND BINARY FORMAT

DECIMAL	BINARY
0	0
1	1
2	10
3	11
4	100
5	101
6	110
7	111
8	1000
9	1001

Notice that the binary numbers follow a repeating pattern just like the decimal system, although they repeat more frequently because you only use two digits. Like the decimal system, when the highest digit is reached (9 in decimal, 1 in binary) the next number adds a new column, that is: 9 to 10, 99 to 100, and so on. The same holds true in binary as well: 1 to 10, 11 to 100.

To convert a decimal number to binary, you look at each number from *right to left* in factors of two. For example, 0, 2, 4, 8, 16, 32, 64, and so on. Examine the binary number 10011, which is 19 in our more familiar decimal thinking.

Move through the binary number from *right to left*. You have one 1, one 2, no 4s, no 8s, and one 16, as shown here:

SIXTEENS	EIGHTS	FOURS	TWOS	ONES
1	0	0	1	1
16	0	0	2	1

For each (one) identified, substitute its decimal equivalent and add it to the result, creating the formula: $16 + 0 + 0 + 2 + 1 = 19$

Now try the binary number 1100110:

(no) 1's, (one) 2, (one) 4, (no) 8's, (no) 16's, (one) 32, and (one) 64:

ONES	TWOS	FOURS	EIGHTS	SIXTEENS	THIRTY-TWOS	SIXTY-FOURS
0	1	1	0	0	1	1
0	2	4	0	0	32	64

$64 + 32 + 0 + 0 + 4 + 2 + 0 = 102$

Let's apply this to our subnet mask concept. The default mask for a class B IP address is
255.255.0.0

In binary, this is
11111111.11111111.00000000.00000000

Now, if you "borrow" a few bits from the third octet to use for the network address, you add, in effect, additional network addresses and reduce the number of available host addresses. Even though this is a class B IP number, if you modify the subnet mask, the network portion includes the first two octets *plus* part of the third octet. Without converting the decimal value into binary, this would not be possible. To properly determine how many bits of the IP address represent the network portion, you need to look at the IP address *and* the subnet mask both in binary format like the sample below:

130.110.30.60   10000010 11011110 00011110 00111100
255.255.255.224   11111111 11111111 11111111 11100000

The network portion is identified at the point where the binary digits of the subnet mask change to zero. So in this example, even though you have a class B address, which normally identifies the network portion as the first two octets, the custom subnet mask redefines the network portion as the first *three* octets, and the first *three* bits of the fourth octet. Using this mask, this IP address provides 2046 networks, and 30 hosts for each network. Taking our example of connecting a network with 25 computers to the Internet, a smart ISP might give you a class B address with a subnet mask of 255.255.255.224. Using this strategy, the ISP would be able to support 2046 different companies who needed fewer than 30 dedicated IP addresses from a single class B IP number.

Since most people don't enjoy converting decimal numbers to binary, I've provided two quick cheat sheets for you in Tables 4-4 and 4-5 that outline the number of networks and hosts available given various subnet masks.

TABLE 4-4 QUICK REFERENCE CHART FOR CLASS B SUBNETS

# OF BITS	MASK IN DECIMAL	# OF NETWORKS	# OF HOSTS
0	255.255.0.0	0	65534
2	255.255.192.0	2	16382
3	255.255.224.0	6	8190
4	255.255.240.0	14	4094
5	255.255.248.0	30	2046
6	255.255.252.0	62	1022
7	255.255.254.0	126	510
8	255.255.255.0	254	254
9	255.255.255.128	510	126

# of Bits	Mask in Decimal	# of Networks	# of Hosts
10	255.255.255.192	1022	62
11	255.255.255.224	2046	30
12	255.255.255.240	4094	14
13	255.255.255.248	8190	6
14	255.255.255.252	16382	2

TABLE 4-5 Quick Reference Chart for Class C Subnets			
# of Bits	Mask in Decimal	# of Networks	# of Hosts
2	255.255.255.192	2	62
3	255.255.255.224	6	30
4	255.255.255.240	14	14
5	255.255.255.248	30	6
6	255.255.255.252	62	2

IP address management

When assigning IP addresses, it is critically important to develop some form of management system. If you happen to assign the same IP address to two devices on the same network, it is likely that both devices will cease communicating. The repercussions of two devices having the same IP address are dependent on the network. Some systems halt communications on both devices; others simply prevent the second device from entering the network. In either case, this is a situation you don't want happening.

It's important to think through your IP strategy, and document your assignments carefully. While there are no set rules for assigning IP addresses, many people try to group numbers in a meaningful way. For example, if you're using a class B address, you might reserve the third octet to identify the operating system. You might have all Windows 95 PCs use IP addresses between 10 and 99, all Windows NT PCs between 100 and 199, and so on. Likewise, it is often wise to reserve either the low- or the high-end numbers for various devices. For example, you might reserve the host IDs from 1 to 10 for routers, and 11 to 20 for file servers. It can be very difficult to re-assign IP addresses later, so spending a little time up front to think out the logic of your numbering pattern will probably save many hours down the line.

Dynamic IP management

If you have a small number of devices, under 25, all located within a single building, manually assigning addresses is simple enough. But as your network grows, or if you're starting out with a larger network, manual addressing quickly becomes a major task. To assist you, the TCP/IP suite offers a method of automatically assigning IP addresses for you, called the *Dynamic Host Configuration Protocol,* or DHCP.

The DHCP protocol provides a network service to manage a range, or pool, of IP addresses for devices on the network. These addresses are *leased* to client computers as needed. When a DHCP client needs an IP address, it sends out a broadcast message on the network searching for a DHCP server. All DHCP servers that hear the request send back an offer to supply the client with an IP address, if the DHCP server has an available IP address to offer. The client then selects one of these servers, usually the first server that responds, and accepts the offer. The DHCP server then assigns an IP address to the client, along with any other TCP/IP configuration the network administrator has defined (I'll discuss these other items shortly). The client device then uses the supplied IP address for the duration of the lease (three days by default). When half of the lease time has passed, the client requests a renewal of the IP information. If the DHCP server is unavailable, or unable to renew the lease for some reason, the client continues to request a renewal at each halfway point of the remaining lease time until it is successful or the lease expires. If the client fails to renew the lease, it needs to locate another DHCP server on the network, or it cannot participate in TCP/IP services.

The Transmission Control Protocol

While IP is responsible for the addressing of devices and formatting datagrams, the Transmission Control Protocol (TCP) provides the transport functions to ensure that all of the data sent from point A is received completely at point B. TCP is a *connection-oriented* and *reliable* service. This means that the TCP protocol creates a connection between the sending and receiving devices *before* data is transmitted.

The service is also considered reliable because the protocol uses a verification method to make sure the data sent is what the receiving device gets. If some or all of the data is lost during transport, the TCP protocol provides a mechanism to retransmit the lost data. TCP is akin to sending a certified postal letter. The letter is tracked throughout the delivery process so you are guaranteed your intended recipient gets the letter.

The User Datagram Protocol (UDP)

The User Datagram Protocol is another transportation service, but unlike TCP, UDP is *connectionless,* and *unreliable.* UDP does not prearrange a connection with the destination device, and provides no system to verify that the data sent ever reaches its destination. UDP is useful in applications such as live audio or visual. The overhead penalty for verifying the delivery of data via TCP would be much too great to support live data transmissions. By the time the sounds or images were corrected and delivered, they would no longer be live. Therefore, applications such as video conferencing or Real Audio use UDP. Since datagrams can be lost, or dropped during transmission, the resulting sound or display can be choppy depending on how fast and busy your connection is.

exam preparation pointer **The exam often refers to the *TCP/IP stack*, which is simply the suite of TCP/IP protocols used in communicating on an IP network.**

IP Routing

I've discussed a number of components necessary for data to be sent across the Internet, but you haven't really seen how routing is accomplished. Routing is the process of finding a path between our devices to send the data down. Routers are the devices mostly responsible for providing this service. Although generic routing in itself is not necessarily part of the TCP/IP protocol, this is the perfect place to discuss how routing is performed.

Within a local area network, all of the computers share the same network number. Even on non-IP networks, the network software differentiates between one network and another. With IP, however, a router is required to send data from one network ID to another. As I said earlier, routers have a direct connection to the local network, and a connection to another router, or perhaps multiple routers.

These routers have their own language and share information among themselves as to what network ID they are connected to. The routers then create "maps" that enable them to send the data to the proper router connected to the desired network ID. For example, look at Figure 4-3.

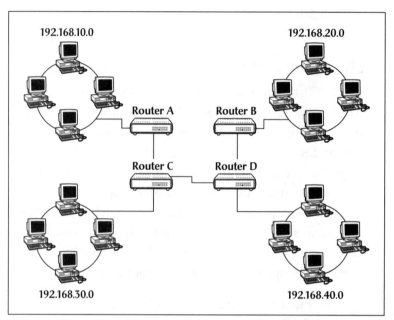

FIGURE 4-3 **Example of four networks connected by routers**

Each router knows about the address of the network to which it is physically connected. For example, Router A knows about network 192.168.10.0, Router B knows about 192.168.20.0, and so forth. When the routers are turned on, they send out a message to whatever router(s) they are connected to, telling the other routers what network they know about. In turn they receive information about what networks the other routers know about. This process is known as *convergence*. Once all of this data is propagated, or fully *converged*, Router A knows that Router D can forward data to network 192.168.40.0, Router B can forward data to network 192.168.20.0, and so on.

This is how modern routing *should* work, but some older routers may not participate in this process nicely. Additionally, other factors could cause this convergence process not to occur, such as incompatible software versions or routing protocol types. Therefore, to ensure that routing still takes place, a method known as the *default route* is used. The idea behind the default route is quite simple. If the router doesn't know specifically where to send the data, it simply passes the data on to the router defined as its *default gateway*. (Default route and default gateway seem to be used interchangeably, depending on whose system you're dealing with.) The router then forgets about the data and leaves it up to the next router in line to deal with the problem.

For example, if Router B in Figure 4-3 receives data destined to network 192.168.10.0 but doesn't know how to get it there, it sends the data on to its default route, router D. Router D doesn't know how to get to the network either, so it passes the data on to its default, which is router C. Likewise, Router C is unaware of a path to 192.168.10.0 so it passes the data along to Router A, which does know about the network and completes the delivery.

The concept of the default gateway (or default router) is not for routers alone. Every device on an IP network should have a default route defined. This way, even though the devices should be able to find their way around, if something precludes this, there is still a chance the default path will work.

When a device is configured as a DHCP client, the DHCP server can supply not only the IP address, but also the proper subnet mask and the IP address of the default router.

NAME RESOLUTION PROTOCOLS

It should be clear that addressing is essential to Internet communications, but you've also seen in Part I that the Internet uses domain names and e-mail addresses. People are not generally fond of having to refer to everything in life using numbers; we are much more comfortable with names. To enable the substitution of common names for arcane IP addresses, the TCP/IP suite provides a number of protocols to convert our friendly names into the proper numeric address. This process is called *name resolution* and comes in a variety of methods. For the i-Net+ exam, we'll look at two of the most important methods of resolving names to addresses: hosts files and Domain Name Services (DNS).

Hosts Files

All IP networks provide a simple method of name resolution known as the *hosts file*. This is a simple text file that contains a list of domain names and their associated IP address. A simple hosts file might look like this:

```
# This is a sample HOSTS file used by Microsoft TCP/IP
#
# This file contains the mappings of IP addresses to host
# names. Each entry should be kept on an individual line. The
# IP address should be placed in the first column followed by
# the corresponding hosts name. The IP address and the hosts
# name should be separated by at least one space.
#

102.54.94.97      rhino.acme.com              # source server
38.25.63.10       x.acme.com                  # x client hosts
206.175.162.15    sales.idgbooks.com          # good books
192.41.63.54      info.net-engineer.com       # great resource site!
127.0.0.1         localhosts
```

The first column of the hosts file is the IP address of the domain. The second column is the actual domain name, and the third column is optional. If included, the third column is simply a comment used to further describe the domain. The # symbol indicates that what follows is a comment. When a local IP device uses a hosts file to resolve an IP address, the file is searched from top to bottom for the domain name. If it's located, the IP address is then passed to the application for further processing. If the domain name is not located, and no other name resolution options are available, the Internet address will be unavailable to the user by means of its domain name. The user must use the numeric IP address to access that location.

For small networks, the hosts file might work for a while, but there are a number of problems with it. First, every time a new domain is needed, the file must be edited to include the addition. If you have more than one computer, the hosts file on each PC would also need to be updated. Second, if the IP address is entered incorrectly, the hosts file method fails, just as if the domain name hadn't been located in the file. Third, and probably most importantly, there simply is no way to include all of the domain names a person is likely to use in a simple text file.

Even if a complete copy could be downloaded, new domains are added daily, so the hosts file would be out of date very quickly.

Domain Name Services

If hosts files are impractical for Internet name resolution, some other method must be used, and in fact one is. *Domain Name Services* (DNS) is the primary name resolution protocol of the Internet. DNS is similar in nature to hosts files in that entries are stored as a database that cross-references IP addresses to their computer names. However, it would be impractical to search such a huge list of entries sequentially, so to overcome this problem, DNS servers are based on a hierarchical formula. Remember from Chapter 2 that every domain on the Internet has a unique name that ends in a *top-level domain name*. For example, idgbooks. com has the top-level domain name of com.

For the i-Net+ exam you are expected to know the common top-level domain names described here, and their corresponding types.

Starting with these high-level domains, DNS servers can break down any given address into smaller and smaller pieces until a specific server is located, as depicted in Figure 4-4.

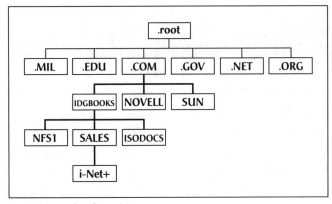

FIGURE 4-4 The domain tree

When a request is made to a primary DNS server, the root is queried first. The result is returned as a list of other servers containing servers within their domain name (COMs, GOVs, EDUs). These servers are then queried further to locate the next lower portion of the target name, and so on, until the full name is resolved.

Suppose you want to view a file located on a server named `internetplus.sales.idgbooks.com`. This is a fictitious computer in the sales department of IDG Books Worldwide, which is a commercial company. To find its Internet address, you might have to consult four different servers like this:

1. A query is made to a central server (the root) to find out where the COM server is. COM is a server that keeps track of commercial organizations. The root server would give you the names and Internet addresses of several servers for COM. (There are several servers at each level, in case one of them is down.)

2. You would then ask one of the COM servers for the address of the IDG-BOOKS server. Again, you would be given names and Internet addresses of several servers for IDGBOOKS. Most likely, not all of those servers would be physically located at IDG Books, to allow for the possibility that the company's computer(s) may be unavailable.

3. Then you would ask IDGBOOKS for the addresses of the SALES servers.

4. Finally, you would ask one of the SALES servers for the address of the `internetplus` computer. The result would be the Internet address for `internetplus.sales.idgbooks.com`. Each level is referred to as a "domain" and the entire name is called the "fully qualified domain name."

While this discussion has primarily focused on Internet name resolution, DNS servers are equally important in private IP networks. The CD included with this book contains SimpleDNS, a very powerful, yet easy to implement DNS server that runs on Windows 95/98 or NT. Even if you don't wish to host your own DNS server on the Internet, this program will speed up Internet access by caching all DNS records requested by your computer (or network of computers) locally, and later fetching them again much faster. If you maintain a local area network based on TCP/IP, SimpleDNS will enable you to call your e-mail server "mail," your proxy server "proxy," and your intranet Web server "web." Users on the LAN can then use these easy-to-remember names instead of IP addresses when setting up your client PCs' Internet programs, and you never have to edit a single hosts file.

CLIENT–SIDE PROTOCOLS

As you can see, the Internet (and networking in general) is filled with various protocols. Just about every service requires its own set of rules to facilitate proper communications. This section discusses a few of the protocols that your client might use.

Dial-Up Connection Protocols

There are two primary standards when using a modem to connect to your ISP. The older of these is *Serial Line IP,* or SLIP. Most modern connections, however, use the *Point-to-Point Protocol,* or PPP. Let's take a closer look at both of these.

Serial-line IP

SLIP is an older protocol for dial-up access to TCP/IP networks. SLIP is commonly used to gain access to the Internet. It can also be used to provide dial-up access between two LANs. SLIP transmits IP packets over any serial link (dial up or private lines) and simply defines a sequence of characters that frame IP packets. SLIP does not provide addressing, packet type identification, error detection/correction or compression mechanisms. Because the protocol does so little, it is usually very easy to implement. SLIP is commonly used on dedicated serial links and sometimes for dial-up purposes, and is usually used with line speeds between 1200bps and 19.2Kbps. It is useful for enabling mixes of hosts and routers to communicate with one another (hosts-hosts, hosts-router, and router-router are all common SLIP network configurations).

With SLIP, both computers in the link need to know each other's IP addresses for routing purposes. As we've seen, with the growing shortage of IP addresses, this requirement alone makes the protocol less attractive. Most ISPs dole out dynamic addresses upon connection and usually charge additional monthly fees for additional IP addresses.

Without a packet type identifier field, SLIP is only capable of transmitting a single network-layer protocol. For example, in a configuration with two Macintosh computers that both run TCP/IP and AppleTalk, there is no way for TCP/IP and AppleTalk to share one serial line while they use SLIP.

The majority of remote connections used today rely on the public telephone system, and the bulk of these connections are through analog phone lines. These lines are susceptible to noise and other interference that can corrupt data packets in transit. Since the SLIP protocol does not provide error detection/correction, other higher-level protocols on the end devices are responsible to request retransmission of bad data. This can add quite a bit of unnecessary overhead to the remote connection.

Fortunately, PPP provides the three major functions that SLIP does not.

Point-to-Point Protocol

Like SLIP, PPP provides dial-up access over serial lines. PPP is designed for simple links that transport packets between two hosts. The links provide full-duplex, simultaneous, bidirectional operation, and deliver packets in order. PPP also provides a common solution to connect a variety of hosts, bridges, and routers. For these reasons, PPP has become the de facto standard for dial-up Internet connections. PPP can encapsulate multiple network-layer protocols, such as IPX and AppleTalk; this makes it very easy to use for connections with a private network as well. The PPP protocol was designed to be easy to configure, and generally, the standard defaults handle all common configurations. That is, the protocol's self-configuration is implemented through a negotiation mechanism where each end of the link describes to the other its capabilities and requirements. To establish communications over a point-to-point link, each end must first send *Link Control Protocol* (LCP) packets to configure and test the data link. After the link is established, the peer may be authenticated. Next, PPP sends *Network Control Protocol* (NCP) packets to choose and configure one or more network-layer protocols (such as TCP/IP or IPX). Once each of the chosen network-layer protocols have been configured, data from each can be exchanged. The link remains configured for communications until explicit commands close the link down, or some external event such as an inactivity timer expiring occurs. The PPP protocol also is capable of automatically reestablishing a failed connection.

Post Office Protocol

Electronic mail on the Internet is sent almost exclusively using a protocol called *Simple Mail Transfer Protocol,* or SMTP, which is discussed in Chapter 9. Unfortunately, SMTP is based on the assumption that you are permanently connected to the Internet and that your system is reachable at any time, which is clearly not the case if you are using a SLIP or PPP connection. This limitation makes it nearly impossible to receive mail reliably via a dial-up connection on your own computer. Instead, Internet e-mail is usually retrieved using an alternative protocol called the Post Office Protocol (POP). Under POP, the ISP's machine accepts mail on your behalf and holds it until you dial in to retrieve it. When you use POP for your mail, your e-mail address is actually an address on the ISP's system, rather than the address of your own machine. POP is a receive-only protocol — it provides no mechanism for sending mail, only for retrieving it. As of the writing of this book, POP version 3 is the most current, so the protocol is often referred to as POP3.

INTERNET CLIENT INFRASTRUCTURE

Now that we know what IP addressing and routing is and some of the more popular client-side protocols, let's take a look at the other components required to support Internet client applications.

Network Connection

If your primary connection to the Internet is provided as part of a private network, you obviously need access to that network first. To be part of a network, your computer needs a *Network Interface Card*, or NIC, a network cable between the NIC and the network system, and a network client software component. In most cases, these components are supplied by the network administrator or the organization's internal Information Systems department. We discuss network connection technologies in detail in Part IV. Any network that can support TCP/IP or a TCP/IP proxy server can provide Internet access to the client computers. This includes the most popular network systems such as Macintosh, Unix/Linux, Windows NT, and NetWare. Depending on what security methods are in place, the client may need to authenticate (log in) to the network with a valid user account and password before access to the Internet is allowed.

Operating System

Whether your connection is provided through a network or not, the client computer, or more specifically, the computer's operating system, must also support the use of TCP/IP. Most modern PC operating systems, such as Windows 95/98, Windows NT, MacOS, Unix, and Linux support the TCP/IP stack.

Since most desktop computers use either Windows 95/98 or NT, the following section will focus in on the process of configuring these systems for Internet access. Mac, Unix, and Linux follow similar processes, although the exact steps are different. If you need to configure one of these operating systems, refer to the documentation that accompanies your particular computer or operating system.

We covered the process for configuring a dial-up connection in Chapter 2, so now we'll look at the connection of a network-attached client computer.

 The installation of TCP/IP should not be performed on a business or school network without first obtaining permission from the network administrator. Only perform this exercise if you have rights to the network you are connected to.

▼ ▼ ▼

TO CONFIGURE TCP/IP, FOLLOW THESE STEPS:

1. Select Start ⇨ Settings ⇨ Control Panel. From the Control Panel window, double-click Network. The Network settings dialog box appears, as shown in Figure 4-5.

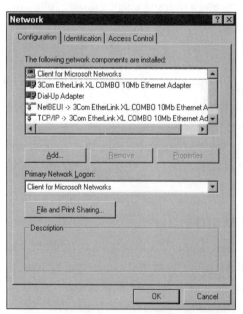

FIGURE 4-5 Windows 95/98 Network settings dialog box

2. Click the Add button. The Select Network Component Type dialog box appears, as shown in Figure 4-6.

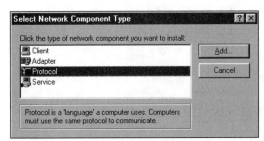

FIGURE 4-6 Windows 95/98 Protocol Selection dialog box

3. Select Protocol, then click Add. The Select Network Protocol Dialog box appears, as shown in Figure 4-7.

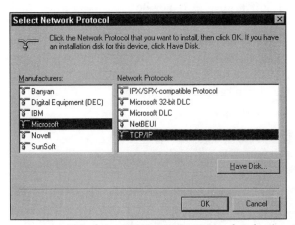

FIGURE 4-7 Windows 95/98 TCP/IP Network Selection Dialog Box

4. From the Manufacturers list on the left side of the dialog box, select Microsoft. From the protocol list on the right side of the dialog box, select TCP/IP. Click OK.

5. The main Network dialog box will be displayed again, and TCP/IP protocol will now appear in the list.

6. Select TCP/IP from the list, and click Properties. The TCP/IP properties dialog box will be displayed, as shown in Figure 4-8. From this screen, you need to define our IP address and subnet mask. If your organization is using static IP addressing, that is, each PC is assigned a specific IP address, enter the unique address and subnet mask for this PC in the appropriate box. If you use DHCP, click the radio button labeled Obtain an IP address automatically.

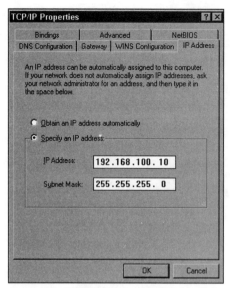

FIGURE 4-8   TCP/IP Properties Dialog Box

7. Select the Gateway tab. Figure 4-9 shows the dialog box for defining the default gateway. If the network has a router to the Internet, you will enter the IP address of the router here. If you don't have this information, the default gateway can be left blank for now.

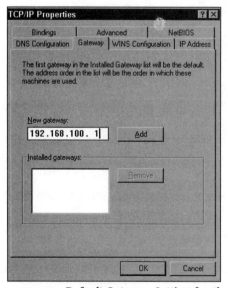

FIGURE 4-9   Default Gateway Setting for the TCP/IP protocol

The last necessary item before TCP/IP is fully installed is our DNS entry. The DNS entries refer to the IP address of one or more DNS servers that you have access to. Usually these servers are provided by your ISP, although they very well could be running on your network as well. In either case, you'll need to obtain the IP addresses of at least one DNS server and insert them in the DNS settings as shown in Figure 4-10. It is always wise to provide at least two DNS servers in the event that one becomes unavailable. Should your only DNS server fail, you will not get name resolution and navigating the Internet will be difficult at best.

 exam preparation pointer

A quick way to test DNS services is to use a known HTTP IP address instead of the corresponding domain name in a Web browser. For example, in the Address/Location field of the browser, enter http://38.170.216.15. If the Web page for IDG Books displays, then you know you have a properly configured Internet connection. Next, try browsing the same page with the domain name. In the Address/Location field, enter www.idgbooks.com. If the page fails to load, you know that DNS services are not functioning.

▼ ▼ ▼

TO CONFIGURE DNS SERVICES, FOLLOW THESE STEPS:

1. Access the TCP/IP Properties box, as shown in the previous series of steps. Select the DNS Configuration tab. You'll see the property sheet shown in Figure 4-10.
2. Check the Enable DNS radio button.
3. Enter your Host name, which in most cases is the name your computer has on the LAN.
4. Enter your Domain Name, which is either your registered domain name, or the domain of your ISP.
5. Enter the IP address of your first DNS server, and then click Add.
6. Enter the IP address of your second DNS server, if you have one, and then click Add.

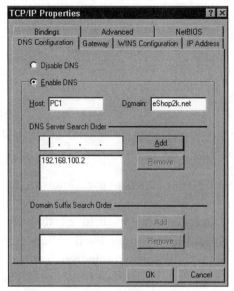

FIGURE 4-10 Configuring the DNS settings for the TCP/IP protocol

■ ■ ■

After all of these settings are made, Windows must be rebooted for the changes to take effect. Once Windows is running again, TCP/IP should be configured on your computer. Windows 95/98 has an excellent tool, called `WINIPCFG.exe`, to view what TCP/IP settings are bound to your network card. To test your TCP/IP configuration, run this utility to make sure the procedure was successful.

1. Select Start ⇨ Run.

2. Enter **WINIPCFG** in the Run dialog box.

   A screen similar to Figure 4-11 will be displayed.

   The Windows NT and Unix/Linux operating systems use the built-in TCP/IP utility called IPCONFIG to display the same information. This is a text-based (DOS-based in NT) utility that is run from the command line (not the graphic interface). To determine what your current IP settings are using this utility, simply go to the command line of the Operating System and enter **ipconfig**. The display will be similar to this:

```
Windows NT IP Configuration
Ethernet adapter N1001:
```

```
IP Address. . . . . . . . . : 203.186.196.8
Subnet Mask . . . . . . . . : 255.255.255.0
Default Gateway . . . . . . : 203.186.196.1
```

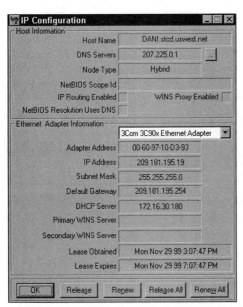

FIGURE 4-11   The Windows 95/98 TCP/IP Tool, WINIPCFG

Client-Side Software

Once the TCP/IP protocol is installed, the second item you need is the proper client software. Just about every Internet service has its own software component. We have already looked at the Web browser, so in this section we'll focus in on other Internet services and the associated client software.

E-mail clients

Arguably, e-mail is as popular as Web browsing. In fact, e-mail service has become somewhat of a commodity. If you don't have access to the Internet, you can still get *free* e-mail service from companies like Juno. Instead of connecting directly to the Internet to send and receive e-mail, you call a local phone number, called a *point of presence* (POP), which in turn routes your mail to and from the Internet. Companies like these make their money by selling advertisements that appear on the client software you use to send and receive your message.

Almost every ISP offers at least one e-mail account with their service. This is typically a POP3 account. When you are ready to check your mail, you use a POP3 e-mail client that connects to the ISP's post office and downloads your waiting messages. Literally thousands of POP3 e-mail clients are available. Among the most popular of these are Microsoft's Outlook/Outlook Express, Qualcomm's Eudora/Eudora Lite, and David Harris's Pegasus.

Microsoft Outlook

Outlook is a client for Microsoft's Exchange Server (discussed in Chapter 8) that integrates task and contact-management capabilities with Exchange's messaging, forms, and scheduling features. A sample of Outlook's display is shown in Figure 4-12. Outlook is included with Microsoft Office 97 and 2000, with Exchange Server, and as a standalone program.

Microsoft calls Outlook a "desktop information manager," bringing together e-mail, group scheduling, and personal information management. Outlook manages e-mail, calendars, contacts, tasks and to-do lists, and documents or files. E-mail can be configured for just Internet mail, just local mail on your company's LAN, or both.

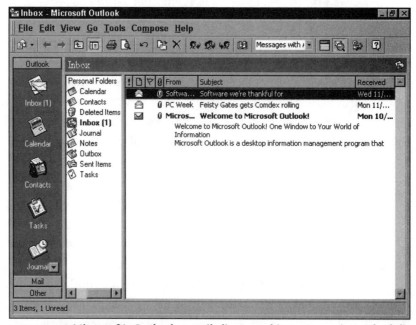

FIGURE 4-12 Microsoft's Outlook e-mail client combines messaging, scheduling, and task-list functions into one application.

Outlook Express

Outlook Express is the updated Internet e-mail and newsreader included with Internet Explorer 4.0 and newer. It was formerly called Internet Mail and News. While it shares the Outlook name, Outlook Express doesn't have the task and contact-management capabilities of the full Outlook version, nor does it support local (LAN) e-mail.

Eudora Pro

Eudora, shown in Figure 4-13, specializes in one area: e-mail. Qualcomm's e-mail client is probably the best-selling application of its kind on the market today. Eudora does not support groupware functions like Outlook, but instead concentrates on being a full-featured Internet e-mail client. Beginners can easily set up and use Eudora without spending hours reading through user manuals, while experienced e-mail aficionados have a tremendous number of options to make e-mail management a real science.

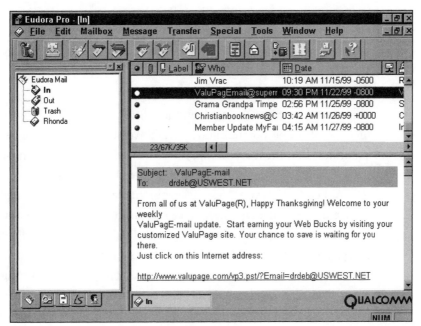

FIGURE 4-13 Eudora Pro only concerns itself with being the most feature-rich e-mail client.

Eudora Lite

Qualcomm's free version of their commercial product is called Eudora Lite. Like Outlook Express, the Lite version has a more limited feature set than the retail version. However, Eudora Lite supports most of the functions basic Internet e-mail users require, such as the capability to store messages in categorized folders, spell checking, and printing. Both versions of Eudora can be downloaded from Qualcomm's Web site at www.eudora.com.

Pegasus Mail

Pegasus Mail is an electronic mail program that can be used in a very wide range of environments, and which is especially well suited to Internet mail. Individual users with a connection to the Internet via an Internet Service Provider can use Pegasus Mail to send and retrieve mail. Pegasus Mail has special support for Novell NetWare local area networks and operates in that environment with almost no maintenance. One remarkable feature of Pegasus Mail is that it's completely free of charge. Normally the free versions of e-mail software restrict certain functionalities to entice you to purchase the full commercial version. Pegasus, however, is a full-featured client that has been updated and maintained for years. The software and documentation can be downloaded from www.pegasus.usa.com.

Multifunction e-mail clients

There are many more choices than those listed here for POP3 e-mail clients, and there are also a host of multifunction and Web-based clients. The best example of a multifunction client is Netscape Messenger, which is the built in e-mail client of the Netscape Communicator software suite as shown in Figure 4-14.

Although Netscape Messenger can run as a standalone application (the browser program does not need to be running at the same time), this component is normally activated while browsing the Web. Like most e-mail clients, the layout is separated into various functional parts. The left-hand pane provides organizational tools such as user-definable folders for categorizing and storing e-mail messages. The right-hand screen display is separated into two sections. The top portion lists a summary of each message contained in the selected category. This summary provides the subject of the message, who sent it and when, and an optional priority code assigned by the sender. Below the summary area, the text for the selected summary item is displayed.

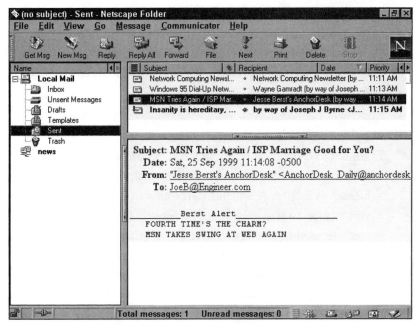

FIGURE 4-14   The Netscape Messenger e-mail client is part of the Netscape program suite

Web-based clients

All of the client applications you've seen so far have one thing in common: they require a POP3 e-mail address located on your ISP's server. To access your e-mail, you must be connected to your ISP, or to the network where your e-mail server is located. Another increasingly popular option is Web-based e-mail. With Web-based e-mail, you can send, receive, and store e-mail from any place you have an Internet connection. Rather than storing the mail on your local computer, the Web-based server houses the necessary components. This provides a great deal of flexibility in managing your e-mail because any Internet connection will work. For example, if you have a Web based e-mail account, but you don't own a computer at home, you can probably find an Internet-connected computer at a local library with which to send and receive your e-mail. Perhaps you can use the computer of a neighbor or friend. With Web based e-mail you don't have to own a computer or pay monthly ISP charges, you just need access to a Web-enabled device.

A number of free Web e-mail services are available. Microsoft's offering is called Hotmail (www.hotmail.com), the search engine company Yahoo! offers Yahoo! Mail (www.yahoo.com), and Mail.com (www.mail.com) offers not only free mail service, but an optional commercial service that enables you to customize your e-mail address. In addition to dedicated Web-based services, many commercial e-mail servers, such as Microsoft's Exchange, Novell's GroupWise, or Deerfield's MDaemon provide a Web-based client in addition to their normal POP3 software.

E-Mail attachments

Although sending and receiving text messages is very convenient, a growing use of e-mail is to transport files. These files might be spreadsheets, graphics, or databases. Just about anything that can be created and stored on a computer can be sent via e-mail as an attachment. As you've seen repeatedly, protocols exist to define the methods used to send and receive e-mail attachments. Of the methods most used for attachments, the most popular method currently is the Multipurpose Internet Mail Extension, or MIME. The MIME standard specifies how messages must be formatted so that they can be exchanged between different e-mail systems. MIME is a very flexible format, permitting one to include virtually any type of file or document in an e-mail message. Specifically, MIME messages can contain text, images, audio, video, or other application-specific data.

Not all e-mail programs support the MIME standard, making it difficult for many e-mail users to deal with encoded documents sent to them. The system that transports e-mail from one computer to another is known sometimes to be unfriendly to non-text information such as images, which is why MIME includes an encoding/decoding mechanism that converts arbitrary information to text and back. This encoding mechanism is known as base64, and seems to be the source of much frustration for many e-mail users using non-MIME compliant software. With the vast number of e-mail clients available, I recommend you insist on one that supports this standard.

exam preparation pointer **S/MIME (Secure MIME) is a version of MIME that adds encryption for secure transmission.**

FTP clients

Unlike e-mail programs, in which non-text files have to be "attached," the File Transfer Protocol, or FTP, is used to directly transfer files over a TCP/IP network such as the Internet, Unix/Linux, Windows NT, or NetWare. It includes functions to log on to the network, list directories, and copy files. FTP operations can be performed by typing commands at a command prompt or via an FTP utility running under a graphical interface such as Windows. FTP transfers can also be initiated from within a Web browser by preceding the FTP server address with `ftp://`. (such as `ftp://microsoft.com`). FTP is designed to handle binary files directly and does not add the overhead of encoding and decoding the data.

 in the real world   **The term FTP is also used as a verb; for example, "let's FTP them the file."**

Like all Internet services, FTP requires a server component to provide client access. FTP requires the client to identify itself by supplying a user name and optional password. Many FTP sites, however, are available to the public. Computer software and hardware companies often use FTP servers to distribute updates and patches for their systems. It is not effective to give everyone a user name and password, nor is it always important to know every person accessing the FTP server. For these situations, many FTP sites allow an *anonymous* user login with the user's e-mail address as the password. Typically, the anonymous FTP directory is isolated from the rest of the system and won't accept uploads from users. In situations where multiple directories and secured login are not required, the Trivial File Transport Protocol, or TFTP, is usually implemented.

Non-graphical interfaces for FTP use a number of standard commands to navigate and control the FTP process. Table 4-6 highlights the commands most often used, and the purpose of these commands.

TABLE 4-6 COMMON FTP COMMANDS

COMMAND	DEFINITION
`ftp [Server name or IP address]`	Starts the FTP application from the command line
`dir`	Lists the contents of the current directory
`cd [remote directory name]`	Change to the [remote directory name]
`get [remote file] [local file]`	

Continued

TABLE 4-6 COMMON FTP COMMANDS *(continued)*

COMMAND	DEFINITION
recv [remote file] [local file]	Copies a file [remote file] from the FTP server to your local computer [local file]
put [local file] [remote file] send [local file] [remote file]	Copies [local file] from your computer to the FTP server [remote file]
quit	Ends the FTP session
help [command]	Provides online help with the optional [command]

IRC

Internet Relay Chat, or IRC, is the Internet service that enables people to communicate together in real time. Clients connect to an IRC server that moderates the process of sending and receiving keyboard-entered messages. Typically, IRC servers allow users to create defined topics of conversation. The server then publicizes the various topics and allows people to join in on the conversations. Many servers also allow private message groups that can only be joined by predefined individuals. Two IRC services are rising as the popular leaders: America Online's Instant Messenger, shown in Figure 4-15, and Microsoft's MSN Messenger Services.

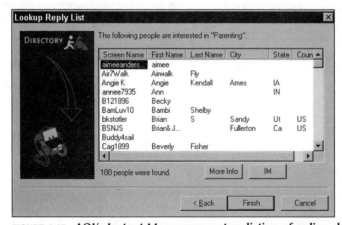

FIGURE 4-15 AOL's Instant Messenger system listing of online chat users

Microsoft's service requires that you create a free e-mail account with their Hotmail service before you can use their IRC application. Once you have filled out the necessary online forms, the rest of the installation process is handled by an installation wizard. Unlike AOL's system, which lets you locate people based on common interests, MSN Messenger requires that you create a user list of known individuals that you'll chat with, as shown in Figure 4-16.

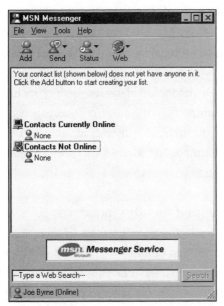

FIGURE 4-16 MSN Messenger Service requires users to create a list of contacts

IRC services are still relatively new, and the full potential for this service is far from being realized yet. During the first few years of the next century, you are likely to see this application mature much as e-mail has in the last part of the 1990s.

Newsgroups

The last Internet service you'll examine is the newsgroup. The newsgroup service, often called a discussion group, is a message board on the Internet. Messages are devoted to a particular topic starting with someone posting an initial query or comment. Others interested in the topic post a reply, and still others reply to those replies. This discussion continues on to form a chain of related postings called a *message thread*.

Newsgroups were popular long before the World Wide Web was even developed. They flourished on private "bulletin board" networks where members usually paid a monthly fee. With the popularity and ease of the Web, many of these bulletin board systems moved to the Internet, ending a short but pioneering life. By the end of 1999, there were more than 50,000 Web-based newsgroups. Some are moderated; some are not, and no single server or online service hosts them all. They originate from many sources and are hosted on many systems. Collectively, these are known as the *Usenet* network, the original name given to this service. It is the system administrator at any given ISP or online service such as AOL or CompuServe that decides which newsgroups are offered and how long postings are available, typically about two weeks.

Newsgroups are organized into topical hierarchies, which include alt (alternative), biz (business), comp (computing), misc (miscellaneous), rec (recreational), and others. As you move to the right in a newsgroup name, the subject focus becomes more limited. For example, the group `alt.music` might discuss every aspect of music, while `alt.music.baroque` and `alt.music.jazz` are more specific topics.

Newsgroup postings amount to what noted computer author Alfred Glossbrenner has called the "collective consciousness." Newsgroup postings represent the wisdom, experiences, and opinions of millions of people around the world on just about any topic imaginable. Unlike a Web site, where the content is regulated by someone or some organization, no one controls or filters what appears in newsgroups. Although the information gleaned there should be taken with a grain of salt, newsgroups can nevertheless be extremely valuable.

Most newsgroups require the user to "subscribe" with a newsreader program. This makes it possible to automatically retrieve all the postings that had not yet been seen whenever the newsgroup was last accessed. Messages can then be read and replied to offline and later uploaded in a single batch. Many modern newsreaders offer this functionality. Newsreaders are built into Netscape Navigator and Internet Explorer.

If newsgroups are treated as a vast database of potentially useful information on a subject, they can be quite worthwhile. An excellent source for locating newsgroups is Deja.com at `www.deja.com` (formerly called Deja News). This is a search engine devoted to newsgroups that not only archives years worth of postings, but also aggressively filters out unwanted and unrelated messages, called *spam*. In Internet circles, the term *spam* refers to the sending of the same message to large numbers of newsgroups or users on the Internet. People spam the Internet to advertise products as well as to broadcast some political or social commentary. This same technique is common with e-mail. Just like unwanted junk mail travels in the regular postal system, so does spam in the Internet system.

Figure 4-17 shows a sample subscription list of newsgroups using the Netscape Messenger program.

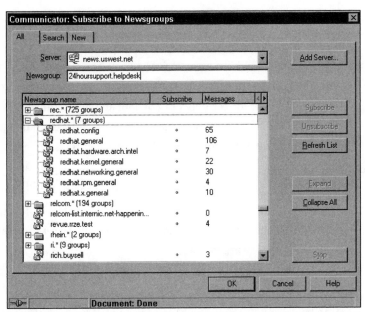

FIGURE 4-17   Newsgroup selection using Netscape's Messenger application

Exam Preparation Summary

We spent a great deal of time talking about Internet protocols and why they're important for the Internet to work. For device to device communications, the TCP/IP suite is the primary protocol that is responsible for Internet device addressing and data routing. It's important to remember that the TCP/IP suite contains a number of related protocols that all interact to provide the communications necessary for the Internet to function. In addition to addressing and routing, name resolution is needed so that humans can find Internet services based on easier to remember names instead of large numeric addresses.

Additional protocols are used for other Internet services as well. Dial-up protocols SLIP and PPP help us connect our computers to an ISP via serial connections. The POP3 protocol assists us in sending and retrieving e-mail when our computers are not permanently attached to the Internet. The MIME protocol is used to send and retrieve non text-based files such as graphics and sounds via e-mail as attachments. When more control is needed when sharing files, the FTP protocol can provide the perfect solution.

- TCP/IP is the "language" of the Internet. IP provides addressing for each and every device on the network.

- IP addresses identify both a network and host. The class of the IP address, when used with the default subnet mask, identifies how many octets of the IP address are used for the network portion, and how many octets identify the host address. Custom subnet masks can be applied to an IP address to modify how many networks a given IP address identifies.

- TCP is the primary protocol for routing and transmission of data across the Internet. TCP is both reliable and connection-oriented. UDP is a similar function, but is neither connection-oriented nor reliable. UDP is useful for applications such as live audio, where the data must be sent in real time and checks for reliability are impractical.

- Networks are created by routers, or devices acting as routers that pass data between one numbered network and another. Routers use their own protocols to learn where other networks are located. When no other routing protocol is used, the concept of *default routing* is used to let downstream routers locate the proper end devices.

- Name resolution is the process of cross-referencing domain names to their IP address. Hosts files can be used for very small networks, but the Domain Name Services (DNS) is the name resolution method used on the Internet. DNS is based on a hierarchical system starting with the top-level domains and working down to specific servers.

- Some of the common client-side protocols include SLIP and PPP for dial-up serial connections to an ISP, and POP3 which is used by e-mail clients to send and receive messages stored on a remote e-mail server.

- Many components are required on the client side to complete the Internet infrastructure, including the Network Operating System for network-connected devices, the local Operating System for end computers, and special client software for the specific Internet services requested.

- Some of the client applications include e-mail programs for messaging, FTP programs for efficiently transferring files, IRC software to participate in real-time communications (chat), and newsreaders for reading and replying to messages posted on electronic "bulletin boards" such as *Usenet*.

APPLYING WHAT YOU HAVE LEARNED

The following review questions give you an opportunity to test your knowledge of the information presented in this chapter. The answers to these assessment questions can be found in Appendix B. If you missed some, review those sections in this chapter before going further.

Instant Assessment Questions

1. An IP datagram contains which two of these components?

   A. Subnet mask

   B. User data

   C. Source address

   D. Domain name

2. According to the TCP/IP protocol, Internet hosts are:

   A. Text files for name resolution

   B. Routers that assist in the transportation of Internet data

   C. Devices other than servers connected to the Internet

   D. Any device connected to the Internet

3. Which of these IP Addresses are valid host numbers?

   A. 191.162.100.20

   B. 127.0.0.0

   C. 12.10.101.0

   D. 101.1.101.1

4. Subnet masks are only included when they differ from the default value for the IP class being used.

A. True

B. False

5. Which of these connection types can be used to connect two routers?

A. ISDN

B. Serial analog

C. Ethernet

D. "T" channel

6. The service used to automatically assign IP addresses is:

A. Domain Name Services

B. Dynamic Numbering Services

C. Static Addresses Protocol

D. Dynamic Host Core Protocol

7. Which of these are valid Top-Level Domains?

A. K12 — Schools from Kindergarten through 12th grade

B. CITY — Local Government Organizations

C. MIL — Military Sites

D. NET — Internet Service Providers

8. The "Central Server" in the DNS tree is known as what server?

A. Root

B. Top Level

C. DNS Host

D. Master

9. What utilities show the TCP/IP settings configured on Windows-based computers?

A. ShowIP

B. WinIPcfg

C. Control Panel ⇨ Networks ⇨ IP

D. ipconfig

10. What three commands are valid when using FTP?

   A. send

   B. exit

   C. recv

   D. get

Client Side Troubleshooting and Security Issues

About Chapter 5

The old adage, that the only sure things in life are death and taxes, I'm sure was coined before the advent of the personal computer. The modern version of this saying should include the fact that nothing goes as planned when computers are involved. It seems that no matter how carefully planned a project is, inevitably something goes wrong. In this chapter, I'll look at some of the more common problems that can occur when dealing with Internet connectivity. Another inherent problem with modern Internet use is the potential for unscrupulous individuals to access your computer and compromise your personal data. Therefore, I'll look at areas of concern with the client components and what security steps you should consider when planning your Internet travels.

IDENTIFYING PROBLEMS RELATED TO LEGACY CLIENTS

Arguably, older hardware and software present some of the most troublesome problems in working with computers and the Internet. These *legacy* devices or code were built without reference to standards now in place, which can cause them to conflict with modern devices or software. Thanks largely to the Y2K problem, much hardware and most DOS applications have been replaced with Windows, Macintosh, or Linux/UNIX based components.

The Disk Operating System (DOS)

DOS, or *Disk Operating System*, was one of the first operating systems widely used on IBM PC compatible computers. Although DOS is a very powerful and stable environment for computing, many applications written for it date back many, many years. Although extremely popular with computer-literate folks, DOS required the user to use many computer commands directly and didn't offer any protection from accidental misuse. In simple terms, DOS is not considered user friendly. With the growth in graphical environments such as the Mac and Windows, users became accustomed to the features and ease of use not found in DOS, so its popularity has declined steadily to near non-existent in the late 1990s. There is still a large number of DOS-based computers in the world, however. You may happen to own one of these legacy systems, or you may be asked to configure one for Internet access at some point.

When it comes to Internet clients for DOS, older versions of UNIX, or Apple, the choices are rather slim. Most of the available programs are developed for specific markets or applications. These programs usually will not support many features of modern Web, e-mail, or file transfer applications. For example, many Web sites include graphics that cannot be viewed with these legacy programs. The text portion would be available, but none of the multimedia components. In the early years of Web page development, most sites consisted of mostly text. As graphics and other visual objects began to increase in popularity, many Web designers provided "text-only" versions for older browsers along with their newer graphics-based pages, but this courtesy is quickly fading. Legacy e-mail and newsreader programs have the potential for a longer life span. The content in both of these services is still primarily text based, which legacy applications handle well.

However, as these services mature, many of the older applications will quickly become obsolete. Whenever dealing with legacy Internet clients, it is always wise to carefully examine the real cost of keeping these systems in place. Even though the initial expense of new hardware and software might appear steep, the potential ongoing costs of maintaining the older systems may indeed be more expensive.

exam
preparation
pointer

The i-Net+ exam will expect you to understand that DOS-based clients are primarily text-based applications that are not well suited for most Web browsing needs.

WINSOCK

A much more common software problem relates to the Windows Application Programming Interface (API) knows as *Windows Sockets,* or WINSOCK. WIN-SOCK is a software component that provides a common interface between a Windows application and the TCP/IP protocol. The Windows socket routines are implemented by the dynamic link library WINSOCK.DLL that is included with Windows 95/98. When programmers create TCP/IP applications designed to run under Windows 95/98, they normally strive to be WINSOCK compliant. It is not uncommon for a new application to include a copy of the WINSOCK.DLL file within the installation routine to ensure that the file is present, or because the application contains certain modifications to provide additional functionality. This can be the cause of all sorts of problems. Because most Windows-based TCP/IP applications rely on the routines included with WINSOCK.DLL, any modifications to this library can cause applications that formerly functioned to fail. Some installation programs will ask you if you want to replace the existing file, but many do not. Even Microsoft has been known to make changes to the DLL file between revisions of the Windows operating system, or with their own Internet applications. Unfortunately, there is no surefire method to avoid this problem, except to keep a backup copy of the WINSOCK.DLL file handy before installing new software that might replace the known good copy.

exam
preparation
pointer

For the i-Net+ exam, you should understand the consequences of an overwritten WINSOCK.DLL file. In many cases, this situation will cause previously working TCP/IP applications to fail. The remedy for this situation is to replace the current WINSOCK.DLL file with a previous version, perhaps from the original Windows 95/98 CD, and test the applications again.

Software Patches and Updates

Nearly all software is updated from time to time. Many larger applications, including operating systems, are updated by means of *patches* or *service packs*. Even with the most extensive testing possible, many software flaws can go undetected until put in use by the general computing public. As these flaws are discovered, the developer usually prepares fixes that are collected into a single service pack. To identify what patches have been applied to a given piece of software, software is often *serialized* with a specific version number. For example, the very first time a program is released, it may be assigned the version number 1. When the first service pack has been applied to the program, its version number is updated to 1.1 and so on. When major changes have occurred within the program the version number is usually incremented on the whole number, such as version 2, 3, and so on. While it is not always necessary to upgrade to every new service pack or major change release, you should be aware of the changes and understand how they affect the program.

 in the real world **Software versions do not necessarily reflect the actual number of times a program has been updated. Some software companies give higher version numbers to their first release of a product because some consumers do not like to purchase a "version 1" product.**

When an application fails to function as expected, or stops functioning as it once had, one of the first troubleshooting steps should be to consult the vendor's Web site to see if a patch or service pack has been released. If so, a list of issues that the update resolves is usually available. This document should be reviewed to determine if your problem has been corrected by the update. When a call is placed to a vendor's support line, they will often ask you to apply the latest patches to your software before performing any other troubleshooting exercises with you. This is especially true for major software components such as the operating system itself.

 in the real world **From a security standpoint, you must install patches that fix potential security holes. As soon as a new exploit is discovered, tens of thousands of "script kiddies" will scan the Internet looking for servers and clients they can break into. You have a short window of time to download and install the patch before your systems can become a target.**

As with the service pack, it is not often necessary to update your software to the latest released version. For example, many people still use Windows 95 although Windows 98 has been available for quite some time. Unless the new software contains features that you really need or want, you may be better off staying with what you know works in your particular situation. However, you should also be aware that as software gets further and further behind the current version, support may be difficult if not impossible to obtain. For example, the Windows 3.*x* platform is still used by a large number of people, but almost all third-party support for the products is gone. Microsoft still provides limited technical support, but often their solution to major problems is to recommend upgrading to the 9*x* release. In addition, software and hardware manufacturers quit developing products for older software releases shortly after the new products begin to ship. There are many cases where customers had to upgrade their systems simply because an existing component failed and there were no legacy replacements available.

A wise approach to keeping your software up-to-date is to rigorously document every application you own. Under most circumstances, this document should include the product and vendor name, the version number, where to go for support, and the date that you installed the new software or upgraded to a new version. A sample software inventory is shown in Table 5-1.

TABLE 5-1 Sample Software Inventory List

Product and Vendor Name	Version	Support Information	Date Installed or Updated
Microsoft Windows 95	4.0.0.0	(425) 635-7000 `www.microsoft.com/support`	2/15/1998
	4.0.0.2		9/10/1998
Netscape Communicator	2.0	`http://home.netscape.com/support`	1/9/1997
	3.0		3/1/1998
	4.6		6/12/1999
PowerSoft PowerPOS	1.0	(800) 555-1212	3/5/1996
	1.2		5/5/1996

The software inventory could just as easily be kept on a computer database that would make it easier to update and search. The important thing to remember is that a well-documented software list will greatly increase your ability to keep your existing software current and will provide quick access to support information in the event that technical support is required.

CLIENT–SIDE SECURITY ISSUES

Whenever a physical connection is created between your computer or network and another network such as the Internet, a potential for unwanted intrusion can occur. It would be great if everyone on the Internet were a good, upstanding citizen, but the reality is that there are a number of people who use the Internet for not-so-nice purposes. Although most crimes and computer invasions that occur over the Internet are usually aimed at organizations and their servers, security should be implemented even at the desktop level in many cases. Every operating system and service's default settings are insecure when right out of the box, so when you are configuring your clients, you never want to leave these default settings in place. Everything must be locked down before exposing it to the open Internet.

Virus Protection

Probably the single most common Internet-related security problem is the virus. Viruses can attack just about any computer they contact. Typically, computer viruses are spread in three distinct ways:

1. Downloading and *executing* a program or document macro file from an Internet site (Web or FTP). A macro file is a pseudo-program that provides short cuts to repetitive functions within applications, most notably the Microsoft Office Suite. With the advent of Visual Basic for Applications (VBA) and other customizing features of the Office Suite, macro viruses are showing up more frequently. I emphasize *executing* here because the infected program (or macro) must be run on your computer before the virus can infect your system. This means that you have the opportunity to check the downloaded file for viruses before it has a chance to do any harm.

2. As an attachment to an e-mail message. Again, only programs and macros can carry viruses, not the e-mail messages themselves, and the program or macro must be executed before the virus can infect your system.

3. Viruses are often transferred between computers by sharing removable media with others whose computers are infected. For example, if someone in your office gives you an infected floppy disk or CD-ROM that they created, your computer could be infected. Once again, there are good methods available to check for viruses on these media before they have a chance to infect your computer.

Virus infection can manifest itself in many ways. Less dangerous attacks can simply slow your computer down by consuming memory and other resources. Viruses that are more malicious will delete critical files on your computer, often before you are aware of what has happened. Other forms of virus type programs allow others to access your computer across the Internet. One of the most dangerous of this type is called *BackOrifice,* which is a take-off on Microsoft's BackOffice product. This program actually provides remote control functions to the victim's computer. Once BackOrifice is executed on the target machine, anyone on the Internet with the corresponding control program has the ability to remotely control or monitor the infected PC, just as if they were sitting at the keyboard. This type of program is most dangerous to people who have dedicated, always-on Internet connections.

There is good news however. Antivirus (AV) software is generally very successful at detecting and eliminating viruses entering your computers. There are many antivirus programs available, most for under $50. Probably the two most popular commercial versions are Symantec's Norton AntiVirus (www.symantec.com) and McAfee Anti-Virus (www.mcafee.com).

The most important feature to consider when choosing an antivirus system is how easy it is to keep the virus signatures updated. Signature files are the data updates that identify new viruses as they are discovered. Conservative estimates show that almost 250 new viruses are released on the Internet monthly. If you haven't updated the AV software for more than two or three months, it is next to useless. Therefore, the AV solution you select must provide an easy method of downloading and applying the signature updates.

A good AV program starts automatically when the computer boots, or as a service within the Windows operating system. With the antivirus program running, all disk activity is monitored. When files are saved to the disk, the AV program scans them for known patterns that indicate the presence of a virus. In addition, when a program executes, the AV software looks for virus-like activity, such as attempting to delete files, or load itself in non-normal memory ranges. When a possible virus is identified, or suspicious activity is detected, the AV program alerts the user and suggests some form of action to be taken. Typically, the program will either clean the infected program (remove the virus code from the normal program) or delete the program altogether. The end user can define most of these options.

 I really can't stress strongly enough that antivirus software is an absolute necessity if you are going to connect to the Internet. It is equally important that the signature files are updated on a regular basis, no longer than once every 30 days.

Securing the Desktop

A big problem with network security that often goes unnoticed is the practice of leaving a computer unattended and still logged into the network. The computer can't distinguish between authorized and unauthorized persons, so if the machine is left unattended, anyone who sits down at the keyboard has full access to whatever the computer is connected to. Unbelievably, this is one of the top 10 security breaches in most corporations and educational institutions. In fact, a survey conducted by Disaster Recovery Journal research shows that over 70 percent of all computer break-ins are performed internally and not externally from the Internet.

One of the best-known computer hackers is Kevin Mitnick. For a number of years, it appeared that this individual was capable of breaking into any computer system he wished. In fact, the man who helped to catch him, Tsutomu Shimomura, a world-renowned computer security expert, was one of Mitnick's victims. Although Mitnick possessed great technical skills, his biggest asset was his *social engineering* skills. Social engineering is the ability to convince people to provide privileged information. For example, Mitnick often impersonated telephone repairmen or other service providing individuals and succeeded in convincing network users to give him their passwords for "testing" purposes. (If you're interested in an excellent non-fiction account of Kevin Mitnick's escapades and eventual capture, I recommend the book *Takedown* by Tsutomu Shimomura and John Markoff.)

There are a number of ways to secure the local desktop, and help prevent social engineering, but all of them rely on the cooperation of the computer users. Every organization should publish a list of unacceptable computer habits and educate people on the severity of weak security practices. At a minimum, users need to know

1. Never leave a computer unattended when logged into the network. Always make sure you have logged out, or have initiated a password-protected screen-saver.

2. Never, under any circumstances, write a password down.

3. Never disclose a computer password to anyone. A legitimate person will obtain a needed password from a network administrator or other authorized person.

4. Follow accepted guidelines when creating and changing passwords. This includes using a minimum of six characters and mixing numbers and letters. Passwords should not be of a personal nature, such as first or last names, names of pets, names of spouses, or telephone numbers.

Data Encryption

With current technology, the best technique to secure data is the use of *encryption*. Encryption is the process of converting readable data into a scrambled mess. The original text, or *plaintext*, is converted into a coded equivalent called *ciphertext* via an encryption algorithm. The ciphertext is decoded, or *decrypted,* at the receiving end and turned back into plaintext.

The encryption algorithm uses a special code, or key, which is a number converted into binary form. The binary number is typically from 40 to 128 bits in length. The longer the key, the more secure the encryption. The actual data is then scrambled by combining the bits in the key with the bits of the data using a mathematical algorithm. When the scrambled message is received, the process is reversed to "unlock" the code, restoring it to its original readable form.

Many e-mail packages now provide encryption built into the software. You can also find a number of third-party encryption programs to protect any form of sensitive data. One of the best encryption programs available to the public is *Pretty Good Privacy*, which offers 128-bit keys, making it nearly impossible to crack. (It may be possible to decrypt a 128-bit code, but it would probably take many years and extremely powerful super-computer resources.) Pretty Good Privacy can be downloaded for free at `http://www.nai.com/products/security/freeware.asp`. There are two basic methods of encryption: *private-key* and *public-key*.

Private key

With private-key technology both the sender and the receiver use the same key. This is the fastest method, but the sender has to get the key to the receiver via some other secured means before decryption can occur. For example, the key can be exchanged via the postal system or other commercial delivery company. Private key encryption is highly dependent on the secured exchange of the key.

Public key

Public-key technology uses a combination of a private key and a public key. Each recipient has a public key that is either openly published or exchanged with some-one over non-secured channels. The owner has a private key that is never shared with anyone. The public and private keys are mathematically related so that what is encoded with the public key can only be decoded with the private. Thus, the sender uses the known public key to encrypt the message and the recipient uses the private key to decrypt it. Once the sender has encrypted the message, even the sender cannot retrieve it in readable format.

Data Encryption Standard (DES)

Data Encryption Standard or DES is a popular secret key cryptography method based on a 56-bit key. DES uses an IBM algorithm that was further developed by the U.S. National Security Agency. It uses the block cipher method that processes the data in fixed blocks of 64 bits each before encrypting them.

DES decryption is very fast and widely used. The secret key may be kept a total secret and reused often, or a key can be randomly generated for each session, in which case the new key is transmitted to the recipient using a public key cryptography method where the actual key is encrypted prior to transmission.

Encryption levels

Many of the common encryption technologies deploy various levels of security. As we discussed, key lengths are normally between 40 and 128 bits long. 56 bits is very common, as it mixes reasonably strong encryption with acceptable performance. Other techniques are used as well to increase encryption levels to provide stronger security. For example, Triple DES is an enhancement to DES that provides considerably more security. There are several Triple DES methods. EEE3 uses three keys and encrypts three times. EDE3 uses three keys to encrypt, decrypt, and encrypt again. EEE2 and EDE2 are similar to EEE3 and EDE3, except that only two keys are used, and the first and third operations use the same key.

Although encryption is generally found with data transmissions across the Internet, even local data can be secured with the same technology. Many encryption programs exist for data stored on local or network hard drives. When security is required, data encryption offers the best defense.

Secure Sockets Layer

Secure Sockets Layer (SSL) is a security protocol widely used on the Internet to transmit private data such as financial information. When an SSL session is started, the browser sends its public key to the server so that the server can securely send a secret key to the browser. The browser and server exchange data via secret key encryption during that session. SSL was originally developed by Netscape, but has recently been merged with other protocols and authentication methods into a new protocol known as *Transport Layer Security*, or TLS. TLS is backward compatible with SSL and uses Triple DES encryption. It is expected that TLS will eventually replace SSL as the secured standard protocol.

Additional Security for Web Browsers

The two most popular Web browsers, Netscape Communicator and Microsoft Internet Explorer, contain an encryption technology to secure financial or confidential transactions over the Internet via the Web browser. Within the United States, the browser can use 128-bit encryption. Due to export laws, only the 40-bit version may be exported outside of the United States

Many Internet Web sites prevent unauthorized people from seeing the information that is sent to or from those sites. The security protocol for this process is known as *digital certificates*. A certificate is a statement guaranteeing the identity of a person or the security of a Web site. A "Web site certificate" states that a specific Web site is secure and genuine. It ensures that no other Web site can assume the identity of the original secure site.

A security certificate associates an identity using the public key method. Only the owner knows the corresponding private key. When you visit a secure Web site that uses the *Hypertext Transport Protocol Secured,* or https, the site automatically sends your browser a certificate to ensure the authenticity of the page. The browser usually displays an icon on the status bar to indicate when you are viewing data from a secured site.

Digital Certificates are issued by trusted third parties known as *Certification Authorities,* or CAs. One of the most popular CAs is VeriSign, Inc. in Mountain View, California. (`www.verisign.com`). The certification process varies depending on the CA and the level of certification, but most CAs require a driver's license, notarization, and fingerprints. Many CAs also offer *Personal Digital Certificates* that provide the end user with the ability to prove identification for e-mail and e-commerce transactions. VeriSign offers personal certificates from their Web site (a valid credit card is required not only for payment, but as identification).

To view security certificates trusted by your browser, follow these steps.

For Internet Explorer:

1. Select Tools ⇨ Internet Options.
2. Click the Content tab.
3. In the Certificates area, click the Publishers buttons to view the list of current trusted certificates.

For Netscape Navigator:

1. Click the padlock icon in the status bar to open the Security Info window.
2. Select Certificates ⇨ Signers.
3. Choose a certificate from the list.
4. If you click Edit, you can view information about the certificate authority and change options about accepting the certificates that it issues or about sending messages to sites that it certifies.

Both Netscape and Internet Explorer have configurable options to set a number of default safety features. It really pays to understand what these settings mean, and when to apply them. The following list describes the settings for each of the browsers.

Netscape security settings

To configure these options, open the Security window by clicking the padlock icon, select Navigator, and then check the warnings you want displayed.

o **Entering an encrypted site:** Pages on an encrypted site are decrypted without intervention. This setting will remind you to manually secure downloaded files upon completion of your session.

o **Leaving an encrypted site:** After leaving a secured site, it is advisable to remove decrypted files left on your local drive. Web pages are encrypted only during transmission, and can remain on your computer (in cache) in unencrypted format for easy viewing by others.

o **Viewing a page with an encrypted/unencrypted mix:** When other people have access to your computer, or if the information you'd like to view is of a secure nature and others are within view of your monitor, this warning helps you decide if you want to open this page or not.

o **Sending unencrypted information to a site:** This warning reminds you that you are about to send unencrypted information through e-mail from a Web page.

Internet Explorer security settings

Internet Explorer divides the Internet into *zones* with each Web site assigned to a suitable security level. You can tell which zone the current Web page is in by looking at the right side of the Internet Explorer status bar. Whenever you attempt to open or download content from the Web, Internet Explorer checks the security settings for that Web site's zone. There are four different zones:

o **Internet zone:** By default, this zone contains anything that is not on your computer or an intranet, or assigned to any other zone. The default security level for the Internet zone is Medium.

o **Local intranet zone:** This zone typically contains any addresses that don't require a proxy server or reside on your local network. These sites are locations defined by network paths such as \\server\share, and local intranet sites, typically addresses that don't contain periods, such as http://OurIntranet. You can also manually add sites to this zone. The default security level for the Local intranet zone is Medium.

- **Trusted sites zone:** This zone contains sites you specifically trust and believe you can download or run files from without worrying about damage to your computer or data. Sites in this zone are manually created or contain certificates that you have explicitly accepted. The default security level for the Trusted sites zone is Low.

- **Restricted sites zone:** This zone contains sites that you're not sure whether files can be downloaded or run from safely. The default security level for this zone is High.

If you want, you can change the security level for a zone. For example, you might want to change the security setting for your Local intranet zone to Low. Or, you can customize the settings within a zone from the default settings in Low, Medium Low, Medium, and High.

To set a security level for each zone.

1. Select Tools ➪ Internet Options.

2. Click the Security tab.

3. Click the zone that you want to set the security level for.

4. Move the slider up for a higher level of security or down for a lower level of security.

To specify custom security settings for the selected zone, click the Customize Level button. To set the options for a particular security level back to their original settings, click the Default Level button.

Java and JavaScript security issues

I discuss Java and JavaScript in more detail in Chapter 6, but for now, just suffice it to say that these are programming languages often used on Web pages. Java and JavaScript allow Web sites to be much more interactive and useful, however, they can allow access to your computer without your consent or knowledge. Many Web pages use Java, or similar programming languages to provide a better experience to the viewer, and most are not dangerous to your local computer. Even so, the possibility for abuse is very real. All of the major browsers provide options to enable or disable these applications from running. Although you might be tempted to simply turn all these programs off, you will soon find that many great features of the Web will not be available to you. Rather than taking an all-or-nothing approach, the browser should be set to warn you when a Java application is about to run. At this point, you can choose to either allow the program to execute, or not. This will depend on how safe you feel about the content on the particular Web site.

Cookies

This friendly sounding feature of the World Wide Web is probably the single most misunderstood component of Web browsing for most beginners. With the security level of most browsers set to the default level, the user will probably receive a warning message regarding cookies on their first journey in Web-Dom.

Simply stated, cookies are an easy method for a Web browser to store minor information about you, your Web choices, or your Web browser settings on your local hard drive. At first, this may seem like a security problem and an invasion of privacy, but the ability of a cookie to do harm is small.

Take a look at what a common cookie might be used for. Many Web sites, especially e-commerce sites (sites you might make a purchase from) use cookies for a number of reasons. First, Web designers want to make navigating their site as easy as possible. Therefore, the designer may allow you to customize what you view and how your selections are presented on their site. If you're looking through a site like Amazon.com and you're primarily interested in cookbooks, the Web programmer can allow you to customize the site to always show books in the cooking section. To remember this preference after you have left the Web site, a cookie can be written to your local hard drive to save your settings. The next time you visit Amazon, the cookie is read and the Web page modified to your preferences. Likewise, many people do not like having to re-enter their name and address information every time they make a purchase. In these cases, this information can be saved in a cookie for later retrieval.

By design, a cookie can only be read by the Web site that created it. Cookies cannot be used to "steal" information about you or your computer system. They can only be used to store information that you have provided at some point. For example, if you fill out a form giving your favorite color, a server can turn this information into a cookie and send it to your browser. The next time you contact the site, your browser will return the cookie, allowing the server to alter background color of its pages to suit your preferences.

However cookies can be used for more controversial purposes. Each access your browser makes to a Web site leaves some information about you behind, creating a gossamer trail across the Internet. Among the tidbits of data left along this trail are the name and IP address of your computer, the brand of browser you're using, the operating system you're running, the URL of the Web page you accessed, and the URL of the page you were last viewing. Without cookies, it would be nearly impossible for anyone to follow this trail systematically to learn much about your Web browsing habits. They would have to reconstruct your path by correlating hundreds or thousands of individual server logs. With cookies, the situation changes considerably.

Current versions of both Netscape Navigator and Internet Explorer offer the option of alerting you whenever a server attempts to give your browser a cookie. If you turn this alert on, you will have the option of refusing cookies. Before you panic over cookies, it's worth remembering that the vast majority of cookies are benign attempts to improve your Web browsing experience, not intrusions on your privacy.

E-Mail Clients

E-mail in itself is relatively harmless. Most e-mail is simple text that cannot carry viruses or other harmful content with it. However, many people use e-mail to send and receive files as well. This makes sense, since attaching files to e-mail messages is quick, easy, and doesn't require the use of a separate FTP program. Here is where the problem lies: not with e-mail, but with the files that can be attached to an e-mail message. Just like downloading a file from an Internet site, the files that come as e-mail attachments can contain viruses. The best defense for this is a good (and *current*) antivirus software program running on your computer. In addition, since e-mail can be sent *to* someone, as opposed to waiting for someone to request a download, e-mail bound viruses can spread at incredibly fast rates. So fast in fact, that some viruses can cause widespread infections before the antivirus developers can create a defense. Therefore, if you receive an attachment via e-mail from someone you don't know, the best option is to simply delete it. Most honest people will understand a request to resend a file to you if you reply to a message and ask them to clarify what the attached file is, and why they sent it to you.

EXAM PREPARATION SUMMARY

In this chapter, I examined some of the more common problems you're likely to see when attempting to connect a client software component to the Internet. The bulk of this chapter dealt with the aspects of securing the Internet connection from the client side.

- Legacy software, especially operating systems like DOS, often present the biggest challenges. Even with modern operating systems like Windows 95/98, problems can be caused by modified version of the WINSOCK.DLL file. You should identify and apply software patches and upgrades as needed.

- In many cases, computer viruses will be the most common result of bad security practices. Antivirus software is the best-known defense, but only if you are diligent in keeping the virus *signature* files up to date. Even a 60-day-old anti-virus system is almost completely ineffective.

- Common sense plays a big part of client-side security. Users need to be made aware that passwords should be closely guarded and never given to anyone without formal authorization.

- Data encryption technologies should be used whenever secured data needs to be transmitted across the public network. Encryption can be used in the Web browser, e-mail, and file transfers.

- *Private key* techniques use a single key shared between two people. The key must be transmitted via a separate, secured method. *Public key* technology uses two keys: The public key is used to encrypt the data (a one-way process) and both the public and private keys are used in combination to unencrypt (decrypt) the data. The public key process is normally easier to use and allows many people to send secured information without first confirming the encryption process with the recipient.

- Digital certificates provide a method for people or organizations to prove their identity. A digital certificate is obtained from a trusted certificate authority. The certificate is then passed from a Web server to a browser, or to an e-mail client to prove authenticity of the server's identification.

- Web programming technologies such as Java and JavaScripts are very useful to enhance Web sites' usability, but they can also be used maliciously. Likewise, cookies are useful to allow a user to customize their Web site preferences without as big a security risk.

APPLYING WHAT YOU HAVE LEARNED

The following review questions give you an opportunity to test your knowledge of the information presented in this chapter. The answers to these assessment questions can be found in Appendix B. If you missed some, review the relevant sections in this chapter before going further.

Instant Assessment Questions

1. DOS-based applications are not well suited for browsing because

    A. DOS can only address 4MB of memory

    B. There are no DOS-based Web browsers available

    C. DOS-based browsers can't display most Web graphic formats

    D. DOS-based browsers are just as good as other operating system programs

2. Which statements are true regarding the WINSOCK.DLL?

    A. Winsock is an interface between Windows applications and the TCP/IP stack

    B. A Windows Socket is used in tandem with a URL to enhance security

    C. WINSOCK.DLL is part of the Windows family operating system

    D. The WINSOCK.DLL file can be modified by a Windows programmer

3. A software service pack usually

    A. Requires a trained Internet Engineer to apply

    B. Always needs to be applied to Internet client software

    C. Fixes bugs and may add features to existing applications

    D. Should only be applied after understanding its implications

4. Service packs should be applied when security holes are identified in the application:

    A. True

    B. False

5. Viruses can be transmitted

A. In an e-mail attachment

B. By a Microsoft Office document

C. From a program downloaded from an FTP site

D. A VBA macro file

6. A major consideration when choosing an antivirus solution is

A. It should cost no more than $25.00

B. It should never require user intervention

C. It should run on multiple operating systems

D. It should provide easy access to signature updates

7. The best technology currently available to ensure privacy of data is

A. Password protection

B. To store data on removable diskettes or writable CD-ROM disks

C. Data encryption

D. The HTTPS protocol

8. Public-key data encryption can be useful for data

A. Stored on a local hard drive

B. Transmitted across a private network

C. Transmitted across the public network (Internet)

D. Shared by many people collaborating on a project

9. Digital Certificates are issued by

A. The Internet Engineering Task Force

B. Federal/Country Government Agencies

C. Operating System Vendors

D. Trusted third-party corporations

10. A negative side effect of allowing cookies from the Web is

A. Companies can track your online habits

B. Cookies can be used to transfer files from your computer without your knowledge

C. Companies can track your e-mail address and send you junk mail

D. They can consume a great deal of disk space

Web Site Development

Even if your Internet aspirations are not targeted at Web site development, by the end of Part III I think you'll agree that this aspect of the Internet is incredibly fun, challenging, and unique to any other form of communication you have ever seen before. The original concept of the World Wide Web was to make a central repository for every imaginable piece of information that needed to be stored or accessed. No matter what subject you're interested in, the Web is a single location where information about everything seems to exist.

It's easy to be intimidated by the flashy graphics of Web pages and think you simply don't have the creativity or programming talent. But in Part III, you'll see the basic elements of a Web page are quite simple, and using just the basic elements, even a novice Web designer can create stunning and useful pages.

Of course we won't stop there. Even though computer programming is far beyond the scope of the i-Net+ objectives, you'll see how additional programming skills can increase the usefulness and usability of the Internet experience.

Also, we'll cover the possible problems you can run into when putting your Web site on the 'net. Although not every conflict can be avoided, you'll look closely at the typical situations that can pose problems, and see how to test your creations before the problems begin.

i-NET+™

Components of the Web Page

About Chapter 6

Although it is only one of many protocols on the Internet, the World Wide Web contains the greatest resources for e-commerce and mass communications. Although Web pages can be fully constructed with plain basic text, many people feel that style is as important as content. And when e-commerce is at stake, plain text pages simply won't provide the necessary tools to make the Web site useful enough for customers.

In this chapter you'll see how Web pages are constructed, starting with the basic elements of HTML. Then I'll discuss some of the standard HTML editors that you can use to create pages more easily.

PROGRAMMING TERMS RELATED TO INTERNET APPLICATION DEVELOPMENT

Like other technologies, the World Wide Web has its own terminology that you need to be familiar with. The i-Net+ exam will expect you to know the basic meaning and use of these programming terms. You should know the full definition for each acronym and understand where and how it is applied within Web page development.

- **ActiveX:** A brand name from Microsoft for various technologies based on its COM component architecture. (See COM.) The term was originally used to represent only small routines (ActiveX controls) that could be extracted from the Internet. Later, it was used to represent COM and Microsoft's entire component strategy.

- **API:** *Application Program Interface.* As programs have become more complex, the amount of computer instructions for any given task has grown tremendously. Similar routines are often reused within a program, or by many different programs. For example, most Windows programs provide a method of selecting a file from a directory, or selecting a specific printer to print to. In order to maximize the programmer's efficiency, many common routines are built into the operating system or other common files such as DLLs (discussed later). These routines are made available to the programmer by means of an API. Rather than re-creating the common function, the programmer simply *calls* the common routine via a published standard, and the API carries out the request.

- **CGI:** *Common Gateway Interface.* A CGI script is a small set of instructions written in a script language that functions as a bridge between HTML pages and other applications on a Web server. (See script.) For example, a CGI script might be used to send search criteria entered from a Web page to a database application on the Web server. A second CGI script could be used to format the results of that search back to Web page for presentation to the user. CGI scripts have been the initial mechanism used to make Web sites interact with databases and other programs, although client-side technologies such as Java, JavaScript, and ActiveX components are quickly becoming more popular.

Continued

Continued

- **COM:** *Component Object Model.* A component software architecture from Microsoft that defines a structure for building program routines (objects) that can be called and executed in a Windows environment. This capability is built into Windows 95/98 and Windows NT 4.0. Parts of Windows itself and Microsoft's own applications are also built as COM objects. COM provides the interfaces between objects, and *Distributed COM* (DCOM) allows them to run remotely.

- **DLL:** *Dynamic Link Library.* A DLL is a collection of commonly used routines, such as opening or saving a file. Rather than re-creating the programming code each time these operations are required, a program can use an API call to a DLL file to perform the function. This greatly reduces the size of programs, as well as the time needed to develop a program in the first place.

- **SAPI:** *Speech Application Programming Interface.* SAPI is a Microsoft definition of a computer/speech interface. It provides an API for applications and speech engines for both text-to-speech and automatic speech recognition processes.

- **Script:** Computer programs are written in human-readable form called source code. The source code is then run through a program that compiles it into a binary executable, which can be read quickly by a computer, but which can't be read by a human. This is why if you try to view the source code of most of the programs on your computer (Microsoft Word, for example) you will find it's impossible. A *script*, on the other hand, is source code that is compiled every time the script is run. This means a human can read it, make changes

to it, and run it on a computer without going through the intermediate compiler step. This makes scripts convenient for simple Web programming and system administration tasks, but less useful for more complex tasks that require more efficient use of hardware, or more functionality than scripting languages typically provide. JavaScript is a popular scripting language that can be embedded in HTML documents. Microsoft Word, Excel, and other complex applications can run macros that use scripts. Perl is a popular scripting language typically used in CGI programming and system administration.

- **SDK:** *Software Developer's Kit.* An SDK is a collection of software routines and utilities used to help programmers write applications that are usually specific to a vendor's operating system or major application. For example, Microsoft Office provides an SDK to assist programmers with developing add-on functions to the Office suite of products.

- **SQL:** *Structured Query Language.* Pronounced "sequel," SQL is a specialty language used to manipulate the data in a relational database. SQL is a common method of accessing data on a true client/server database where the data i s completely stored on the server for multiple-user access. SQL commands can be used interactively or can be embedded within a programming language to access the database. Some of the major databases that support SQL are DB2, MSSQL, Oracle, Sybase, and INFORMIX. Although the American National Standards Institute (ANSI) standardized the SQL language, each database system has implemented i ts own enhancements. Therefore, moving an application from one SQL database to another generally requires manually converting some of the SQL statements.

ALL ABOUT WEB PAGES

A Web page is really nothing more than a simple text file. In fact, an entire Web site can be created with just a text editor such as Windows Notepad. But except for those whose Web creation needs are minimal, most developers choose an HTML editor with which to create their Web sites. Figure 6-1 is a sample of a text-based editor, HTML-Notes, which is included on the CD that accompanies this book.

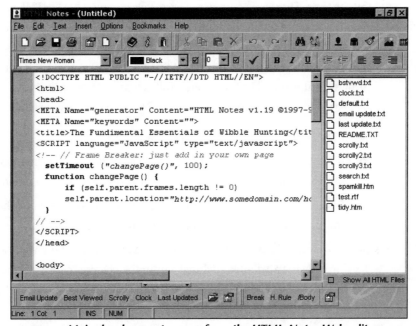

FIGURE 6-1 **Main development screen from the HTML–Notes Web editor program**

The defining characteristic of a Web page is the use of Hypertext Markup Language (HTML) commands. HTML commands instruct a Web browser on how to display a given Web page. HTML commands are known as *tags*, which are embedded within the Web page text, and are always surrounded by angle brackets. HTML is not case sensitive. Some Web authors prefer to write HTML tags in all caps to make their code more readable; others prefer lowercase. Either way, the browser doesn't care.

For example, to present a section of text in italics, HTML tags would surround the text like this:

```
<I>This text will display in italics</I>
```

The `<I>` (or `<i>`, because HTML is not case sensitive) instructs the Web server to begin displaying the text in italics until it encounters the `</I>` tag. The forward slash / indicates that the browser should turn off whatever formatting code follows the slash.

Basic HTML provides a large number of tags, and more are being developed all the time. There are a number of basic tags common to all HTML pages that help identify the text file as an HTML page. Some of these tags are mandatory, while others are optional. One of the most commonly used optional tags is `<!` which identifies a comment. All text on the line following the `<!` is ignored by the browser but is useful to developers to add comments regarding what the section is supposed to do. At a minimum, every HTML page requires the following tags:

- `<HTML>` This tag identifies the beginning of an HTML page.

- `<HEAD>` This section contains Web page identification information such as the page title, description, author, keywords, and other comments.

- `<TITLE>` Text contained after this tag is displayed on the top of the browser window and defines the purpose of the Web page/site.

- `<BODY>` The body section holds the primary content of the Web page. Normally the attributes enclosed within the opening `<BODY>` tag identify the default format of the page, such as the background image, text color, and font type.

The Web page must also include the closing tags for these tags to define the function's ending points. The following sample shows how the HTML code for a simple Web page might look:

```
<HTML>
 <HEAD>
  <TITLE>Tutorial: Sample Page</TITLE>
 </HEAD>
```

```
<BODY BACKGROUND="http://mywebserver/images/background.gif"
 TEXT="#0000FF" LINK="#FF0000" VLINK="#000000">


<CENTER>Sample Web Page</CENTER>
</BODY>
</HTML>
```

When displayed, this Web page would center the phrase "Sample Web Page" on the background image defined as *background.gif*.

As you can see, a new tag has been introduced in the sample: <CENTER>. This particular tag tells the browser to center the following text on the page. There are a number of common tags within the basic HTML language, which we'll take a closer look at here.

Text Formatting

There are several common tags for formatting text. These accomplish things that you would usually do with a word processor, such as

- Bold: <B> and </B>
- Italics: <I> and </I>
- Centering: <CENTER> and </CENTER>
- Font Size: <FONT SIZE="#"> and </FONT>

For example, the following HTML:

```
<FONT SIZE="4">This is font size 4.</FONT>

<FONT SIZE="+2">This is two sizes bigger than the default.
</FONT>
```

The results of the various formatting options are shown in Figure 6-2.

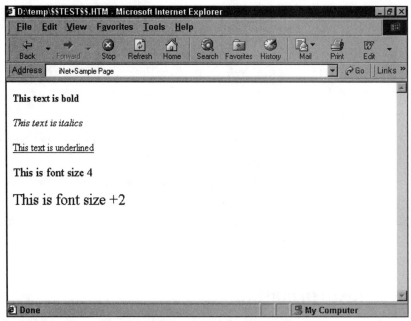

FIGURE 6-2 Web page showing the various formatting options

Headings

There are six headings you can use. They look like regular text, except they're a different size, are in bold face, and have blank lines before and after them. The HTML tag is the letter H followed by the heading level, such as <H1> or <H2>. The lower the heading level, the larger the heading that is displayed.

White Spaces and Blank Lines

White spaces are blank spaces between things, usually text, but sometimes graphic elements. Browsers usually ignore more than one white space in a row, so special tags are used to help format the text the way the author envisioned. These tags include

Indenting

Use the <DD> tag to indent. For example, look at this HTML:

```
This is normal text.
<DD>This is indented text.
```

The output looks like this:

```
This is normal text.
  This is indented text.
```

Blank lines

The `<BR>` tag produces a line break, also called a "soft return." The `<P>` tag starts a new paragraph by setting some space between the previous line and the new one. This is also called a "hard return." These breaks will appear in the output even if the tags are all on one line in the HTML code:

```
This is my first line,<BR>and this is my second,<P>and this is
a new paragraph.
```

The output looks like this:

```
This is my first line,
and this is my second,

and this is a new paragraph.
```

Note that the `<DD>`, `<BR>`, and `<P>` tags do not have "off" tags (with a forward slash). The formatting changes they create happen only once.

Colors

There are many ways to use color in Web pages. There are default colors that the browser uses, but you can define different ones in your page if you wish. You can define colors for

- Some of the text: `<FONT COLOR="#hex_value">` and `</FONT>`
- All of the text in the page: `TEXT="#hex_value"`
- Links that haven't been clicked on: `LINK="#hex_value"`
- Links that have been clicked on: `VLINK="#hex_value"`
- The background color of the page: `BGCOLOR="#hex_value"`

If you decide to change the default background, link, and text colors, make sure that the new colors differ enough so that you can read text on the background and tell when a link has been visited or not. For example, you don't want to have blue text on a blue background

Color tags can use descriptive adjectives such as "red" or "blue" for *Web safe* colors (the primary colors). For other colors or shades of colors, hexadecimal values are required. For example, a light shade of red has a hexadecimal value of ff0800. There are many charts available that cross-reference color shades to their corresponding hexadecimal value, for example, the site `http://www.htmlearn.com/hexcolors.html` is a good example.

Lists

There are a few different kinds of lists, but the two most common are

- Numbered lists: `<OL>` and `</OL>` (OL stands for Ordered list)
- Bulleted lists: `<UL>` and `</UL>` (UL stands for Unordered list)

Each item in a list must have the `<LI>` tag before it (no closing `</LI>` tag is necessary). Items in a list are indented with a number or bullet preceding the text. For example

```
<OL><LI>First item<LI>Second item<LI>Third item</OL>
```

The output looks like this:

1. First item
2. Second item
3. Third item

If you use the `<UL>` tag instead of the `<OL>` tag, the above three items will have small bullets (•) preceding the text instead of numbers.

Links to Pages

A *link* is something that takes the user to another Web page. Links can be created for text or graphics, or you can create a link to launch the default e-mail program to send an e-mail message. The text or image clicked to launch the link is called an *anchor,* and denoted with the anchor (`<A>`) tag.

- To link to a new page from text within a page, the tags `<A HREF="">` and `</A>` are used. Inside the quotes should be the URL of the page you want to link to.

- To link to a page by clicking an image, the tags `<A HREF="">`, `<IMG SRC="">`, and `</A>` are used. The `HREF` quotes should have the URL of the location you want to link to, and the `IMG SRC` quotes should contain the image that you want to display as the link.

- To automatically launch the default e-mail program to send an e-mail message, the tag `mailto:` is used with the `<A HREF>` tag.

Examples:

1. To create a text link on a Web page that takes the viewer to the home page of IDG Books, the following line could be used:

```
<A HREF="http://www.idgbooks.com/">IDG Books Home Page</A>
```

When the Web browser displays this line, the output shows in the default link color, underlined like this:

```
IDG Books Home Page
```

2. The following HTML lines display the graphic image `new.gif` located on the server `myserver` in the `/images` directory and link to the Web site `idgbooks.com`.

```
<A HREF="http://www.idgbooks.com/">
<IMG SRC="http://www.myserver.com/images/new.gif"></A>
```

3. To launch the default e-mail program to send a message to the webmaster at `idgbooks.com` by clicking a linked text area, the following code could be used:

```
<A HREF="mailto:webmaster@idgbooks.com">
```

Adding Graphics

To add graphics to your page, use the `<IMG SRC="">` tag. For example

```
<IMG SRC="http://www.myserver.com/images/picture.gif">
```

Optional parameters can be added to align the graphic on the Web page, such as

```
<IMG SRC="http://www.myserver.com/images/picture.gif"
ALIGN=LEFT>
<IMG SRC="http://www.myserver.com/images/picture.gif"
ALIGN=RIGHT>
```

Usually, content on the same server as the referring Web page is linked to with a *relative link*. For example, if `picture.gif` is in the `images` subdirectory of the directory where your Web page resides, you could use the following for the same effect as in the preceding example:

```
<IMG SRC="images/picture.gif" ALIGN=RIGHT>
```

in the real world

When using graphics, make sure that file sizes are as small as possible (32K or less). Otherwise your page may take too long to load. People can be impatient so you don't want them leaving your site just because the graphics take too long to display.

MORE COMPONENTS AND CONCEPTS OF THE HTML LANGUAGE

As you can see, HTML pages use tags to indicate how a Web browser is to display pages sent from the Web server. At a minimum, each HTML page must contain the beginning and ending tags `<HTML>` and `<BODY>`. Most HTML pages contain other tags as well to form a starting point, or template, for further development. The following code sample shows what an HTML template page might contain:

```
<HTML>
 <META NAME="description" CONTENT="this is the page
description.">
 <META NAME="keywords" CONTENT="keyword1, keyword2, Add as
many of these as necessary.">
```

```
<HEAD>

<TITLE>Title goes here</TITLE>

</HEAD>

<SCRIPT LANGUAGE="JavaScript1.2">
</SCRIPT>

<SCRIPT LANGUAGE="VBScript">
</SCRIPT>

<BODY BGCOLOR="White">

This section contains the actual information the page will
present to the reader. Many additional HTML tags will be
embedded in this section to make the page more appealing
and useable.

</BODY>
</HTML>
```

 tip **Throughout this chapter you will create a number of sample HTML pages based on the template above. To save time, it would be helpful to create a text file on your computer with this template. Start your text editor, type in the template, and save it as HTML_Template.TXT.**

THE META TAG

We've discussed briefly (in Chapter 3) that META tags are mostly informational rather than functional. These tags have no effect on how the browser displays the page. However, many Internet search engines gather the information in these tags to list the pages in their databases. Most search engines understand the "Keywords" and "Description" tags. These lines simply provide author-defined values that the search engines can use. Other engines may use custom META tags the developer can include to assist in further defining the search criteria. For example: copyright notices that should show in search results, or commands to instruct the engine how often the system should check your page for changes. When submitting a site to a search engine service, it is important to review what special META tags the engine will use to ensure your pages get the best results.

USING TABLES

Earlier in this chapter you looked at some simple text formatting tags to create extra blank spaces, indentation, and paragraphs. However, trying to format text and images using just these methods would be extremely difficult. To create more advanced formatting and provide greater control over text and object placement on a page, tables are often used. If you have experience with a word processing program, you've probably used tables in your documents. The concept is the same for HTML pages. A table is a specific object comprising rows (down) and columns (across). The area between the intersections of rows and columns creates a *cell*. Each cell can contain a specific item, such as text or an image. Figure 6-3 shows what a simple table of one row and three columns might look like.

This is a cell	This is a cell	This is a cell

FIGURE 6-3 **Example of an HTML table with one row and three columns**

As you might expect, the TABLE tag is used to define a table as shown here:

```
<TABLE WIDTH="100%" BORDER="0" CELLPADDING="2"
CELLSPACING="0">
```

The Table WIDTH Attribute

The WIDTH value defines how wide the table should be displayed on the page. This value can be a percentage, such as 100% (fills the width of the page), or a fixed amount. A fixed value is the width in *pixels*. A pixel is the smallest display value of the screen and is based on the resolution the viewer has the screen set to.

If the WIDTH value is set as a percent, the Web browser might resize the table and change how the contents fit within the cells. If a pixel value is specified, the table will not rescale to fit a Web browser's window, regardless of the screen's resolution or how the person viewing the page resizes the window. If you specify a fixed size that doesn't fit within the viewable area of the browser, the viewer will need to operate the horizontal scroll bar to see the entire contents of the table. Unless it is crucial that the table contents not be resized, the percentage value is the better choice.

The Table BORDER Attribute

The BORDER value defines how *thick* the edges of the table will display. This is a fixed pixel value. A value of zero (0) tells the browser not to display the border at all, in effect making the table invisible to the viewer. Most browsers will display table borders in a slightly three-dimensional format, which adds a feeling of depth to the display.

The Table Cell Attributes

The cells of a table contain the objects you want displayed. The cells can be treated as individual objects in the sense that each cell can contain its own color, can be resized separately from the other cells, and can have the objects within it aligned differently than objects in other cells.

The CELLPADDING attribute

The CELLPADDING value defines the space between cell contents and the inside edges of the cell. This is a fixed value defined in screen pixels. A value of 0 will place the objects within the cell right next to the edge of borders. The higher the value, the further away from the borders the cell contents will be placed. A value of 2 is normal for this attribute.

The CELLSPACING attribute

The CELLSPACING is a value in pixels that defines the amount of spacing to be placed between all the cells in a table. This value offsets entire contents of a cell from the surrounding border edges.

Figure 6-4 is an example of a one-row, three-column table with the following table attributes: WIDTH="100%" CELLPADDING="2" CELLSPACING="11" BORDER="3"

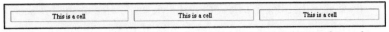

FIGURE 6-4 **Example of an HTML table with a CELLPADDING of 2 and CELLSPACING of 11**

Table Cell Properties

While the CELLPADDING and CELLSPACING attributes of the TABLE tag define the margins of the cells with the table, the <TD> and <TR> tags define the specific features of each cell. The following code shows how these tags are used to create a table of three rows and three columns with text centered in each cell.

```
<!Create row 1, cells 1-3
<TABLE>
 <TR>
    <TD WIDTH="33%" VALIGN=TOP><P>Cell 1</TD>
    <TD WIDTH="33%" VALIGN=TOP><P>Cell 2</TD>
    <TD WIDTH="33%" VALIGN=TOP><P>Cell 3</TD>
  </TR>

<!Create row 2, cells 4-6
  <TR>
   <TD WIDTH="33%" VALIGN=TOP><P>Cell 4</TD>
   <TD WIDTH="33%" VALIGN=TOP><P>Cell 5</TD>
   <TD WIDTH="33%" VALIGN=TOP><P>Cell 6</TD>
  </TR>


<!Create row 3, cells 7-9
  <TR>
   <TD WIDTH="33%" VALIGN=TOP><P>Cell 7</TD>
   <TD WIDTH="33%" VALIGN=TOP><P>Cell 8</TD>
   <TD WIDTH="33%" VALIGN=TOP><P>Cell 9</TD>
  </TR>
  </TABLE>
```

The Cell WIDTH attribute

The value for the cell's `WIDTH` is either a percentage of the table width, or a fixed number of pixels. As with the table width value, if the cell `WIDTH` value is set as a percent, the Web browser might resize the cell and change how the contents appear. By specifying a pixel value, the cell will not rescale regardless of the screen's resolution or how the person viewing the page resizes the window.

The Cell VALIGN Attribute

The `VALIGN` attribute allows for a specific placement of the object within a cell. This value can be set to Top, Center, or Bottom. This attribute is for the *vertical* alignment of the object. To specify a horizontal alignment, the normal `<ALIGN=>` tag is used. For example, the following code sample creates the top row of your table with the text aligned left, center, and right in each of the three cells respectively.

```
<TABLE>
<TR>
   <TD WIDTH="33%" VALIGN=TOP>
     <P ALIGN=LEFT>Cell 1
   </TD>
   <TD WIDTH="33%" VALIGN=TOP>
    <P ALIGN=CENTER>Cell 2
   </TD>
   <TD WIDTH="33%" VALIGN=TOP>
      <P ALIGN=RIGHT>Cell 3
   </TD>
</TR>
</TABLE>
```

The Cell BGCOLOR Attribute

Web pages look best in color, and a powerful use of tables and cells is to add color at specific areas on the page. To add a color to a particular cell in a table, the `BGCOLOR` attribute is used. For example, the following code sample adds the colors Aqua, Yellow, and Silver to the first three cells of row one in your table.

```
<TABLE>
   <TR>
     <TD WIDTH="33%" BGCOLOR="AQUA" VALIGN=TOP>
```

```
        <P ALIGN=LEFT>Cell 1</TD>
      <TD WIDTH="33%" BGCOLOR="YELLOW" VALIGN=TOP>
       <P ALIGN=CENTER>Cell 2</TD>
      TD WIDTH="33%" BGCOLOR="SILVER" VALIGN=TOP>
       <P ALIGN=RIGHT>Cell 3</TD>
    </TR>
  </TABLE>
```

To make the text in Cell 2 really stand out against the yellow background, a nice blue color could be used. To accomplish this, simply modify the Cell 2 line to assign a value to the COLOR attribute of the FONT tag, like so:

```
<FONT COLOR="BLUE"> <P ALIGN=CENTER> Cell 2 </FONT></TD>
```

WYSIWYG HTML Editors

What You See Is What You Get (WYSIWYG, pronounced "whiz-ee-wig") editors make creating and maintaining Web pages very easy. Although it is recommended that you understand at least the basics of HTML creation, these editors can provide either a finished product, or an excellent base to which to add your customizations. These programs work much like a word processor or desktop publishing application. You start with a basic template and then add text, graphics, and other Web elements as you see fit. Many of these programs contain added features such as spell checking, table creation, and automatic conversion of colors to their hexadecimal values. Among the many commercial WYSIWYG editors, Netscape's Composer (part of the Netscape browser package), Microsoft's Front Page, and Microsoft Word provide WYSIWYG page creation. The accompanying CD contains a wonderful WYSIWYG editor called WebExpress by MicroVision development. Figure 6-5 shows the primary development screen from this application. Compare this to the text-based HTML editor shown in Figure 6-1. WebExpress walks you through the complete creation process with very helpful Wizards, templates, and a gallery of graphics. It supports many of the advanced Web features including multimedia, sound, video, and interactive forms. I highly recommend you install this trial version and create a few Web pages. Examine the pages it creates and you'll have an excellent reference point for designing your own Web site.

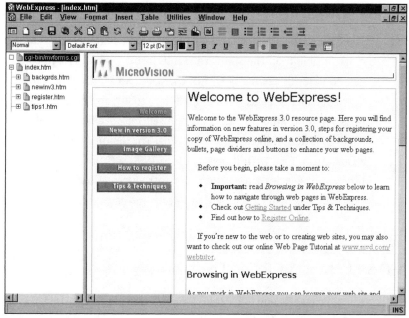

FIGURE 6-5 Development screen from the WebExpress WYSIWYG editor program

IMPROVEMENTS ON STANDARD HTML

While basic HTML supports many features and provides an excellent framework for development of highly presentable Web pages, other enhancements are being developed and improved to make Web pages even more extensible.

Dynamic HTML

Dynamic HTML (DHTML) is a general term for Web pages that are customized dynamically for each user. For example, a DHTML page may be formatted instantly based on the return values from a search. Contrast this with static HTML pages that never change.

To support dynamic implementation of HTML pages, specific enhancements to HTML tags are required that enable Web pages to function more like regular software. For example, fonts can be changed or images selected without having to jump to another page. DHTML is based on the Document Object Model (DOM) interface that enables HTML tags to be dynamically changed via Java or another scripting language. DHTML standards do not yet exist; therefore Netscape Communicator and Internet Explorer use different methods to implement DHTML.

Extensible Markup Language

The EXtensible Markup Language (XML) is a document format for the Web that is more flexible than the standard HTML format. While HTML uses only predefined tags to describe elements within the page, XML allows tags to be defined by the developer of the page. Thus, tags for virtually any data items, such as product, sales rep, and amount due, can be used for specific applications, allowing Web pages to function like database records. The definition of these tags is provided in a Document Type Definition (DTD). In 1999, a flavor of XML defining the characteristics of a sales transaction was introduced. Commercial XML, or *cXML*, is expected to provide a standard for electronic commerce transactions.

HANDS-ON EXERCISES

In following lab, you will create a simple Web page to see how the basic HTML tags affect the page's display.

 To perform these exercises you will need a text editor that will save your work in plain ASCII text (no special formatting). Windows NotePad is recommended. You will also need a Web browser with Java support (Internet Explorer version 4 or higher, or Netscape Navigator version 4 or higher recommended) installed on your computer.

1. To create your basic Web page, start your text editor and type in the following lines:

```
<HTML>
 <HEAD>
   <TITLE>My Sample Web Page</TITLE>
 </HEAD>

<BODY TEXT="#0000FF" LINK="#ff0000" VLINK="#000000">

<H1>This is the page Heading</H1>
   <CENTER>This text is centered</CENTER>
       <B>This text is bold</B>
```

```
        <BR>
        <I>This text is italics</I>

    <!this line will be replaced later>

    <P>The following items are in a numbered list</P>
    <OL>
        <LI>Item one
        <LI>Item two
        <LI>Item three
    </OL>

    <P>The following items are in a bulleted list</P>
    <OL>
        <LI>Bullet item one
        <LI>Bullet item two
        <LI>Bullet item three
    </UL>
    </BODY>
    </HTML>
```

2. Next, save this file to the root of your primary drive. Click File ➪ Save As.

3. In the Save In box, select C:\.

4. In the File Name box, type in SAMPLE1.HTML.

5. Click Save.

Now load your sample page in the browser to see how it looks.

1. Start your browser by clicking the icon, or selecting it from the program list.

2. If prompted to dial-up your ISP, click no (if you don't have an option, continue with the connection).

3. Click File ➪ Open.

4. Navigate to the root of the C: drive and locate the file SAMPLE1.HTML.

Our sample page should be displayed in blue text. Now change the color of the item lists.

1. Bring up the text editor. (Re-open the SAMPLE1.HTML page if needed.)

2. Locate the line that reads: `<!this line will be replaced later>`.

3. Replace this line with: `<FONT COLOR="#ff0800">`.

4. Click File ⇨ Save.

5. Bring the browser back to the top.

6. Click Refresh (or Reload in Netscape).

> The page should now display your numbered and bulleted list in red.
>
> Now create a second page and create a link from the first page to the second.

1. Bring up the text editor.

2. Click File ⇨ New.

3. Enter the following text.

```
<HTML>
<HEAD>
 <TITLE>My Sample Web Page 2</TITLE>
</HEAD>
  <BODY TEXT="#0000FF" LINK="#ff0000" VLINK="#000000">
  <H1>This is the Heading on Page 2</H1>

  <FONT COLOR="green">
      <P>this is a color test
      <FONT COLOR="blue">


  <P>
  <A HREF="c:\sample1.html"> Click here for Page 1 </A>
  </P>
</BODY>
</HTML>
```

4. Click File ⇨ Save As.

5. In the Save In box, select C:\.

6. In the File Name box, type in `SAMPLE2.HTML`.

7. Click Save.

8. Click File ⇨ Open.

9. Navigate to the root of the C: drive and locate the file `SAMPLE1.HTML`.

10. Scroll down to the end of the file. Just above the final command `</html>` enter the following line:

```
<P>
 <A HREF="c:\sample2.html"> Click here for Page 2 </A>
 </P>
```

11. Click File ⇨ Save.

12. Bring the browser back to the top.

13. Click Refresh (or Reload in Netscape). The original sample page now has an underlined link at the bottom that reads *Click here for Page 2*.

14. Click the new link.

The second page you created above will be displayed. Notice also that the FONT COLOR tag changed the color of the embedded text to green. As you can see, this color was defined using the adjective "GREEN" instead of a hexadecimal number. You also have another link back to your sample Page 1.

For reference, your completed SAMPLE1.HTML code should look like this:

```
<HTML>
 <HEAD>
  <TITLE>My Sample Web Page</TITLE>

</HEAD>
    <BODY TEXT="#0000FF" LINK="#ff0000" VLINK="#000000">

    <H1>This is the page Heading</H1>
    <CENTER>This text is centered</CENTER>
    <B>This text is bold</B>
    <BR>
    <I>This text is italics</I>
    <FONT COLOR="#ff0800">
    <P>The following items are in a numbered list</P>
       <OL>
       <LI>Item one
       <LI>Item two
       <LI>Item three
       </OL>
```

```
<P>The following items are in a bulleted list</P>
   <UL>
   <LI>Bullet item one
   <LI>Bullet item two
   <LI>Bullet item three
   </UL>

<P>
<A HREF="sample2.html"> Click here for Page 2 </A>
</P>
</BODY>
</HTML>
```

The finished SAMPLE2.HTML code looks like this:

```
<HTML>
<HEAD>
   <TITLE>My Sample Web Page 2</TITLE>
</HEAD>
   <BODY TEXT="#0000FF" LINK="yellow" VLINK="#000000">
      <H1>This is the Heading on Page 2</H1>
      <FONT COLOR="green">
      <P>this is a color test
      <FONT COLOR="blue">
      <P>
      <A HREF="c:\sample1.html"> Click here for Page 1 </A>
      </P>
   </BODY>
</HTML>
```

EXAM PREPARATION SUMMARY

In this chapter you looked at numerous tools used to develop and enhance Web pages. As in many areas of the Information Technology field, there are a number of new acronyms and terms to be learned. You looked at the basic components of a Web page and some of the tools you can use to make creating your pages easier.

Now review the key concepts for this chapter to make sure you understand the material you just read:

- HTML, or Hypertext Markup Language, is the language used to create Web pages. HTML uses *tags* to instruct a Web browser on how the page is to be displayed. HTML tags have a defined beginning and ending, such as `<B>` to start bold display, and `</B>` to end bold display. While many HTML editors exist, a complete Web site can be written in HTML with nothing more than a simple text editor.

- The `META` tags in an HTML page are useful to include non-display information like a description of the page, search engine keywords, and special codes that help search engines index your site properly.

- One way to control the format of text and objects on your page is to use tables. A table can contain many rows and columns, each of which can be sized independently. The area of a table defined by the points where rows and columns meet is called a cell. Cells can contain any valid HTML object. Objects within a cell can be formatted using the `CELLPADDING`, `CELLSPACING`, and `VALIGN` attributes. This provides a great deal of flexibility for controlling the format of a page.

- Many improvements to the basic HTML protocol have been developed, and continue to be developed. Two of the more popular enhancements are Dynamic HTML (DHTML) and Extensible Markup Language (XML).

APPLYING WHAT YOU HAVE LEARNED

The following review questions give you an opportunity to test your knowledge of the information presented in this chapter. The answers to these assessment questions can be found in Appendix B. If you missed some, review those sections in this chapter before going further.

Instant Assessment Questions

1. An API is

   A. A collection of commonly used programming routines

   B. An extension to HTML to provide Active Pages

   C. An interface that provides simple access to common programming routines

   D. A set of predefined values within an operating system

2. The proper syntax to center a line of text in bold type on a Web page is

   A. `<CENTER-BOLD>`This is sample text`</CENTER-BOLD>`

   B. `<CENTER><B>`This is sample text`</CENTER></B>`

   C. `<CENTER><BOLD>`This is sample text`</CENTER></BOLD>`

   D. `<CENTER><B>`This is sample text`<\CENTER><\B>`

3. Predefined colors can be set for which Web page elements?

   A. All of the text on the page

   B. Links that have already been clicked

   C. Links that have not been clicked

   D. Solid backgrounds

4. Hyperlinks can be defined on which two elements of a Web page?

   A. The status bar

   B. The Back and Forward buttons

   C. Any text

   D. A graphic image

5. The `WIDTH` attribute of the HTML `TABLE` tag can contain

   A. A percentage of the viewable page to display the table

   B. A tag to control the three-dimensional view of the border

   C. A fixed integer defining a non-resizable area for the table

   D. The point size of the table border

6. Two attributes for formatting objects within a cell are

   A. `CELLWIDTH`

   B. `CELLSPACING`

   C. `CELLPADDING`

   D. `CELLPOSITION`

7. The two HTML tags used to create cells within a table are

    A. TD

    B. CL

    C. CELL

    D. TR

8. To format an object in the exact center of a cell, which two attributes are used?

    A. <CENTER>

    B. <ALIGN=CENTER>

    C. <ALIGN=MIDDLE>

    D. <VALIGN=CENTER>

Advanced Web Techniques

About Chapter 7

As you've seen, a lot of tools are available for Web development. Web programmer jobs abound, and the career path will probably remain one of the hottest for years to come. In Chapter 7 you'll delve deeper into the Web language of HTML and see more of the advanced techniques at your disposal.

There are a number of methods to gauge the popularity of your Web site, but one of the best is to have your visitors send you feedback. Providing an online method of communication often is extremely desirable, and that's exactly what Web forms do. In this chapter, you'll learn how forms work by using the form tags to create a visitor response page.

You'll also look at some of the scripting and programming options that can be used to take your Web pages beyond the capabilities of HTML. This book won't explore any of these languages in depth, but you'll need to know what they are for the exam.

When HTML isn't quite enough to accomplish your goals, multimedia extensions and browser plug-ins fill the gap nicely. There are a number of popular plug-ins for static images, audio, and video. You'll see what these programs do, and which ones are the most appropriate in a given situation.

A number of special file formats for images, documents, and video are used on the Web. You'll learn why and where they should be used.

Finally, I'll end the chapter discussing some important aspects of testing your work before setting it loose on the world. It's important that all your hard work doesn't get skipped over simply because of a few common mistakes. So settle in and let's take a closer look at developing professional-looking HTML pages!

USING FORMS

An HTML form is a special *interactive* portion of a Web page that contains control elements such as check boxes, radio buttons, and text boxes. Users generally complete a form online by entering text, selecting menu items, and so on, before submitting the form.

The first step in creating a form is to define the user section within an HTML page, specifying which fields are presented and what information collected. When someone fills out the form and clicks a "Submit" button, the information on the form is sent to a server for processing.

On the server, CGI is used along with a server-based program (written per-haps in Perl, C++, or Visual Basic) to process the form's data. The processing pro-gram's function is to accept the information sent from the HTML form and do something with it. Forms are commonly used to e-mail data or automatically update a database.

You should remember that it is possible to put multiple forms in an HTML document, but not to put a form inside another form.

To create a form, use the FORM tag. The FORM tag requires two additional parameters: ACTION and METHOD. The ACTION parameter contains the URL of the program that processes the form's data. The METHOD parameter is either GET or POST. The selected parameter determines how the exchange of data between the client and the program starts to process the form. The GET method appends the form's data to the URL specified by the ACTION attribute (with a question-mark as a separator), and this new URL is sent to the processing agent.

Technically speaking, the method paramater appends the form's data to a *Uniform Resource Identifier*, or URI. The URI is the addressing technology from which URLs are created. URLs such as HTTP:// and FTP:// are specific subsets of URIs, although the term URL is mostly used.

With the HTTP POST method, the form data is included in the body of the form and sent to the processing agent.

The POST method is preferred for most applications.

For example, a valid HTML tag to begin a form might look like this:

```
<FORM ACTION="www.mywebsite.com/cgi-bin/forms.cgi"
METHOD="POST">
```

In this example, the form data will be sent to a CGI program called forms.cgi located at www.mywebsite.com in a subdirectory (folder) called cgi-bin. The form will be submitted to the program using the POST method.

Inside the form, other tags are used to create the interactive elements the user will use to add information to the form. Along with standard HTML tages, the special forms tags include the following:

○ INPUT TYPE

- SELECT

- TEXTAREA

Let's take a closer look at each of these form tags.

The Form INPUT Tag

To accept data, you need to define an input field like this:

```
<INPUT TYPE= NAME= OPTION=>
```

Note that there is no INPUT ending tag. This tag defines a field where the user may enter information on the form. Each input field assigns a value to the variable identified as NAME. The value assigned to the TYPE= parameter defines what kind of data the variable will contain. The following list outlines the various parameters defined by TYPE.

- TEXT and PASSWORD accept character data (letters and numbers)

- CHECKBOX is either selected (1) or not (0)

- RADIO allows selection of only one of several radio fields

- SUBMIT is an action button that sends the completed form to the query server

- RESET is a button that resets the form variables to their default values

The OPTION parameter has special meanings depending again on what type of data is being used. These options include the following:

- SIZE= is an integer value specifying the number of characters allowed for the TEXT and PASSWORD data types.

- VALUE="" The value contained within the quotation marks is a "default" value for that field. If the user doesn't change the value of this field, whatever value is defined as VALUE= is accepted as the user's entry.

- CHECKED No value is assigned to this attribute (no equal sign). When included as an option, the CHECKED option sets the default for a check box or radio button to be selected (checked).

The following code samples show some valid INPUT statements using these parameters:

```
<P>Enter your name (maximum of 40 characters)
```

```
<INPUT TYPE="TEXT" NAME="Item1" SIZE=40>
<P>Check this box to receive more information
<INPUT TYPE="CHECKBOX" NAME="Item4a" VALUE="ON">
<p>Select your age range from the following list:
Under 20<INPUT TYPE="RADIO" NAME="Item 5" VALUE="ON">
21 - 30 <INPUT TYPE="RADIO" NAME="Item 5" VALUE="ON" CHECKED>
31 - 40 <INPUT TYPE="RADIO" NAME="Item 5" VALUE="ON">
Over 40 <INPUT TYPE="RADIO" NAME="Item 5" VALUE="ON">
```

The Form Select Field

Selections allow you to present multiple, fixed options to the user. You can choose
to display this as a pop-up or pull-down menu, which means that the user can only
select one item. You can also display this as a scrolling list, from which the user
can select several items, not necessarily contiguous. The tags used for this type of
form element are as follows:

```
<SELECT NAME="" SIZE=x MULTIPLE>
```

The value enclosed in quotes after the NAME= option defines the variable that
will contain the selected value(s). The integer defined by the SIZE= option determines how many items are to be displayed at one time. The word MULTIPLE, if
included, specifies that more than one item may be selected from the list. If omitted, only one selection will be accepted.

To display the list of items to select from, the HTML tag <OPTION> is used.
To set one item as the *default* in the list, the SELECTED attribute is included in the
OPTION tag. For example, the following code snippet asks the viewer to select his
or her favorite desserts. All three items will be displayed since no SIZE option is
included, and the option *Baked Alaska* will be highlighted as the default selection.

```
<SELECT MULTIPLE>
<OPTION>Apples
<OPTION SELECTED>Baked Alaska
<OPTION>Cherries
</SELECT>
```

The next sample will display a scrolling menu with six items visible at a time
(the SIZE= option is set to 6) and will allow multiple entries to be made.

```
<P>Choose your favorite cards
<SELECT NAME="Item 7" SIZE=6 MULTIPLE>
<OPTION>Jack of Spades
<OPTION>Queen of Diamonds
<OPTION>10 of Clubs
<OPTION>King of Hearts
<OPTION>2 of Diamonds
<OPTION>5 of Clubs
<OPTION>Ace of Spades
<OPTION>8 of Hearts
<OPTION>4 of Clubs
<OPTION>5 of Diamonds
<OPTION>Queen of Hearts
<OPTION>Joker
<OPTION>King of Clubs
<OPTION>6 of Diamonds
</SELECT>
```

The Form TEXTAREA Tag

The TEXTAREA tag is used when a large block of data (such as written comments in an e-mail form) needs to be entered by the user. This tag displays a region on the screen and accepts free-form data entry. The TEXTAREA tag has two mandatory attributes.

- NAME= This attribute defines the name of the variable that will hold the entered data.
- COLS= and ROWS= These two integer values define the size of the text entry window.

    An example of this tag:

```
<TEXTAREA NAME="comments" COLS="40" ROWS="5"> </TEXTAREA>
```

The above sample will display a text box 40 characters long and five lines deep and store the entered data into a variable named comments.

Figure 7-1 is a sample of a form commonly found on Web pages. This form is used to gather some opinions from viewers to see how they like the Web site.

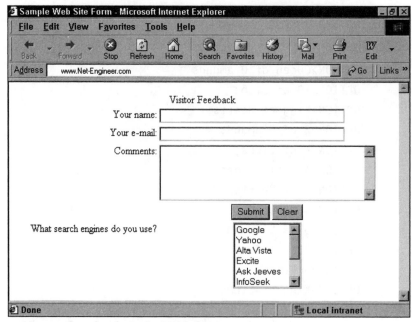

FIGURE 7-1 Sample of a typical Web form

The HTML code used to create this page is

```
<HTML>
<HEAD>
 <TITLE>Sample Web Site Form</TITLE>
</HEAD>
<BODY TEXT="#0000FF" LINK="#ff0000" VLINK="#000000">
   <P ALIGN=CENTER>
     <FORM ACTION="cgi-bin/mvforms.cgi" METHOD="POST">
       <CENTER>
         <P ALIGN=CENTER>
           <TABLE CELLPADDING="2" CELLSPACING="0" BORDER="0">
            <TR>
             <TD COLSPAN="2" VALIGN=TOP>
              <P ALIGN=CENTER>
                 <FONT FACE="Verdana"><B><FONT SIZE="3">Visitor
                 Feedback</FONT></B></FONT>
             </TD>
```

```
</TR>
<TR>
 <TD VALIGN=TOP>
  <P ALIGN=RIGHT>
   <FONT FACE="Verdana"><FONT SIZE="2">Your
   name:</FONT></FONT>
 </TD>
 <TD VALIGN=TOP><DIV ALIGN=LEFT>
  <P ALIGN=LEFT>
   <INPUT TYPE=TEXT NAME="aaName" SIZE="40"
   MAXLENGTH="125">
 </TD>
</TR>
<TR>
 <TD VALIGN=TOP>
  <P ALIGN=RIGHT>
   <FONT FACE="Verdana"><FONT SIZE="2">Your
   email:</FONT></FONT>
 </TD>
 <TD VALIGN=TOP><DIV ALIGN=LEFT>
  <P ALIGN=LEFT>
   <INPUT TYPE=TEXT NAME="zzClientEmail" SIZE="40"
   MAXLENGTH="125">
 </TD>
</TR>
<TR>
 <TD VALIGN=TOP>
  <P ALIGN=RIGHT>
   <FONT FACE="Verdana"><FONT
   SIZE="2">Comments:</FONT></FONT>
 </TD>
 <TD VALIGN=TOP><DIV ALIGN=RIGHT>
  <P ALIGN=RIGHT>
   <TEXTAREA NAME="abComments" COLS="40"
   ROWS="5"></TEXTAREA>
```

```
          </TD>
        </TR>
        <TR>
         <TD VALIGN=TOP></TD>
         <TD VALIGN=TOP><CENTER>
          <P ALIGN=CENTER>
          <INPUT TYPE=SUBMIT NAME="xxSend" VALUE="Submit">
          <INPUT TYPE=RESET NAME="xxClear"
            VALUE="Clear"></TD>
        </TR>
      <TR>
        <TD VALIGN=TOP>
         <P>What search engines<br>do you use
        </TD>
        <TD VALIGN=TOP> <DIV ALIGN=CENTER>
         <P ALIGN=CENTER><SELECT NAME="Item 7" SIZE=6
         MULTIPLE>
            <OPTION>Google
            <OPTION>Yahoo
            <OPTION>Alta Vista
            <OPTION>Excite
            <OPTION>Ask Jeeves
            <OPTION>InfoSeek
            <OPTION>Lycos
            <OPTION>Northern Light
            <OPTION>EuroSeek
            <OPTION>GOTO
         </TD>
        </TR>
       </TABLE>
      </FORM>
    </BODY>
  </HTML>
```

DATABASES

Many times Web applications are created to access information maintained in a database. In very simple terms, a database is an organized method of storing and retrieving information from a computer system. Obviously databases are generally more complex than just being a simple storage device, but the underlying reason for all databases is to do just that. Databases are often required to make a page interactive with the viewer. For example, if a Web site is tied to a company's inventory system, a potential customer would be able to see the current level of items on hand before making a purchase. A database tied to the Web page also eases the updating of the Web site. Using the same example, if a number of products had a 10 percent price increase, the Web administrator could simply make this change in the database once and the affected Web pages would automatically reflect the new pricing. Without a database back end, the administrator would have to manually change each page that contained an inaccurate price and repost the pages to the site. This is not only time consuming, but prone to human errors. There are a number of ways to connect a database to a Web site, but the most common method is to use a CGI script as the glue between the user interface (Web page) and a separate program just as a Perl or Visual Basic script. This program is then responsible to retrieve and store the actual information in the database. Many modern Database development systems include predefined scripts and an *Application Program Interface*, or API, that make connecting the databases to HTML formats extremely easy.

There are two primary types of database systems, *flat* and *relational*. A flat database contains all the information regarding the subject matter in a single record. A relational database spreads *related* information about the subject across many records tied together by a common thread. Relational databases are much more efficient, and are the preferred method for maintaining large volumes of information. Let's take a closer look at the differences between these two technologies.

For this example, assume you are creating a database to track customers and their purchases from your online company. Table 7-1 details the information you need to track.

TABLE 7-1 DATA REQUIRED FOR TRACKING CUSTOMERS AND TRANSACTIONS

NECESSARY DATA	DESCRIPTION
Customer ID	Each customer is assigned a unique number
Customer name	The business name of the company
Billing address	The company's street address
City	City where the company is located
State	The state code, used for tax purposes too
Zip code	The postal code for the company
Contact name	Name of the person to contact
Purchased item ID	Your part number for a purchased item
Sale amount	The amount you billed the customer
Purchased date	The date the customer placed the order
Shipped date	The date you shipped the product
Date payment received	The date you collected for the sale

The Flat Database

In a flat file database, you'd be pretty much finished. When a customer makes a purchase, you'd simply gather the necessary information and create a new record in your database. The new record would be added to the end of the existing database file. This method solves your basic problem. That is, you have an electronic record of every transaction made by your customers. However, if you want a report that shows all of the transactions you've had with a *specific* customer, the report program is going to have to read *every* record in the database to select only the data for the requested customer. If your database contains hundreds of thousands of records, it is quite likely that this simple report could take hours to generate. It's easy to see that this would be unacceptable.

To overcome this problem, many databases provide a method to *index* the data to increase data retrieval efficiency. When new records are added to the database, a second index file is created as well. The new index file is sorted in a specific order and points to the physical location of the actual data within the database. For example, you could create an index file sorted by customer. If you wanted to sort by zip code, you would need another index file to do that. Now when you want your report, the report program simply reads through the index file that has grouped all customers together. Once the report program has located the first index of the requested customer, it can use the information to locate the actual details from the primary database. The report program then reads the next index record and checks to see if it's for the same customer. If so, the details for that transaction are retrieved. This process continues until the customer ID in the index file changes, at which point you know that you've collected all the required data. Figure 7-2 shows how this might look. The report program is reading the index file looking for all transactions for a company called ComOne. When the name on the index record matches ComOne, the physical record number within the database is known, so the report program can directly read details from the database.

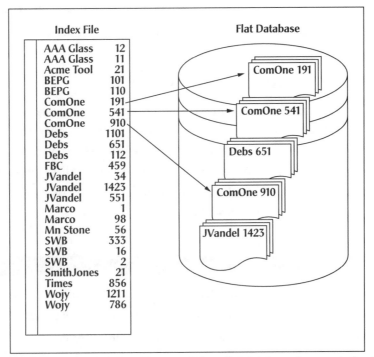

FIGURE 7-2 Locating specific records in a flat database from an index file

The index method is clearly the preferred method for organizing information. However, this also requires that an index file be created for every possible way the information might be accessed. For example, if you also need reports that show who has purchased a specific item (sorted by the item) you need to maintain an index file sorted by item number as well. This becomes even more complex when, for example, you want to see all products sold within a given date range to customers only in selected geographic areas (customers by zip code). As you can see, you either need to maintain a large number of index files, or the reporting programs will still need to perform a large amount of additional processing. There is one other drawback, possibly less obvious, to the flat file database. If you examine how your data is stored, you'll see that every new record is duplicating a lot of data — the address for ComOne is repeated in every ComOne record, as if it were a new customer. This method creates a database that requires a large amount of unnecessary storage space. In addition, keeping the data current can be very complicated. For example, suppose ComOne moves. To update the change of address, you need to go into every record in the database to make the changes. When dealing with the potential of thousands or hundreds of thousands of records, this is not only inefficient, but it creates a large possibility for mistakes.

The Relational Database

The relational database concept is to create a large number of smaller detail records tied together with one or more common items. Rather than maintaining a single large file with every piece of data stored in the same place, a relational database uses many small *tables* within a single database. These tables then point to other tables that hold *related* information. To visualize this, look at how the same customer transaction file is designed in Table 7-2a.

TABLE 7-2A THE RELATIONAL DATABASE CUSTOMER MASTER TABLE

TABLE CONTENTS	*DESCRIPTION*
Customer ID (*key*)	Each customer is assigned a unique number
Customer name	The business name of the company
Billing address	The company's street address
City	City where the company is located
State	The state code, used for tax purposes too
Zip code	The postal code for the company

TABLE 7-2B THE RELATIONAL DATABASE CUSTOMER CONTACT TABLE

TABLE CONTENTS	*DESCRIPTION*
Customer ID *(key)*	Each customer is assigned a unique number
Purchase order number *(key)*	The PO relating to a particular sale
Contact name	Name of the person to contact

TABLE 7-2C THE RELATIONAL DATABASE PRODUCT TABLE

TABLE CONTENTS	*DESCRIPTION*
Product item ID *(key)*	Unique identification of the item
Product description	Description of the item for reports, etc.
Quantity on hand	The number of items available to sell

TABLE 7-2D THE RELATIONAL DATABASE PRODUCT SALES HISTORY TABLE

TABLE CONTENTS	*DESCRIPTION*
Purchase order number *(key)*	The PO used in this transaction
Product item ID *(key)*	Our part number of a purchased item

TABLE 7-2E THE RELATIONAL DATABASE PURCHASE ORDER HISTORY TABLE

TABLE CONTENTS	*DESCRIPTION*
Purchase order number *(key)*	The PO used in this transaction
Customer ID *(key)*	Unique customer identification
Date of sale	Date this order was placed
Amount of sale	Amount this product sold for

TABLE 7-2F THE RELATIONAL DATABASE CUSTOMER SALES HISTORY TABLE	
TABLE CONTENTS	*DESCRIPTION*
Customer ID (*key*)	Unique customer identification
Purchase order number (*key*)	The PO used in this transaction

Record keys

In the relational model, the data are separated into smaller groups. Notice that I have identified certain items as *keys* within each table. Keys are used to cross-reference *related* data in other tables (a function similar to the index files in the flat database model). The database program automatically maintains key items in sorted order. Notice that some tables have more than one key. In these situations, the table's key comprises all fields identified as a key value. For example, the Purchase Order History Table (Table 7-2e) will be sorted by purchase order number *and* customer ID.

Normally, a table's key must be unique. If the key is not unusual enough to guarantee a unique value, the database program can append the physical record number to the key to make the value unique. A major requirement of designing a relational database is to properly identify the key elements. Let's walk though a few examples showing how detailed reports can be retrieved from a relational database.

Sales by customer

Following the example with the flat database, you can generate a report of all sales made to a particular customer. The report program uses the Customer Sales History file (Table 7-2f) to drive the remainder of the inquiries. Reading sequentially through these records, each purchase order key is used to reference the data in the Purchase Order History file (Table 7-2e) to retrieve the purchase date and sales amount. The purchase order number is also used to acquire the product ID from the Product Sales History table (Table 7-2d). The product ID is then used to retrieve the product description from the Product Master file (Table 7-2c). Figure 7-3 shows how this report would be constructed from the various tables.

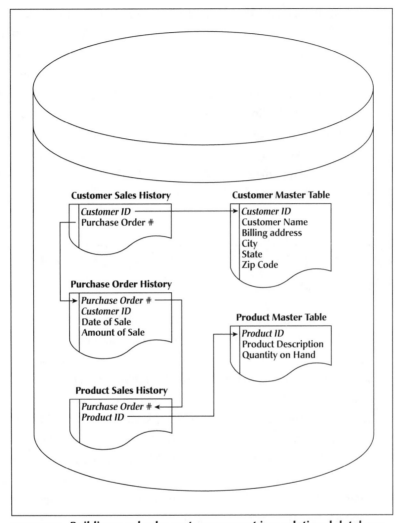

FIGURE 7-3 Building a sales by customer report in a relational database

Sales by product

The Product Sales History file can be used to drive the data retrieval for a Sales by Product report. Similar to the Sales by Customer report, the necessary data is gathered from the individual tables based on keys stored in related tables. If a more granular report is required, such as one listing only sales made in a particular region between two specific dates, the report program can easily include or exclude the details as each record is retrieved.

On the surface, this method may seem a lot more complex, but in reality, once the design of the tables has been done, the underlying database application maintains all of the related data. As you can see, data are only entered once. If a customer changes his or her address, only a single record needs to be updated. When records are changed or deleted, the underlying database engine takes care of cleaning up all the linked records. In addition, this method is designed for rapid retrieval of any specific piece of information and does not require maintaining multiple, separate index files. All modern databases are based on the relational model. The only time you would be dealing with a flat database is when it is proprietary, or you have to deal with legacy software.

ADVANCED PROGRAMMING TECHNIQUES WITH SCRIPTING TOOLS

Simple Web pages using no more than basic HTML tags make up a large part of the Web. However, with e-commerce becoming increasingly popular, basic pages don't provide the tools necessary to promote real-time, safe financial transactions. And many companies are starting to use the Internet for applications beyond e-commerce, such as collaboration on projects or keeping schedules organized. All of these functions require programming techniques beyond the capabilities of simple HTML.

Although the disciplines of computer programming have filled volumes of books independently, the i-Net+ exam will cover only simple concepts of Web-supported programming. One chapter can't possibly cover the complex details of programming, but I will describe how various languages are commonly used, and for what purposes they are most suited.

As I mentioned earlier, scripting is a simple method of creating program statements that execute independently of other programming languages. Scripts are usually limited to specific functions used to augment the running of an application. They can be run on either the client or the server side.

Server-Side Scripting

Server scripting can be used to create HTML pages dynamically on the Web server that are then sent to the browser. For example, you can use server scripting to query a database and format the results into a static HTML page that is sent to the user. Server scripting takes place before the page is sent to the browser. Server-side scripts are normally used in conjunction with other server programming components, such as Perl or Microsoft's Active Server Pages (ASP).

Client–Side Scripting

A client-side script is a program that may accompany an HTML document or be embedded directly into it. The program executes on the client's machine when the document loads, or at some other time such as when a link is clicked. Scripts provide a simple means for programmers to extend the basic abilities of the HTML language. Client scripting is used to make your pages more interactive after they have been sent to the browser. For example

- Scripts can be used to dynamically modify the contents of a document while it is being loaded into a user's browser.

- Scripts may be incorporated into Web-based forms to process data as it is entered. A script may dynamically fill out parts of a form based on the values of other fields. Scripts can also be used to validate data to ensure that it conforms to predetermined ranges of values, or that fields are mutually consistent.

- Scripts may be linked to form controls, such as buttons, or to perform tasks such as displaying images, loading documents, or executing other programs for use by user interface elements.

 exam preparation pointer

Client–side scripting depends on the browser that supports it, so it is important that you are aware of the types of browsers that might access your page and plan accordingly.

Because HTML does not rely on a specific scripting language, Web programmers must explicitly tell the browser what language each script is in. This may be done either through a default declaration or a local declaration by including a META declaration between the <SCRIPT> and </SCRIPT> tags. A META tag is a non-executable HTML element that identifies the contents of a Web page or prepares the browser for non-displayed content. META tags contain such things as a general description of the page, keywords for search engines, copyright information, and scripting declarations.

For example, the following code snippet could be used to declare a *JavaScript* routine within an HTML page:

```
<SCRIPT LANGUAGE="javascript">
...some JavaScript...
</SCRIPT>
```

SPECIFIC SCRIPTING LANGUAGES

Scripts are small, single-function programs used heavily in Web programming to make pages more functional and to connect other server components and applications to the Web pages. Although the same knowledge of programming is generally required to write scripts as it is to create full application programs, scripts are usually smaller in size, and often easier to debug. In the following section, we will look at the most popular scripting languages and how they are used to enhance the usability of the Web pages.

JavaScript

With all of the scripting languages available for Web developers, JavaScript is arguably the most popular. There are several versions of JavaScript supported by certain browsers and browser versions. Unfortunately, this can often lead to confusion and incompatibilities. Netscape originally introduced JavaScript 1.0, which was the language specification supported in Netscape Navigator 2.0. Subsequently, Navigator 3.0 and later supported new enhancements that comprised JavaScript 1.1. The European Computer Manufacturers Association (ECMA), an international association dedicated to establishing standards in the information and communications fields, has recently standardized the JavaScript specification.

Although programming for any single version of JavaScript is relatively simple, writing code that functions across disparate browsers and versions, most notably Navigator 4 and MSIE 4, is one of the major challenges and topics of discussion in JavaScript programming circles.

You may specify that a section of code only be executed by browsers which support a particular version of JavaScript by using the LANGUAGE attribute like this:

```
<SCRIPT LANGUAGE="JavaScript1.2">
```

JavaScript is commonly embedded within HTML code. However the SCRIPT tag's SRC attribute can be used to include an external file containing JavaScript code.

```
<SCRIPT LANGUAGE="JavaScript" SRC="myjavascript.js">
</SCRIPT>
```

The external file is a simple text file containing JavaScript code. Although some Version 3 browsers support the SRC attribute, it only functions reliably across platforms in the Version 4 and higher browsers.

Like most other programming languages, JavaScript is composed of statements that make assignments, compare values, and execute other sections of code. If you have some programming experience, you will be familiar with JavaScript's usage of variables, operators, and statements. Table 7-3 summarizes the main elements of JavaScript grammar.

TABLE 7-3 THE MAIN ELEMENTS OF JAVASCRIPT

ELEMENT	*DESCRIPTION/FUNCTION*	*EXAMPLE*
Variables	Labels that refer to a changeable value.	The variable total might possess a value of 100.
Operators	Operators are used to calculate or compare values.	Two values may be summed using the addition operator (+): total+tax.
Expressions	Any combination of variables, operators, and statements that evaluate to some result.	total = 100; if (total>100)
Statements	A statement pulls all grammatical elements together into a full thought. JavaScript statements may take the form of conditionals, loops, or object manipulations. Semicolons are used between multiple statements on the same line.	if (total>100) {statements;} else {statements;} while (clicks<10) {statements;}

Continued

TABLE 7-3 THE MAIN ELEMENTS OF JAVASCRIPT *(continued)*

ELEMENT	DESCRIPTION/FUNCTION	EXAMPLE
Objects	Objects contain constructs that possess a set of values, with each value reflected by an individual *property* of that object. Objects are a critical concept and feature of JavaScript. A single object may contain many properties, with each property acting as a variable reflecting a specific value. JavaScript can reference a large number of "built-in" objects that refer to characteristics of a Web document.	The `document` object contains properties that reflect the background color of the current document, its title, and other attributes.
Functions and Methods	A JavaScript function is similar to a procedure or subroutine in other programming languages. A function is a discrete set of JavaScript statements that perform a specific action. The function may accept incoming values (parameters), and it may return an outgoing value. A function is "called" from a JavaScript statement to perform its task. A method is simply a function that is contained within in an object.	A function which closes the current window, named `close()`, is part of the `window` object; thus, `window.close()` is known as a method.

A simple JavaScript example

The following JavaScript adds a *pull-down* menu to an HTML page so the user can select an Internet search engine site to jump to. The list of search engine URLs is defined within the script itself in the *options* section. Two steps are required to install this script within an existing HTML page.

1. Copy this code into the HTML document between the <HEAD> and </HEAD> tags of the document:

```
<SCRIPT LANGUAGE="JavaScript">
function formHandler(form){
var URL = document.form.site.options
[document.form.site.selectedIndex].value;
window.location.href = URL;
// End -->
```

```
}
</SCRIPT>
```

2. Copy this code into the HTML document between the `<BODY>` and `</BODY>` tags of the document:

```
<CENTER>
<FORM NAME="form">
<SELECT NAME="site" size=1>
<OPTION VALUE="">Go to....
<OPTION VALUE="http://www.yahoo.com">Yahoo
<OPTION VALUE="http://www.metacrawler.com">Metacrawler
<OPTION VALUE="http://www.altavista.digital.com">Altavista
<OPTION VALUE="http://www.webcrawler.com">Webcrawler
<OPTION VALUE="http://www.lycos.com">Lycos
</SELECT>
<INPUT TYPE=button value="Go!"
onClick="javascript:formHandler()">
</FORM>
</CENTER>
```

JScript

JScript is Microsoft's newest implementation of JavaScript and is designed as a general-purpose scripting language with special appeal to programmers familiar with C, C++, and Java. This means that JScript "borrows" features from these languages where appropriate, but is a language in its own right and includes many features not found in C or Java. Internet Explorer 4.0 and 5.0 include robust support for the ECMA standardized JavaScript, which, although it shares much with Netscape's JavaScript 1.2, is not exactly equivalent. Because of its strong adherence the ECMA standards, JScript is pretty much guaranteed to run in any browser, anywhere.

JScript is a completely dynamic language. That is, you can effectively redefine your program on the fly. While this has a number of potential disadvantages, it does give you the ultimate flexibility in your scripts. This is particularly useful in Dynamic HTML (DHTML) programming, since DHTML allows you to dynamically manipulate the object model.

VBScript

VBScript is a subset of the full Visual Basic programming system from Microsoft for developing both client- and server-side scripts. VBScript is especially popular with existing BASIC language programmers because it provides an easy path to Web development. Visual Basic has brought BASIC developers some of the advantages of more complex languages, while not losing sight of the fact that the language is easy to use and understand. All the skills learned with Visual Basic instantly apply to VBScript.

Because of its Visual Basic foundation, VBScript offers a number of advantages over other scripting languages. For example, VBScript contains a powerful subset of the error handling provided by Visual Basic. This includes the error object and on-error resume-next functions. Error handling is especially important when developing server-side code, so these enhancements in VBScript make it very desirable for many programmers.

Selecting the Proper Scripting Language

For many developers, the choice of programming language takes on an almost religious zeal. Java programmers are almost never convinced that BASIC is a viable alternative. Likewise, BASIC programmers generally object strongly to learning an unfamiliar syntax and a different way of thinking. Therefore, the factors that affect your decision about which language to use usually come down to what the target platform is (the client side or the server side), the language features, and your personal preference and existing knowledge.

For server-side development, the ability to script external objects is probably going to be more important than language features, because that's where most of the server functionality will be implemented. For example, the ability to cope with errors quite probably outweighs the ability to use extended language features.

If your client-side scripting needs dictate a broad-reaching support of both Netscape and Microsoft browsers, then your choice of languages is pretty much limited to JavaScript or JScript. Netscape does not support VBScript and IE does not fully support JavaScript. There are still many differences in HTML object-model conformance among the leading browsers. However, if you adhere to features in HTML 3.2 and ECMA standards, most of your interactive Web pages should be OK.

OTHER ADVANCED PROGRAMMING TOOLS

Scripting tools add an easy method to extend the basic HTML language to enhance the usability of Web pages. However, scripts are somewhat limited in scope and function. To create truly interactive Web pages, you need to use more sophisticated programming methods. The next section will cover a number of the more popular programming languages available for the Web and show where they can be applied to the greatest advantage.

Java

By far, Java is the easiest and most popular Web-based programming language. The original design goal of Java was to create a "Write Once, Run Anywhere" platform. Simply stated, Java is intended to provide a programming language that is independent of the underlining operating system or computer on which it is run. In theory, a Java application should run as well on a UNIX computer as it would on an Apple Macintosh or Windows-compatible PC. It is possible that this lofty goal may some day be achieved, but unfortunately, political and economic realities have precluded Java from reaching this pinnacle so far. Although there are a number of variations of the basic Java theme, for the most part, Java can still successfully execute across a wide variety of platforms. For Java to accomplish this task, the language is not compiled into an executable program like other languages, but into an intermediary format that is interpreted and executed by a separate *Java Interpreter* component often called the *Java Virtual Machine*, or JVM.

The Java platform consists of the Java Application Program Interfaces (APIs) and the JVM. Java APIs are libraries of compiled code that you can use in your programs. They let you add ready-made and customizable functionality to save programming time. Java programs are run (or interpreted) by the JVM. This is very similar to the process used by Visual Basic and other interpreted languages. Rather than running directly on the native operating system, the program is interpreted by the JVM for the native operating system. This means that any computer system with the JVM installed can run Java programs regardless of the computer system on which the applications were originally developed.

There are two general flavors of Java programming: Java applications and Java applets. A Java application is a standalone program, normally launched from the command line, that has more or less unrestricted access to the host system. An *applet* is a program which is run in the context of an applet viewer or Web browser, and which has strictly limited access to the host system. For example, an applet cannot normally read or write files on the host system, while an application normally can. Both applications and applets can be used within a Web-based page depending on the features required.

A Java program has to be converted to a form the JVM can understand so any computer with a JVM can interpret and run the program. Compiling a Java program is the process of taking the readable text (also called *source code*) and converting it to bytecodes, which are platform-independent instructions for the JVM.

The Java compiler is invoked at the command line on UNIX and DOS/ Windows operating systems as follows:

```
javac MyJavaProgram.java
```

Once the program has been successfully converted, it can be run on any JVM, or interpreted and run as an applet in any Web browser with a JVM built in, such as Netscape Navigator or Internet Explorer. The JVM converts the Java bytecodes to platform-dependent machine codes so your computer can understand and run the programs.

The following example is for your information only. The iNet+ exam will not expect you to actually write application code. Additionally, this sample is not meant to teach the concepts and intricacies of the Java language, but to show some basic components of the language to help you identify what a Java program might look like.

It is customary for many programming tutorials to begin with a simple program known as the "Hello World" program. Simply, this is an application that prints the string "Hello World" to the display. The following sample is the Hello World Application as written in Java.

```
class HelloWorld {
 public static void main (String args[]) {
  System.out.println("Hello World!");
 }
}
```

The initial `class` statement may be thought of as defining the program name, in this case HelloWorld.

In Java, the source code is broken up into parts separated by opening and closing braces, the { and } characters. Everything between is called a *block* and exists more or less independently of everything outside of the braces.

Blocks are important both syntactically and logically. Without the braces, the compiler would have trouble figuring out where one class ended and the next began. In addition, the blocks make it easier for someone else to read and understand your code. The braces are used to group related statements together. In the broadest sense everything between matching braces is executed as one statement.

Blocks can be hierarchical. One block can contain more subsidiary blocks. In this example, one outer block defines the HelloWorld class and within that block is a method block called `main`. When the main method is executed it simply performs one function, printing the phrase "Hello World" on the monitor.

Perl and PerlScript

Perl stands for Practical Extraction and Report Language. It is a programming language written by Larry Wall that combines syntax from several UNIX utilities and languages. Perl is a language with an eclectic heritage. Perl derives from the ubiquitous C programming language and to a lesser extent from sed, awk, the UNIX shell, and at least a dozen other tools and languages. Perl's process, file, and text manipulation facilities make it particularly well suited for tasks involving quick prototyping, system utilities, software tools, system management tasks, database access, graphical programming, networking, and Web programming. These strengths make it especially popular with system administrators and CGI script authors. Larry Wall never intended for Perl to take the place of robust compiled languages like C, but many developers have found that Perl lets them accomplish many of the same tasks with much less code.

PerlScript is an ActiveX scripting engine that lets you write PerlScript code for any ActiveX host, including servers and browsers. PerlScript joins the ranks of JavaScript and Visual Basic Script as an easy-to-use Web-scripting language.

You can use PerlScript to perform typical Web client scripting tasks such as triggering events when a button is clicked, performing calculations, manipulating text and data, and so on. Because PerlScript is a standard ActiveX Control, it works only with Microsoft Internet Explorer. It is simple to embed PerlScript into an HTML page, as you would any other script language. The following sample is a simple PerlScript embedded into an HTML document. The script simply displays the phrase "This is text from an embedded PerlScript." in a window when the page is loaded in a Microsoft browser.

```
<HTML>
<HEAD>
<TITLE>Web page with embedded PerlScript</TITLE>
<SCRIPT language="PerlScript">
sub ShowExample {
    $window->document->write("This is text from an embedded
    PerlScript.<br><hr>");
}
</SCRIPT>
</HEAD>
<BODY onLoad="ShowExample()">
</BODY>
</HTML>
```

Virtual Reality Modeling Language

The Virtual Reality Modeling Language (VRML) is a 3-D graphics language used on the Web. After a VRML page is downloaded, its contents can be viewed, rotated, and manipulated. Simulated rooms can be "walked into." The VRML viewer is launched from within the Web browser. The viewer is installed as a *plug-in* to the browser. The viewer program is stored on the hard drive and the VRML file type is associated with the viewer application. The first VRML viewer was WebSpace from SGI, whose Open Inventor graphics library was the basis for developing VRML. WebFX and WorldView are other Windows viewers, and Whurlwind and Voyager are Mac viewers.

From the beginning, the designers decided that VRML would not be an extension to HTML, since HTML was designed more for text than graphics. In addition, VRML requires a more finely tuned network than HTML.

For example, the following code snippet contains a simple 3D image view of a red cone and a blue sphere, lit by a directional light:

```
Separator {
    DirectionalLight {
        direction 0 0 -1 # Light shining from viewer into world
```

```
      }
PerspectiveCamera {
      position        -8.6 2.1 5.6
      orientation -0.1352 -0.9831 -0.1233 1.1417
      focalDistance            10.84
   }
Separator { # The red sphere
      Material {
            diffuseColor 1 0 0    # Red
         }
      Translation { translation 3 0 1 }
      Sphere { radius 2.3 }
   }
Separator {    # The blue cube
      Material {
        diffuseColor 0 0 1    # Blue
         }
            translation -2.4 .2 1
         rotation 0 1 1    .9
      }
      Cube {}
   }
}
```

C

C is a high-level programming language developed at Bell Labs that is able to manipulate the computer at a low level, like assembly language. During the last half of the 1980s, C became the language of choice for developing commercial software. C can be compiled into machine languages for almost all computers. For example, UNIX is written in C and runs in a wide variety of microcomputers, mini-computers, and mainframes.

C is written as a series of functions that call each other for processing. Even the body of the program is a function named `main`. Functions are very flexible, allowing programmers to choose from the standard library that comes with the compiler, to use third-party functions from other C suppliers, or to develop their own. Many software vendors have developed C compilers and development tools over the years. The most popular versions have come from Microsoft (Microsoft C) and Borland (Turbo C).

The following C example converts Fahrenheit to centigrade:

```
#include <stdio.h>
void Main ()
{
    float fahr;
    printf("Enter Fahrenheit ");
    scanf("%f", &fahr);
    printf("Celsius is %f\n", (fahr-32)*5/9);
}
```

C++

C++ was initially designed and implemented by Dr. Bjarne Stroustrup at AT&T Labs (then AT&T Bell Labs). The first commercial release happened in 1985. The language gained widespread use in industry and academia during the 1980s, and by around 1990 the major computer and software tools suppliers started to provide C++ to their users as a major implementation tool. After explosive growth of the C++ user population in the 1980s and early 1990s, when C++ usage doubled every 7.5 months, the use of C++ has settled into a pattern of steady growth (on the order of 15 to 30 percent per year). More than 400 books are currently in print about C++ programming. C++ is an *object-oriented* (OO) programming language. Object-oriented techniques are the most popular methods to develop large, complex software applications and systems. Object-oriented programming allows you to create procedures for objects whose exact type is not known until runtime. For example, a screen cursor may change its shape from an arrow to a line depending on the program mode. The routine to move the cursor on screen in response to mouse movement would be written for "cursor," and would work in whatever shape is required at runtime. It would also allow a new shape to be easily integrated into the program.

C and C++ are similar to a great extent. Incompatibilities do exist, though, and many idiomatic constructs used in C are frowned upon by C++ experts. C++ programmers generally consider code that does not exploit those features of C++ that make it possible to write "better" programs—programs that are more readable and easier to write and maintain—to be in *poor style*. The differences between the two languages are significant enough to ensure that one has to be clear about the language being used. However, you should not forget that C++ is largely a superset of C, and that it is possible (though perhaps not desirable) to write code that works correctly in both languages.

Visual Basic

Visual Basic is a simple, easy-to-learn language and programming environment that you can use to build real applications for Windows. Visual Basic is widely used in industry for developing rapid prototypes of new programs. A subset of the language (Visual Basic for Applications, or VBA) is used in many other Microsoft products including Excel, Word, and Access.

For many years, the BASIC language was thought of as a beginner's language, derived perhaps from its acronym's meaning: Beginner's All-Purpose Symbolic Instruction Code. In reality, BASIC is a very powerful development tool that has constantly improved for many years.

One of Visual Basic's initial enticements is its drag-and-drop design method of developing the Graphic User Interface (GUI). Objects such as edit boxes, list boxes, menus, push buttons, and so on, can quickly be located on a development pallet, lending itself to easy creation of a working application. Although this graphic technique lends itself to easier programming methods, the finished code is not necessarily small and compact. You may recall that our simple "Hello World" program in Java consisted of just a few lines. In Visual Basic, the following program lines are required to accomplish the same task.

```
Object = "{F5BE8BC2-7DE6-11D0-91FE-00C04FD701A5}#2.0#0";
"AgentCtl.dll"
Begin VB.Form Form1     Caption           =     "Hello, World"
     ClientHeight       =    1680
     ClientLeft         =    60
     ClientTop          =    345
     ClientWidth        =    4680
     LinkTopic          =    "Form1"
     ScaleHeight        =    1680
     ScaleWidth         =    4680
     StartUpPosition    =    3    'Windows Default
```

```
        Begin VB.TextBox TextBox          Appearance        =     0
'Flat
        Height              =     615
        Left                =     240
        MultiLine           =     -1 'True
        TabIndex            =     1
        ToolTipText         =      "Type something in here for the
Genie to say, then press the Say it! button"
        Top                 =     120
        Width               = 4335
    End
    Begin VB.CommandButton Button
        Caption      = "Say it!"
        Height       = 495
        Left         = 1920
        TabIndex     = 0
        ToolTipText  = "Type some text into the text box, then
press this button to hear Genie say it"
        Top          = 960
        Width        = 1215
    End
    Begin AgentObjectsCtl.Agent Agent1
        Left         = 240
        Top          = 960
     _cx      = 847
     _cy      = 847
    End
End
Attribute VB_Name = "Form1"
Attribute VB_GlobalNameSpace = False
Attribute VB_Creatable = False
Attribute VB_PredeclaredId = True
Attribute VB_Exposed = False
Dim Genie As IAgentCtlCharacterEx
Const DATAPATH = "genie.acs"
```

```
Private Sub Form_Load()
  Agent1.Characters.Load "Genie", DATAPATH
  Set Genie = Agent1.Characters("Genie")
  Genie.LanguageID = &H409
  TextBox.Text = "Hello World!"
End Sub
Private Sub Button_Click()
  Genie.Show
  Genie.Speak TextBox.Text
  Genie.Hide
End Sub
```

The majority of these commands were automatically generated by simply dragging the graphic items onto the pallet, or by adding simple attributes to those objects, but as you can see, the final program requires a substantial number of commands.

CGI

There really is no programming language called CGI. CGI stands for *Common Gateway Interface*. It is a *gateway* that allows you to execute program code on the Web server and return the results to the Web browser. CGI provides even more tools to help the Web developer create interactive, dynamic Web sites. CGI programs can be written in C, C++, Java, Visual Basic, Perl, or just about any language that can run on your Web server. The Web server doesn't care what language you write in, as long as you follow the rules. The following code is an example of using a CGI library to create an HTML 4.0 page with the contents "Hello World".

```
module: Hello-World-cgi
define method main (argv0 :: <byte-string>, #rest noise)
  write-html(make(<http-header>));
  write-html(make(<html-dtd>, type: #"transitional"));
  let html-header = make(<html-head>,
  contents: make(<html-title>,
  contents: "Hello World"));
  let html-body = make(<html-body>,
```

```
bgcolor: "#FFFFFF",
text: "#333333",
vlink: "#CCCCCC",
alink: "#666666",
link: "#999999",
contents:
vector(make(<html-p>,
       tag: "<P>",
       end-tag: #f,
       contents: "Hello World!\r\n"),
              make(<html-comment>,
              contents: "Dylan is cool.")));
write-html(make(<html-doc>, contents: vector(html-header,
html-body)));
end method;
```

POPULAR MULTIMEDIA EXTENSIONS (PLUG-INS)

Even though basic HTML is quite powerful, even more so with custom programming, there are more ways to enhance the capabilities of a Web site. Developing standards to any Internet protocol takes time. Often, companies develop enhancements that people want right away. In a marketplace that places a premium on rapid delivery, it is often not practical to wait for a volunteer organization to accept a new standard. That's where plug-ins are useful. Plug-ins add capabilities to the HTML language as separate but integrated programs. Nearly all plug-ins extend the multimedia capabilities of the Web, but others deal with document presentation and other features where HTML is still weak.

Multimedia is a generic term used to describe the audio and visual properties of the Web. Although simple graphics enhance the Web experience, they are no substitute for full motion video. Since the Web servers are only responsible to deliver content to the browser, they have the ability to transmit just about any type of data imaginable. This includes sounds, structured music, animated graphics, and video. WebCams (Web-based, real-time video cameras) are becoming quite popular, and with the advances in high-speed data transmission, they will certainly become commonplace. For decades, we have been told that the telephone of the future would include live video as well as voice. With TCP/IP-based communications, voice and video transmissions are available today.

To exploit the capabilities of TCP/IP communications, many companies have developed proprietary extensions to Web browsers. To make them as widely acceptable as possible, they implement their software as *plug-in* programs. This simply means that when you click on a Web object that requires one of these plug-ins, the program starts up automatically, separate from your browser. It is very possible that the plug-in is designed to be integrated within your browser's windows, thereby appearing to be part of the actual browser. The following list describes some of the more common Web extensions and their functions.

- **QuickTime,** from Apple Computer: A Web plug-in to deliver *streaming* video and audio across the Internet. The source can be live, or stored on Web servers as files. QuickTime works both on the Apple and Windows platform and is so popular it is often considered a Web standard.

- **QTVR,** from Apple Computer: QuickTime VR is another Apple product that provides cross-platform virtual reality technology that makes it possible to explore places as if you were really there. All major applications that play QuickTime movies can also play QuickTime VR movies. At the intersection of commercial photography and new media technology, QuickTime VR moves the photographic image from the flat, 2-D world into a more immersive experience, complete with 3-D imagery and interactive components.

- **Flash,** from Macromedia: Macromedia Flash is used for vector graphics and animation. Web developers use Flash to create detailed, resizable, and extremely small navigation interfaces, technical illustrations, long-form animations, and other dazzling effects for Web sites and other Web-enabled devices (such as WebTV). Flash graphics and animations are created using the drawing tools in Flash or by importing artwork from other vector illustration tools.

- **Shockwave,** from Macromedia: Shockwave is a plug-in that provides rich media playback (fixed files, not live video) on a Web page. With this tool, you can view interactive Web content like games, business presentations, entertainment, and advertisements from your Web browser. Of the many media players available, Shockwave is among the most popular.

- **RealPlayer,** from Real Networks: Real Networks was among the first companies to create Web support for live audio. Their first product, RealAudio, provided real-time listening capabilities to a handful of national radio stations. As the RealAudio standards became more popular, many more radio stations worldwide joined in. This popularity boosted Real Networks' products to the point where RealMedia is itself a Web standard. RealPlayer is the company's compilation of their live audio and live video technologies. Many broadcast companies, such as CNN, transmit their productions live on the Internet using the Real Network's product line.

- **Windows Media Player,** from Microsoft: Windows Media Player is Microsoft's extension for delivering a variety of multimedia files. Windows Media Player is integrated into Windows, which makes it easy to access multimedia content, whether stored locally on a hard drive or on the Internet.

TYPES OF MULTIMEDIA FILES AND FORMATS

By now you should understand that the Web flourishes with multimedia components. Although almost any type of file can be transported across the Internet, not all file types are supported by the mainstream browsers. A great multimedia presentation that isn't understood by the viewer's browser doesn't do much good.

When designing a good Web page, it is important to keep in mind the standard, accepted multimedia formats supported by most popular browsers. There are accepted standards for fixed-image formats, as well as sounds, music, and video. The following section describes these standard file formats.

Standard Graphic Formats

Graphics are the most common enhancement to Web pages. They're also one of the oldest, so there are several different formats to choose from. When choosing a graphic format, you usually have to choose between size and quality. Images with more colors look better, but they're larger and take longer to load. If the audience for your page is using a low-bandwidth connection, you may be better off using a smaller, less complex format.

- **GIF:** *Graphics Interchange Format* is a popular graphics format developed by CompuServe. It supports 8-bit color (256 colors) and is widely used on the Web because the files compress extremely well. The smaller the file, the faster it displays. GIFs include a color table that includes the most representative 256 colors used. For example, a picture of the forest would include mostly greens. This method provides excellent realism in an 8-bit image.

- **GIF89a:** *GIF89* allows one of the colors to be made transparent and take on the background color of the underlying page or window. This feature is often useful on Web pages to make the image appear to be part of the page instead of simply added to the page. In addition, GIF89a supports animation. Animated GIF files are sequences of images displayed one after the other to simulate movement. Although this is a simple method to draw a viewer's attention somewhere, animated images can also take twice as long to load.

- **JPEG:** *Joint Photographic Experts Group*, pronounced "jay-peg." This format is an ISO/ITU standard for compressed images that is very popular on the Web due to its high compression capability. Variations of the JPEG format are used for full-motion digital video (see MPEG in the next section). JPEG and GIF are the two most common image formats used on the Web and do not require other plug-ins to be viewed.

- **PNG:** *Portable Network Graphics*, a bitmapped graphics format endorsed by the World Wide Web Consortium. It is expected to eventually replace the GIF format, because there are lingering legal problems with GIFs. (CompuServe owns the format, and Unisys owns the compression method.) In addition, GIF is a very basic graphics format that is limited to 256 colors. PNG provides advanced graphics features such as 48-bit color, built-in color correction, tight compression, and the ability to display at one resolution and print at another.

- **TIFF:** *Tagged Image File Format* was developed by Aldus and Microsoft and handles monochrome, grayscale, 8-, and 24-bit color. TIFF allows for customization, and several versions have been created, which does not guarantee compatibility between all programs. This compatibility issue makes the TIFF format undesirable for Web use. TIFF is the standard graphics format used by most fax applications.

- **BMP:** BitMaP file, sometimes called a "bump" file. The *BMP* format is a Windows and OS/2 native graphics file format. Every Windows application has access to the BMP software routines in Windows. BMP files provide formats for 2, 16, 256, or 16 million colors (1-bit, 4-bit, 8-bit, and 24-bit color). Although the popularity of Windows and Windows-based applications on the Web is extensive, this format has not become widely accepted on the Internet.

Standard Document Formats

Although it's easy to present text on your Web page, sometimes you want to provide a separate document, for the user to print out, or to use while offline. There are a few formats that enable you to do this:

- **PDF:** *Portable Document Format* is the file format used by the Adobe Acrobat document exchange system that allows documents created on one platform to be displayed and printed exactly the same on another regardless of which fonts are installed in the computer. The fonts are embedded within the PDF file, thus eliminating the requirement that the target machine contain the same fonts. Although PDF files are not directly embedded into a Web page, the Adobe Acrobat Reader plug-in has become an Internet standard and integrates seamlessly into the browser, giving the appearance that the PDF file is actually embedded into the Web page.

- **RTF:** *Rich Text Format* is a Microsoft standard for encoding formatted text and graphics. The RTF format is widely accepted and supported on many platforms and is generally a good option for creating formatted documents for sharing across the Internet.

- **PostScript:** This is another Adobe-developed format that is used extensively on many computer platforms. It is the de facto standard in commercial typesetting and printing houses. *PostScript* commands do not drive the printer directly. They are language statements in ASCII text that are translated into the printer's machine language by a PostScript interpreter built into the printer. Fonts are scaled by the interpreter, which eliminates the need to store a variety of font sizes on disk. PostScript Level 2 adds data compression and enhancements, especially for color printing. Level 3 adds more enhancements, native fonts, and the ability to directly support formats including

HTML, PDF, GIF, and JPEG. *Encapsulated PostScript* (EPS) is a subset of PostScript used to exchange a single graphic image in the PostScript format.

Standard Video Formats

With the arrival of high-bandwidth connections, it's now more realistic to integrate video into your Web site.

- **MOV:** This is a native Apple Movie format viewable with the QuickTime (and QTVR) browser plug-ins. The MOV format supports very good compression and is an excellent format to use if you have access to the Macintosh platform to create the video.

- **MPEG:** *Moving Pictures Experts Group*, pronounced "em-peg," is an ISO/ITU standard for compressing video. MPEG-1 is commonly used on CD-ROM and Video CDs and provides resolutions of 352 × 240 at 30 frames per second with 24-bit color and CD-quality sound. Many hardware MPEG boards provide scaling that boosts the image to full screen. MPEG-2 is a broadcast-quality standard that provides better resolution than VHS tapes. MPEG-2 is used in DVD movies. For the best playback, MPEG-encoded material requires an MPEG board, and the decoding is done in the board's hardware. MPEG uses the same intraframe coding as JPEG for individual frames, but also uses interframe coding, which further compresses the video data by encoding only the differences between periodic key frames, known as *I-frames*.

- **AVI:** *Audio Video Interleaved* is a Microsoft Windows multimedia format. The AVI specification interleaves standard waveform audio and digital video frames (bitmaps) to provide reduced animation at 15 frames per second at 160 × 120 × 8 resolution. Since the AVI format is native to Windows, many Web browsers can view AVI embedded files.

- **Streaming media:** This is a process of transmitting audio and video over a data network such as the Internet. The term implies a one-way transmission to the viewer, in which both the client and server software cooperate for uninterrupted motion. The client side buffers a few seconds of video data before it starts sending it to the screen, which compensates for momentary delays in packet delivery. Other applications, such as video conferencing, require real-time two-way transmission for effective results.

PREPARING TO PUBLISH A WEB SITE

Now that you have all the components needed to create your Web site, there is one last, but very important step—and that's testing. Hopefully there is a reason you're creating a Web site in the first place, so you want to be sure it functions as you expect it to. There are five basic tests that you want to perform before the site goes "live," as discussed next.

Checking Hot Links

One of the fastest ways to lose viewers on your site (and potential customers) is to have links to important areas that fail to work. Most people will not tolerate even one broken link and will likely leave your site altogether rather than figure out where it is that you wanted to take them.

Many HTML editors will check your links as you create and edit pages. If your editor doesn't support this functionality, you can either check each link manually (risky), or obtain an additional HTML utility program to test your links. One area many of the editor checks will miss are links to other Web sites. If you send your viewers to other areas of the Internet, make sure you test these links. It is also a good idea to regularly test these links, as pages, and Web sites, tend to move from time to time.

Testing Different Browsers

As you've seen numerous times, different browsers support different features. If possible, try not to develop pages with "browser-specific" components. However, even though some features are supposed to be supported across many platforms, it is highly recommended that you test your particular site to be sure. Not only should different browsers be tested, but different versions of browsers. Each time a new browser version is released, new features are added (and some removed). Not all of your visitors are going to upgrade to the latest and greatest version, so you'll want to find out if some of your dazzling code is going to fail on some of those less-than-new browsers.

Testing with Various Speed Connections

A common problem when designing a Web site is simply that your design environment is normally very fast. Performance from a server located on your private network is going to be much better than it will be across the Internet. Many beginners get caught up in the development of elaborate Web pages, view them on their local browser, and forget completely that a 400K animated image will take forever to display on a 33.6Kbps dial-up connection. When testing your handiwork, adjust your connection speeds to see how well your site performs at dial-up speeds of 28.8, 33.6, and 56K. You might be very surprised to see the differences.

Load Testing

The performance of the Web server itself may cause your Web site to experience less than desirable effects. If your servers are overworked, your pages may not be delivered fast enough to retain the attention of your audience. If you're fortunate enough to own the Web server(s), you may be able to fine tune them, or replace them altogether. On the other hand, many people rent Web service from their ISP or other Web publishing organization. If you suspect that the load on the servers supporting your site is hindering your site's performance, you may be able to have your provider move your pages to a different server. If that is not feasible, you may need to look at other providers, or entertain the thought of hosting your Web site yourself.

Access to the Site

As simple as this sounds, you should test the ability of viewers to access your site. A number of factors can prevent your prospective visitors from getting to your site. This is especially possible if you are hosting your Web site yourself. It is quite possible that you can get to your site via a local connection, but others can't get there across the Internet. (Usually this is a DNS or firewall problem.) After you make your site live, try connecting to your Web site from outside your organization. If you have multiple ISP accounts, make sure your site is accessible from each of these accounts. It is also a good idea to have other people test your site just to be sure.

EXAM PREPARATION SUMMARY

As you've seen in Chapter 7, there's a lot to Web design and programming. As popular as the Web is, there will be employment for good Web designers for years and years to come. This chapter covered the very basics of Web design. You've learned more than enough to put together some pretty snappy Web pages. Now let's review some of the highlights for this chapter to make sure you understand the material you just read

- Forms provide an easy method of making a site interactive. Forms enable your viewers to send specified information to the owners of a Web site. CGI is used to bridge the process of sending the data from the browser to the server-based program that manipulates the information. There can be multiple forms on a page, but one form must begin and end before the next form starts. The FORM SELECT tag can make filling out forms easier for the viewer by providing them a list of options to select from.

- Web design can be enhanced with many development tools, such as scripts that are executed on demand rather than being compiled ahead of time. Scripts can be created for the server (server-side) or the client. Among other possibilities, server-side scripting can be useful for querying a database for specific results then passing the data to the Web page. A client-side script can be used to validate entries made on an online form.

- Java is a common and popular foundation for Web-related programming. Java itself is a highly portable and powerful programming language. Smaller applications, or applets, written in Java and JavaScript can be embedded into an HTML page to increase a Web site's usability.

- In addition to HTML-specific programming tools, many other languages are commonly used to access and manipulate data on a Web server prior to being displayed on a Web page. C, C++, and Visual Basic are among the most popular of these programming languages.

- Databases play a large role in current Web technology, especially in e-commerce. There are two primary types of databases: flat and relational. Flat databases normally rely on predefined index files to cross-reference data in the primary file. Relational databases contain data spread out across tables within a database and use keys to retrieve related data stored in other tables. Relational databases make better use of file systems since data does not need to be duplicated across the tables.

- In addition to programming custom applications, multimedia extensions and plug-ins add feature-rich options to HTML pages. Plug-ins are useful for video, audio, and 3-D virtual reality enhancements. Plug-in components are separate applications that seamlessly integrate into a Web page although they are not part of the HTML language.

- There are a number of multimedia file formats in use on the Web. For standard images GIF, GIF89, and JPEG are the most commonly used formats. Adobe's PDF format is arguably the best document format, while MOV, MPEG, and AVI formats round out the top video formats.

- Once your Web site is created, you should test the following five items:

  - Check for broken links.

  - Test your pages with various browsers and browser versions.

  - Test your site with various connection speeds.

  - Test the performance of the Web server. Make sure it isn't serving too many other sites and pages to affect your site.

  - Make sure there is access to the site from the Internet. Use multiple Internet accounts to browse your site if possible.

APPLYING WHAT YOU HAVE LEARNED

The following review questions give you an opportunity to test your knowledge of the information presented in this chapter. The answers to these assessment questions can be found in Appendix B. If you missed some, review those sections in this chapter before going further

Instant Assessment Questions

1. Data collected from a form can be sent to

   A. The site visitor via e-mail

   B. A corporate database

   C. The webmaster of the site via e-mail

   D. A custom-written program for further processing

2. The `FORM` tag requires which two additional attributes?

A. A `GET` or `POST` directive

B. A `TYPE` and `ACTION` attribute

C. A vertical and horizontal positioning area

D. An `ACTION` and `METHOD` directive

3. Which tag(s) must be included to send the data collected in an HTML form?

A. `<INPUT TYPE=SUBMIT>`

B. `</FORM>`

C. `</FORM></SUBMIT>`

D. `<SUBMIT/RESET></FORM>`

4. SQL is

A. A specialty language to manipulate data in a relational database

B. A flat database

C. A relational database

D. A Microsoft tool to manipulate data in other manufacturers' databases

5. Which of the following are primary elements of JavaScripts:

A. Operators

B. Verbs

C. Spell Checking

D. Expressions

6. A PerlScript can be properly used in any Web browser of version 4 or higher.

A. True

B. False

7. C is a high-level programming language written as a series of

A. Programming commands

B. Objects

C. Functions

D. Scripts

8. A relational database links common database items by means of

   A. Self-maintained index files

   B. Unique values called keys

   C. Unique key values that include the physical record number

   D. Unique data predefined by the needs of the end user

9. Which of the following image formats are supported on all browser platforms?

   A. BMP

   B. TIFF

   C. JPEG

   D. GIF

Networking, Infrastructure, and Security

In Part IV we'll turn our attention to the physical components required to provide businesses with Internet access across the company as a whole. But, before you begin looking at connection options and security issues, you'll need to know what Internet services you'll be using *and* providing. Part IV begins with a look at the server side of the Internet as well as Internet services.

Many companies have a Web presence, even if it's nothing more than a posting of their address and a display of their products. Likewise, e-mail has become a necessity for almost every business. With both of these technologies, there comes a time when the business has to decide whether to provide these services for themselves or pay monthly fees to an outside service. However, these are only two Internet services that can be beneficial to a company. Other Internet technologies, such as newsgroups and multimedia presentations, can also be quite useful so companies should understand how to deploy these services. Even if all of a company's Internet services are outsourced, network infrastructure and security will need to be addressed.

Part IV concludes with a list of troubleshooting items and tools useful for the Internet connections, servers, and security components. With the fast-growth pace of the Internet and Internet-related business, companies require 100 percent uptime. As an Internet professional, your job will often revolve around ensuring that services are available and operational around the clock. Hardware and software problems, as well as security breaches, can all impact a company's ability to conduct business and cost millions of dollars in lost revenues.

i-NET+™

Core Components of the
Internet Infrastructure

About Chapter 8

In this chapter you'll look at some of the devices used to access the Internet. Even as this book is being written, companies are busy building newer, faster, and smaller devices based on Internet technologies. We often think of computers when discussing the Internet, but there are many more devices that can offer Internet services.

Most of this chapter will focus on the server side of the Internet. You will look at how information is provided to devices, as well as see firsthand how data is routed, stored, and shared throughout the Internet or privately using Internet technologies.

This chapter contains hands-on exercises that will walk you through the installation and configuration of many popular Internet server services. Most of the software required for this chapter is located on the CD included with this book. Please refer to Appendix D for a complete list of the software, and for installation and licensing information.

By the end of this chapter, you will have a fully functional Web server (two of them in fact!) and an FTP server. If you have registered a domain name, I'll show you how to install your own e-mail server to provide you with all the e-mail addresses you could want. In addition, if you have a static IP address, your friends, family, and coworkers can visit your Web site from across the Internet.

So fire up the computer. You'll want to read this chapter right in front of the keyboard.

HARDWARE PLATFORMS

The desktop computer, be it a PC, a Mac, or other terminal device, is a popular Internet client, but by no means is this the only method available. As the Internet grows, businesses will spend enormous amounts of capital to develop cheaper and more convenient devices to connect to it. For the Internet to become a dominant marketplace, it is imperative that access to the Net be simple, fast, and cheap.

One rule of technology is that early adopters fund the initial investments. A company must spend a great deal of money and resources to bring a new technology to market and recoup at least part of its investment. The hope is that the new product will appeal to a large audience so volume sales will eventually turn into profits. Let's take a look at some Internet devices that are changing the traditional view of Internet services.

Internet access is quickly reaching into all areas of our lives. As businesses become more mobile the need for small, portable Internet devices increases dramatically. Some people simply aren't interested in all of the Internet services that currently require a desktop computer, so products that deliver Web access and e-mail on a common television set are becoming hot items. Perhaps the Holy Grail for an Internet connected device, however, is the modern telephone. Advances in Internet technology are quickly making the dream of free long-distance voice calls a reality.

Handheld Devices

The end of 1999 might be remembered as the year the handheld Internet device gained credibility. At the end of that year, the 3Com corporation announced that it was creating a new corporation based around its incredibly successful Palm personal organizer. Alternatively, Microsoft's Windows CE is held by many as the handheld operating system of choice. As hardware components become smaller and cheaper, and consumer demand for easier Internet access increases, handheld devices are becoming commonplace.

Most people think of the Palm organizer and other personal organizers as "the" handheld device. However, modern pagers, cellular phones, and other specialty devices also fall into the handheld category. So popular are these devices becoming, that ISPs and Web-based businesses are clamoring for new standards. The *Handheld Device Markup Language*, or HDML, specification is already in its second version and will probably be accepted as an Internet standard before 2001. The HDML protocol is being designed as a simple language for creating hypertext-like content for small-display, handheld devices. Handheld devices are characterized primarily by a limited display size. A typical display is capable of displaying 4-10 lines of text 12 to 20 characters wide and may be graphical (bitmapped) or text-only. Network bandwidth is usually low due to limitations of the network technology or simple economics. The same holds true for other resources such as memory, processing power, and battery life. Although some devices do have large amounts of memory or processing power, these are the exception. As consumer demand increases, and product pricing comes into line with what most people are willing to pay, these constraints will quickly disappear.

Internet access for handhelds is still rather limited. A large percentage of these devices still rely on standard modem technology. Speeds from 33.6Kbps to 56Kbps almost always require a wired telephone connection. Cellular connectivity is widely available but realistic speeds are normally constrained between 4800bps to 9600bps. These speeds are often acceptable for short e-mail messages, but the process still requires the use of a cellular telephone which itself can be hindered by battery life.

Wireless technology has improved dramatically in the late 1990s, but cost and service coverage put this option out of reach for most people. Wireless speeds can easily reach 10Mbps, but some implementations still require some amount of wired connection and are often dependent on a series of tower, wall, or roof-top mounted point-to-point installations.

WebTV

Targeted at the less-technical home users, WebTV is a device that can be connected to a television to enable access to the Web, e-mail, and real-time chat. To access WebTV service, a special Internet receiver is required. The Internet receiver connects to the television and existing phone line. Internet access is then provided over the dial-up telephone connection to a WebTV enabled Internet Service Provider. Although files can't be saved (there is not fixed storage media like a hard drive) the Internet receiver usually has a parallel printer port for generating printed copies.

The physical characteristics of a television display compared to a computer monitor make the WebTV system a little different from a programming standpoint. There are some additional HTML tags available for the WebTV audience, while some standard tags don't work, or work differently on a TV display. If you want to test your HTML pages to see how they will appear on WebTV, a simulation viewer is available for free download on the WebTV home page at: `http://www.webtv.com`.

Internet Phone

Are you tired of searching for the "best" long distance calling rates? If you have a friend or business contact with an Internet-connected computer and both of you are willing to accept slightly less than crystal clear communications, an Internet telephone may work for you. The concept is fairly simply. Using a computer sound card and microphone, voice signals are digitized into normal IP packets and transported across the Internet just like data. Many telephone handset manufactures have also introduced standard telephones with an Ethernet jack to connect directly into your computer or computer network.

Real-time voice communications take place either in half or full duplex, depending on the capabilities of the sound cards. *Half duplex* is similar to talking on a citizens band radio — only one person can talk at once. *Full duplex*, on the other hand, is just like a normal telephone conversation. Both parties can talk and listen simultaneously, which is much more natural. To converse in full duplex mode, both sound cards must support full duplex communications. When using the Internet to communicate with voice, the only charge you'll ever pay is the initial price of the software. Many Internet phone software packages exist, with normal street prices around $50.

PC-to-phone service is also available, but requires an intermediate service known as an Internet Telephone Gateway. These services have Internet connections to accept the incoming "call" and route it through a standard telephone wire connection. These services make it possible to call any existing telephone number, worldwide, from your Internet telephone. The cost for this service varies from provider to provider, but some services are as low as $10 per month for unlimited long-distance calling. The greatest savings, however, will be realized when making international calls. The quality of a PC-to-phone conversation is normally acceptable for non-business use, but will still not duplicate the existing plain-old telephone system.

Before Internet voice transmissions become commonplace, Voice over IP (VoIP) will have replaced many point-to-point business connections. For example, it is not uncommon for a company with offices in different cities to lease a dedicated connection between the two locations for telephone communications. These are typically T1 lines that are fully capable of transporting data as well as voice. Without the interference and uncontrolled routing on the Internet, Voice over IP on a dedicated connection is very reasonable. Since data packets can be transmitted much more efficiently than analog signals, a company can save significantly by using smaller (and cheaper) dedicated lines, or by converting to a lower cost ISDN, DSL, or cable type of connection.

If you're interested in further investigating Voice over IP, the following sites may be of interest:

- `http://www.pulver.com/iphone/`
- `http://www.vocaltec.com/`
- `http://www.net2phone.com`

INTERNET SERVER COMPONENTS

Throughout this book, I've referred to various Internet servers many times. Remember that the Internet is based on the *client/server* model. While the client requests information, the server provides that information. This is also known as *push* technology. A browser asks for specific information, and the server "pushes" that data from the server. Each Internet service has a related server. Many times, these are unique physical computers, but it is possible to have many different software *services* running on a single physical computer *server*. The determining factor when deciding whether to run a particular service on a dedicated PC is usually one of performance. I'll cover these issues a little later on.

Intranets, Extranets, and Virtual Private Networks

Although most people think of a Web site as a place on the Internet, there are many more uses for Web-based technologies. When a Web server is used within the confines of a private computer network, it forms what has become known as an *intranet*. The components, features, and use of an intranet are exactly the same as an Internet except that the scope of the audience is limited to a private group of people.

An intranet can be used to share important company documents, to post corporate-wide or department-wide announcements, or even to tie into a corporate database to provide real-time access to inventory details. Anything that an Internet Web service can offer can also be privatized into a corporate intranet.

When two or more corporations need an easy and effective way to exchange information, usually data that changes quickly, such as inventory levels, they can combine their private intranets into an *extranet*. Like the intranet, any service that can be used by a Web server is available on an extranet. It is very likely that the extranet portion of this configuration is only a small part of a larger intranet. For example, a company may have an intranet to communicate corporate information among its own departments, but it might also permit access to a group of Web pages that update quantity-on-hand inventory levels to its resellers.

The connection between intranets that form an extranet is normally a dedicated connection between locations, although it can be *tunneled* between sites across the Internet. Tunneling is a process of encrypting the data sent across the Internet. This process creates a *Virtual Private Network,* or VPN. The network is *virtual* because it is not a physical link and *private* because the data between the two sites is encrypted.

Although Web services are the most common with intranets and extranets, all of the other Internet type processes can also be included. As I discuss Internet servers throughout this chapter, keep in mind that all of them can be used across the Internet, or as part of a private intranet or extranet.

exam preparation pointer

The i-Net+ exam will refer to various forms of networks and ask you to identify them as Internets, intranets, or extranets. Make sure you understand the differences and uses for these various networks.

WEB SERVERS

One of the most popular Internet servers is the HTTP, or Web, server. As you might imagine, this is the software that provides, or serves up, HTML pages at the request of a browser. Web servers are available for just about every platform: UNIX, NT, NetWare, Apple, and others. UNIX and NT are probably the platforms of choice for most, but Novell is quickly becoming a very serious Web platform.

On the UNIX side, the Apache server is one of the most popular (a Windows NT version of Apache is also available, and a NetWare version is under development). Apache is developed as an "open-source" project. This basically means that the software is free. The source code is freely distributed so anyone can use, customize, or modify the resulting program. Individuals in collaboration with the *Apache Software Foundation*, or ASF, develop all bug fixes, improvements, and add-ons. The ASF exists to provide a foundation for open, collaborative software development projects by supplying hardware, communication, and business infrastructure. The Apache Web server is only one project this group is currently involved in.

Microsoft also has a Web server product called Internet Information Server, or IIS, which is included with the BackOffice suite of server software or can be purchased separately. IIS's Active Server Pages offer an application environment that combines HTML, scripts, and reusable ActiveX server components to create dynamic Web-based solutions. IIS also contains dynamic full-text searching components integrated into the software product.

Netscape's FastTrack Server is another popular Intel-based Web Server. Novell's NetWare operating system includes a customized version of FastTrack as its Web server product.

There are literally hundreds of additional Web server packages. Many are freely available, and others are commercial products. They run from very simple to highly configurable. Most Web server programs have fairly small minimum requirements since not a lot of computation processing is required to serve HTML pages.

There are a few common configuration components found in most Web servers. For example:

- By default, the Web server will listen for, and respond to, browser requests on the TCP/IP port number 80.

- The server will look to a predefined directory on the computer for the location of the HTML pages to send to the browser.

- When a specific HTML page is not specifically requested, the Web server will use a default page, normally named `index.htm`.

- Most servers will generate usage logs that can be enabled or disabled.

- The server can allow predefined associations of certain *MIME* tags with file extensions. Multipurpose Internet Mail Extensions, or MIME, allows a Web server to communicate to a browser what type of file is being sent. The browsers recognize a set of standard MIME tags. Although MIME is more often associated with e-mail, the HTML implementation is nearly identical. MIME is an official Internet standard that specifies how messages must be formatted so that they can be exchanged between different systems. MIME is a very flexible format that encompasses virtually any type of file or document. Specifically, MIME messages can contain text, images, audio, video, or other application-specific data.

The accompanying CD contains two non-commercial Web servers: *JWeb,* written by Jeff Heaton (`http://www.heat-on.com`) and *Xitami* from the iMatix Corporation (`http://www.imatix.com`). Later in this chapter I'll walk you through the installation of these programs to demonstrate how a Web server works.

note 🖉 **The i-Net+ exam will not contain questions about specific Web servers. I chose the two applications on the CD simply to demonstrate basic concepts of Web servers in general. You do not need to memorize the specific configuration tasks covered in the following exercises.**

JWeb is a small (87K) single executable program with minimal configuration requirements. Figure 8-1 shows JWeb's browser-based configuration screen. It runs on a Windows 95/98 or NT computer. Although it's small, the speed with which server pages are sent is very impressive. JWeb allows the administrator to configure the TCP/IP port to use, the location of the Web pages to serve, a default document name, log file creation, and MIME-type configuration.

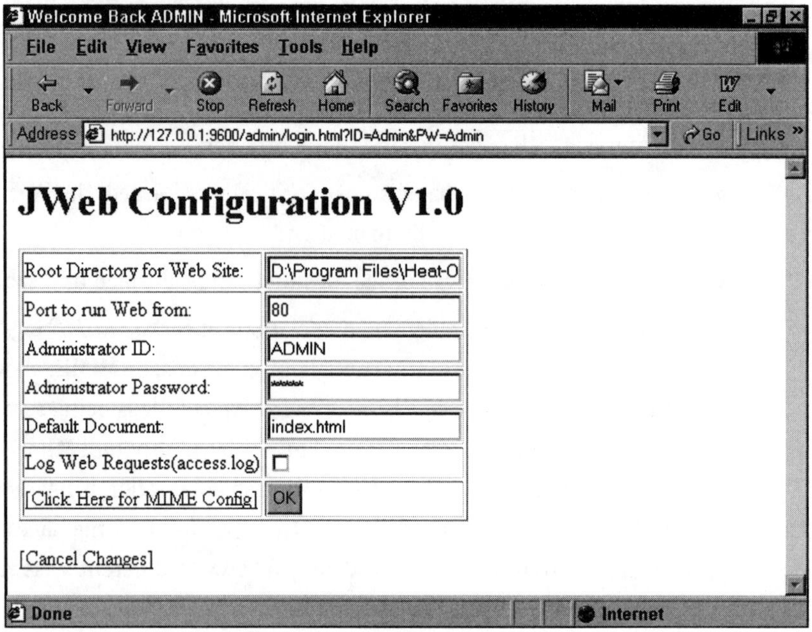

FIGURE 8-1   JWeb's configuration is done through an HTML page

The Xitami Web server is an excellent example of what a more feature-rich server offers. Amazingly enough, Xitami is freely distributable through the open source code philosophy. However, as with many open source code projects, this in no way means that Xitami is limited in any way or is not as functional as other commercial packages. When fully installed, Xitami requires less than 2MB of disk space. It runs on all UNIX platforms, OS/2, OpenVMS, Windows 3.x, Windows 95, and Windows NT. Xitami is targeted to a much larger audience than JWeb as is evident from its features, which include the following:

- Support for HTTP, FTP, CGI, and SSI protocols, server-side image maps, user-defined MIME types, customizable error messages, multilingual HTML documents and multilingual CGI scripts

- Basic authentication per directory, FTP access rights per user and per directory, on-the-fly user and password management, UNIX setuid, and restricted access by IP address

- Custom log file formats, programmed log file cycling, asynchronous reverse DNS lookups

- Virtual hosting to allow more than one Web "site" to be hosted by a single session of the program

- Configuration through editable files or through a Web-based administration interface (WBA) that includes virtual host wizard, server control (restart, terminate), active connection monitor, and full configuration of server options, security, users, and so on

- Direct support for CGI scripts in Perl and other languages, plug-in extensions, SSI protocol for dynamic Web pages, and filter protocol for arbitrary Web page filters.

Hands-On Exercise: Using the JWeb server

Web server software is generally no more difficult to install and configure than any other software package. Most Windows-based packages come with self-installers that only require you to know where on your computer's hard drive you want to place the installed files. The single prerequisite, however, is that TCP/IP is set up and working on your server machine.

For these exercises, start by making a stand-alone site (a browser talking to the server on the same machine). If you have the hardware available, you can connect your system to a network or the Internet to let other people access your pages. This is a checklist of things to do:

- You need a network adaptor. Under Windows 95, this can be the dial-up adaptor, rather than a physical network card.

- TCP/IP must be installed and ready to use. Refer to Chapter 4 if you need to install TCP/IP on your PC.

- Install the Web server and test the default page.

- Add pages to your site and adjust the configuration as required.

In this exercise, you'll install the JWeb server, copy some HTML pages into its directory, and connect to it with your browser. For this exercise, use the following parameters. You should substitute your actual settings where appropriate.

- Installation Path: `C:\Program Files\Heat-On Software\JWeb`
- HTML Page Path: `C:\Program Files\Heat-On Software\JWeb\WWWRoot`
- Local IP address: `192.168.1.1`

USING A STATIC HOST NAME FOR A WEB SERVER USING A PPP DIAL-UP INTERNET CONNECTION

To connect your computer to a network, you need to give it a fixed IP address and a domain name. This is a job for a network administrator. On a dial-up PPP connection you get a temporary IP address which can be used (http://193.23.54.12/) but it changes each time you connect. Some providers will give you a fixed IP address, sometimes at extra cost.

There are many Internet services that will provide you with a static host name (mycomputer.somedomain.com) even though you may have a dynamic IP address. This lets others access your computer the same way every time, instead of having to enter a different IP address every time you reconnect to the Internet.

One company that is very well known for providing this service is Winip (http://www.dragonmount.net/software/winip/). Winip works with Windows 95/98, as well as with Windows NT 4.0 and is freely distributed. With Winip, your PC gets a fully qualified domain name. Your IP address, even if dynamically assigned, may be reached while you are online through a single hostname, recognized on the whole internet. People may connect to your machine's FTP, WWW, IRC, or other server by using your new hostname.

Follow the installation procedures outlined in Appendix D for the JWeb server. If you change the default path during the installation, make sure you substitute the correct path for the rest of these steps.

1. Using a text or HTML editor, create the following HTML page:

```
<HTML>
<HEAD>
<TITLE>Sample HTML Home Page for the JWeb Server</TITLE>
</HEAD>
<BODY BGCOLOR="White">
<H1>
This is a sample home page for our Web Server Demonstration
</H1>
</BODY>
</HTML>
```

2. Save this page as index.htm in the C:\Program Files\Heat-On Software\JWeb\WWWRoot directory.

3. Click Start ⇨ Programs ⇨ JWeb ⇨ JWeb to start the Web server. (If the JWeb server is already running, double-click its icon in the Windows system tray.)

4. On the JWeb control panel, click Configure.

5. Your default Web browser will start displaying the JWeb Administration login page. Enter Admin as both the username and password then click LOGON.

6. In the Default Document field, change the current setting to `index.htm` The default document will be displayed when a browser connects to the Web server without specifying a document name. This can be any HTML page but it is customary to name the default page `index.htm` or `index.html`.

7. Click OK to save the changes.

8. In the URL address field of your browser, enter: `http://192.168.1.1`.

Next I'll demonstrate the use of the TCP/IP port property.

1. Double-click the JWeb icon in the System Tray.

2. On the JWeb control panel, click Configure.

3. Your default Web browser will start displaying the JWeb Administration login page. Enter Admin as both the username and password then click LOGON.

4. Change the value for the Port to run Web from field from `80` to `8080`.

5. Click OK to save the changes.

6. Close the browser.

7. On the JWeb control panel, click Stop ➪ Start to reset the Web server.
   Start your browser program and enter `http://192.168.1.1` in the URL address field. You'll receive a message stating that the requested page cannot be displayed (your actual message will vary depending on the browser you are using). This error has occurred because the Web browser is now listening on port 8080 for HTTP requests.

8. To connect to the Web server and display the default page, type `http://192.168.1.1:8080` in the URL address field of your browser.

If the Web server is configured to use a TCP/IP port other than 80, the correct port number must be included with the URL address to connect to the server. Although this is not a perfect security method, it is one way that a Web server can be made a little bit safer.

Hands-On Exercise: Using the Xitami Server

Although JWeb is simple to use, easy on computer resources, and serves HTML pages rather fast, you can see that it doesn't offer many options. In the next exercise, you'll perform the same tasks using the Xitami Web server. For this exercise, you'll use the following default values. You should substitute your actual settings where appropriate.

- Installation Path: `C:\Xitami`
- HTML Page Path: `C:\Xitami\webpages`
- Administrator Name: `Admin`
- Administrator Password: `Admin`
- Local IP address: `192.168.1.1`

1. Install the Xitami Web server by following the directions in Appendix D. If you change the default path during the installation, make sure you substitute the correct path for the rest of these steps. The Xitami application installs with a common set of defaults that are appropriate for most people.

2. To test your installation, start your browser, and enter `192.168.1.1` in the URL field. The Xitami home page will be displayed.

3. Double click the Xitami icon in the Windows system tray to display the Xitami Web Server Properties dialog box. This screen provides a quick status of the Web server and allows you to suspend or terminate the server service. In addition, a check box in the upper-right-hand corner allows you to set the server to automatically start when Windows begins. If you are on a network, the Web server won't begin until this PC has successfully logged into the network. Now let's take a look at some of this application's advanced administration features.

4. Click Setup on the Xitami dialog box. A login dialog box will be displayed. Enter the username and password you created during the installation process (Admin / Admin in this example).

5. The Xitami Administration Web page as shown in Figure 8-2 will be displayed. Click the CONFIGURATION icon.

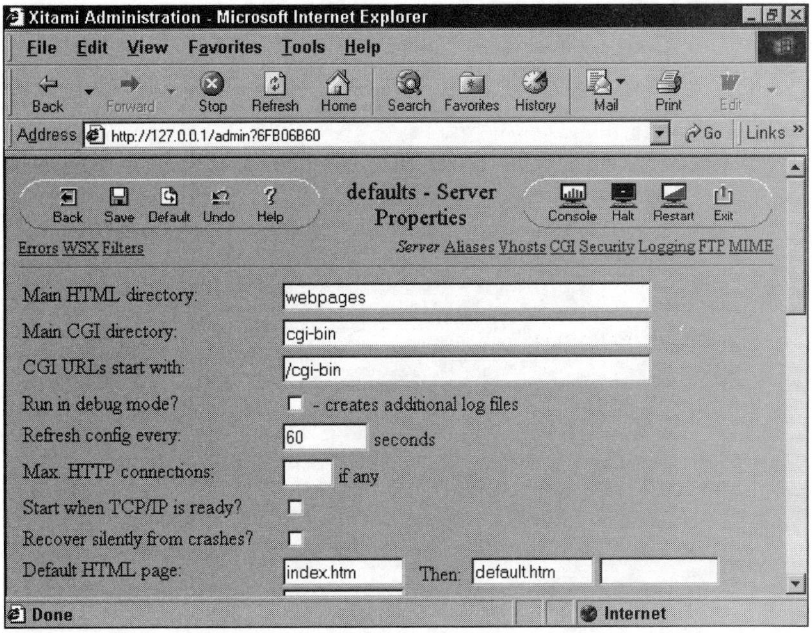

FIGURE 8-2 A portion of Xitami's Administration Configuration Page.

Although there are too many options to cover here individually, you can use the online help for detailed descriptions of each additional option. The following discussion covers some of the major options not offered by simpler Web servers.

On the configuration page, the first three data fields allow you to define where you want to store your Web pages and CGI scripts. About halfway down the page you can specify the file name to use as your default page. Xitami also allows you to define three additional "default" pages in case previous pages are damaged or missing.

A little further down, as shown in Figure 8-3, you can see some advanced options. The data field, labeled IP Port Base, is where you can change the default TCP/IP port the server listens on. Note that the value you see here is relative to port 80, not 0. In other words, if you enter 80 into this field, Xitami will use port 160, not 80.

At the top of the page are a number of text hyperlinks. Click the Security link. The first dialog box (Figure 8-4) allows you to define a file that holds your passwords. By clicking the Define button, you can add, change, or remove passwords and private directories.

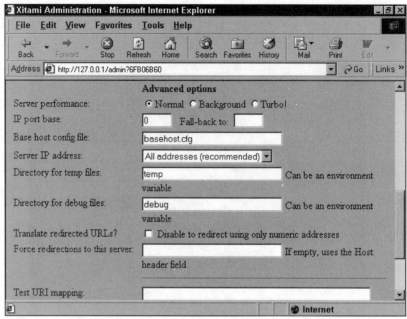

FIGURE 8-3   Some advanced configuration settings of Xitami's Web server

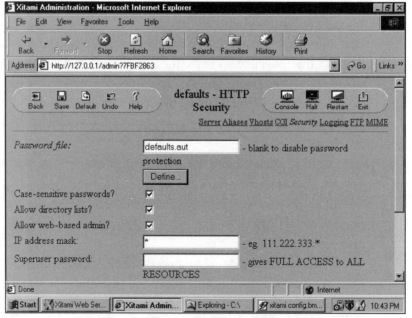

FIGURE 8-4   Xitami offers a number of password-protected areas fully administered within the configuration Page.

E-MAIL SERVERS

E-mail is arguably the second most used service on the Internet. Most companies and individuals have one or more e-mail addresses that may be hosted by ISPs or privately. Although e-mail servers generally require more computer horsepower than Web servers, an e-mail server can be nearly as easy to set up, configure, and maintain.

It is relatively easy to justify the cost of owning an e-mail server. Most ISPs charge from $2 to $5 per e-mail address *per* month. Taking the average cost of $3.50, a company with just 10 employees will spend $420 per year for e-mail accounts. In addition, as people join and leave the organization, the ISP will likely charge additional fees to maintain the e-mail changes. A company that owns its own e-mail server bears only the initial cost for the hardware and software, and normally can create as many valid e-mail addresses as are needed. In addition, since the e-mail accounts are maintained locally, names can be added, changed, and deleted at will with no additional charges.

A plethora of e-mail applications is available. Features can range from the simple — basic message transportation — to the advanced. Advanced applications can send automated responses to incoming mail, or maintain mailing lists that people can join or leave as they choose. The UNIX standard for e-mail servers is an application called sendmail. Microsoft's package is Exchange, while Novell's is called GroupWise. Both Exchange and GroupWise combine additional features such as shared calendars, group scheduling, and *universal in-boxes*. The universal in-box is a single client application that centralizes e-mail, voice mail, and faxes in one interface.

There are two primary Internet protocols associated with Internet e-mail. The Simple Mail Transport Protocol, or SMTP, is used to send messages between e-mail servers on the Internet. The Post Office Protocol version 3, or POP3, is used by e-mail clients to request and transport messages to and from an e-mail server.

 exam preparation pointer **For the exam, you need to know that the SMTP protocol uses port 25 (usually send) and the POP3 protocol uses port 110 (usually receive)**

Many private e-mail servers use the ETRN extensions to the SMTP service to gather their local mail from the ISP's e-mail server. With ETRN, the private e-mail server ("sender-SMTP") requests that the ISP server ("receiver-SMTP") starts processing its mail queues for messages that are waiting at that server for the client machine. If any messages are at the server for the client, they are sent to the client.

Although the same process can be accomplished using the POP3 protocol, ETRN is somewhat more secure.

The following is a simple example of how mail is transported across the Internet. Examine Figure 8-5: An Internet-connected PC (a) is sending an e-mail message to Sales@IDGBOOKS.com. The process this message will follow is outlined below.

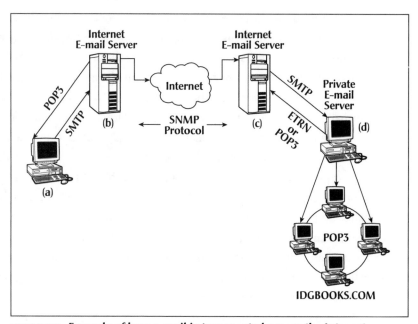

FIGURE 8-5   Example of how e-mail is transported across the Internet

1. PC (a) uses the SMTP protocol to send the message to the local ISP.

2. Server (b) looks at the domain portion of the intended recipient (IDGBOOKS.com). If this server is the *authoritative* server for that domain then no further processing will take place. However, since this server is not the authority for the domain, it queries its domain name server (DNS) to locate a *Mail Exchange,* (MX) record for IDGBOOKS. com. MX records within DNS are pointers to e-mail servers. The MX record query informs server (b) that server (c) is responsible for handling e-mail for the IDGBOOKS.com domain.

3. Server (b) transfers the message to server (c) using the SMTP protocol.

4. Server (c) attempts to transfer the message to the private server at `IDGBOOKS.com`. However, to minimize costs, this server uses a dial-up connection that is not always on. Therefore, server (c) will `queue` the message for later processing. Simply stated, the server creates a holding area known as a queue to save incoming messages until they're requested.

5. On a regular interval, the private server (d) at `IDGBOOKS.com` dials up to the ISP and sends an ETRN request to the mail server (c) to check for new mail. If there is mail waiting in the queue, the ETRN protocol sends a message to start the "de-queuing," or sending, of the mail from server (c) to server (d).

6. Server (d) now reads only the first part of the e-mail address, the name portion to the left of the @ sign, and places the messages into the appropriate local queue for that user.

7. Users on the local network use a standard e-mail client to send a POP3 protocol request to the local e-mail server (d) to request its message. Any messages waiting in the local queue for that user are sent down to the e-mail client.

As you can tell, the e-mail system is predicated on domain names. Until the message is delivered locally, the MX records in the DNS system are only concerned with what e-mail domains are used. E-mail servers within a domain are designated as being *authoritative* for that domain which is reflected in the MX records. Therefore, a prerequisite to maintaining an e-mail server is to register a domain name for the company. The basics of domain name registration are covered in Chapter 2.

Because you are not likely to have a registered domain name yet, we won't do a hands-on exercise to set up an e-mail server. However, I have included an extremely powerful, yet easy to use software package on the CD. *MDaemon* is an SMTP/POP3 e-mail server for Windows 95 and NT. This is typically the kind of e-mail server software required to send e-mail to users on a LAN or the Internet. MDaemon allows an organization to implement an inexpensive but powerful e-mail system that will allow users to e-mail one another locally and on the Internet.

MDaemon can send and receive e-mail to the ISP at a user-defined interval as low as one minute. It can also be configured to dial an Internet access account automatically to check for and send new e-mail. Other features include MultiPOP, which allows MDaemon to check an unlimited number of POP3 accounts at numerous ISPs, and WorldClient, which adds a Web-based e-mail client to allow users to access their e-mail account from any place on the Internet.

MDaemon supports several types of Internet connections including dial-up modems, ISDN, T1 circuits, and many others, making MDaemon a scalable solution capable of growing with an organization's e-mail communications needs. A host of other features make MDaemon one of the most powerful SMTP/POP3 mail servers available, including mailing lists, aliasing, auto responders, auto forwarding, multiple domains, remote administration, and many other features.

FTP SERVERS

Although e-mail attachments are a popular method for sending files across the Internet, the *File Transport Protocol,* or FTP, is still a more robust and secure process. FTP servers are generally small, fast, and easy to install and configure. The only large resource required by most FTP servers is the amount of disk space used to hold the files sent and received.

FTP servers provide many mechanisms to control the access and use of the files sent and received. Most FTP servers allow security to be administered on directory and file basis, and also provide unique settings for each user and the ability to put users into "groups," simplifying maintenance for a system with a large number of users. Users can also be restricted or permitted at the IP level, meaning that you can allow or deny access to users based on their machine location. This is desirable if you want to let certain people within your network or intranet gain access to the FTP server, but deny access to all others across the Internet.

The FTP protocol also allows for remote execution of programs, and remote printing. For example, an employee working from home or on the road could send a document to the FTP server and specify that it be "uploaded" to a printer port. The resulting document would be redirected to the printer for hard copy output.

Anonymous FTP

Many computer systems throughout the Internet offer files through anonymous FTP. This means that you can access a machine without having to have an account on that machine (i.e. you don't have to be an official user of the system). These anonymous FTP servers contain software, documents of various sorts, graphic images, song lyrics, and an abundance of other information. Archives for electronic mailing lists are often stored on and made available through anonymous FTP. A standard way to connect to an anonymous FTP server is to enter *anonymous* as the username and the user's e-mail address as the password.

Trivial File Transport Protocol

When security is not a requirement, the *Trivial File Transport Protocol*, or TFTP, can be used. As with FTP, files are transferred between computers. But unlike FTP, no login or password authentication occurs. TFTP is commonly used to upload software patches and revisions to small hardware devices such as hubs and routers.

exam
preparation
pointer

For the exam, you need to know that the default port for the FTP protocol is 21.

To effectively support an FTP server on the Internet, a static IP address is highly recommended. FTP clients generally connect directly to the server's IP address, although many newer clients also use DNS to resolve a hostname to its IP address. If you have a dial-up account, you need to determine the IP address for that session for an FTP client to reach your server. Again, this is a good reason to ask your ISP for a dedicated IP address.

Hands-On Exercise with an FTP Server

In this exercise you'll examine the FTP features of the Xitami Web/FTP server. If you haven't installed the Xitami application, please do so now. Also included on the CD is a standalone FTP server called FTP SERV-U, which is a full-featured server for Windows 95/98 or NT. The full installation of FTP SERV-U requires less than 3MB of disk space. Refer to Appendix D for more information.

As in previous exercises, you should use the following default values, substituting your actual settings where appropriate.

- Installation Path: `C:\Xitami`
- FTP Files Path: `C:\Xitami\ftproot`
- Administrator Name: `Admin`
- Administrator Password: `Admin`
- Local IP address: `192.168.1.1`

1. Start your browser. In the URL Address field, enter `192.168.1.1`.

2. The displayed page will list the files in the `\ftproot` directory, which by default is on the file `index.txt`.

3. Click the file named `index.txt`: The contents of this simple text file will be displayed in your browser.

Next, add a few more files into the `ftproot` directory and watch the effect these have in your browser.

1. Start the Windows text editor. Select Start ⇨ Run. Enter Notepad, and click OK.

2. In the Notepad application, type in: `This is a test FTP document`

3. Select File ⇨ Save as. In the File Name field, enter: `sample1.txt`. Click Save.

4. On your browser, click refresh/reload.

Now you should see two files: `index.txt` and `sample1.txt`. The reason these files were saved into the `C:\Xitami\ftproot\Pub\` directory rather than the `ftproot` directory is that your browser is logged in as *anonymous*. All anonymous logins are restricted to the public directory.

Although browser-basedFTP is convenient for downloading files, it severely limits much of the power of FTP. There are a number of graphical FTP clients available, but Windows also has a DOS-based FTP client that I'll use here to demonstrate the various features of FTP.

1. Select Start ⇨ Run. Enter `ftp 192.168.1.1`, and click OK.

2. The Xitami welcome screen will be displayed and ask you for a username.

3. Type `Guest` and press Enter.

4. The `ftp>` prompt will be displayed.

5. Type `dir` and press Enter.

6. The two files you saw in the Web browser will be listed.

7. Type `Bye` and press Enter.

8. Type `Exit` and press Enter.

9. Open the Xitami Web Server Properties box by double clicking the Xitami icon in the system tray.

10. Select Setup.

11. If the login box did not remember you username and password, enter Admin for both.

12. Select OK.

13. Select Configuration.

14. From the text hyperlinks in the top right corner, click FTP. Take a few minutes to examine the options available on this screen. This is where most of your FTP options are set, including the port number and message definitions.

15. Click the Define Button associated with the User Configuration field.

16. Click the Admin hyperlink under User Name.

17. In the Password field, enter admin (make sure you use all lowercase letters).

18. Select Save.

19. Notice that the User admin now has the password of admin; now select Save.

20. Select Restart; the FTP server will restart and the new user information will be read in.

21. Select Start ⇨ Run. Enter FTP 192.168.1.1, and Click OK. The Xitami welcome screen will be displayed and ask you for a username.

22. Type admin and press Enter.

23. You will now be prompted to enter a password; type admin and press Enter.

24. The admin login will be confirmed and the ftp> prompt displayed.

25. Type dir and press Enter. Notice that you now have a lot more files listed. The admin account automatically logs into a different directory than the Anonymous user does.

26. Type help and press Enter. The list of valid FTP commands is listed.

exam preparation pointer
The i-Net+ exam will expect you to know that the get command is used to transfer files *from* the FTP server to your local machine (download), the put command is used to send (upload) a file *to* the FTP server, and the command bye closes the FTP session.

27. Type cd pub and press Enter. This command changes the directory (cd) to the public directory.

28. Type dir and press Enter. You should now see two files. One is the sample.txt file you created earlier.

29. Type `get sample1.txt`. The file `sample1.txt` will be transferred to your computer, in the directory where the FTP program was started. (This varies depending on the Windows platform you are using.)

30. Type `cd` (make sure you have a space after cd and that you use two dots). This command moves you up one level in the directory tree on the FTP server (in this case, it changes your directory to the `pub` directory).

31. Type `put sample1.txt` to send the file to the FTP server in this directory.

32. To confirm that the file was transferred type `dir` and press Enter. The `sample1.txt` file is now displayed in the directory listing.

33. Type `bye` and press Enter to close the FTP session.

If you are uncomfortable with the command line, you might be thinking that FTP is a lot of work just to send a few files back and forth. However, applications based on the FTP protocol can add a great deal of functionality to your normal work chores. For example, a shareware program called WebDrive (`http://www.riverfrontsoftware.com`) uses FTP to modify the Windows Explorer utility so that you can assign an FTP site to a drive letter and treat that drive just as if it were local to your PC. Using this program, you can save, retrieve, delete, and rename files on an FTP server using the Windows commands you normally use. If your company has an extranet, you can use a program like this to automate the process of saving and retrieving common files for novice users without ever having to teach them to use FTP.

PROXY SERVERS

A proxy server is a dedicated application that acts as a middleman between the client and the Internet. One of the primary purposes of a proxy server is to share a single Internet connection among a number of client computers. This is extremely beneficial when the connection to the Internet is accomplished with a dial-up line. Without a proxy server, people on the network that wanted to connect to the Internet would need access to their own modems and telephone lines. Obviously this would be rather costly. With a dedicated connection, a proxy server also offers the benefit of providing extra security, because the proxy usually is configured with two network cards. One card is connected to the Internet, while the other is connected to the local network. This helps hide the computer addresses on the local network, making an Internet attack even more difficult.

A proxy server can be protocol specific, such as only serving the Web, or it can incorporate any number of Internet applications. Just like the other Internet server services this chapter has covered so far, proxy servers are widely available in prices ranging from free to a few hundred dollars. Most proxy servers are easy to install and configure, and make few demands on computer resources. The configuration of a proxy server is, for the most part, so easy that the installation routine handles all of the necessary settings.

On the CD, I've included one of the finest Windows-based proxy servers on the market, Wingate by Deerfield.com. With WinGate installed on your network, accessing the Internet from either the WinGate server computer or any of the client computers will appear virtually the same. Network users can use almost any Internet application as they would with their own Internet connection. WinGate also initiates an Internet connection or disconnection with an Internet request from client computers, so users on client stations can initiate Internet access even if they are not using the WinGate server computer with the modem or other Internet connection.

WinGate contains a secure firewall component that prevents intruders from accessing your internal network through your Internet connection. All Internet requests are routed through the WinGate software, thus WinGate accomplishes this security by identifying in-bound requests for access to the network and verifying that the IP address of the request is allowed to access the internal network. WinGate also binds the communications ports necessary for outsiders to access an internal network. Refer to Appendix D for complete installation instructions.

CERTIFICATE SERVERS

To ensure confidential communications and safeguard intellectual property, many companies are deploying *digital certificate* technology. Digital certificates address the problem of verifying someone's identity over the Internet. Unlike encryption technologies, which only address user's privacy, digital certificates allow companies and individuals to use other kinds of security such as authenticity (guaranteeing that you are who you say you are) and integrity (ensuring that a document hasn't been altered by an unauthorized party). A *certificate authority*, or CA, refers to either the software or service that issues digital certificates.

Digital certificates work via public key encryption. The user of a certificate holds two keys: a public key (which allows anyone to encrypt data to send to a specific user) and a private key (which is accessible only to the user, who may send encrypted information and decrypt information sent to the user's public key). By themselves, the keys are just strings of numbers. That's where the certificate authority comes in. It verifies to a requesting party that users are who they say they are by verifying that their public keys were in fact issued to them. A certificate server enables network administrators to issue and manage digital certificates in house, ensuring that data is secure while in transit both over the network and over the Internet. Certificate servers can also generate *Secure-Socket Layer* (SSL) certificates for Web servers. This is a critical requirement for any business that conducts commerce over the Internet.

NEWS SERVERS

A slightly lesser known Internet service is Internet News, or Usenet. In a nutshell, newsgroups are a means of "public discussion." Newsgroup articles (messages) look like e-mail but can potentially be read by millions of people all over the world. Newsgroup topics literally cover just about any topic imaginable and, like e-mail, can contain multimedia components as well as text. Not all news servers carry every newsgroup topic.

Internet service providers, schools, universities, and private companies distribute the articles via *news servers*, which contain databases of articles. There is no central server on Usenet. A newsgroup article propagates from one server to another, starting from the server where it is first posted. When an article is posted in a newsgroup, the message first goes to the local news server. This server then sends copies of the article to its neighbors; that is, to servers with which it has agreed to exchange articles. Those servers in turn send copies to their neighbors until eventually every server that carries the newsgroup has a copy.

News servers use the *Network News Transfer Protocol*, or NNTP. Special client software is required to read and post Usenet messages. Free newsgroup clients ship with Netscape Communicator and Microsoft Internet Explorer. News servers, on the other hand, are not quite as common. Due to the high overhead of maintaining newsgroup servers, most organizations rely on ISPs and universities to provide this service. One popular shareware news server called Cassandra is produced by Atrium Software (`http://www.atrium-software.com/cassandra/cassandra_e.html`). Cassandra provides all of the basic newsgroup features and runs on the Windows platform.

DIRECTORY SERVERS

LDAP (Lightweight Directory Access Protocol) is the Internet directory protocol. Developed at the University of Michigan at Ann Arbor in conjunction with the Internet Engineering Task Force, LDAP is a protocol for accessing and managing directory services. A *directory* consists of entries containing descriptive information about your network. For example, a directory might contain entries describing people or network resources, such as printers or fax machines.

The descriptive information is stored in the attributes of the entry. Each attribute describes a specific type of information. For example, attributes describing a person might include the person's name (common name, or *cn*), telephone number, and e-mail address. An attribute can have more than one value. For example, a person might have two common names (a formal name and a nickname) or two telephone numbers.

A directory service might be used to look up someone's telephone number. Another application might use the directory service to retrieve a list of e-mail addresses. LDAP is a protocol defining a directory service and access to that service. LDAP is based on a client/server model. LDAP servers provide the directory service, and LDAP clients use the directory service to access entries and attributes.

Network directories are used throughout the Internet to provide fast, detailed information about many subjects. One of the most well-known uses of a directory is the People Finder service by Web sites such as WhoWhere (`http://www.whowhere.com`). These sites allow you to search and display telephone numbers and addresses of people around the world from public sources.

MIRRORED SERVERS

Mirror servers are Internet sites dedicated to duplicate data stored on other sites. A mirrored site might duplicate a newsgroup, an FTP site, or a Web site. One primary purpose of a mirror site is to have a place near you from which you can browse in a speedier manner. Although accessing a server that is geographically closer to you does not guarantee faster access, spreading the workload of a heavily accessed server among mirrored servers that are geographically close to those accessing them can improve access times. Another benefit of mirror sites is that they can host information in different languages. This way, people all over the world can connect to a mirrored site to retrieve important information in a language more familiar to them. There is no specific "mirror" software or special protocol. The mirror site is simply a duplicate of the site it is mirroring.

CACHE SERVERS

In Chapter 3, I discussed the use of caching to assist in increasing the performance of Web browsing. Cache servers build on this concept but on a much larger scale. Most proxy servers include a cache component, caching a few megabytes of information for use by any person accessing the proxy server, but a dedicated cache server goes way beyond this. Most cache servers are configured to fetch large amounts of data from predefined Web sites. The amount can range from a few hundred megabytes to thousands of gigabytes. The Novell Corporation has developed one of the fastest cache servers on the market, called Novell's FastCache. This product is included in their firewall/proxy product, BorderManager, but is also available as a standalone Internet device.

Cache Servers can be located at many strategic locations throughout the Internet. At the local level, cache servers can greatly increase Web browsing for an entire company. ISPs are beginning to implement cache servers to not only increase performance for their customers, but to reduce the amount of data that must leave their physical location. When an ISP's subscribers can retrieve the information they need from a cache server, they're not using the bandwidth to go out to other servers on the Internet. Likewise, the major Internet Access Points can deploy cache servers for the same reason. As the use of the Internet grows and bandwidth demand increases, cache servers promise to be a major component of the Internet to help keep data moving as quickly as possible.

Caching is also useful to sites that host their own Web servers. *Reverse cache* is the process of duplicating Web pages from a corporate Web server, and placing it out for public access. Using this technology, a single Web server can be cached by multiple Web cache servers to load balance the incoming demands for the Web site. An added benefit to deploying cache servers is that the primary Web server can be located within a company's firewall, completely secured from outside attacks. Should a cache server be hacked into, it won't cause a major problem since the original data will overwrite whatever changes an attacker has made.

List Servers

List servers are systems that allow you to post an e-mail message to the server and have it distributed to everyone on the list. If your name is on the list, you receive copies of all the messages others send to the list. List servers are similar to newsgroups in that they allow exchange of ideas and discussions but they differ in that they get far less commercials and usually stay on topic.

Many companies who have developed Web sites have also instituted e-mail list servers as an additional channel to communicate with customers. List servers are for the most part self-maintaining. People usually join and leave e-mail lists by sending specially addressed messages to the list server. The functions of a list server are normally part of the standard e-mail server, although a separate list server can be installed to reduce the traffic on the primary e-mail server. The included e-mail server on the CD, MDaemon, has list server capabilities.

Telnet

Telnet is a remote terminal emulation protocol that provides text-based access to a host running a telnet service. Most UNIX networks use or allow telnet, as do many active hubs, switches, and routers. Telnet is the main Internet protocol for creating a connection with a remote machine. It gives the user the opportunity to be on one computer system and do work on another, which may be across the street or thousands of miles away. Where modems are limited by the quality of telephone lines and a single connection, telnet provides a connection that's error-free and nearly always faster than the latest conventional modems. With telnet, you log on as a regular user with whatever privileges you may have been granted to the specific applications and data on that computer.

Telnet works over TCP/IP port 23 by default. A telnet server can be used for a wide variety of purposes, such as allowing an administrator an easy method of connecting to the network remotely, or allowing remote users easy access to corporate printers. Most Telnet servers are rooted in UNIX or Linux, although many third-party packages exist for NT. One of the more popular Telnet server applications is the Georgia SoftWorks Windows NT Telnet Server available at `http://www.georgiasoftworks.com/gswtelnet.html`

EXAM PREPARATION SUMMARY

You covered a lot of territory in Chapter 8. You looked at both the clients and the servers that make the features of the Internet possible. You also looked at some ways to set up your own servers to provide Internet and intranet services. Now let's review some of the highlights for this chapter to make sure you understand the material you just read.

- You saw that many small devices, such as pagers and handheld devices, offer Internet access for very specific services. In addition, inexpensive devices that connect to a television make access to some Internet services a going proposition for those who don't need or want a personal computer. You also took a look at Internet telephony, a means of making inexpensive long-distance phone calls over the Internet.

- You looked at Web servers in depth, and saw how even a small (under 8K) Web server can help you reach the world. For those times when security or added functionality is required, more sophisticated programs exist that enable you to build very powerful Web sites complete with high-level security and e-commerce capabilities.

- You also looked closely at e-mail server applications and how they are used to enhance your ability to share information on the Internet. The SMTP, ETRN, and POP3 e-mail protocols work in tandem to ensure messages are delivered from person to person quickly and efficiently. You saw that the Domain Name Service, specifically the Mail Exchange records in DNS, is critical to making e-mail delivery possible.

You also looked at many other common Internet servers, such as

- FTP servers, for transferring files when e-mail attachments are too limited or inefficient

- Proxy servers, for increasing response times to Web users and providing added security

- Certificate servers, for ensuring confidential communications

- News servers, for providing public discussion groups

- Directory (LDAP) servers, for providing a method to access and manage large amounts of information about network resources

- Mirror servers, for holding duplicates of another server's content and reducing demand on the original

- Cache servers, for making Internet content more accessible to the user and providing security

- List servers, for providing public discussion forums, like Usenet, but using e-mail as the medium

- I closed the chapter with a discussion of telnet, a UNIX-born protocol that provides remote access services. Telnet is a text-based system with user/password authentication. Using telnet, users can access server resources with acceptable performance, even using voice-grade dial-up connections.

APPLYING WHAT YOU HAVE LEARNED

The following review questions give you an opportunity to test your knowledge of the information presented in this chapter. The answers to these assessment questions can be found in Appendix B. If you missed some, review those sections in this chapter before going further.

Instant Assessment Questions

1. WebTV is most useful for

   A. Savvy Internet users who demand the fastest Internet connections possible

   B. Conversing with people across the Internet with good quality voice service

   C. Less technical people who want simple Internet services with little fuss

   D. Remote areas where dial-up access is not a local call

2. Internet "telephone" calls can be made, provided

   A. The local phone company offers an Internet gateway

   B. At least one user has a multimedia system including a sound card and speakers

   C. You are willing to accept less than clear communications

   D. Your telephone can be upgraded to support TCP/IP communications

3. When a company provides linked text computer communications to employees who are not connected to the Internet, it has implemented

   A. An internet service provider (ISP)

   B. A shared network

   C. A cached proxy network

   D. An intranet

4. When two separate companies want to link their computer systems but ensure that private data remains secure, they can implement

   A. A virtual private network

   B. An extranet

   C. A Web server

   D. A telnet server

5. By default, Web servers respond to requests on TCP/IP port

   A. 8080

   B. 8

C. 80

D. Whatever port the Web administrator defines

6. The Multipurpose Internet Mail Extensions, or MIME, is used to

   A. Specify how messages must be formatted in order to be exchanged between different systems

   B. Specify the route that message will take between the Web server and the browser

   C. Define how to convert one file format into another

   D. Allow a browser to display any type of file the server is able to send

7. TCP/IP ports 110 and 25 are used by what two protocols?

   A. HTTP uses 110

   B. SMTP uses 25

   C. FTP uses 25

   D. POP3 uses 110

8. MX records define the username in a fully qualified domain name (FQDM).

   A. True

   B. False

9. Certificate servers are useful in preventing

   A. One person from impersonating another

   B. Documents from being tampered with

   C. Unauthorized access to a Web site

   D. Network users accessing restricted Web sites

10. Newsgroup servers use which protocol?

   A. Network News Transfer Protocol (NNTP)

   B. Internet News Transfer Protocol (INTP)

   C. Usenet Transfer Protocol (UTP)

   D. Usenet News Transfer Protocol (UNTP)

Networking Hardware and Software Components

About Chapter 9

Some standard components are required for a network to operate, such as computers to act as servers, the server software, and some form of physical connection to the Internet. Additionally, cables and connecting devices must be properly selected and utilized to avoid costly performance problems down the line. Because Internet connections are often deployed company wide on a private network, it is important to understand the basic makeup of a local area network to understand what Internet options and services fit best within the environment.

In this chapter, you'll look at the basic hardware components of a network including cable types and connections. You'll look at network routing and the importance of routing technologies within both local area and wide area networks.

Choosing the proper network software is also a very important consideration, so you'll review the popular network software and learn where different technologies are best deployed.

There are many options to choose from when shopping for a dedicated, high-speed Internet connection. Bandwidth requirements and costs both need to be carefully examined. Selecting the wrong solution can be very costly, so you'll look at each of the most common connection types and review the pros and cons of each.

NETWORK INTERFACE CARDS

One of my favorite computer sayings is "hardware makes software happen." Without the hard computer and network components, even the best software in the world won't be very helpful. Many security, performance, and reliability issues are directly related to the underlying hardware.

When computers are connecting to a *Local Area Network* (LAN), each must contain a *Network Interface Card*, or NIC. This is the primary hardware device that provides connectivity between the computers. Within the LAN these NICs must all talk on the same protocol and use a compatible wire system. Collectively, this cable system and common protocol is called the *topology* of the network. Although multiple protocols can be used across a single topology, a well-designed LAN is configured with only one.

The NIC is normally an add-in computer board that is installed into an available slot inside the computer (see Figure 9-1). The two most common slots are *Industry Standard Architecture*, or ISA, and *Peripheral Component Interconnect*, or PCI. ISA is an older technology and normally requires manually configuring the add-in board before use. The PCI technology provides a high-speed data path between the CPU and peripheral devices. PCI provides *"plug and play"* capability that can automatically configure the PCI cards at startup. Many "network ready" computers have a NIC built directly into the computer's main system board, which frees up one of these slots for other devices.

The Network Interface Card contains a ROM chip that contains a unique address known as the *Media Access Control* address, or MAC address. Each manufacturer of network cards is assigned an identification number. As each NIC is produced, the manufacturer adds a sequential number to its identification number to create the unique MAC address for that card. This way, each NIC, regardless of manufacturer, is assigned a unique address. Although high-level protocols such as TCP/IP identify each computer with a unique address of its own, routing data across a network eventually requires locating the specific MAC address of the desired computer. I'll provide a closer look at how data is routed between computers shortly.

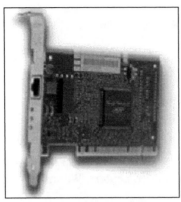

FIGURE 9-1   Standard Network Interface Card

NETWORK CABLES

Many forms of network cable have been used to provide the physical path for transferring data between computers and devices. Modern networks are now built around two basic cable types: Category 5 (or CAT5) twisted pair, and fiber optic.

Copper Cable

CAT5 is the cable of choice within a local network. CAT5 looks very similar to standard telephone wire, only slightly larger. The cable itself is composed of eight thin copper wires twisted into pairs (hence the reference to *twisted pair wire*). CAT5 wire can be either shielded or unshielded. *Shielded twisted pair*, or STP, wire has a thin metallic sheathing around the wires to help reduce outside interference. *Unshielded twisted pair*, or UTP, does not contain this sheathing. The ends of CAT5 cable are terminated with a *Registered Jack-45,* or RJ-45. An RJ-45 plug is a telephone-type connector that holds up to eight wires. Figure 9-2 is an illustration of an RJ-45 connector.

The pairs of CAT5 cable must be wired in the proper order for communications to take place. As long as the send and receive pairs match on each device, it doesn't really matter in which order they are connected. There is, however, an industry standard method.

The four wire pairs are color coded with the standard of Pair 1 being blue, Pair 2 as orange, Pair 3 as green, and Pair 4 as brown. Colors are always shown with the base color first, then the stripe color. The RJ-45 connector is wired as shown in Table 9-1.

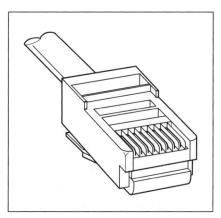

FIGURE 9-2 An RJ–45 connector terminates the ends of CAT5 twisted pair cables.

Pin	Color	Function
TABLE 9-1 RJ–45 WIRING DEFINITIONS		
Pin 1	White/Orange	Transmit –
Pin 2	Orange/White	Transmit +
Pin 3	White/Green	Receive –
Pin 4	Blue/White	
Pin 5	White/Blue	
Pin 6	Green/White	Receive +
Pin 7	White/Brown	
Pin 8	Brown/White	

 note   **Holding the cable in your left hand, with the RJ–45 pins facing up, Pin 1 is the furthest away from you.**

To connect two computers directly together, or to connect two hubs together (hubs are discussed later), a *cross over* cable is necessary. A cross over cable simply means that the transmit wires are *crossed over* the receive wires. To test the functionality of the network card, a *loop back* cable is required. A loop back cable simply closes the data signal and returns a response to the sending device.

Fiber Optic Cable

Fiber optic cable is a thin glass wire designed for light transmission, capable of transmitting trillions of bits per second. In addition to the huge transmission capacity, optical fibers offer many advantages over electricity traveling through metal wire. Light pulses are not affected by random radiation in the environment as electrical pulses are. The error rate in transmitting light pulses is significantly lower than in electrical pulses. Fibers allow longer distances to be spanned without repeaters in between that regenerate fading signals. Fibers are more secure, because taps in the line can be detected. Lastly, optical fiber installation is stream-lined due to the dramatically lower weight of the material compared to copper cables.

For years, the telephone companies have used fibers extensively to rebuild their communications infrastructure. For example, by 1999 more than 12 million miles of fiber had been laid in the United States alone.

As Figure 9-3 shows, fiber optic cable is constructed of a transparent core made of pure silicon dioxide ($SiO2$), through which the light travels. This core is so transparent that you could see through a three-mile thick window made out of it. The core is surrounded by a shielding layer that reflects light, keeping it in the core. The outer sheathing is surrounded by a layer of kevlar fibers for strength and an outer sheath of plastic or Teflon.

There are two primary types of fiber. *Multimode* fiber is very common for short distances and has a core diameter of from 50 to 100 microns. For intercity cabling and highest speed, *singlemode* fiber with a core diameter of less than 10 microns is used.

In addition to wide area connectivity, fiber optic cables are often used as the *backbone* of a LAN so high-speed data transmissions can traverse the network. Slower speed copper is used from the computer to the backbone.

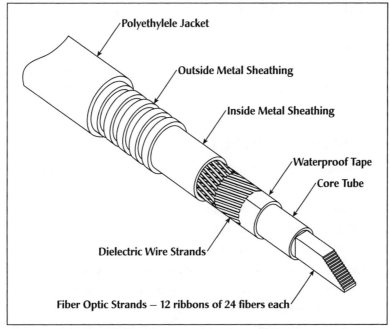

FIGURE 9-3 Fiber Optic cable is manufactured with many layers to protect the thin glass fibers at the center.

NETWORK CONNECTING DEVICES

A number of devices connect the PCs within the LAN, LANs with other LANs, and LANs to *Wide Area Networks* (WANs). Choosing the proper device depends on where the data needs to be routed to, performance issues, costs, and security requirements. Within the LAN environment, a cable connects the NICs to a *multiplexor*, which is a generic term used to describe a device that merges several low-speed transmissions into one high-speed transmission and vice versa. Normally this device is a *hub* or a *switch*.

Network Hubs

Hubs simply join communications lines together in a star configuration. There are two types of hubs: passive and active. A passive hub, which is the most common, does nothing extra to the data, where an active hub regenerates the packets to maintain a stronger signal. Neither of these types is intelligent, meaning they can't route data between devices. Hubs are generally inexpensive and easy to install. If you run out of available ports on a hub (the connector where the cable from the NIC is installed) you can add another hub (up to three) by using a cross over cable. For small workgroups of between 2 and 20 computers, hubs are an acceptable solution.

Network Switches

A switch is similar to a hub in that it concentrates all the cables from the NICs. But unlike a hub, a switch is capable of routing data between two specific devices. Network switches are often preferred over hubs because they can increase bandwidth. For example, a 16-port 10BaseT hub shares the total 10Mbps bandwidth with all 16 attached devices. If the hub is replaced with a switch, each sender/receiver pair gains the full 10Mbps capacity. Each port on the switch can give full bandwidth to a single server or client station, or it can be connected to a hub with several stations.

In Figure 9-4, there are two networks. The data on the shared hub LAN, on the left, has a maximum of 10Mbps for *all* devices. If more than one PC needs to communicate with the server, each of those PCs will have a percentage of the 10Mbps. The switched environment on the right, however, provides a maximum of 10Mbps for *each* device. When two or more PCs send data to the server, the switch allocates a full 10Mbps connection for *each* of the computers. The proper method of designing a network using switched technology is to create a backbone 10 times faster than the connections to the end devices. In this example, you would have a 100Mbps connection from the switch to the server and 10Mbps connections to the desktop PCs. This arrangement ensures that the connection between the switch and server doesn't become overly congested by the desktop's abilities to transfer data at the full speed of the connection.

Bridges

Many times it is necessary to connect two or more networks together. Sometimes a single network becomes too large and performance is negatively affected, so splitting it up into two or more segments is necessary. One device commonly used for this purpose is a *bridge*. A bridge performs two purposes. One is to extend the length and number of stations that a segment can support. The second is to reduce the traffic flow to known destinations on the same segment. When a bridge is placed between two segments, it only passes data between the segments when it knows the destination device resides on the remote segment. As long as the destination is on the same side of the bridge, the data is not allowed to cross over onto the other segments. The exception to this is when a network broadcast is generated. Since no specific destination is identified by the broadcast, the data is sent to all segments on the network.

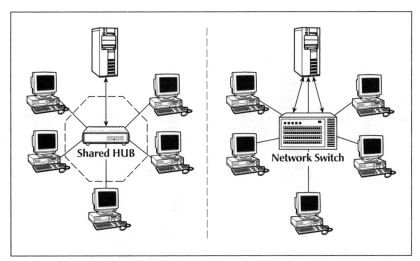

FIGURE 9-4 Network hubs (left) share the total bandwidth of the cable where switched networks (right) provide the full bandwidth to each device.

Bridges are intelligent devices in that they will learn where devices are based on the conversations occurring on the network. Examine the diagram in Figure 9-5. This LAN consists of three *segments*, or *collision domains*: S1, S2, and S3. Station A has data to transmit to Station K. Station A builds a frame that identifies Station K as the destination address. Station A also includes its own address in the frame's source address field.

When Station A transmits the frame, the bridge copies the data frame from Segment S1, then reads the source address — Station A in this case. Because the bridge copies the frame from the port attached to segment S1, it *learns* that Station A exists on Segment S1. Because the bridge has not yet determined where Station K is located, it forwards the frame to all active ports except the one connected to S1 (the segment the frame came in from). When Station K sees that the frame is addressed to it, it sends back an acknowledgement. The bridge copies this frame and now knows that Station K is on segment S3. From this point on, the bridge will forward all traffic between these devices directly through the proper ports keeping the data off of Segment S2. If Station A sends data to Station B, the bridge recognizes that Station B is on the same segment as Station A, and does not forward the data to the other segments keeping them free of unnecessary traffic. This is known as *transparent bridging* because the directing of traffic is transparent to the end user. When connecting a private network to the Internet, many connection types, such as DSL, (discussed shortly) use bridging technologies.

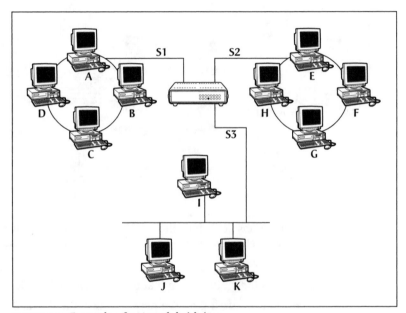

FIGURE 9-5   Example of network bridging

Network Routers

Like bridging, routers are used to connect two or more (potentially extended) segments. The segments may or may not be of the same topology or protocol. (In other words, the router may be on a LAN or WAN, or placed between two networks talking different languages, such as Ethernet and token-ring.) For a router to do its job, routing information must be contained within the data packet. Broadcasts and multicasts are never propagated across a router because the exact destination information is not contained within the packets. Just as a mailman needs to know the exact street address to deliver the mail, so must a router know exactly what device the data is intended for. Routers are only interested in local hardware addresses (the MAC address of the Network Interface Card). Routers are intelligent devices that are able to keep track of known network segments and share that information with other routers.

Routers can be used to segment LANs to balance traffic, but unlike a bridge, routers can also be used to filter traffic for security purposes. Most routers are specialized devices optimized for communications. However, router functions can also be implemented by the Network Operating System within the file server. For example, the NT and NetWare Operating Systems can route data from one network to another if each LAN segment is connected to a separate NIC in the file server.

Routers often serve as an internetwork backbone, interconnecting all networks in the enterprise. This architecture connects several routers together via a high-speed LAN topology. As networks become more and more complex, and the need to extend network services across larger and larger geographic areas increases, the routing of data becomes a critical factor in network technology. Where bridges connect to network segments, routers typically connect two or more LANs. These LANs can be physically located in the same building, or across countries, continents, or hemispheres. There are a number of ways routers on each end can be connected, but the most common means are by dedicated lease lines, packet switching technology like frame relay, or the Internet.

exam preparation pointer

For the purposes of the i-Net+ exam, you should be familiar with the basic components of a WAN and the fundamental routing concepts.

Regardless of what physical lines are used, the device to connect the in-house line to the external digital circuit is often a *Digital (or Data) Service Unit,* or DSU, and a *Channel Service Unit,* or CSU. These devices are often combined into one component so that both voice and data signals can be carried across the same line. The DSU/CSU is similar to a modem, but connects a digital circuit rather than an analog circuit. The DSU provides connectivity for the digital signal and the CSU is used to strip off optional channels of the data line for voice. The data flow is then fed out to another port, commonly using a v.35 serial cable, which then attaches to the router. The router has a LAN connection, such as an RJ-45 port, to connect to the LAN. Routers are usually programmable so that certain types of data packets can be blocked from passing through the router. This blocking function is typically used for security, which is discussed in more detail in Chapter 10.

Routers use flat lookup tables stored in RAM to make forwarding decisions. These tables are either static or dynamic. Static routing requires the network administrator to physically calculate the routes between segments and enter these addresses into the router's databases. Static routing is only recommended for small networks with only one or two routers.

Dynamic routing uses special routing protocols that let routers exchange data with each other. The two most common routing protocols are *Routing Information Protocol*, or *RIP*, and *Open Shortest Path First*, or OSPF. RIP performs route discovery based on *hops,* or the number of routers that must be crossed to reach various segments. OSPF bases its routing calculations on the available bandwidth instead of hops. These protocols exchange their tables with other adjacent routers so that each router on the network will know how to get a data packet from any one point to another. Based on the routing tables, any router on the network should be able to direct a packet either to the desired segment (if that segment is attached to the router) or onto another router which will forward the packet based on its routing tables.

Even with this table exchange, there are many possibilities that can occur that would keep a router from knowing which router to send data to. Therefore, a concept called the *default route* is used. When a packet is received with a destination address that the local router does not have in its routing tables, it simply passes the packet on to its default route and lets that router deal with the problem. Many implementations of the TCP/IP protocol suite use the term *default gateway*, which is synonymous with default route. When designing a routed network, it is important that special attention be paid to the default routes of each router. A data packet will typically be passed on by a maximum of 16 routers (called a *hop*) before the packet is considered undeliverable and is discarded.

When a client workstation is configured for IP, a default gateway address is usually defined within the TCP/IP properties. When the workstation needs to send data beyond its local network, the data flows to this default gateway (the router) and lets the router handle the process of finding the destination location. This is typical on a LAN on which Internet access is required. Since Internet addresses are always outside of the private LAN, a router is used to pass the data to the Internet systems. In this scenario, the router has a local IP address (a private address for the LAN) and a public address connected to the Internet.

Follow the steps of how routers fit together to provide Internet access to the network by examining the design in Figure 9-6.

1. The browser on PC (A) sends a request to display the home page at www.IDGBooks.com, which has an IP address of 38.170.216.15.

2. Because this is not the local area network address (192.168.1.*x*) the request is sent to the default gateway defined for this PC, which is the local port on the router with the IP address of 192.168.1.100.

3. The router doesn't have an entry in its routing table for the 38.*x.x.x* network, so it passes the data on to its default gateway, which is the serial port at IP address 209.196.101.1.

4. The ISP's router doesn't have an entry for the 38.*x.x.x* network either, so it sends the data on to its default gateway at IP address 10.1.5.2.

5. At this point, the ISP's routers are able to pass the data through the Internet to the appropriate router with a connection to the Web server at IDGBooks to complete the path.

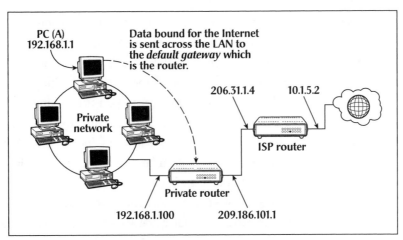

FIGURE 9-6 Routing Internet requests from private network

Network Gateways

When services from two different systems are required, such as connecting an IP network with a non-IP network, a *gateway* device is necessary. Gateways are also used when two different applications need to share information. For example,

Microsoft's Exchange message server and Novell's GroupWise system are not compatible in their default configurations. However, a PC with software that understands both applications can be connected between the two systems to act as a *gateway*. This way, the PC becomes an *application gateway* that allows users of either message system to exchange messages with each other.

NETWORK OPERATING SYSTEMS

Although hardware is the highway that provides the path for data to flow, the network software is just as important if any of the hardware is to be useful. At the heart of the network is the *Network Operating System,* or NOS. The NOS provides the services necessary to share files, printers, and other peripherals and supplies the necessary security components to keep the data safe. There are two types of Network Operating Systems: peer-to-peer, and client/server.

Peer-to-Peer Networks

A peer-to-peer network consists of two or more "equal" computers. Any PC on a peer-to-peer network can share its resources (disk space, printers, modems, and so on) with other computers on the network, and may likewise request resources from any other connected PC. All of the Microsoft Windows products since Windows for Workgroups have offered peer-to-peer networking functions (such as sharing files and printers), while other NOS-specific products like LANtastic are more robust and offer more network-like features, including slightly better security policies and the ability to handle a larger number of users. Peer-to-peer networks are fine for small numbers of PCs, when you only need basic file and print sharing, and security is not a major issue. The performance of most of these NOSs is acceptable in most cases. One major drawback to a peer-to-peer network is that the computers that have resources to share must be powered on to be accessed. This is often more than a mere inconvenience.

Client/Server Networks

The client/server model uses one or more dedicated computers (the *servers*) which provide all network functions to end-user computers (the *clients*). This type of network is very scalable from two to thousands of users. The servers can perform very advanced authentication for security purposes, track file usage and changes, provide centralized, automated backups of critical data, and overall perform better than peer-to-peer systems. Generally, businesses invest heavily in server hardware and less on desktop systems to leverage the benefits of the client/server environment.

There are many NOS products on the market, but the three most common include

- UNIX
- Microsoft Windows NT
- Novell NetWare

UNIX

There are many flavors of UNIX by a number of different vendors, as well as many versions of Linux, which is a freeware derivative of UNIX. For the most part, UNIX and Linux are quite different from the Microsoft and Novell platforms that are both based more on traditional DOS concepts. UNIX is predominately a character-based system (although a graphical interface called X Window is popular) and typically runs over serial connections to dumb terminals. The strength of UNIX is its portability across multiple vendor hardware platforms, vendor independent networking, and the strength of its application-programming interface. Most of these NOSs are written in C with only a very small amount written in assembly language. This makes it relatively easy for a computer vendor to get UNIX and Linux running on many different systems.

Vendor-independent networking allows users to easily network multiple UNIX systems from many different vendors. An excellent reference for UNIX fundamentals can be found at `http://www.ugu.com/`.

Microsoft Windows NT

Windows NT is Microsoft's high-end, 32-bit NOS. In the past few years it has become very popular and provides an easy software development platform for programmers to write for. NT offers file and print sharing, and because of its multi-threading architecture it is well suited as an application server. For example, a company with heavy database needs might deploy an NT server specifically to offer database services, with other servers providing file and print services. Native NT also offers cost-effective Internet-related services like Web publishing and e-mail. Prior to NT, most of these Internet services were done with more expensive UNIX systems.

Windows NT is sold in two flavors: Workstation and Server. These are nearly identical in most cases. The Workstation version is intended for high-end client users, and the server provides multiuser server services. The current version of NT is based on a *Domain* concept. In this environment, clients belong to a *Domain,* or *specified group* of network users centered around a main server called a *Primary Domain Controller, or PDC,* which provides the authentication of users within the group. Multiple domains may exist within an NT network, but unless users are specifically defined in multiple domains, they are unable to access domains outside of their primary group. This method allows for a single network topology to consist of many smaller groups of LANs, each managed by a different network administrator, or if properly configured, by a single administrator.

Novell NetWare

NetWare is the grandaddy of PC-based NOSs. Novell created NetWare in the 1980s and dominated the market until recently when NT began to gain in popularity. NetWare's base service has always been file and print sharing, and a very robust security model.

Until the release of NetWare version 5.0, NetWare's native protocol was IPX, which is extremely well suited for LANs, but not as efficient as IP is for WANs and Internet access. Many Internet-related services found in Windows NT were added to NetWare starting with Version 4. Version 5 continued in this direction by adding support for true IP as the core protocol. In addition, Novell developed a directory service unparalleled in the industry today. *Novell Directory Services*, or NDS, gives NetWare the ability to manage and maintain any network object (hardware, software, or users for example) quickly and easily. It is also the foundation for providing users their own "Network Persona" so that no matter where they enter the network, all of their personal settings are available to them.

NDS is a distributed database, based on the international X.500 standard, that stores information about hardware and software resources available within a given network. It provides network users and administrators global access to all network resources through a single login and a single point of network administration. All network resources are represented as objects that are maintained in a hierarchical directory tree. Unlike the domain concept, in a directory service model users are part of the whole network (enterprise) and obtain access to any service or resource in the network simply by having rights granted to them by an administrator. The directory simplifies administration and increases security by creating a single point of login and administration for the entire network no matter how large or dispersed it may be. Currently, this is the single biggest advantage of NetWare over other NOSs.

INTERNET BANDWIDTH TECHNOLOGIES

Most businesses require a dedicated high-speed connection to the Internet, but choosing the best service is often difficult. Most of the time, the choice is based on the perceived bandwidth requirements, and cost. Identifying bandwidth needs is the difficult part. Many businesses look at the available options, then purchase the fastest connection type they can afford. Although this is pretty reasonable, a company's assumptions regarding Internet use may not be as accurate as they appear.

When looking at the various bandwidth options, it is critically important to analyze what Internet services will be used, and to what extent. For basic Web browsing and light e-mail, slower connection speeds, such as 56Kbps, are acceptable. In businesses that need to transfer large files between sites, faster connection technologies are easier to cost justify. How a business comes to this determination will vary from company to company, but an extremely inaccurate estimate can be costly. The hardware requirements for dedicated connections can be rather expensive, so a careful and thought-out process needs to be conducted prior to making a commitment to one technology over another.

In this section, you'll look at the currently available dedicated connection technologies to understand exactly what your options are. I stress that these are *currently available* because there are numerous new technology that can potentially make any of today's standards obsolete almost overnight. Although I've discussed some of these technologies briefly already, understanding them is an important part of most Internet careers, and they will be covered at some length on the i-Net+ exam.

T-Carrier Technology

The T-carrier technology is a digital transmission service from a common carrier introduced by AT&T in 1983 as a voice service. With the proliferation in Internet demand, T services have grown steadily since the mid-1990s. T1 and T3 lines are widely used to create point-to-point private data networks as well as dedicated connections to the ISP for Internet services. T-carrier lines use four wire cables. One pair is used to transmit; the other to receive.

The cost of the lines is generally based on the length of the circuit. Thus, it is the customer's responsibility to utilize the lines efficiently. Multiple lower-speed channels can be combined, or *multiplexed* onto a T-carrier line and demultiplexed (split back out) at the other end. Some multiplexors can analyze the traffic load and vary channel speeds for optimum transmission.

T1/E1

The T1 classification is very common for medium-sized businesses. Larger companies may even utilize multiple T1 lines for different uses, such as voice on one line, and data on another. T1s transmit data at 1.544Mbps point-to-point dedicated. This is a digital circuit provided by the telephone companies. The monthly cost is typically based on distance. T1 lines are widely used for private networks as well as interconnections between an organization's Private Branch eXchange, or PBX, or LAN and the telephone company.

A T1 line uses two wire pairs (one for transmit, one for receive) and *time division multiplexing* (TDM) to interleave 2464Kbps voice or data channels. The standard T1 frame is 193 bits long, which holds (24) 8-bit voice samples and one synchronization bit with 8,000 frames transmitted per second. T1 is not restricted to digital voice or to 64Kbps data streams. Channels may be combined and the total 1.544Mbps capacity can be broken up with DSU/CSUs as required.

The E1 line is the European counterpart that transmits data at 2.048Mbps.

T3/E3

When multiple T1s are insufficient to provide the bandwidth required, the next step is a T3 connection, which transmits data at 44.736Mbps point-to-point. A T3 line provides (672) 64Kbps voice or data channels. T3 channels are widely used on the Internet by ISPs and corporations whose primary business is derived from Internet services.

The E3 line is the European counterpart that transmits data at 34.368Mbps.

Frame relay

When analyzing bandwidth usage, one factor that is often overlooked is the *type* of traffic sent across the link. With T-carrier technology, a company has the full use of the "pipe" at all times. However, this also means that they are paying a fixed amount whether they are using 10% or 100% of that line. Looking closely at Internet traffic, it is rare that the whole connection will be fully utilized all of the time. More often, the traffic will be *bursty*. At any given time, a small amount of bandwidth is required (for example, when users are just browsing the Web). However, as people send e-mails with documents attached, or programs are sent through the FTP server, momentary use of the bandwidth will spike higher than average. To accommodate this type of use and maximize the efficiency and costs of the high-speed connection, frame relay was created.

Frame relay refers to the technique of passing *frames*, or blocks, of information across a digital network using a connection number applied to each frame. This number distinguishes individual connections. At the edges of the network, this number identifies the source and destination. Routing is controlled on an end-to-end basis by the network protocol, such as the TCP/IP protocol suite.

Four important features characterize frame relay:

o High transmission speeds

o Low network delay

o High connectivity

o Efficient bandwidth use

Frame relay is especially well designed for networks that use packet-oriented technologies, like TCP/IP. It is specifically designed to address the problem of variable burst sizes and unpredictable traffic patterns. One method of making frame relay as efficient as possible is to eliminate as much error checking of the data as possible. Frame relay, therefore, depends on the end-to-end protocols to check data validity. Good frames will traverse the connection very quickly and bad frames are simply dropped. The network protocol is in charge of identifying that frames are missing, and requesting a retransmission of the missing data. Since most physical connections are now made with fiber optic technologies, the number of bad frames that need retransmitting is well within the acceptable performance range.

An important factor when selecting a frame relay service is to understand the *Committed Information Rate*, or CIR, and the *Committed Burst Rate*, or CBR. To fully understand these, let's use an analogy of driving on a modern highway. Imagine a highway system that permits you to travel 60 miles during a one-hour period. In fact, the rules of the road stipulate that you're guaranteed a distance of 60 miles in any one-hour period, but no more. If you exceed the 60-mile guaranteed distance, you are ticketed. Now suppose your car will travel at 0 or 90 miles per hour. To travel the 60 miles in 60 minutes you must stand still for 20 minutes and drive 90mph for 40 minutes. If you're ticketed for speeding, rather than going to court to pay a fine, you're allowed to continue on to your destination. However, if there is a traffic jam along the way, your car is forced off the highway into the ditch.

In frame relay, the guaranteed rate of 60 miles per hour corresponds to the *Committed Information Rate*, or the rate in bits per second the network agrees to transfer your data. The speed at which the car actually travels, 90mph in our analogy, corresponds to the rate of the physical connection between the user equipment and the network. The total 60 miles corresponds to the *Committed Burst Size*, or the maximum number of bits the network agrees to transfer during any measurement interval, or one hour in our analogy.

The next problem we face is what happens in the event of a traffic jam. Frame relay uses a process called *rate enforcement*, which states that frames in excess of the CIR will be carried only if bandwidth is available; otherwise the data will be discarded.

When selecting a frame relay service, therefore, it is important to understand what the CIR and CBI values are. If you exceed the CIR, the service provider may allow the additional traffic but impose steep per-bit penalty charges.

X.25

The X.25 protocol allows remote devices to communicate with each other across high-speed digital links without the expense of individual leased lines. Packet Switching is a technique whereby the network routes individual packets of data between different destinations based on addressing within each packet.

X.25 was the first international standard for packet switching networks. It was developed in the early 1970s and was designed to become a worldwide public data network similar to the global telephone system for voice. X.25 provides a connection-oriented technology for transmission over highly error-prone facilities, which were more common when it was first introduced. Error checking is performed at each node, which can slow overall throughput and renders X.25 incapable of handling real-time voice and video.

Since the physical connections throughout most parts of the world have increased reliability of digital communications, X.25 networks have mostly dropped from favor and have been replaced with frame relay technology instead.

ATM

Asynchronous Transfer Mode, or ATM, is a high-speed networking protocol that enables simultaneous transmission of voice, data, and real-time video/multimedia traffic. It offers scalability to accommodate future demand for advanced applications, quality of service (QoS) to guarantee efficient transmission of delay sensitive traffic, and flexibility to connect multiple devices, regardless of the application. ATM supports speeds ranging from 2.5Mbps to 622Mbps and ultimately gigabit speeds. And it can be used in both high-speed LAN and WAN environments.

ATM is based on a 53-byte data cell with a 5-byte header and a 48-byte data field, also called the *payload*. The anatomy of the payload depends on the application data being transmitted, but the structure of the cell header remains constant to ensure quick data transmission and the necessary level of QoS from the ATM network.

This fixed-length data cell was chosen to optimize the latency of data, video, and voice transmission, so the delays inherent to one type of traffic won't affect the others. ATM is a connection-oriented networking scheme that relies on *switched virtual circuits*, or SVCs. In contrast with dedicated, point-to-point links, SVCs are created on the fly through ATM switches, adapters, and other network hardware. These circuits remain active only as long as data is being transmitted.

To date, local and wide area communications have remained logically separate. On the LAN, bandwidth is free and connectivity is limited only by hardware and implementation cost. The LAN has carried data only. In the WAN, bandwidth has been the overriding cost, and such delay-sensitive traffic as voice has remained separate from data. New applications and the economics of supporting them, however, are forcing these conventions to change.

The Internet is the first source of multimedia to the desktop and immediately breaks the rules. Such Internet applications as voice and real-time video require better, more predictable LAN and WAN performance. In addition, the Internet also requires that the WAN recognize the traffic in the LAN stream, thereby driving LAN/WAN integration. ATM has emerged as one of the technologies for integrating LANs and WANs. ATM can support any traffic type in separate or mixed streams, delay-sensitive traffic, and no delay-sensitive traffic. Although ATM potentially offers enormous benefits, implementing ATM is often costly and usually requires assistance from the ATM vendors.

DSL

Digital Subscriber Line, or DSL, is a technology for bringing high-speed band-width to homes and small businesses over ordinary copper telephone lines. There are many forms of DSL so the general technology is often described as xDSL. Like more costly "always-on" services, DSL enables continuous transmission of text, motion video, and audio. Typically, individual connections will provide from 256Kbps to 512Kbps, although theoretical limits exceed 8Mbps. A DSL line can carry both data and voice signals with the data part of the line continuously con-nected. DSL installations began in 1998 and will continue at a greatly increased pace during 1999 in a number of communities in the United States and elsewhere. Compaq, Intel, and Microsoft, working with telephone companies, have developed a standard and easier-to-install form of *Asymmetric Digital Subscriber Line*, or ADSL, called G.Lite that is expected to accelerate deployment. Within a few years, DSL is expected to replace many other forms of dedicated and dial-up connections in many areas and to compete with cable modems in bringing multimedia and 3-D graphics to homes and small businesses.

Traditional phone service (sometimes called "Plain Old Telephone Service" or POTS) was created to exchange voice information transmitted as an analog signal. For normal dial-up connections, the telephone company filters information that arrives in as digital data, puts it into analog form for your telephone line, and requires your modem to change it back into digital. In other words, the analog transmission between your home or business and the phone company is a band-width bottleneck.

The Digital Subscriber Line technology assumes digital data does not need to be changed into analog form and back. Digital data is transmitted to your computer directly as digital data and this allows the phone company to use a much wider bandwidth for transmitting it to you. The analog signal used for voice doesn't require the entire bandwidth available on the standard copper wire; therefore the digital signal can share the remaining area allowing the same line that provides voice to simultaneously provide the data stream.

Most DSL technologies require that a signal splitter be installed at a home or business, requiring the expense of a phone company visit and installation. However, it is possible to manage the splitting remotely from the central office. This is known as splitterless DSL, "DSL Lite," G.Lite, or Universal ADSL and has recently been made a standard. Most telephone companies now offer a discount to users if they elect to install the home/office equipment themselves. Normally, this simply requires connecting the telephone line just as you would a normal modem, with the wall line entering into the DSL modem on one port, and another line feeding the telephone handset. The DSL modem also has an RJ-45 Ethernet jack which can be connected directly to the NIC of a computer (using a CAT5 crossover cable) or into a hub or switch.

DSL modems follow the data rate multiples established by North American and European standards. In general, the maximum range for DSL without repeaters is 5.5 km (18,000 feet). As distance decreases toward the telephone company office, the data rate increases. Another factor is the gauge of the copper wire. Heavier 24-gauge wire carries the same data rate further than 26-gauge wire. If you live beyond the 5.5-kilometer range, DSL service may still be available if the local phone company has extended the local loop with optical fiber cable.

ISDN

Like DSL, *Integrated Services Digital Network*, or ISDN, is a set of standards for digital transmission over ordinary telephone copper wire. ISDN requires adapters at both ends of the transmission, so your ISP also needs an ISDN adapter. ISDN is generally available from your phone company in most urban areas in the United States and Europe. The term *integrated* refers to the fact that ISDN is capable of sending voice, video, and data signals across its connection.

There are two levels of ISDN service, the *Basic Rate Interface*, or BRI, which is intended for the home and small enterprise, and the *Primary Rate Interface*, or PRI, for larger users. Both rates include a number of B (bearer) channels and a D (delta) channel. The B channels carry data, voice, and other services. The D channel carries control and signaling information.

The Basic Rate Interface consists of two 64Kbps B channels and one 16Kbps D channel. Thus, a Basic Rate user can have up to 128Kbps service. The Primary Rate consists of 23 B channels and one 64Kpbs D channel in the United States or 30 B channels and 1 D channel in Europe.

Cable

A *cable modem* is a device that enables you to hook up your PC to a local cable TV line and receive data from 256Kbps to about 1.5Mbps. This data rate far exceeds that of the prevalent 56Kbps telephone modems or ISDN, and is about the same rate of DSL service. A cable modem can be added to or integrated with a set-top box that provides your TV set with channels for Internet access. In most cases, the cable modem hardware is furnished as part of the cable access service and is not purchased directly and installed by the subscriber.

A cable modem has two connections: one to the cable wall outlet and the other to a PC or to a set-top box for a TV set. Although a cable modem does modulate between analog and digital signals, it is a much more complex device than a telephone modem. It can be an external device or it can be integrated within a computer or set-top box. Typically, the cable modem attaches to a standard NIC card in the computer.

All of the cable modems attached to a cable TV company's coaxial cable line communicate with a *Cable Modem Termination System*, or CMTS, at the local cable TV company office. All cable modems can receive signals from and send them to only the CMTS, but not to other cable modems on the line. Some services have the upstream signals returned by telephone rather than cable, in which case the cable modem is known as a *telco-return* cable modem.

The actual bandwidth for Internet service over a cable TV line is up to 27Mbps on the download path to the subscriber with about 2.5Mbps of bandwidth for interactive responses in the other direction. However, since the local provider may not be connected to the Internet on a line faster than a T1, a more likely data rate is closer to 1.5Mpbs.

Table 9-2 is a handy chart to summarize the various connection methods I've discussed, what medium they use, and the most common situation the services would be found in.

TABLE 9-2 COMPARISON OF DIFFERENT CONNECTION TECHNOLOGIES

CARRIER TECHNOLOGY	SPEED	PHYSICAL MEDIUM	APPLICATION
Cable modem	256Kbps to 52Mbps	Coaxial cable in some systems, telephone used for upstream requests	Home, business, school access
Digital Subscriber Line (DSL)	256Kbps to 8Mbps	Twisted-pair (used as a digital, broadband medium)	Home, small business, and enterprise access using existing copper lines
E1	2.048Mbps	Twisted-pair, coaxial cable, or optical fiber	32-channel European equivalent of T1

CARRIER TECHNOLOGY	SPEED	PHYSICAL MEDIUM	APPLICATION
E2	8.448Mbps	Twisted-pair, coaxial cable, or optical fiber	Carries four multiplexed E1 signals
E3	34.368Mbps	Twisted-pair or optical fiber	Carries 16 EI signals
E4	139.264Mbps	Optical fiber	Carries 4 E3 channels, Up to 1,920 simultaneous voice conversations, Internet backbone
E5	565.148Mbps	Optical fiber	Carries 4 E4 channels, Up to 7,680 simultaneous voice conversations
Frame relay	56Kbps to 1.544Mbps	Twisted-pair or coaxial cable	Large company backbone for LANs to ISP, ISP to Internet infrastructure
ISDN	BRI: 64Kbps to 128Kbps	BRI: Twisted-pair	BRI: Faster home and small business access
	PRI: 23 (T1) or 30 (E1) assignable 64Kbps channels plus control channel; up to 1.544Mbps (T1) or 2.048Mbps (E1)	PRI: T1 or E1 line	PRI: Medium and large enterprise access
Regular telephone service (POTS)	Up to 56Kbps	Twisted-pair	Home and small business access
T1	1.544Mbps	Twisted-pair, coaxial cable, or optical fiber	Large company to ISP, ISP to Internet infrastructure
T2	6.312Mbps	Twisted-pair, coaxial cable, or optical fiber	Large company to ISP, ISP to Internet infrastructure
T3	44.736Mbps	Coaxial cable	ISP to Internet infrastructure, Smaller links within Internet infrastructure

EXAM PREPARATION SUMMARY

By the end of Chapter 9 you have most of the puzzle pieces necessary to connect a computer or private network to the Internet. I discussed the major hardware components, network operating systems, and took a detailed look at the popular connection technologies. Now let's review some of the highlights for this chapter to make sure you understand the material you just read:

- At the heart of the hardware components is the *Network Interface Card*, or NIC. Modern NICs use the PCI bus. Although the TCP/IP protocol uses unique IP address for each NIC, the actual routing of data is dependent on the *Media Access Control*, or MAC, address.

- The NIC is connected to some form of *multiplexor* on the network, usually a network *hub* or *switch*. The hub is a non-intelligent device that joins communication lines together in a star configuration.

- A network *switch* is similar in purpose to the hub, but has some intelligence built in. The switch is capable of basic routing of data packets between ports. While devices connected to a hub simply share the available bandwidth, the switch creates a dedicated path between devices at the full capacity of the bandwidth.

- To connect all the network devices together, special network cable is used. The two most common cable types are *Category 5* copper, and *fiber optic*. CAT5 is composed of eight wires twisted into pairs. The ends of CAT5 cable are terminated with plastic *Registered Jack-45*, or RJ-45, plugs.

- Fiber optic cable is made from extremely thin silicon dioxide. Fiber optic cable is capable of transmitting larger amounts of data over much greater distances than copper.

- When multiple networks need to be connected, two common connecting devices are the *bridge* and the *router*. Bridges are useful to help reduce network traffic caused by a growing number of network devices on a single segment. Bridges are also used to extend the overall length of a network segment.

- Routers, like bridges, help to reduce network congestion, but also offer intelligent routing capabilities beyond the scope of a bridge. Routers share information between other routers to determine the proper paths for data transmissions. The two most common routing protocols are *Router Information Protocol,* or RIP, which determines best routes based on the number of routers, or hops, between the source and destination, and *Open Shortest Path First,* or OSPF, which selects routes based on available band-width. When a destination is unknown to a router, the data is passed to the device defined by the *default route address* (also called the *default gateway*).

○ *Network gateways* are used as a connector between two different systems, such as an IP network to a non-IP network. *Application gateways* are used to connect different applications to share similar services.

○ At the heart of the network, the *Network Operating System,* or NOS, provides the services necessary to provide access security, share files and devices, and provides basic control over the connectivity of connected com-puters. There are two primary NOS technologies, peer-to-peer and client/server.

○ To connect networks, and specifically to connect a private network to the Internet, there are a number of connection technologies available. The process of selecting the proper service is based on required bandwidth, and affordability. The more bandwidth a technology provides, the most costly the solution.

○ *T-carrier lines* provide high-speed, point-to-point services from 1.55Mbps (T1) to 44.736Mbps (T3). The E1/E3 European counterparts provide 2.048Mbps and 34.368Mbps, respectively.

○ *Frame relay* is a packet switching technology developed to maximize the available bandwidth. Frame relay is best suited when average traffic is *bursty* — when traffic is normally minimal with peak times of large usage. Frame relay improves overall performance by eliminating error checking by the transmission protocol. Bad packets are forwarded across the connection with the good packets. Higher-level protocols on the end devices are responsible for detecting errors and arranging for retransmission of bad frames.

○ The *X.25* protocol is similar in concept to frame relay, but includes error detection within the transmission process. This additional process adds to the overhead of transferring data, which makes it less desirable when reliable WAN links are available and when real-time voice and video data is used.

- *Asynchronous Transfer Mode*, or ATM, is a highly sophisticated connection technology that is best suited in situations where a large amount of high-speed bandwidth is required. ATM supports speeds from 2.5Mbps to 622Mbps and provides guaranteed transmission of delay-sensitive traffic.

- *Digital Subscriber Line*, or DSL, is a technology for bringing high-speed bandwidth to homes and small businesses over ordinary copper telephone lines. Typical speeds for DSL connections range from 256Kbps to a theoretical limit around 8Mbps.

- *Integrated Services Digital Network*, or ISDN, like DSL, is a set of standards for digital transmission over ordinary telephone copper wire. ISDN is provided in two forms, *Basic Rate Interface*, or BRI, intended for the home and small business, and *Primary Rate Interface*, or PRI, for larger users. BRI speeds achieve 128Kbps by means of two 64Kbps channels and one 16Kbps channel for signaling.

- *Digital cable* is quickly becoming the high-speed alternative for home and small business users. Although cable speeds can reach rates as high as 27Mbps, most current cable companies throttle down the connections from 256Kbps to 512Kbps.

APPLYING WHAT YOU HAVE LEARNED

The following review questions give you an opportunity to test your knowledge of the information presented in this chapter. The answers to these assessment questions can be found in Appendix B. If you missed some, review those sections in this chapter before going further.

Instant Assessment Questions

1. The collection of the cable system and a common protocol is called the network

   A. Star configuration

   B. Bandwidth

   C. Topology

   D. Connectivity System

2. The PCI technology provides

    A. A connector for the network cable system

    B. Plug-and-play capability

    C. A "network ready" PC

    D. An Industry Standard Architecture

3. Routing takes place between

    A. Two cable systems connected by a hub

    B. Two MAC addresses

    C. Two IP Addresses

    D. A bridge and a hub

4. Category 5 cable consists of

    A. 4 wires

    B. UTP sheathing

    C. Standard telephone wires

    D. 4 wire pairs

5. Advantages of fiber optic cable include

    A. Protection from radiation and electrical pulses

    B. Longer distances capabilities with inexpensive repeaters

    C. Line taps are easily detectable

    D. Light weight

6. Network switches provide

    A. Faster speeds than network hubs

    B. The ability to connect more than 3 switches

    C. Dedicated bandwidth between 2 devices

    D. The ability to route data between 2 ports

7. Routers require _____ to be included in the data packet.

    A. Routing information

    B. MAC addresses

    C. A username and password

    D. A default route address

8. The Routing Information Protocol performs route discovery based on available bandwidth.

A. True

B. False

9. A CSU/DSU connecting a T1 line to a router is used to

A. Make the physical connection between the telco and the private network

B. Separate channels for voice and data

C. Maintain OSPF routing tables

D. Filter packets for security reasons

10. Common connection types from the slowest to fastest are

A. T1, Frame Relay, DSL, ISDN

B. ISDN, DSL, T1, E1

C. X.25, Frame Relay, E1, T1

D. T1, G.Lite, T2, E3

Network Troubleshooting and Security

About Chapter 10

Itt would be nice to work in an industry in which problems were rare and readily identifiable, but unfortunately, that isn't an option for those who work with computers. In fact, many problems go undetected until they become serious to the point of failure. It's not uncommon to completely misdiagnose a problem, fixing a symptom instead of the root cause. As more and more businesses move large parts of their commerce to the Internet, they cannot afford even short periods of downtime, so what might be a simple failure is "fixed" with a major hardware overhaul. Another challenge posed by Internet technology is security. Keeping private information secure without hindering Internet use by employees is not often easy to do. Economic concerns and the time required to maintain the security measures must be accounted for when creating security systems. With the whole world having a potential connection to the private network, knowing what methods hackers use, and the available tools to counter attack them, is extremely important. Although no method is guaranteed to prevent every possible network attack, there are a number of basic measures that should be implemented before going online.

In this chapter, I'll cover the systematic techniques of proper problem diagnostics and troubleshooting. I'll show you some common problems Internet sites face, and what tools are available to assist you in resolving them. Since security is such an important issue, I'll spend the second half of this chapter covering the common risks associated with an Internet site, how hackers attack systems, and what tools and techniques are at your disposal to counter these intruders. Although there is no magic formula that works in all cases, keeping an Internet site humming need not cost countless sleepless nights or break the corporate bank account.

TROUBLESHOOTING PROCEDURE

A big part of being an Internet professional is being able to diagnose and resolve problems. Since many problems are network related, it is important to learn some proper troubleshooting techniques. It's not uncommon to find that a fix for one problem has created other problems, and often, the symptoms do not clearly identify what is really happening. A systematic approach to solving problems can easily be divided into the following seven steps.

1. **Identify and document the problem.** This may seem self evident, but many times people spend more time trying to fix symptoms and never correct the actual cause of the problem. This step is also the starting point for the

problem resolution document. Often you will come up against problems that have been encountered before, either by yourself or someone else. If you keep good records, you will save countless hours of reinventing the wheel the next time. It is also important to remember that you may not be around the next time a problem arises. Knowing what you did may be invaluable to the next person working on the system.

2. **Isolate variables causing the problem.** Many problems can have multiple potential causes. The best way to find the exact cause of a problem is to eliminate items that are not part of the problem. For example, if you are experiencing a connection problem with your ISP over a dial-up connection, try dialing into a different service provider. Perhaps changing the modem to a different brand or speed may yield different results. Does the problem continue if a different phone line is used? If you have a possible hardware problem, you may want to remove any electrical devices near the PC. If you are troubleshooting a software error, find out whether it only occurs on this one PC, or is department wide. The main goal is to eliminate as many outside influences as possible.

3. **Duplicate the problem.** If a user complains that a specific program causes a general protection fault, have them run the program again and see if it reoccurs. If the program *always* fails at the same point, it is easier to diagnose. If the error is still intermittent, then other factors need to be examined. Perhaps there is a Windows DLL file that is causing the problem. Perhaps the problem only occurs on a particular Web page, or Web site. The more you can duplicate the problem, the more likely it will be that a pattern will form.

4. **Develop a plan to correct the problem.** Once you have identified the problem, outline it in as much detail as is practical and decide what steps you plan to take to correct the situation. If your plan requires exclusive use of the PC for any length of time, make sure the people who rely on that machine know in advance how long you estimate the repairs will take. If you need to take a server offline, be sure to provide advanced warning to those who use the services on that computer. If you'll be requiring outside assistance, make sure you document who they will be, and what role they will play. If you have contacted a vendor's software support line and they have instructed you to download and apply a patch, make sure you write down whom you talked to, where the patch came from, the name of the patch, and what, if any, installation instructions accompanied the software.

5. **Implement the corrective action.** Follow your implementation plan and document any deviations. If further assistance was required, note it in your problem resolution document.

6. **Test the results.** This is *extremely* important. Far too often, people fix a problem only to the point that the initial symptom is gone. It is very possible that other problems will occur as the result of fixing another.

7. **Document the findings.** Now that the problem is resolved, complete the documentation. If you've followed the suggested outline, most of your work will already be done. Make sure you fill in any items undone from previous steps. If your fix required additional software, and it's practical, include a diskette with the software implemented. If outside help was required, make sure you note any important telephone numbers, e-mail addresses, or Web sites. You should develop some form of filing system so that this and other problem resolution documents can easily be retrieved in the future. There are a number of electronic systems that can be used, or just a plain old file cabinet works wonders!

The point to all of this is really twofold. First you need to get at the root of the problem, and second you need to fully document the process from problem to resolution.

PROBLEMS WITH INTERNET CONNECTIVITY

As people's reliance on Internet services increases, ensuring uninterrupted connectivity becomes an increasingly critical issue. Many businesses consider e-mail as an equally important communications tool as the telephone. Additionally, Web services are the cornerstone of some company's entire commerce. As more companies harness the power of the Internet for daily business practices, connectivity problems become even more crucial. Even though many Internet career paths will not require in-depth knowledge of connectivity issues, understanding basic concepts of connectivity and performance problems will be a real asset to anyone involved with providing Internet expertise. In the next section, we'll look at many common problems that can negatively affect Internet access and performance and how to deal with these situations.

Diagnosing Slow Server and Network Performance

Many performance issues have their roots in physical problems. When cables, NICs, hubs, and other hardware components begin to fail, the results may not be readily obvious. For example, if a NIC begins to fail, it may start "dribbling" garbage on to the wire. Since the bits are not properly formed and do not contain a specified destination address, the network infrastructure will assume the information is a broadcast and will begin flooding the network with this bad data. This situation is commonly called a *broadcast storm*. Depending on the severity of the malfunction, the results can range from a simple degradation in network performance to a complete collapse of the LAN. This situation is much more common than most network administrators realize. Even a minor broadcast storm often degrades network performance noticeably, but not enough to cause serious data loss. Without a serious analysis of the problem, many people will upgrade other components of the network, which masks the problem, making it appear that the network is functioning normally again. For example, when overall performance drops, many vendors will suggest that the backbone isn't fast enough to support the current number of workstations. Their solution is to increase the network backbone speed from 10Mbps to 100Mbps. Once implemented, the perceivable difference is great. Data is now traversing the network 10 times faster than before. However, the erroneous broadcasts are also 10 times as fast, so the resulting increase in network speed may only be 3 or 4 times. Nevertheless, compared to the previous situation, the end user sees a faster network. The problem, however, still exists and will likely only get worse. Additionally, the cost of this "fix" may be thousands of dollars when all that was required was an inexpensive NIC.

Cables are notorious for causing performance problems too. A split in a wire, or the placement of a space heater near the cable lines can easily cause data to be corrupted resulting in excessive retransmission requests. When looking at the cable structure, take care to check for potential electrical devices near all cables. External interference is a common cause of network performance problems. Patch cables from the wall jack to a user's desk can also cause the overall length of the cable to exceed acceptable distances. Once again, the data on the network is negatively impacted. Many cable testing instruments are available on the market, or a specialist can be contracted as needed.

Software is another potential culprit in slow server performance. When symptoms arise, a detailed review of what software has been added, removed, or updated should be performed. Many software installation programs will copy their versions of common DLLs to the computer, possibly overwriting existing files. The new version may not function as well as it should, which might cause problems with the network's, or a server's performance.

If the results of your tests do not reveal hardware or software problems, the server's resources, specifically memory, should be checked. Network servers require much more memory than an average workstation. As new services are loaded on the server, or more people use the server, memory may become too limited to support the new requirements. All vendors of commercial network operating systems provide formulas to calculate the recommended amount of memory required to support the types of applications used, the amount of disk space, and number of user connections. If the server has less than the recommended amounts, more memory should be added and performance retested.

Disk fragmentation is another possible cause of slow server performance. As files are written to a hard disk, the operating system keeps track of the exact location where each part of a file resides. Since data is written and updated randomly, files eventually get *fragmented*, meaning that pieces of the whole file are scattered around the drive. Fragmentation can reach a point where assembling the pieces of each file takes so much processing time that performance suffers noticeably. Defragmentation utilities are available for most network operating systems and should be used on a scheduled basis to maintain peak disk performance.

E-Mail

E-mail servers can decrease in performance for a number of non-physical reasons unique to the process of managing e-mail. One common problem is the result of users sending and receiving large files as e-mail attachments. This problem increases with slower connection speeds. While attaching files to e-mail is a simple process, users should be instructed to use FTP when they need to transfer large files (greater than 1MB).

Other performance problems can be attributed to the number of SMTP threads the server is configured to create. As mail is sent or received, the server can, if not limited, create new processor threads. If the amount of mail is large enough, and the length of time messages take to transfer becomes extended, the server's ability to process normal server functions could be severely affected. Most e-mail server software allows you to configure the maximum number of processor threads it will create at any given time. To analyze this type of problem, you should review the server's activity logs daily. Each server platform has its own method of logging server activity so you'll need to see how they are tracked for the server in question.

Web Sites

One of the primary performance bottlenecks for a Web server is memory and cache. For Windows NT based servers, it is normally a good idea to control the *virtual memory* settings manually rather than letting Windows handle the task. Windows uses a dynamic algorithm to determine the best settings for the virtual memory swap file. This process can take several seconds during which time other processes are suspended. If the swap file size changes often (which typically happens), your Web server will show signs of slowness. Therefore, manually set the minimum and maximum virtual memory settings to one and a half to three times the amount of physical memory in the computer.

A RAM disk is another way to increase Windows NT Web server performance. A RAM disk is simply a method of using a small portion of the computer's memory to simulate a hard drive. Since retrieving data from RAM is much faster than the same process from a hard drive, a RAM disk can greatly increase performance for read-only files such as Perl libraries. Placing commonly used Web pages and graphics on a RAM disk will also boost the server's performance.

Speaking of graphic files, larger graphics will have a direct impact on server performance. Not only will your visitors get frustrated waiting for the graphic files to display, but your server will spend precious processing time pushing those files out. As we talked about in Chapter 7, graphic, video clips, and audio file should always be kept to the smallest sizes possible.

DIAGNOSTIC TOOLS FOR IDENTIFYING AND RESOLVING INTERNET PROBLEMS

Many other performance issues are related to problems within the TCP/IP protocol settings, such as the default gateway settings and DNS settings. The following section discusses the common tools used to identify and diagnose these problems.

IPConfig

The `ipconfig` utility will quickly display the current TCP/IP settings defined on your local PC. `Ipconfig.exe` is a DOS-based program. This is an especially useful utility to see exactly what IP settings were assigned to the PC from the DHCP server. The `ipconfig` utility not only returns your IP address but also the subnet mask, default gateway address, and DNS server addresses for all network cards in your computer. The following is a sample output of the `ipconfig` utility run from the DOS prompt on a Windows NT PC:

```
Windows NT IP Configuration
0 Ethernet adapter :
    IP Address. . . . . . . . . : 209.186.192.3
    Subnet Mask . . . . . . . . : 255.255.255.248
    Default Gateway . . . . . . : 209.186.192.6
```

The `ipconfig` utility can provide additional information by using optional command switches, and is used to release or renew IP configuration from a DHCP server. The optional switches supported by the Windows NT version of `ipconfig` are as follows:

```
ipconfig [/? | /all | /release [adapter] | /renew [adapter]]
```

- `/?` Display the help message.
- `/all` Display full configuration information.
- `/release` Release the IP address for the specified adapter.
- `/renew` Renew the IP address for the specified adapter.

If no adapter name is specified for the release or renew switches, the IP address for all adapters bound to TCP/IP will be used.

The following sample is output from the `ipconfig /all` command:

```
Windows NT IP Configuration
    Host Name . . . . . . . . .: user.certificationplus.com
    DNS Servers . . . . . . . : 219.186.191.1
                                214.142.80.10
                                219.186.191.1
    Node Type . . . . . . . . : Broadcast
```

```
        NetBIOS Scope ID. . . . . . :
        IP Routing Enabled. . . . . : Yes
        WINS Proxy Enabled. . . . . : No
        NetBIOS Resolution Uses DNS : No

Ethernet adapter N1001:
        Description . . . . . . . . : Compaq Ethernet NIC
        Physical Address. . . . . . : 08-50-8A-2C-62-E5
        DHCP Enabled. . . . . . . . : Yes
        IP Address. . . . . . . . . : 219.186.191.3
        Subnet Mask . . . . . . . . : 255.255.255.248
        Default Gateway . . . . . . : 219.186.191.26
```

This display provides quick access to many important IP settings that otherwise would require a number of steps to obtain. Most notably are the IP addresses of the network card, DNS servers, and default gateway, all of which are needed when testing connectivity with IP. In addition, this utility shows you the physical MAC address of the network card, the Internet Domain name, and your computer's name within that domain.

WINIPCFG

For Windows 95/98, Microsoft offers a graphical version of ipconfig called winipcfg.exe shown in figure 10-1. This utility is not installed on the desktop by default but can be found in the Windows directory. It has all the same functions as the DOS-based ipconfig.

Ping

Ping is probably the most used of the tools mentioned here. Ping was named for the sound a sonar detection device makes on military submarines. The purpose of the sonar is to send a signal at a potential target and listen for the "ping" sound it makes upon its return after successfully bouncing off the target. You can use ping to see if another IP device on the network is active. For example, go to a DOS prompt and type

```
PING xxx.xxx.xxx.xxx
```

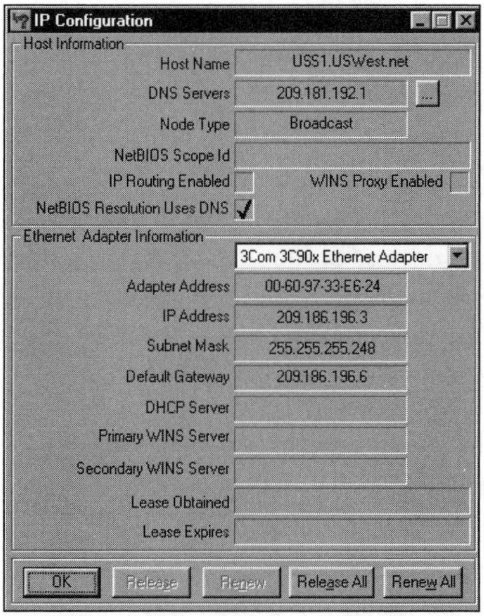

FIGURE 10-1 The Windows 95/98 WINIPCFG utility is a graphical replacement for ipconfig.

where the xxxs represent the IP address that you wish to test. If the device is active, and reachable from your PC, the utility will return a message. The specific message will vary depending on which version of the ping program you use. In addition to the confirmation message, the ping utility will return the number of milliseconds it took to send and receive the ping from the target device. If the ping was unsuccessful, you will see a message saying that the request timed out, or that the destination host was unreachable.

The following is an example of the output from the `ping.exe` program in Windows 98:

```
C:\ping 209.181.192.1

Pinging 209.181.192.1 with 32 bytes of data:
Reply from 209.181.192.1: bytes=32 time=24ms TTL=253
Reply from 209.181.192.1: bytes=32 time=26ms TTL=253
Reply from 209.181.192.1: bytes=32 time=25ms TTL=253
Reply from 209.181.192.1: bytes=32 time=25ms TTL=253
Ping statistics for 209.181.192.1:
```

```
Packets: Sent = 4, Received = 4, Lost = 0 (0% loss),
Approximate round trip times in milliseconds:
Minimum = 24ms, Maximum =  26ms, Average =  25ms
```

exam preparation pointer

The ping utility can also be used to test for properly configured TCP/IP on your local device by pinging the IP address 127.0.0.1 (This is the reserved "local device," or loopback IP address.) If your results are successful, then IP is properly functioning on this device. You can also use ping to test proper DNS configuration. If you ping a host name successfully, then DNS is resolving the IP address correctly.

Ping is also an excellent tool to verify that you are receiving proper name resolution. If you ping a host by name (such as `ping idgbooks.com`) you should get a successful result which indicates that name to IP resolution is functioning properly. If the ping utility returns the error message "unknown host," or "destination host unreachable," then name resolution is not being performed. You can now use ping or other tools to troubleshoot your name resolution problems.

Tracert

The trace routing utility, called tracert, goes a bit further than ping in that it also tells you how many *hops* away the target device is. Remember that a *hop* is a router that forwards the request on to another segment, so four hops means that the tracert packet had to be forwarded by four routers to reach its destination.

Tracert is especially useful in troubleshooting router problems. Because the results of a tracert show each router hop, you can quickly determine which router in a path has failed to forward the packet. Tracert also provides the response time, which helps determine how efficient a specific route is. If you notice that a particular router is slow, you can further diagnose why there is a hang up at that point.

For example, the following command shows how to use tracert from a command prompt, and a sample of what the results might be:

```
tracert 209.181.192.1

Tracing route to stcd.uswest.net [209.181.192.1] over a
maximum of 30 hops:
```

```
1    28 ms    29 ms    27 ms   219.182.191.254
2    29 ms    29 ms    28 ms   219.18.200.6
3    28 ms    29 ms    29 ms   stcd.smb.net [219.180.92.1]
```

```
Trace complete.
```

This output shows that the route to device 219.180.92.1 crossed two routers (219.182.191.254 and 219.18.200.6). Likewise, we can see that the times the packet took to reach these routers are all under 30 milliseconds each. Not too bad!

ARP

The *Address Resolution Protocol*, or ARP, is the fundamental method of resolving an IP address to a device's MAC (hardware) address that is required for host-to-host communications to occur. Once the IP and MAC address have been obtained, both of them are stored in the ARP cache to improve performance. This cache is cleared automatically after two minutes if the resolution process for this host has not reoccurred. The ARP resolution is a four-part process consisting of an ARP request and an ARP reply as outlined below.

1. When a device tries to communicate with another device on the network, the ARP process is initiated. ARP first looks in its ARP cache to see if an entry for the requested host exists. If found, the process is complete.

2. If no entry is found in the cache, the ARP protocol builds a broadcast packet that basically asks, "Who has this IP address, and what is your hardware address?" The packet consists of the source host's IP address and the IP address of the host to be located.

3. Because the packet is sent as a broadcast, all devices *on the local segment* will receive and process the request. Every device whose IP address does not match will simply ignore the packet, although every device must check it first.

4. When the target device receives the packet it sends an ARP request back directly to the sending device (since the IP address of the sending device is known, this response does not need to be broadcast to all devices). The returned packet includes the target's hardware address. Both the hardware and IP address are inserted into the ARP cache for possible future use, and communications between the two devices can now commence.

If the destination address is not on the local segment, the ARP packet addresses the destination to the default router. From there the router initiates the same form of ARP request across the remaining segments.

The ARP utility allows you to display and modify the IP-to-Physical address translation tables. In fact, the ARP utility lets you make permanent entries to frequently accessed hosts, preventing them from being flushed out of the cache. The format for using the ARP utility is as follows:

```
ARP     -s inet_addr eth_addr [if_addr]
ARP     -d inet_addr [if_addr]
ARP     -a [inet_addr] [-N if_addr]
```

- -a Displays current ARP entries by interrogating the current protocol data. If inet addr is specified, the IP and Physical addresses for only the specified computer are displayed. If more than one network interface uses ARP, entries for each ARP table are displayed.

- -g Same as -a. Windows 3.x and some other operating systems do not support the -a parameter.

- Inet_addr Specifies an Internet address.

- -N if_addr Displays the ARP entries for the network interface specified by if_addr.

- -d Deletes the host specified by Inet addr.

- -s Adds the host and associates the Internet address inet_addr with the Physical address eth addr. The Physical address is given as six hexadecimal bytes separated by hyphens. The entry is permanent.

- Eth_addr If_addr Specifies a physical address. If present, this specifies the Internet address of the interface whose address translation table should be modified. If not present, the first applicable interface will be used.

For example:

```
> arp -s 157.55.85.212    00-aa-00-62-c6-09
```

This command adds the IP address 157.55.85.212 for the network interface card with the MAC address of 00-aa-00-62-c6-09 to the ARP table as a static entry. The following command displays the current contents of the ARP table:

```
> arp -a
```

Netstat

The netstat utility is a useful tool for checking network configuration and activity. It is, in fact, a collection of several tools lumped together. By default netstat displays statistics for the primary network interface. However, statistics for all interfaces can be displayed by settting the -a command-line switch. Other netstat options display active or passive sockets on the system, which is useful for finding what ports on the network servers are activly listening for a connection. Many network hackers use a netstat utility to scan network ports looking for anything that might be useful for attacking the system. Another use for this utility is to see how your Internet connection is performing. Many real-time graphic-based netstat utilities are available to perform ongoing monitoring of your Internet connections. One such tool is NetStat Live, which you can download for free from `http://www.analogx.com/contents/download/network/nsl.htm`.

Command-line options for the netstat utility in Windows 95/98/NT:

```
netstat  [?] [-a] [-e] [-n] [-s] [-p proto] [-r] [interval]
```

- ? Displays all available command line options.

- -a Displays all connections and ports.

- -e Displays Ethernet statistics.

- -n Displays addresses and port numbers in numerical format

- -p *proto* Displays connections for the protocol specified by *proto*. *Proto* may be TCP, UDP, or IP. If used with the -s option the display will show protocol statistics.

- -r Displays the routing table.

- -s Displays per-protocol statistics. By default, statistics are shown for TCP, UDP, and IP.

- interval Redisplays the selected statistics pausing between each display the number of seconds defined by *interval*. If omitted, netstat will display the current configuration only once.

Network Analyzers

A network analyzer is necessary to really "see" what is happening with the communication flow of a network. Some analyzers are software-only solutions, while others are a combination of software running on special hardware platforms. Network analysis is not unlike the process a doctor uses to determine the cause of a health problem, or the process used during an annual checkup. The analyzer is placed on the network to listen to the flow of traffic and provide vital pinpoint information used to identify potential problems. There are many problems that simply can't be properly diagnosed without the use of a network analyzer. For example, if one PC cannot connect to a server, a network analyzer can be used to quickly answer the following questions:

- Can the PC communicate on the cable system at all? If not, the problem is internal to the PC.
- Can the server communicate on the cable system?
- Could the PC find a route to the server? If not, there is a cable, router, or bridge problem.
- Was the PC able to authenticate to the server? If not, there is probably a NOS problem.
- Did the PC make a proper request for services? If not, the client software is probably not configured properly.
- Did the server reply to the PC? If not, the server software is probably not configured properly.
- If the server did reply, was there a failure or denial of service?

As you can see, without the network analyzer, identifying all of these potential problems would at least take considerable time. A trained network analyst with the proper tool should be able to answer these questions and more in less than an hour. There are a number of network analyzers available on the market. For Novell NetWare-only systems, Novell's proprietary LANalyzer is a low-cost (under $500.00) software solution. For other platforms, or where any mix of NT, UNIX, and NetWare servers are used, a more robust system like Network Associates Sniffer is required. The Sniffer system comes in a software-only product for about $3,500.00 or a software/hardware combination for about $7,000.00.

BASIC SECURITY TOOLS AND METHODOLOGIES

There are many myths and misunderstandings around network security. Although *no* network can be made completely secure, there are many steps you can take to minimize your susceptibility to a network attack. The single most important fact to understand, however, is that *most* security breaches are internal, rather than external. In other words, if all of your efforts to secure a network are focused on attacks from the Internet, you are only protecting yourself from the least likely security hole on your system. Common sense should dictate basic network security methods with the local area network, such as enforcing sensible passwords and physically limiting access to network servers. Does this mean that you should forgo all external security measures? Of course not. But it is important to understand that the whole network needs securing, not just the connections between the internal and external links. That said, I am going to concentrate on the external security methods used to protect a local area network from unauthorized intrusions from the Internet.

Firewalls

The primary security component for keeping a private network secured is a *firewall*. Firewalls come in many different forms, from software that runs on a PC, to routers that provide programmable filtering of data, to proprietary hardware devices. All of these solutions attempt to perform the same basic function: keeping unwanted traffic from entering into the network while allowing traffic from the LAN to get out to the Internet. The firewall is placed between the Internet connection and the private network where all inbound and outbound traffic can be analyzed. Many people think of a firewall as a single technology, when in fact there are a number of methods that can be used to create a firewall.

Protocol screening

The most basic of firewall technologies is *protocol screening*. Figure 10-2 shows how this firewall works. Data is filtered, or blocked based on the type of protocol it is. For example, workstations on private network are allowed to send out HTTP and SMTP packets, but all attempts to connect to an FTP server outside the private network are blocked. In addition, incoming data for HTTP is allowed, but FTP and Telnet requests are blocked. Although this type of firewall is easy to set up, and inexpensive, it also presents the greatest risks. Since each computer is allowed direct access to the Internet, each must have a registered IP address that is not hidden from the outside world. The most common attack from the Internet is a process known as *IP spoofing*. Spoofing is the process of building IP datagrams with a source ID of an IP address from the private network. Properly constructed, the firewall can be tricked into believing that the incoming data originated as a request from the private network. Once this path has been established, a hacker can exploit any weaknesses on the internal servers.

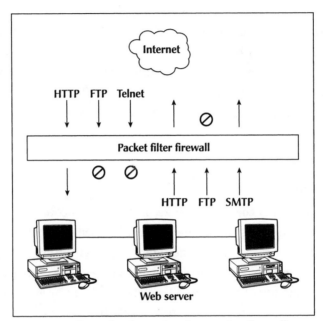

FIGURE 10-2 Example of a protocol screening firewall

Internet proxy

I talked about Internet proxy servers in Chapter 8. The proxy server acts an interpreter between the private IP network and the Internet. A proxy server can also add additional firewall security to the network. As seen in Figure 10-3, all of the internal IP addresses are hidden from the Internet making it more difficult for a hacker to use IP spoofing. Also, the proxy server normally hosts a company's Internet services, keeping sensitive data away from the outside connection. The proxy server, sometimes called a *multihomed* server because it has a "home" on two separate networks, can provide an additional security feature known as *Network Address Translation*, or NAT. NAT is the process of substituting the IP address on the private network with a valid IP address for the Internet. This way, all outbound IP traffic has the same registered IP address, further hiding the internal IP address structure.

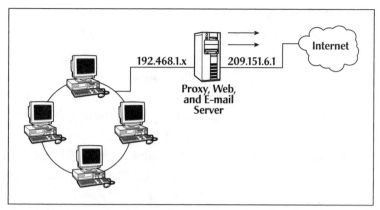

FIGURE 10-3 Example of a proxy server firewall performing Network Address Translation

Tri-homed proxy

Another method of decreasing the likelihood of an attack on internal Internet servers is to add another NIC in the proxy to create a *tri-homed proxy*. Shown in Figure 10-4, the Internet servers such as Web, e-mail, and FTP are placed on a separate subnet (192.168.1.x in the figure). This subnet is often referred to as the *demilitarized zone,* or DMZ.

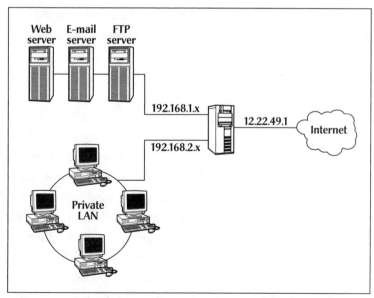

FIGURE 10-4 Example of a Tri-homed Proxy server with a demilitarized zone for Internet servers

Packet filtering

A more secure firewall technology is called *packet filtering*. In this scenario, the firewall software looks at a much wider scope of the datagram to determine if it is allowed to pass. This technology filters data based on different criteria, including service type, port numbers, interface (NIC), source, and destination address. Packet filters can permit access that generally falls outside the normal rules. For example, you may restrict all incoming HTTP access except those from a predetermined list of IP addresses. With this filter in place, you can deny the general Internet population access to your internal Web server while allowing access to on-the-road employees with assigned static IP addresses.

Packet filters normally do two things:

1. Permit packets that match a filter rule and deny others, while optionally specifying some exceptions

2. Deny packets that match a filter rule and permit others, while optionally specifying exceptions

In both cases, the firewall configuration is very precise. All services must be well documented so that the proper filters can be defined. Although this technology provides a stronger security environment, it tends to be more restrictive on the LAN user as well. Packet filtering does not concern itself with who you are on the network, only where you plan to go. In other words, having complete administrative rights to your network grants you no more rights around the firewall than anyone else.

Circuit-level gateways

Circuit-level gateways work in a fashion similar to NAT, but with a bit more flexibility. With NAT, IP translation is provided for any internal address. A circuit-level gateway, on the other hand, looks at more of the packet to determine whether or not it should be denied. A circuit-level gateway can filter based on IP address, or Domain Name, or in some cases, username. Username filtering is normally supported on networks where the NOS is based on a directory, such as Novell's NDS, or Microsoft's Active Directory. With directory-based network authentication, the circuit-level gateway ensures that your username, or other identifying information, is granted *before* a connection is allowed. This provides great flexibility to a network administrator and reduces the chance for unexpected results due to filter exceptions. The downside to circuit-level gateways however, is that special software must be installed at each workstation. Also, since the process requires additional processing to read more of the packet, there is a slight performance penalty to circuit-level gateways.

Access Control Lists

Access control lists forward or block network traffic based on criteria specified within the access lists. These criteria could be the source address of the traffic, the destination address of the traffic, the protocol type, or other information. Sophisticated users can evade or fool basic access lists because no authentication is required. If you do not configure access lists on your router, all packets passing through the router could be allowed onto all parts of your network.

For example, access lists can allow one host to access a part of your network, and prevent another host from accessing the same area. In Figure 10-5, PC (A) is allowed to access the accounting network while PC (B) is denied access.

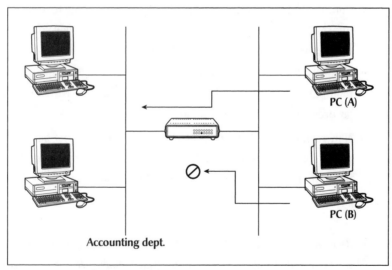

FIGURE 10-5 **Example of a router using Access Control Lists to control access to the accounting department**

Access lists should be configured for each network protocol configured on the router interfaces so that inbound traffic, outbound traffic, or both, are filtered on an interface. Access lists must be defined on a per-protocol basis. In other words, you should define access lists for every protocol enabled on an interface if you want to control traffic flow for that protocol.

Authentication: Certificates, Digital Signatures, and Non-Repudiation

The Internet is a public network and therefore susceptible to many security problems. This is especially true with Web-based commerce. Depending on the transaction or service, different levels of security are required. For example, the security requirements for someone trying to access product information are vastly different than the security requirements for someone placing a $100,000 purchase order. Web-enabled businesses must consider their specific business objectives and the importance of implementing various security measures.

The process of user authentication is critical. The identity of both the sender and receiver of data must be verified. For example, how does your bank know it is you trying to access your online account? How do you know you are really accessing your bank's Web site, and not an impostor? The following authentication issues must be addressed.

- **Confidentiality.** Unauthorized people must not be able to access sensitive information. For example, no one should be able to view your credit card number while it is being transmitted to a Web shopping site.

- **Integrity.** Data must not be altered or compromised by unauthorized manipulation. For example, no one should be able to turn a one million dollar order into a one billion dollar order.

- **Non-repudiation.** The sender of a transmission must not be able to deny (or repudiate) the transmission. For example, the person who authorized the ten million dollar purchase order must be unable to credibly deny placing the order.

Public key infrastructure, certificates, and digital signatures

There are a wide range of technologies that can address one or more of these three critical requirements, but a *Public Key Infrastructure* (PKI) is the only system that can address all of these requirements. As stated in earlier chapters, public key technology is a system that provides the basis for establishing and maintaining a trustworthy networking environment through the generation and distribution of keys and certificates. An individual or organization creates a pair of electronic *keys* and makes one key public for others to send them encrypted data. Both keys are required to unencrypt the data.

A *certificate* is an electronic identification issued and maintained by a Certificate Authority, or CA. A CA is a trusted third party similar to a passport office, or a Certified Public Accountant. Certificate authorities are responsible for issuing, revoking, renewing, and providing directories of digital certificates. Certificate authorities must follow rigorous procedures for authenticating the individuals and organizations to which they issue certificates. All digital certificates are "signed" with the certificate authority's private key to ensure authenticity. The certificate authority's public key is widely distributed.

To better understand the relationship between keys and certificates, look at this simple example:

In public key cryptography, if Alice wants to send a secret message to Bob, she must obtain a copy of his public key. Before doing so, however, she needs to make sure that the public key really belongs to Bob.

Certificates (also called Digital IDs) address this problem. A certificate is an electronic document that binds a public key to a particular individual or organization. Before issuing a certificate, a good CA will go though a series of authentication procedures to make sure that Bob is who he claims to be, and that the public key in the certificate really belongs to Bob. Bob's server ID will then contain the following information:

- The common name of Bob's organization (e.g. `www.bobco.com`)
- Additional identifying information (e.g. IP and physical address)
- Bob's public key
- Expiration date of the public key
- Name of the CA that issued the ID (such as VeriSign)
- A unique serial number

The certificate is then encrypted (signed) with the CA's private key. Therefore, if the end users trust the CA, and have the CA's public key, they can be ensured of the certificate's legitimacy.

The Secure Socket Layer technology

For Internet transactions, a special security function known as the *Secure Socket Layer* or SSL is widely used. SSL is a technology developed by Netscape and adopted by all vendors producing Web-related software. It negotiates and employs the essential functions of mutual authentication, data encryption, and data integrity for secure transactions.

The SSL protocol runs above TCP/IP and below higher-level protocols such as HTTP or IMAP. It uses TCP/IP on behalf of the higher-level protocols. In the process it allows an SSL-enabled server to authenticate itself to an SSL-enabled client, allows the client to authenticate itself to the server, and allows both machines to establish an encrypted connection.

exam preparation pointer

For the exam, you should know that Secure Socket Layer (SSL) 2.0 supports server authentication only; SSL 3.0 supports both client and server authentication.

SSL server authentication allows a user to confirm a server's identity. SSL-enabled client software uses public-key cryptography to check that a server's certificate and public ID are valid and have been issued by a certificate authority in the client's list of trusted CAs.

SSL client authentication allows a server to confirm a user's identity. Using the same techniques as those used for server authentication, SSL-enabled server software can check that a client's certificate and public ID are valid and have been issued by a certificate authority listed in the server's list of trusted CAs.

An encrypted SSL connection requires all information sent between a client and a server to be encrypted by the sending software and decrypted by the receiving software, thus providing a high degree of confidentiality. Confidentiality is important for both parties to any private transaction. In addition, all data sent over an encrypted SSL connection is protected with a mechanism for detecting tampering — that is, for automatically determining whether the data has been altered in transit.

exam preparation pointer

There are two accepted encryption standards. Global encryption standards are based on a 40-bit algorithm, and a 128-bit encryption standard which is restricted from export outside the United States. Recent changes in the United States now permit the export of 56-bit encryption. For the exam, it is important to know that strong encryption (128 bit) is not permitted for export.

SET (Secure Electronic Transactions)

The SET specification is an open technical standard for the commerce industry developed by Visa and MasterCard as a way to facilitate secure payment card transactions over the Internet. Digital certificates create a trust chain throughout the transaction, verifying cardholder and merchant validity, a process unparalleled by other Internet security solutions. Message data is encrypted using a randomly generated key that is further encrypted using the recipient's public key. This is referred to as the "digital envelope" of the message and is sent to the recipient with the encrypted message. The recipient decrypts the digital envelope using the original private key to unlock the original message.

Intrusion Detection and Auditing

I stated earlier in this chapter that no network can be made completely secure. No matter how sophisticated you get with firewalls, encryption, and other security measures, there is always a chance that someone will compromise your hard work and gain access to your network. A hacker can scan your computer looking for open ports. When the hacker finds an open port, he can attempt to connect to your computer via that port using a Telnet application or other specialized networking tools. From there, the hacker may be able to retrieve files, place files (including viruses) on your computer, or watch your Internet communications. All of this can be done without anything showing up on the screen.

Another common way hackers access computers is to send a *Trojan horse* application. Like the mythical gift from the Greeks to the residents of Troy, a Trojan horse is an application that looks innocuous and may even behave as expected, but has a virus or other malicious program lurking inside. Some Trojans allow a user to access your computer at any time you are on the Internet. One of the most common Trojan applications is called BackOrifice. Originally designed as a remote maintenance and administration tool for corporate networks, BackOrifice quickly became a tool for hackers to access computers and steal information.

One common misconception about hackers is that they are all teenagers sitting at a computer diligently trying to break into your system. In reality, most hacking is actually done by automated programs called "bots" (short for robot) or spiders. A bot is merely an automated script or program designed to systematically carry out scans and attacks. A spider is an automated program that can search areas of a network for a particular vulnerability. Therefore, detection is just as important as prevention.

To assist with the detection of unauthorized use of your network, there are many third-party utilities you can use. Most of these utilities run as a background service and monitor access in and out of the TCP/IP ports. Some of the more powerful utilities will automatically block suspicious inbound traffic and *backtrace* the connection. This backtrace feature is extremely useful to gather legal evidence against a potential intruder.

One of the finest detection utilities is the BlackICE suite of products from the Network ICE corporation. BlackICE Pro is specially designed for corporate networks and provides intrusion detection, identification, and protection on networked workstations and servers. With a powerful network-monitoring engine, BlackICE Pro can react instantly to any suspicious activity. When used with the ICEcap Management console, a comprehensive Intrusion Defense Network is formed to protect your extended enterprise. For home and small office users, the $39.95 version of BlackICE defender is well worth the cost. You can review these products at http://www.networkice.com.

Another excellent utility is Network Associates' CyberCop Scanner. This software-based solution examines computer systems and network devices for security vulnerabilities in NT and UNIX network environments. CyberCop scans workstations, servers, hubs, and switches, using a proprietary packet test to provide thorough perimeter audits of firewalls and routers. One of CyberCop's best features is its extensive reporting system that offers summaries, detail reports, and field resolution advice. CyberCop can be used as a stand-alone application, or as part of a collection of integrated security tools developed to provide network risk assessment scanning, intrusion monitoring, decoy services, and custom audit research tools. Network Associates can be found at http://www.nai.com.

One of the original detection utility developers is Axent (http://www.axent.com). Axent has developed a large number of products to cover everything from single PCs to large WANS. One of their most popular products, Intruder Alert, monitors systems and networks in real time to detect security breaches and suspicious activities, responding automatically according to an established security policy. Intruder Alert works across the entire enterprise including LANs, WANs, intranets, and the Internet.

IDENTIFYING SUSPICIOUS ACTIVITIES

There are many ways to detect an intrusion. Even with third-party utilities, complete detection involves the constant review of server logs and audit trails.

Unfortunately, most of the data in these logs are caused by normal system operations. Experience and familiarity with a network is required to screen out the authorized events so that real intrusions do not go undetected. Most business class server software applications provide some degree of activity logging and audit trail files. These logs should be reviewed on a weekly basis, or when suspicious activity occurs. Some things that might signal an intrusion are

o **Failed Logins.** Everyone occasionally errs when typing in a password, which results in failed logins. First thing in the morning and after lunch would be normal times for this to happen. A failed login at two in the morning might indicate someone trying to get in. Three failed logins on different accounts and on different hosts within fifteen minutes in the middle of the night would probably indicate a hacker attempting to gain access.

o **Increase or decrease in disk usage.** System administrators may notice that the average disk utilization has suddenly increased or decreased. This could also be an intruder adding or deleting files.

o **Logins from unknown IP addresses.** If you notice a pattern of failed or successful logins from unknown hosts, this could also be an intruder's mark. Generally, most intrusion detection is *management by exception*. This means looking for things that are out of the ordinary. The security administrator must be able to recognize these events and may have to piece the information together from various sources. Intrusion detection is very similar to a mystery novel.

DENIAL OF SERVICE ATTACKS

The Denial of Service (DoS) attack is aimed at devices and networks with exposure to the Internet. Its goal is to cripple a device or network so that external users no longer have access to your network resources. Without hacking password files or stealing sensitive data, a denial-of-service hacker simply fires up a program that will generate enough traffic to your site that it denies service to the site's legitimate users. DoS attacks are very common but they are not a joking matter. In the United States, they are a serious federal crime under the National Information Infrastructure Protection Act of 1996 with penalties that may include years of imprisonment. Many countries have similar laws. There are basically two types of DoS attacks.

1. **Operating system attacks**, which target bugs in specific operating systems and can be patched against defensively. It is imperative, therefore, to set up a system to monitor all security announcements for your particular network operating system. You can be assured that as soon as a vulnerability is discovered, there will be many hackers quickly working on ways to exploit it. When a security patch is made available, it should be applied to the network servers immediately.

2. **Networking attacks**, which exploit inherent limitations of networking and often cannot be patched or defended against. These are the type of attacks that we try to prevent by using a quality firewall. As weaknesses are detected in our security systems, we need to change or add new components to plug the hole.

Ping Floods

Two lethal attacks, the well-known Ping of Death and the newer Teardrop attack, exploit known bugs in TCP/IP implementations. The Ping of Death uses a ping system utility to create an IP packet that exceeds the maximum 65,536 bytes of data allowed by the IP specification. The oversize packet is then sent to an unsuspecting system. Systems may crash, hang, or reboot when they receive such a maliciously crafted packet. This attack is not new, and all OS vendors have fixes in place to handle the oversize packets.

The recently developed Teardrop attack exploits weaknesses in the reassembly of IP packet fragments. During its journey through the Internet, an IP packet may be broken up into smaller chunks. Each fragment looks like the original IP packet except that it contains an offset field that says, for instance, "This fragment is carrying bytes 600 through 800 of the original (nonfragmented) IP packet." The Teardrop program creates a series of IP fragments with overlapping offset fields. When these fragments are reassembled at the destination host, some systems will crash, hang, or reboot.

SYN Floods

Another well-known weakness in the TCP/IP specification leaves it open to a *SYNchronize-ACKnowledge,* or SYN attack. During the three-way handshake that precedes the conversation between two applications the first program initiates the session by sending a TCP synchronization (SYN) packet to the receiving application. The receiver sends back a TCP acknowledgment (SYN-ACK) packet and then the initiator responds with an ACK acknowledgment. After this handshake, the applications are set to send and receive data.

But a SYN attack floods a targeted system with a series of TCP SYN packets. Each packet causes the targeted system to issue a SYN-ACK response. While the targeted system waits for the ACK that follows the SYN-ACK, it queues up all outstanding SYN-ACK responses on what is known as a backlog queue. This backlog queue has a finite length that is usually quite small. Once the queue is full, the system will ignore all incoming SYN requests. SYN-ACKs are moved off the queue only when an ACK comes back or when an internal timer (which, by default is a relatively long interval) terminates the three-way handshake.

A SYN attack creates each SYN packet in the flood with a bad source IP address, which under routine procedure identifies the original packet. All responses are sent to the source IP address. But a bad source IP address either does not actually exist or is down; therefore the ACK that should follow a SYN-ACK response will never come back. This creates a backlog queue that's always full, making it nearly impossible for legitimate TCP SYN requests to get into the system.

One way to minimize the possibility of a SYN attack is to configure the firewall to filter out all incoming packets with known bad source IP addresses. Packets that come into your system with source IP addresses that identify them as generated from your internal system are obviously bad. Other IP addresses that should be filtered are 10.0.0.0 to 10.255.255.255, 127.0.0.0 to 127.255.255.255, 172.16.0.0 to 172.31.255.255, and 192.168.0.0 to 192.168.255.255.

Mail Flooding

The same concept as a ping or SYN attack can be mounted against an e-mail server to prevent legitimate users from sending or receiving mail. The process is the same, where the attacker will send a continuous flood of e-mail directly to the server, effectively "clogging" the server's process.

Often times, people will look for mail servers that don't require authentication. Once found, the intruder can use the server to forward *spam* mail. Spam is a word coined to describe multiple copies of the same message e-mailed to large numbers of newsgroups or users on the Internet. People spam the Internet to advertise products as well as to broadcast some political or social commentary. To avoid detection, spammers send their mail through a server that doesn't authenticate the sender, effectively hiding the originator's source address. Whenever you have an e-mail server with the SMTP protocol, all inbound servers should follow a standard authentication process to avoid these types of problems.

ACCESS SECURITY FEATURES FOR INTERNET SERVERS

Even with firewalls, security patches, and other high-level safety measures, the basic security features of the network need to be implemented and enforced. If a hacker is successful in bypassing the external security layer, you might still be able to thwart the loss of valuable data by utilizing the NOS itself. The two features mentioned next are common options for all client/server network operating systems although their exact implementation may differ.

User Names and Passwords

Each person on a network requires a unique identification, or username, but not all NOSs require these usernames to have passwords associated with them. Whenever a network is connected to the Internet, it is imperative that a password policy be implemented.

Password authentication is only as useful as your ability to keep passwords private. If passwords are too easy to guess, they don't provide the intended security. If passwords are too difficult for the authorized users to remember, people will begin writing them down, or take other methods that will compromise the privacy of the passwords. For example, many years ago, I started a new job as a network administrator. I asked my new employer for the supervisor password (the account that had full access to the LAN) but the previous administrator had failed to let anyone know what the password was. However, it took less than 30 seconds to properly log into the network. I simply looked under the keyboard and sure enough, there it was, taped to the bottom. This is the number one place people will "hide" their password in case they forget it.

There are no "rules" governing passwords, but there are some generally accepted standards. When defining a security policy, examine the use and benefits of the following guidelines and implement those that make the most sense for your installation.

- **Mix alpha and numeric characters.** It is much more difficult to guess a person's password if it contains both letters and numbers. A hacker often tries to guess passwords by starting out with the names of children, pets, or other close relatives of valid network users. Similarly, birth dates, anniversaries, and telephone numbers are common guesses. By mixing numbers and letters, passwords become many times more secure. For example, guessing a person's password as Jimmy is much easier than guessing Jim99my.

- **Mix upper and lower case letters.** For the same reason you mix numbers and letters, character case can increase security. For example, you might use JiMmy or jImmY. Before relying on this method alone, be sure that the NOS you are using is case sensitive so it makes a distinction between J and j.

- **Minimum length.** As a rule, passwords should be no less than four characters long. There are a number of *brute force* password cracking programs easily accessible from the Internet. These programs systematically try combinations of letters hoping to find the right combination for the password. The more characters in the password, the longer it takes a program like this to find a valid combination. Three or fewer characters can normally be decoded in a relatively short amount of time — in some cases, under two minutes.

- **Maximum length.** Passwords that are longer than eight characters offer minimal additional security, and often make the password difficult to remember. When users can't remember their passwords, they begin to write them down where others can find them.

- **Force periodic changes.** As inconvenient as it might feel to some people, passwords should be changed at least quarterly. This helps enforce the idea that passwords are important, and it may thwart a hacker who has already gained access. Suppose someone does learn a user's password and it goes undetected. At the very least, this hole will be plugged sometime in the next few months.

○ **Disallow the repetitive use of the same password.** If you require users to change their passwords every three months, but they simply switch back and forth between two passwords, security might be compromised. Most operating systems have the ability to enforce the frequency of password changes, and how often passwords can be reused. If you set a policy that requires changes four times a year, then repetition should be allowed no more than every third change.

○ **Where possible, limit the need for passwords to one.** If people need to remember multiple passwords the likelihood that they will create a written copy increases. For example, if you have both NetWare and NT on your LAN, create users on both systems with identical passwords. This way, the NOS that authenticates the user passes the username and password on to the other operating system. If these are the same on both servers, the person will only need to login once for both systems.

○ **Force accounts to automatically expire.** If the operating system provides for it, make sure that all user accounts expire within a few days of the required password change if the password has not been updated. For example, suppose an employee leaves the company and his or her computer account isn't purged. This person can potentially enter the system later, and even if they need to change their password (due to the force password change option) they are still able to access their old account. If the account automatically expires after the grace period of the last forced change date, only an administrator will be able to access this account.

File-Level Security

One primary reason for not using peer-to-peer networks is that they lack the ability to provide secure access to the file system. A good client/server operating system will have mechanisms to add access control to individual files and directories on the servers. Each NOS has its own method of securing files and the level at which files can be secured, but when possible, all users should be restricted to *read-only* access to most files. For personal files stored on the server, and where absolutely necessary to perform their jobs, write and delete access should be granted to controlled sets of files or directories. A regular review of user access rights to the file system should be implemented to see if unauthorized access is taking place.

USING ANTIVIRUS SOFTWARE

A computer *virus* is defined as a program that causes damage to computer files and has the ability to replicate itself from computer to computer. No doubt, viruses are nasty beasts and we're not going to eliminate these things any time soon. According to the Security Research Alliance, more than 40,000 viruses exist today. While it's impossible to prevent all viruses from infecting your networks, you can minimize their impact by taking steps to limit their access to your computers, and by being prepared to deal with them should the need arise. There are many myths about computer viruses, and many truths, but to completely ignore the possibility that one can infect the network is irresponsible. The cost of protecting the network is minimal when compared to the cost of repairing their damage after the fact.

The first step is to choose an antivirus program. There are literally hundreds of packages you can choose from, and they all perform basically the same tasks. The focus is on scanning computer programs as they are saved on disk, and optionally when they are accessed. If a program appears to have been tampered with, the virus software usually issues a warning to the network administrator.

Where to Deploy the Scanning

The two primary issues that need to be addressed before implementing a protection program are deciding where to place the scanning process, and how the virus detection updates will be obtained and applied.

In a network environment, two main areas can be reviewed for antivirus protection: just the server, or the server and the workstations. Due to cost and administrative issues, many companies implement the antivirus protection only at the file server level. This reduces administrative time, and protects the critical data. With this arrangement, you can be assured that a virus will not enter the server from a workstation, nor will a workstation become infected from the server. However, this method leaves open the possibility that a virus can infect a workstation from a local floppy disk, or from the Internet or other dial-up connection. If users store their critical data on the server, and the process of restoring workstation applications is not overly costly, this method may be the better choice.

Antivirus software can be deployed on each workstation as well. This is a more complete solution, but requires additional administrative time to install and maintain, and, depending on the product selected, may add a small amount of performance overhead to daily operations. If the network uses some peer-to-peer services, it might be worth the extra cost and effort to deploy antivirus software on the workstations.

Keep the Software Up-to-Date

The most critical issue with an antivirus policy however, is keeping the virus *signatures* up to date. A virus signature is the updates issued by the antivirus software vendor that are used by the application to identify new virus patterns. Each month, hundreds of viruses, or variations of old viruses, are identified. If the signature files are out of date, even by as little as 45 days, the antivirus system is practically worthless. When selecting an antivirus software program, the most important factor to look for is the vendor's ability to provide signature updates *at least* every 30 to 60 days. You can find this information simply by logging on to the company's Web site and seeing how often previous signature files have been posted. Most of the commercial antivirus vendors allow free signature file downloads.

The last point to consider when choosing an antivirus solution is how the vendor supplies its signature updates. As I mentioned, most vendors allow free downloads from their Web sites, but this method places increased responsibilities on the network administrator. Under most circumstances, companies can cost justify yearly subscription fees to have the antivirus signatures delivered to them electronically.

Push technology

Many vendors incorporate *push* technologies to distribute their signature files. The push technology is a method of utilizing the Internet to automatically send files and notices to subscribers. Push technologies make it possible not only to receive virus signature files automatically, but also in some cases to automate the installation process. As these technologies become increasingly sophisticated, the administrative overhead of running antivirus software on all devices within the network may become a non-issue.

Pull technology

Like push methods, the pull technology is designed to automate the process of software distribution. With pull technology, the virus software contains a scheduling mechanism that is configured to automatically log onto the vendors support site on a regular basis and *pull* down the signature files and application updates. The same process normally will install the files as well. This process offers a little more safety, in that a failed connection can be identified and re-requested at a later time. With push technology, the client may not even be aware that an update was attempted.

WEB-BASED SERVERS AND SECURITY REQUIREMENTS

One last consideration: I've briefly mentioned in previous chapters that Internet technologies are not restricted for use on the public Internet. The same Web technology that people use on the Internet can also be used to easily organize and share information privately. However, even within the confines of a private network, there are security issues that need to be considered. Let's take a look at the other two methods where Web services are used, and what steps should be taken to secure them.

The Intranet

Technically speaking, an intranet is exactly the same as the Internet except that the network services are localized without a connection to the outside world. Intranets are gaining in popularity because corporate information can be organized and centralized in electronic format, greatly reducing the cost of paper memos. Since an intranet is based on the same components as the Web, any type of business correspondence can be posted on the corporate intranet, such as text documents, graphics, training videos, spreadsheets, and forms.

Like much interoffice correspondence, not every piece of information is intended to be seen by every employee. There are many times when interdepartmental communications must remain confidential. In these situations you can use the features of Java or Perl to password protect the documents just like you would on an Internet Web site. In other situations, such as with a payroll department intranet, all or most of the information must remain private. In these cases internal firewalls should be used. The function of an internal firewall is exactly the same as the firewalls between the private network and the Internet. The firewall is intended to allow authenticated users to access intranet services outbound, while preventing unauthorized access inbound.

Extranet

The information on an intranet can be very dynamic, in the sense that product or financial data can be built into a Web page and feed from an online database. This information is often useful to a company's partners. For example, a distribution company might keep its inventory on an intranet so that current stock levels, price breaks, and other real-time information is readily available to its customers. However, putting this type of information on the Internet might be too risky, even with the best firewalls and encryption methods. Rather than placing the intranet on the Web for a limited number of people to access, an extranet would be a better option. An extranet is simply the combining of two or more private intranets. Although it might be the connection medium of the extranet, security is enhanced because you know exactly who is allowed on the site. The firewalls can be programmed to allow connections only from a specific IP address or IP address range. A *virtual private network* (VPN) can be created within the connected intranets to increase security even further. A VPN is a method of creating an encrypted "tunnel" of information flow between two known sites. Most modern VPNs use the *Point-to-Point Tunneling Protocol*, or PPTP. The Point-to-Point Tunneling Protocol uses the RSA encryption to virtually guarantee the privacy of the data between the two points.

Securing the information between partner sites is only one security concern however. Even though these customers trust each other to do business together, there is important information that must remain confidential. Just like connecting a private network to the Internet, anytime an external connection is established, there is always a potential for abuse. In the same vein that we need to deploy firewall technology between our LAN and the Internet, the same methods must be used between the connections of an extranet. Since the inbound connections are much more limited, and we know specifically who will be granted access, standard routers with packet filtering capabilities are normally used to provide firewall protection within an extranet.

EXAM PREPARATION SUMMARY

In this chapter I covered a lot of important aspects of keeping servers up and running. The two most common problems servers develop are physical failures and intentional security breaches.

- When dealing with physical problems, develop a systematic approach to troubleshooting and diagnosing the problem. There are seven primary steps in a solid structured approach: Identify and document the problem, isolate the variable causing the problem, duplicate the problem, develop a corrective action plan, implement the corrective action, test the results, and document the findings.

- When dealing with server performance issues, often the primary problem is a physical failure with the network cards, cables, hubs, or switches. If you suspect your servers are suffering from broadcast storms, or other problems with data flow, a network analyzer might be required to truly see what is happening with the cable system. If a proper analysis indicates that the number of users has increased to the limit of the network, it is often reasonable to upgrade the overall speed of the LAN. If physical issues are ruled out, software problems, especially corrupt or older versions of DLL files, might be the culprit. Documenting what software has been installed on the server and when can greatly increase your ability to spot these types of problems.

- The TCP/IP protocol itself can become the source of poor performance. Fortunately, the protocol suite provides a number of tools for diagnosing TCP/IP related problems, such as ping, ipconfig, tracert, ARP, and netstat.

- When dealing with security issues, a firewall is the best form of protection money can buy. There are a number of methods firewalls use to determine what incoming data is acceptable, and what is not.

- Proxy servers add an addition level of security by utilizing multiple network cards to separate the private network from the public Internet. Proxy servers can also provide Network Address Translation to mask the IP addresses on the private network.

- Packet filtering technology provides a higher level of security because the firewall actually reads the data within the datagrams to determine if the data is allowed to pass through.

- Circuit-level gateways offer the most options when determining what is good data and what is not. This type of filter can restrict or allow data based on protocol, IP address, domain, or user.

- Authentication and non-repudiation are other forms of security required for Internet commerce. These items are not targeted so much with malicious attacks against an Internet server, but attacks to the data sent between browsers and servers.

- Even with the latest and greatest firewall technologies, nothing can guarantee complete security. For that reason, it is important to use some common sense and some intrusion detection tools.

- Some of the most common Internet related attacks are Denial of Service. These attacks aim to send abnormal data packets to a server in an attempt to keep the server so busy with the bad data that it can't process legitimate requests. Ping floods, such as the Ping of Death, or the Teardrop attack, are the most common. Another common DoS attack is a SYN flood, where incomplete synchronize and acknowledge handshakes keep the server occupied on bad source IP addresses, preventing it from serving authorized users.

- Mail flooding is a similar attack, waged against an e-mail server. Sometimes the goal of the attack is to simply overwhelm the server and shut it down, or the attacker wants to abuse the server to forward large amounts of mail. When used as a mass-mailing target, the hacker can masquerade their real address with your domain name, making it appear that you are responsible for the unsolicited mail.

- Basic security measures can greatly increase the safety of internal systems. Everyone who is authorized to use a network should be assigned a unique username and password. Every user account should be configured to authenticate with a password. Password policies need to be defined and enforced. Passwords should be created that include a mix of letters and numbers, with a minimum length of four characters but not more than eight. Users should be forced to change their passwords on a regular basis, and not allowed to repeat the same password more than once in four changes. If your systems require multiple passwords, it may be a good idea to synchronize the passwords. Like login security, the network operating system's file security features need to be understood and implemented. Most NOSs provide methods to grant or deny access to disk files based on a username. These features should always be used before opening the network up to the Internet.

- Computer viruses are a fact of computer life, and strong antivirus measures must be part of the overall security strategies. Antivirus software can be implemented only at the server level to maintain the integrity of data on the servers, or it can be deployed on every workstation as well to greatly reduce the chance of a virus proliferating on the network in the first place.

- Web technologies are not limited to Internet use. Intranets and extranets can be used to share information between trusted partners. Although these partners may trust each other in some respects, the same firewall security methods used to keep unauthorized people from the Internet out should be deployed to maintain privacy on the local intranets.

APPLYING WHAT YOU HAVE LEARNED

The following review questions give you an opportunity to test your knowledge of the information presented in this chapter. The answers to these assessment questions can be found in Appendix B. If you missed some, review those sections in this chapter before going further.

Instant Assessment Questions

1. A part of the first step to systematically approaching the diagnostic process is to create a

    A. List of possible causes

    B. Inventory of software

    C. Problem resolution document

    D. Corrective action document

2. Server performance degradation caused by a NIC flooding the cable system is commonly called

    A. A ping flood

    B. A broadcast storm

    C. Packet saturation

    D. A teardrop attack

3. What two things can be done to increase a Web server's performance?

    A. Defragment the hard drive

    B. Reduce the size of the server swap file

    C. Convert all graphic files to the GIF format

    D. Place Web pages and graphic files on a RAM disk

4. What utility could you use to determine the TCP/IP settings of an NT computer?

A. ping

B. netstat

C. arp

D. ipconfig

5. Which utility is useful in identifying where routing bottlenecks are occurring?

A. tracert

B. winipcfg

C. netstat

D. arp

6. What type of firewall technology is most useful for preventing incoming FTP requests?

A. FTP filters

B. Content filter

C. Protocol screening

D. Tri-homed proxy

7. A security protocol created by Visa and MasterCard for secure credit card transactions across the Internet is

A. SET

B. SSL

C. SHTTP

D. Digital signatures

8. Global encryption standards are based on 128-bit algorithms.

A. True

B. False

9. To minimize administration time while maintaining the integrity of critical data, antivirus software could be implemented

A. By the ISP

B. By the firewall

C. On the servers

D. At the workstations using pull technology for updates

10. What two technologies are used to facilitate the sharing of organized information between two businesses?

A. Virtual Private Networks (VPN)

B. Intranets

C. Point-to-point tunneling protocols

D. Extranets

Understanding the Business Side of the Internet

The Internet has grown quickly because the business world saw its enormous potential. Most i-Net+ certified individuals haven't gone through their training just to put up a personal Web server, but to participate in the business market of the Internet, whether directly or indirectly. As we've seen throughout this book, putting the necessary components together is not all that difficult, but it's only half of the job. In this last section, you're going to look at the Internet from a business perspective. The final objectives of the i-Net+ exam cover the principles and concepts that all organizations need to understand before taking their businesses to the Internet.

i-NET+™

The Role of E-Commerce within a Business Strategy

About Chapter 11

This chapter covers the fundamentals of doing business online that make up the final 10 percent of the i-Net+ exam.

The broadest way to categorize e-commerce transactions is by whether a company is doing business with other businesses or with consumers. Although business-to-business commerce is in some ways easier, business-to-consumer commerce presents a number of new challenges that many companies may never have thought of before.

Besides being a new way for buyers and sellers to meet, the Internet creates new problems and opportunities for marketers. Rather than focusing advertising campaigns on smaller, specifically targeted groups, the Internet provides the means to reach millions of potential customers globally and build relationships with them through interactive means. Often, this requires a new way of thinking, and totally different methods of advertising.

Prior to the proliferation of electronically shared information, copyright laws were fairly easy to understand and follow. However, it is extremely easy to copy information from one Internet source and paste it into another. It is important to know what your rights are, and steps required for protecting yourself from others who might wish to plagiarize your original works. In addition, to avoid infringing on the protected material of others, you need to have a good idea of how the copyright laws work.

Some of the biggest challenges for businesses moving to the Internet, however, are the issues related to conducting commerce in a global environment. Most of us are pretty clear about the laws and regulations within our own borders, but international commerce rules vary greatly from country to country.

Although I will not attempt to cover each of these issues in great depth, the remainder of this book will be spent examining how these issues impact business on the Internet.

E-COMMERCE TERMS AND CONCEPTS

The so-called "killer app" driving much of the Internet's exponential growth is *e-commerce*. The term e-commerce generically describes a new method of conducting business. Buying and selling goods and services over the Internet holds tremendous potential that has already changed many attitudes toward traditional marketing, manufacturing, and distribution systems. E-commerce provides existing businesses new markets and reduced costs, while also giving small startup companies opportunities unavailable just a few years ago. For example, a company that sells a physical product might never have had the capital to advertise beyond its local market. However, with a small investment in Internet technologies, this company can reach millions of potential buyers around the globe without additional salespeople or expensive advertising campaigns. For the individual, or small company, e-commerce provides a method of reaching the same global pool of customers equally. The small business may never need a capital investment for real estate, inventory, or advertising. There are many e-commerce success stories of people who turned a hobby into a full-time business because of the affordable costs associated with online business. I predict that in less than five years the term *e-commerce* will fade away, as the general term commerce will presume e-commerce as a natural extension of the business process.

Business to Business

Within the scope of modern e-commerce, two distinct branches have emerged: business to business, and business to consumer. Although there may be some overlap, most business plans clearly define one or the other of these paths. There are some specific methods of transacting business between two or more companies that differ from selling directly to the consumer. I've already discussed extranets, where companies link their intranets together to facilitate the transportation of business information, in previous chapters.

Electronic Data Interchange, or EDI, is about doing business and carrying out transactions with trading partners electronically. EDI covers most things that are done using paper-based communication; for example, placing orders with suppliers and carrying out financial transactions. This is why the term *paperless trading* is often used to describe EDI.

More formally, EDI is described as the interchange of structured data according to agreed message standards between computer systems, by electronic means. Structured data equates to an unambiguous method of presenting the data content of a document, be it an invoice, order, or any other document type. The method of ensuring the correct interpretation of the information by the computer system is defined by the standard. Electronic exchange of information in the context of pure EDI effectively means without human intervention.

With EDI, businesses can eliminate the need to re-enter data from paper documents and thus prevent clerical errors. Estimates suggest that 70 percent of all computer input has previously been output from another computer. Each re-entry of data is a potential source of error. It has also been estimated that the cost of processing an electronic requisition can be one-tenth the cost of handling its paper equivalent. In addition, EDI can reduce the need for personnel involved in orders and accounts processing

EDI may seem difficult to distinguish from electronic mail (e-mail) as both involve the transmission of electronic messages between computer systems. What differentiates EDI from e-mail is the internal structure and content of the data message. The content of an e-mail message is not intended to be processed in any way by the receiving system, while EDI messages are intended for and are therefore structured for automatic processing.

Business to Consumer

The largest percentage of e-commerce is arguably business to consumer. Although traditional purchasing methods - traveling to a store, selecting products, and paying for them at the checkout counter - still account for the majority of all consumer buying, electronic purchasing is gaining acceptance. As more people begin accessing the Internet, and online credit card transactions become more accepted, these ratios will surely shift.

Internet commerce

The two main benefits to online shopping are convenience and lower costs. Obviously, if an e-commerce site is designed so that customers can easily find and purchase goods, shopping online is more convenient. Customers have 24-hour access and can easily compare products, prices, and merchants. Since it is easy to jump from site to site, the online seller must keep its prices as competitive as possible, or offer some other form of value-added service. For example, some companies offer free shipping, or special services to notify the customer when new products of interest become available. Amazon.com is an excellent example of a company that not only prices its products competitively, but also offers a host of value-added services. In its book line, for example, Amazon.com customers can enter their billing and shipping information once, then initiate all future transactions with a single click. Customers can also sign up for Amazon.com *eyes*. When new books from their favorite authors are released, this program instantly sends them an e-mail message notifying them of its ship date. This same technology can be used to keep people informed of new music or videos that they are interested in.

In addition to competitive pricing, many consumers are drawn to Internet purchasing for the tax advantage. Unless the business is operated within the taxing authority the buyer lives in, there are generally no sales or value-added taxes on Internet purchases. This advantage may not remain, but while the current laws remain in effect, the savings on taxes often cover the shipping fees.

Other companies are concentrating on customer service issues. For example, the Toys-R-Us Corporation has developed its system to complement its "brick and mortar" businesses. If a buyer wishes to return an item purchased on the Internet, he or she simply needs to return it to any of the Toys-R-Us stores for a refund or exchange. This is often much more convenient than having to repackage the merchandise and ship it back to the company. I would bet that other traditional businesses with physical stores will soon offer free shipping if a customer is willing to pick up his or her purchases. This concept allows the customer 24-hour shopping without paying extra for shipping.

In this early stage of business-to-consumer e-commerce, companies are searching for less traditional methods to attract the attention of new Internet customers. For example, the online auction format has recently soared in popularity. These Internet sites allow people to list items for sale to the highest bidder. Other people, mostly looking for bargains, bid on the items for a set period of time, usually a few days. The person with the highest bid then arranges for payment and delivery of the product. The Internet auction house charges a small fee, often 1-2 percent of the sale price, to provide the Internet tools that make the auction possible. Some companies only sell their own products using the auction method, but the market trend has been for both companies and individuals to auction goods to other individuals. Without question, the largest Internet auction site is eBay (www.ebay.com), although many such sites are growing in popularity, such as Amazon.com (www.amazon.com/auctions) and BoxLot (www.boxlot.com).

Merchant systems

To effectively conduct e-commerce on the Internet, a Web site must contain special features for handling online transactions. Many online shoppers pay by credit card, so the site must be capable of securely processing these transactions. A *merchant system* consists of the secured Web features and a bank willing to process the credit card payments. A bank, or a third-party processor on behalf of the bank, provides merchant account services to the merchant. These services include authorization of credit cards, settlement of funds through the bankcard associations (MasterCard, Visa, for instance), depositing of funds to checking accounts, merchant billing, and account activity reporting. These services are not limited only to Internet purchases but can also be used for orders taken by telephone, fax, or in person. Until recently, most small businesses relied on their local banks for this service. But with the explosion in online trading, many large financial institutions and third-party companies are offering these services as well. Many local banks required a business to be well established, funded, and not have any credit problems by the principle owners before granting merchant accounts. These requirements alone made it difficult for many new businesses to offer credit card processing to their customers. Since nationwide institutions can spread the risk over a larger number of businesses, they are able to offer merchant systems to a wider range of small businesses with less overall risk.

To process real-time transactions, the merchant must obtain an authorization from the bank prior to completing the sale. This can be accomplished in many ways. Most non-Internet stores, such as restaurants and retail shops, use a card reader and modem. The card is swiped through the reader and the amount keyed in. This information is then called into the merchant bank for electronic authorization. This system works fine, but many online customers expect authorization to be performed during the purchase process. To accomplish this, the Web merchant must be available to take the credit card information from the Web form or e-mail, then manually process the authorization on another line. This generally eliminates the possibility of 24-hour service, or requires a hefty investment in additional hardware and employees.

To automate the process, many merchant systems use a *payment gateway*. A payment gateway is a secondary service that gives merchants the ability to perform real-time credit card authorizations from a Web site over the Internet without having to process the transactions themselves. When an online shopper submits an order, the payment information is routed to the payment gateway to obtain the purchase authorization. The transaction is automatically submitted for settlement so the funds can be processed and transferred to the merchant's account. Notification is then sent via e-mail so the product can be shipped. If the authorization is denied, the merchant then sends notice to the customer with an explanation from the merchant system's bank. Depending on the system selected, the gateway process can be done in just a few minutes, or all transactions can be processed in batches, perhaps once or twice daily. Payment gateways improve security by keeping customer credit card data behind firewalls so the merchant doesn't have to worry about someone hacking into their system.

Online cataloging

One of the most important aspects of an e-commerce Web site is easy navigation and location of products. If potential customers can't find the product and information they are looking for within a few minutes, the Web makes it easy to jump to a competing site — something that would be more troublesome for a customer in a physical store.

Cataloging of products is an important consideration for an e-commerce site. A comprehensive catalog system should be built on a hierarchical system, beginning with general topics, such as clothing, electronics, or books. Below the main categories, more specific classifications should be used, such as women's clothes, clothes for teens, and so on. Again, at this level, even more categories or specific items can be listed. Graphics complementary to the hierarchical level should be used to provide visual guidelines to the customer.

Each item should also include a brief description of the product highlighting its features and benefits. When a customer selects one of these product summaries, a more detailed description, possibly including a comparison of similar products, could be displayed. As each level is viewed, more graphics can be added to enhance the appeal of the product. Remember however, to keep graphic sizes small enough so as not to slow down the loading of the individual pages.

When creating an online catalog, the primary decision is whether to make it static or dynamic. A static catalog is simply made with a series of separate Web pages. As information on these pages changes, the page must be manually edited. A static catalog generally requires less programming knowledge (just good HTML skills) although they tend to take more time overall to maintain.

A dynamic catalog normally consists of a generic HTML template with placeholders for graphics, descriptions, and pricing. The details for the product are maintained in a database. When the page is displayed, the dynamic information is read from the database and displayed in the appropriate places by a program interface (usually CGI). There are many advantages to using a dynamic catalog for e-commerce sites, including the ability to quickly maintain price changes, and incorporate real-time inventory levels. For example, if a dynamic page is connected to the backend accounting system that maintains orders and inventory control, the customer can see immediately how many products the merchant has in stock and ready to ship. If no products are on hand, the page can easily display the date more items are estimated to be available.

Relationship management

The traditional shopping experience usually relies on interaction between the customer and a store employee. Some customers like having sales clerks to show them a variety of items, or to help them locate products. Most department stores have customer service desks to help customers with special orders, returns, or other personal services. Even checkout persons can influence a customer's opinion of that business. With online shopping, much of this personal interaction is missing. To build customer loyalty, then, other relationship management features must be incorporated into an e-commerce site.

I discussed some of the value-add features sites like Amazon.com use to build customer relationships, but in this early stage of e-commerce, no single customer relationship model has emerged. Businesses are testing many ideas. One concept that is slowly emerging is the process of mixing live human assistance within the Web process. For example, if a customer is browsing through a site's products, he or she can click a special button that will create a real-time audio and video transmission of a human sales assistant. This person can then answer questions the customer might have, as well as direct them electronically through the Web site to places of interest. This technology will require much higher bandwidth than is generally used by most consumers today, but clearly shows how traditional interactive service can be brought to Web shopping.

Customer self-service

One feature many Internet shoppers like is the ability *not* to have to deal with store personnel. Self-service businesses are nothing new, but the Web offers businesses many new tools to help consumers help themselves.

One of the most common items found on e-commerce sites is the shopping cart. Much like a real-world cart, customers can place items in and out of their electronic shopping carts while browsing through the site. As items are added or removed, the total price is calculated so the customer knows how much his or her current selections will cost.

Other tools that assist in creating a self-service site include the cross-referencing of related items. For example, if a customer is looking at a specific music title, the Web page might have links to similar groups, or to other releases by the same band. If the title cut from the CD was used in a movie, a link might lead the customer to the videotape. Some companies allow people to create a *gift registry,* making it easy for friends and relatives to purchase gifts for them. This concept has been used for years by couples planning to be married, or having a baby. All of these tools are targeted toward helping customers find the products they want, and making it easy for them to make purchases.

Internet Marketing

The golden rule for setting up a new business has always been location, location, location. Having your business in a high-traffic, easily accessible location is deemed critical to the success of almost any business. Marketing an Internet site may not require obtaining prime real estate, but it does require Internet knowledge and creativity.

Three of the most common Internet marketing techniques used today include

- Listing in a search engine, directory, or portal
- Banner advertising
- Established media advertising

Search engines, directories, and portals

The term *search engine* is often used generically to describe both true search engines and *directories*, although they are not the same. The difference is how listings are compiled.

Search engines create listings automatically by using special programs often called a *crawler* that visit Web sites and build information from the existing content. When a Web page changes, search engines will eventually find these changes and update their listings. Most crawlers gather page titles, descriptions, and keywords from meta tags contained within the HTML body of the pages.

A directory service, such as Yahoo!, depends on humans for its listings. A Web author submits a short description to the directory for the entire site, or the directory editors write one for sites they review. A user search then looks for matches in the descriptions submitted. Changes in the Web pages will have no effect on the directory listing. Things that are useful for improving a listing with a search engine have nothing to do with improving a listing in a directory. The only exception is that a good site, with good content, might be more likely to get reviewed than a poor site.

Some search engines maintain an associated directory. Being included in a search engine's directory is usually a combination of luck and quality. Sometimes you can submit your site for review, but there is no guarantee that it will be included.

Portals are Web sites that offer more than products or services to their customers. For example, a computer business might create a portal site that provides real-time news feeds relating to the information technology field, product reviews of new hardware and software, and helpful "how-to" articles. Along with these interesting side items, the business will promote its products and services and possibly other related items from other companies. Portal sites often offer free e-mail, Web space, or other incentives to keep the viewer coming back. In fact, the hope of a portal site is to have the visitor make that site his or her "home" page. These types of Web sites require enormous investments in programming and network infrastructures but often pay off in additional advertising revenues as well.

Banner advertising

As marketers began looking for ways to bring more traffic to their sites, the idea of advertising Internet sites on the Internet made the most sense. Banner ads have proven to be a popular and inexpensive method of Internet advertising. If you've been on the Internet already, then you've most likely seen banner advertisements. A banner is typically a 468 × 60 pixel graphic, much like a mini billboard, that links directly to another site. The effectiveness of banner advertising is open to debate. Many quality researchers have come to completely different conclusions, perhaps indicating that the merit of the banner defines its effectiveness.

A banner ad is like the envelope of a direct mailing. Once the prospective customer has opened the envelope, you can show color images, persuasive copy, and glitzy presentations - but the whole package will wind up in the trash unopened unless there's a compelling reason to open it up. Like a color brochure or the contents of a direct mail ad, the Web site you're inviting your prospects to visit has no perceived value to them. It's just something you're trying to impress them with, so it had better be good and entertaining.

A growing annoyance to most Web users is the sheer volume of banner advertising. If you decide to market your site in this way, where you place the ads may be as important as what your banner says. Not only do you want to advertise on sites that generate a lot of traffic, but you also don't want your ads placed on sites where it will be lost in a sea of other banners. There are a number of "banner brokers," or banner exchanges, that act as a mediator between advertisers and the sites who host advertisements. These brokers enforce rules as to how banner ads are placed, and control the number of ads any one site or page can contain.

How banners are paid for varies almost as much as the advertising concept itself. Some advertisers pay a flat fee for the space on a Web site, much like a newspaper advertiser would. Others pay a small amount, perhaps a penny or two, to the site owner when someone clicks on the ad. This is known as a *click through*. Still others pay a percentage of any sales they make as the result of someone coming to their site from a banner ad. Since banner advertising is still relatively new, many of these payment methods are negotiable.

Established media advertising

Advertising is a major business in and of itself. Many forms of advertising exist to sell everything imaginable using many channels. Television and radio ads generally reach the most people and generate the best returns, although print media ads are very effective for a targeting an audience. The Internet, and Web sites in particular, is no different a commodity than anything else advertised through traditional methods. Many new e-commerce ventures will spend hundreds of thousands of dollars to advertise their new businesses on television, magazines, and other established media. Although these methods remain too expensive for small businesses, they are still highly effective for large companies that can afford this option.

CREATING YOUR OWN E-COMMERCE WEB SITE FOR UNDER $200

Throughout this book, I've covered all the technologies required to set up a Web server. The following list summarizes the necessary steps to quickly get your site up and running, and what it costs. In order to accomplish this task, you must have a dedicated Internet connection with a static IP address, such as an xDSL or cable connection. For an example of a finished product, I created a new Web site at www.eShop2k.net while writing this book. The graphics for the page headings were created online by a free service at: www.cooltext.com. Please feel free to visit this site for examples and ideas.

1. Register your domain name. ($70) Register.com at www.register.com is one of the newest domain registrars and will not only register your name, but supply the DNS server entries as well. When your registration is complete (about 48 hours) return to register.com and modify your DNS settings to change your domain address to the static IP address of your Web server.

2. Install and configure the Xitami Web server on your computer according to the directions in Appendix D (free).

3. If you don't have a firewall to protect your server, purchase a copy of BlackICE from `www.networkice.com` ($39.95).

4. Create your e-commerce site, either from scratch, or with the WebExpress software included on the CD. (Register for $69.95)

5. If you require the ability to accept credit cards and other online payments, review the services of iCat (a division of Intel) at `www.icat.com`. (Prices vary depending on number of items to be sold.)

6. Submit your site to multiple search engines for free at `http://www.selfpromotion.com/` (please send the owner a voluntary donation).

7. I highly suggest you add a hit counter to your site to see how much traffic is being generated. A very detailed counter can be obtained for free from Sitemeter.com at `www.sitemeter.com`.

8. If you want matching e-mail for your new Web site, return to Register.com and request an addition to the DNS database for an MX record which points to your static IP address. Install the MDaemon e-mail server according to the directions in Appendix D. When the DNS database has been fully propagated (about 48 hours) you will have the ability to create new Internet e-mail address for your registered domain name. ($199.95 for six accounts)

If you don't have the hardware for a Web server of your own, or you don't have a dedicated connection to the Internet, an excellent alternative is to have your site hosted by a third-party company. I have first-hand experience with Internet Communications, Inc. at `www.icom.com` and have found their services to be of high quality. ICOM provides 45MB of server space (more than enough for a very professional small business e-commerce site). The base hosting package, including a full POP3 account (easily extendable with MDaemon) begins at $99 per year with a one-time setup fee of $45. For a sample of a site hosted by Internet Communications, visit my primary Web site at `www.Net-Engineer.com`. They also offer a series of e-commerce ready accounts that include the merchant systems and shopping carts in the monthly fee.

COPYRIGHT, TRADEMARKS, AND LICENSING

Just as the Internet makes it easy to distribute documents, the Internet makes it just as easy to copy that information for other uses. Copyright laws seemed to be a bit easier to understand when the major media were books, radio, and television. It is pretty clear to most people that it is illegal to simply copy someone's work from a book for your own personal gain. However, with the ease with which documents can be distributed on the Internet, the laws governing copyrights become a little more skewed. For example, is the content on your Web page automatically protected? How effective is adding the © copyright symbol? Is copyrighted material protected outside your legal authority? When creating Internet materials, you must know the answers to these questions to avoid infringing on other's copyrights and to protect your own.

Scope of Your Copyright

Before discussing how copyrights are used, you need to understand the scope of copyright protection, or what can and cannot be protected. In general terms, works of expression are protected by copyrights. In the U.S. Copyright Act of 1976, works of expression are defined as literary, dramatic, and musical works. Therefore, works of choreography, pictorial, graphic, audiovisual, sound recordings, and architectural works may all be protected under the copyright law. As soon as an original expression is put in tangible form, it is eligible for copyright protection.

For example, when a new graphic file is created with a graphic arts program, the original graphic creation is protected as soon as it is saved to disk or printed, as this is a fixed tangible form. Likewise, this book was protected the moment I finished typing and saved the document to my hard drive. Therefore, almost everything posted on the Internet is copyrighted material, including text and graphics on Web pages, the contents of e-mail and newsgroup messages, and downloadable programs.

Although this list seems pretty all-inclusive, not everything is eligible for copyright protection. Things that by their definition are not covered are ideas, thoughts, facts, blank forms, titles, names, and phrases. Many people mistakenly believe that their ideas should be protected, but unless they have created a tangible item from their ideas, no absolute protection is granted.

Items not clearly defined as protected

As with any legal question, there are some very gray areas. Two Internet-related copyright issues that are constantly discussed but not firmly defined are the use of links to graphics on other Web sites (using the HTML IMG tag) and linking directly to another Web page without permission. Although there are no definitive answers to these questions, the circumstances that raise these legal issues are interesting and worth investigating.

From our definition of the copyright laws above, it should be clear that it is illegal to simply copy a graphic from some other site and use it on your Web page. However, if your HTML code used the IMG tag to link to, and download from, another Web site, you are not physically taking the graphic image. Although this issue has been raised many times, no case has been followed through far enough for a legal precedent to be established. The best advice in these situations is to always get the author's permission first, or don't use the material in question.

How about linking to another Web site? Understandably, this is not only common practice, but is directly in line with the premise of the Web technology in the first place. But is it legal? The courts have never formally ruled on this issue either. Many experts argue that a URL is simply another address, such as a telephone number, which by definition of its purpose is not copyrightable. However, while it may be legal to publish a person's telephone number, you'll probably get in trouble if you publish something like "To speak to a real idiot, call 555-1212." In context, this situation might also happen on the Web. Suppose for example, that a Web author creates a link to another site with very useful information. Above this link the author indicates that the work is his or hers. Although the material has not been "taken," the intention is clearly to deceive the reader into thinking the Web author created the material being linked to. This would obviously be an infringement on the owner's copyright.

Even if there are no legal requirements with regard to the use of images and links that you plan to use, it is always wise to obtain permission from the owner first. In general, if you are quite confident that you are not doing anything wrong in setting up an HREF link, then you probably are not doing anything wrong. Millions of HREF links have been set up in the World Wide Web, and the sky has not fallen and common sense has prevailed. Nonetheless, if you have any misgiving or doubt about a particular link, then the ethical thing to do is to write to the owner of the site and ask if there is any objection. This will give them an opportunity to view the page containing the link, and to consider whether there is any reason to object to it.

Fair use

Under the copyright laws, some works can be used without fear of infringement under the fair use definition. Generally, items covered by the fair use clause are items deemed to be newsworthy or used for educational purposes. Factors considered in determining whether a use is fair use or an infringement are as follows:

1. The purpose and character of the use. Is the material in question being used for profit?

2. How much of the total work is employed in the course of the use?

3. What effect will the use have on the market for or value of the work being copied?

One typical invocation of fair use is in the publication of reviews. Under fair use, a book reviewer can quote from the book being reviewed without infringing on the owner's copyright (provided, of course, that the reviewer doesn't quote the work in its entirety).

Copyright notification

Given the definition of what is automatically protected, the issue of whether or not specific notification is required comes to mind. Originally, the courts ruled that protected material *did* need to be identified with the proper terms and symbols. However, more recent decisions have overturned this requirement. Therefore you cannot argue that material not identified as protected is in the public domain. Although works no longer require a copyright notice, it is still customary to attach such a notice on copyrighted material. A proper copyright notice consists of these four elements:

1. The copyright symbol ©
2. The term "Copyright" with the year of copyright
3. The name of the copyright holder, and
4. The phrase "All Rights Reserved"

How to License Copyrighted Materials

Although the Copyright Act protects you just for creating original material and saving it to a tangible form, you may desire to "officially" register works with the U.S. Copyright Office. The registration process is not terribly difficult and the fees are reasonable. Although the certificate of copyright provided by the Copyright Office is not necessarily suitable for framing, there are two distinct advantages to obtaining a registered copyright. First, you cannot actually sue someone for infringing on your copyright unless you have registered the material with the Copyright Office. And second, if you register your work prior to the date of infringement, you can collect statutory damages from the party that violates your copyright. If you fail to do this, you are only entitled to actual damages, which, depending upon the situation, may be hard to prove and end up being nominal.

For example, suppose my Web site is not registered (yet still protected since it is a tangible item) and the illtakeyourstuff.com owner steals content from my site verbatim. If I wanted to sue, I'd have to quickly register my site first. Assuming illtakeyourstuff.com didn't have a valid legal defense, I could collect for my losses, and any profits made by the infringer. Since neither site operates for profit, my awards probably wouldn't even cover the cost of bringing the suit.

Assume however, that I had registered my site before illtakeyourstuff.com began publishing. If I prove infringement, then I might be able to recover statutory damages in lieu of actual non-existent damages. Statutory damages awards can be up to $100,000, plus attorney fees and court costs, depending upon the nature of the infringement. Clearly then, this option will affect the decision of whether to register a formal copyright or not.

Pending legislation regarding U.S. copyright laws

In response to "The Report of the President's Working Group on Intellectual Property Rights," a bill known as the National Information Infrastructure Copyright Protection Act of 1995 has been introduced in both the United States Senate and the House of Representatives. The purpose of the bill is to increase and clarify the scope of copyright protection as an incentive for copyright owners to make their works available on the Internet, for the benefit of the public at large. The bill clarifies that a transmission of a publication is a part of the distribution right for purposes of copyright protection. A transmission is defined in the new bill as something that is distributed by any device or process whereby a copy or phonorecord of the work is fixed beyond the place from which it was sent. In addition, the new bill bans de-encryption devices because of the important role encryption plays in protecting transmitted copyrighted content. A variety of civil remedies are provided under the bill for frustrating encryption systems, including injunctions, impounding, actual or statutory damages, attorney's fees, or destruction of infringing products or devices. Damages are available even if the copyright owner has not registered his or her copyright prior to the infringement. The bill also includes criminal sanctions.

The copyright process

One helpful—and free—aid you should obtain is a Copyright Information Kit, which can be requested from the Copyright Office, Library of Congress, Washington, D.C. 20559. The Copyright Information Kit includes copyright application forms and circulars explaining a great deal about the operation of the Copyright Office. Specify what type of work you are creating, so that you receive the right kit. A hotline telephone number (202-707-9100) has been established by the Copyright Office to expedite requests for registration forms

To register a work, you simply need to send a completed application form, $30, and one or two copies of the work *in the same envelope or package* to:

Library of Congress
Copyright Office
Register of Copyrights
101 Independence Avenue, S.E.
Washington, D.C. 20559-6000

The following guidelines help determine how many copies of the work must be submitted:

- If the work was first published in the United States on or after January 1, 1978, two complete copies or phonorecords of the best edition must be submitted.

- If the work was first published in the United States before January 1, 1978, two complete copies or phonorecords of the work as first published.

- If the work was first published outside the United States, one complete copy or phonorecord of the work as first published.

Although there are more than a dozen possible application forms available from the copyright office, the following list contains the forms generally associated with Internet related documents. Electronic copies of the following forms are on the CD. For a complete list of all copyright forms, please visit the home page of the US Copyright office at `http://lcweb.loc.gov/copyright/`.

- Form TX is for published and unpublished non-dramatic literary works. This is the general application used for works with text, such as an article, book, or Web page and covers most items.

- Form VA is the appropriate form for the visual arts such as pictorial, graphic, and sculptural works, including photography and illustration. If you have original graphics on your Web site and want to benefit from registering these images, this form should also be submitted.

- Form SE is used for works issued or intended to be issued in successive parts bearing numerical or chronological designations and intended to be continued indefinitely, such as periodicals, newspapers, magazines, newsletters, annuals, or journals. If your Web site contains any form of ongoing series, or if you publish an electronic newsletter, you should include this form with your application.

Public domain

Non-copyrighted material is generally considered to be in the *public domain* and may be freely used by anyone for whatever purpose they see fit. The creator may place works into the public domain, or the work will become public domain when the copyright expires without being renewed.

Under U.S. copyright laws, a work that is created on or after January 1, 1978, is given a term enduring for the author's life plus an additional 70 years after the author's death. In the case of "a joint work prepared by two or more authors who did not work for hire," the term lasts for 70 years after the last surviving author's death. For works made for hire, and for anonymous and pseudonymous works (unless the author's identity is revealed in Copyright Office records), the duration of copyright will be 95 years from publication or 120 years from creation, whichever is shorter.

How to copyright your material anywhere

United States copyright protection is available for all unpublished works, regardless of the nationality or domicile of the author. Published works are eligible for copyright protection in the United States if any one of the following conditions is met:

- On the date of first publication, one or more of the authors is a national or domiciliary of the United States, or is a national, domiciliary, or sovereign authority of a treaty party, or is a stateless person wherever that person may be domiciled; or

- The work is first published in the United States or in a foreign nation that, on the date of first publication, is a treaty party. For purposes of this condition, a work that is published in the United States or a treaty party within 30 days after publication in a foreign nation that is not a treaty party shall be considered to be first published in the United States or such treaty party, as the case may be; or

- The work is a sound recording that was first fixed in a treaty party; or

- The work is a pictorial, graphic, or sculptural work that is incorporated in a building or other structure, or an architectural work that is embodied in a building and the building or structure is located in the United States or a treaty party; or

- The work is first published by the United Nations or any of its specialized agencies, or by the Organization of American States; or

- The work is a foreign work that was in the public domain in the United States prior to 1996 and its copyright was restored under the Uruguay Round Agreements Act; or

- The work comes within the scope of a Presidential proclamation

There is no such thing as an International Copyright that will automatically protect an author's works throughout the entire world. Protection against unauthorized use in a particular country depends basically on the national laws of that country. However, most countries do offer protection to foreign works under certain conditions, and these conditions have been greatly simplified by international copyright treaties and conventions.

The Universal Copyright Convention (UCC) and the Berne Convention for the Protection of Literary and Artistic Works are two global, multilateral copyright treaties. The United States was a founding member of the UCC, which came into force on September 16, 1955. Generally, a work by a national or domiciliary of a country that is a member of the UCC or a work first published in a UCC country may claim protection under the UCC. If the work bears the notice of copyright in the form and position specified by the UCC, this notice would satisfy and substitute for any other formalities a UCC member country would otherwise impose as a condition of copyright. A UCC notice should consist of the copyright symbol accompanied by the name of the copyright proprietor and the year of first publication of the work

Consequences of not being aware of copyright issues

Copyright laws are defined like any other law in the United States. Ignorance of the law is no defense against breaking the law. As discussed earlier, the penalties for copyright infringement can consist of a simple cease and desist order, to the imposition of fines up to $100,000. It should be noted here as well that most insurance policies do not cover losses due to copyright infringement. For the most part, you will find that owners of copyrighted material, suitable for reproduction on the Internet, are usually willing to give permission for its use so long as you clearly identify the source of the information. Where profits are derived from the work, the owner may request a small percentage that should be negotiated and defined within the confines or a legal contract. When in doubt, always check with a competent legal advisor, obtain permission from the owner, or look for another noncopyrighted source.

Working in a Global Environment

For many people, thinking *globally* is somewhat difficult. Most of us have always lived and worked within the confines of a single country. Unless you reside on the border between two countries, you may never have to worry about transporting goods and services, taxes, or different currencies. However, as world economies grow, partially fueled by the Internet, even small businesses will likely be confronted with issues of a global nature.

Working in a Multivendor Environment with Different Currencies

E-commerce presents some unique challenges for most businesses. Not the least of these are currency exchanges. Customers want to see prices in their native monetary forms, and need to make payments that way too. When creating Web pages, either static or dynamic, the possibility that customers may want to make purchases with foreign currency should be taken into account. Offering a monetary exchange feature is extremely helpful. This type of functionality is generally easier to incorporate into a dynamic Web page where the daily change in monetary valuations can be quickly updated.

When processing payments from a Web page, the payment gateway discussed earlier is a very useful tool. Since a third-party financial institution handles the transactions, it should be equipped to handle the currency exchange problems for you. If a major credit card company or international bank provides your e-commerce authorization system, it can also assist in properly converting between the various denominations for you. Before opening your e-commerce site up for worldwide access, you need to address the methods used to process transactions from around the globe.

International Issues — Shipping and the Supply Chain

In addition to currency exchange problems, e-commerce businesses must also contend with shipping and supply issues. Although most major transportation companies such as United Parcel Service, Federal Express, and even the United States Post Office, ship to most international sites, additional costs can quickly make product prices uncompetitive. In addition to the added costs, servicing, spare parts, and other product-related customer service issues need to be addressed. If international customers need to return an item, or if they need replacement parts for items they purchased from your site, they will expect you to be able to handle these situations with minimal additional costs or delays resulting from their distant locations. Again, careful and thoughtful planning before your site goes live is required.

Multilingual or Multicharacter Issues (Unicode)

Obviously, since the Web is a global environment, there are language barriers that must be dealt with when doing e-commerce across borders. The Unicode Consortium has been involved with developing a standard method of creating multicharacter sites. Unicode provides a consistent way of encoding multilingual plain text and brings order to a chaotic state of affairs that has made it difficult to exchange text files internationally. The Unicode Standard provides the capacity to encode all of the characters used for the written languages of the world. It uses a 16-bit encoding that provides code points for more than 65,000 characters. To keep character coding simple and efficient, the Unicode Standard assigns each character a unique 16-bit value. While 65,000 characters are sufficient for encoding most of the many thousands of characters used in major languages of the world, the Unicode standard provides an extension mechanism called UTF-16 that allows for encoding as many as a million more characters. This is sufficient for all known character encoding requirements, including full coverage of all historic scripts of the world.

Legal and Regulatory Issues

Existing international companies are well versed in the laws, tariffs, and regulatory issues of the countries they do business in. However, these companies have invested thousands, if not millions, of dollars in establishing their international business processes. Most companies new to international commerce do not have these resources at their disposal. However, if your business plans on selling in the international marketplace, proper legal advice with international law and financial understanding is an absolute necessity.

exam
preparation
pointer

The i-Net+ exam will not expect you to understand the detailed implications of doing business internationally, only that you are aware that additional considerations must be taken prior to starting a business that reaches beyond your native borders.

WHAT THE FUTURE HOLDS

Clearly the originators of the Internet are as surprised as anyone at the incredible growth of these technologies. The Internet has changed many paradigms in business, communications, and society. As recently as the mid-1990s, most businesses maintained long-term business plans that spanned five to eight years. Today, a long-term business plan rarely exceeds three years. Where the Internet will take us, or even what it will look like in the next decade is anybody's guess, and most predictions are just that, a guess. However, there are a few things on the horizon that will most likely become commonplace on the Internet. Many services that are still slow in gaining acceptance today will become the standard method of operation as school age children grow up with this Internet technology.

IPv6

IPv6 is short for "Internet Protocol Version 6". IPv6 is the next generation protocol designed by the IETF to replace the current version Internet Protocol, IP Version 4 (IPv4). Early references to IPv6 are sometimes called IPng for IP, Next Generation.

Most of today's Internet uses IPv4, which is now nearly twenty years old. IPv4 has been remarkably resilient in spite of its age, but it is beginning to have problems. Most importantly, there is a growing shortage of IPv4 addresses, which are needed by all new machines added to the Internet.

IPv6 fixes a number of problems in IPv4, such as the limited number of available IPv4 addresses. It also adds many improvements to IPv4 in areas such as routing and network autoconfiguration. IPv6 is expected to gradually replace IPv4, with the two coexisting for a number of years during a transition period.

6bone is an independent outgrowth of the IETF IPng project that resulted in the creation of the IPv6 protocols intended eventually to replace the current Internet network layer. The 6bone is currently an informal collaborative project covering North America, Europe, and Japan.

One essential part in the IPv4 to IPv6 transition is the development of an Internet-wide IPv6 backbone infrastructure that can transport IPv6 packets. As with the existing IPv4 Internet backbone, the IPv6 backbone infrastructure will be composed of many Internet Service Providers and user networks linked together to provide the worldwide Internet.

Until the IPv6 protocols are widely implemented and fully tested for interoperability, production ISP and user network routers will not readily place IPv4 routers at risk. Thus a way is needed to provide Internet-wide IPv6 transport in an organized and orderly way for early testing and use.

The 6bone is a virtual network layered on top of portions of the physical IPv4-based Internet to support routing of IPv6 packets, as that function has not yet been integrated into many production routers. The network is composed of islands that can directly support IPv6 packets, linked by virtual point-to-point links called "tunnels." The tunnel endpoints are typically workstation-class machines having operating system support for IPv6.

Over time, as confidence builds to allow production routers to carry native IPv6 packets, it is expected that the 6bone would disappear by agreement of all parties. It would be replaced in a transparent way by production ISP and user network IPv6 Internet-wide transport.

The 6bone is thus focused on providing the early policy and procedures necessary to provide IPv6 transport in a reasonable fashion so testing and experience can be carried out. It would not attempt to provide new network interconnects architectures, procedures, and policies that are clearly the scope of ISP and user network operators. In fact, it is the desire to include as many ISP and user network operators in the 6bone process as possible to guarantee a seamless transition to IPv6.

Voice over Public IP

As we discussed previously, voice signals transported over an IP network, especially over the Internet, will be a major milestone for both the Internet, and personal communications. Voice over IP (VoIP) is a term used for a set of facilities to manage the delivery of voice information using the Internet Protocol. In general, this means sending voice information in digital form in discrete packets rather than in the traditional circuit-committed protocols of the public switched telephone network. A major advantage of VoIP and Internet telephony is that it avoids the tolls charged by ordinary telephone service.

Although the technology for VoIP exists today, the quality of the communication is not high enough for business and most personal needs. People are used to picking up a handset, having a dial tone, and being able to place their telephone calls. The expectation is that the quality of the sounds between the telephone parties will be clear, without interference, and without choppiness. As improvements to the Internet infrastructure continue, and all digital, high-speed connections to the end user becomes commonplace, VoIP will be the standard transportation mechanism for all voice *and* video calls.

Changes in the Mega-Mall Mentality

The holiday shopping season of 1998 was the birthmark of Internet commerce. Even though less than 3 percent of all holiday purchases were attributed to Internet sales, estimates indicated that there would be constant and steady growth of consumer acceptance. This prediction clearly held true, as early analysis of holiday shopping for 1999 had exceeded the 4 percent mark even before the first of December. As today's children come of consumer age, and larger percentages of households connect to the Internet, the traditional methods of "mega-mall" shopping will change. Granted, there are some items, especially clothing, that may never be as popular electronically as they are in person, but thousands of everyday items that don't require close examination will be purchased over the Internet in greater numbers. The sheer convenience, competitive pricing, and increased selection will continue to attract more consumers and will likely be the shopping method of choice for most people within the next five to eight years.

The Internet Stock Phenomenon

Many financial analysts have predicted a downturn in the current stock market levels for the past few years. Increasingly, however, the old rules of Wall Street are changing. The market is no longer limited to retirement plans and business insiders. The Internet has created a whole new avenue for stock investors by providing easy access, timely news, and inexpensive trading fees. Is the Internet a major factor in the record-setting performance of the stock market? Perhaps, but if not a major factor, surely it is more than a mild influence. More people, across wider economic backgrounds, are buying and selling stocks then ever before because the Internet has empowered them to do so. Where traditional stockbrokers were uninterested in the smaller volumes of stocks a new trader might want to place, do-it-yourself Internet brokers will accept trades for one, or one thousand shares.

To help spur interest in online trading, most Internet brokers provide vital research information, real-time quotes, and customizable portfolio tools to their customers. Combine these benefits with transaction costs from $8 to $20 per trade, and many people previously kept out of the mainstream stock market have become serious investors. To what extent these new traders will impact the overall actions of the stock market is still unknown, but clearly these tools have provided additional financial options to many people.

EXAM PREPARATION SUMMARY

With the conclusion of this chapter, you have covered all the concepts required to successfully pass the i-Net+ exam. Now let's review the information presented in Chapter 11.

- There are two main categories of e-commerce: business-to-business and business-to-consumer. Business-to-business e-commerce uses tools like the extranet and Electronic Data Interchange (EDI) technologies to share information between business partners. EDI is a common method for carrying out financial transactions with a goal of reducing paper and manual processes.

- Business-to-consumer technologies include advanced Internet solutions such as merchant systems, online catalogs, and shopping carts to make online shopping and transactions easy, secure, and expedient.

- Internet marketing offers solutions that allow even the least-funded business to get global attention. Search engines, directories, and portals are all popular and powerful tools to aid people in finding your site. Banner ads also have merit, but placement is key. If your budget can afford it, traditional marketing methods, such as television and radio advertising are also very effective.

- The sheer volume of information, and the ease with which it can be copied from one medium to another, even between Web sites, often obscures the idea of copyright protection. It is important to understand that all tangible works are automatically protected by U.S. copyrights (protection in other countries varies). Although you may not need to register your work, having a formal copyright provides the owner(s) with additional recourse in a legal dispute.

- Geographic borders clearly do not bind the Internet. This greatly enhances the ability of companies to do business on a global level. However, there are many issues involved in multinational commerce. Currency exchanges, shipping, and supply distribution all present challenges to businesses doing business outside their current country's regulations.

- The future of the Internet is being written each and every day. This new communication tool is so new that many of its services and features are being developed and fine-tuned on a trial basis. Where the Internet will unfold in the future is still up for debate.

- IPv6 will be a major upgrade in the way devices are addressed, and data is routed in the next generation of the Internet. Voice over the public Internet, using the IP protocol (VoIP) will most likely replace the telephone infrastructure we use today. People's opinion of shopping malls and retail stores will change as e-commerce replaces traditional shopping practices. And people will be further empowered to control financial futures with the help of online stock trading.

APPLYING WHAT YOU HAVE LEARNED

The following review questions give you an opportunity to test your knowledge of the information presented in this chapter. The answers to these assessment questions can be found in Appendix B. If you missed some, review those sections in this chapter before going further

Instant Assessment Questions

1. Because of its business advantage, the EDI process is sometimes called

   A. Electronic ordering

   B. Paperless trading

   C. Order interchange

   D. Structured ordering

2. According to the i-Net+ definition, a merchant system consists of these features:

A. Secured Web page

B. Shopping carts

C. A credit authorization account

D. Firewalls

3. Advantages to payment gateways are

A. They provide unattended, real-time credit card authorization

B. They normally costs less per transaction than other systems

C. All authorizations or denials are normally completed in less than two minutes

D. They eliminate the need for advanced firewalls

4. Two advantages to using dynamic HTML catalog pages are

A. They provide better forms tools to gather credit information

B. Customers can calculate tax and shipping charges in real-time

C. Price changes can be maintained quickly

D. Inventory levels can be adjusted in real time

5. Search engines differ from directories because

A. Search engines will automatically locate changes in Web pages

B. Directories will automatically locate changes in Web pages

C. Directories are easier to get listed in

D. Search engines use editors to evaluate the content of a site

6. Banner ads are normally

A. Placed in e-mail based advertising materials

B. 468 × 60 pixel graphics

C. Automatically updated

D. Not as effective as other marketing techniques

7. Original material is considered protected by copyright only when

   A. Registered with a copyright authority

   B. Indicated with the proper notice

   C. When tangibly committed to real media

   D. The source origin is with the United States

8. Material used for non-profit results can be copied under the fair use exclusion.

   A. True

   B. False

9. Web pages can be created in multiple languages by

   A. Using the Unicode standards

   B. Only by using separate static Web pages

   C. Only by using separate dynamic Web pages

   D. Encoding the text portions in internationally accepted ASCII format

10. What objectives must be defined when doing e-commerce internationally?

    A. Consideration of available shipping methods

    B. Escrow accounts for sales tax payments

    C. Ability to accept payments in different currencies

    D. Ability to secure the Web site with encryption methods that do not violate export regulations.

i-Net+ Examination Blueprint

The appendix contains the complete blueprint for the CompTIA i-Net+ exam, including the approximate percentage that exam objective domain is covered on the exam.

This examination blueprint includes weighting, test objectives, and example content. Example topics and concepts are included to clarify the test objectives; they should not be construed as a comprehensive listing of the content of this examination.

Table A-1 lists the domains measured by this examination and the approximate extent to which they are represented.

TABLE A-1 TABLE OF OBJECTIVE DOMAINS AND PERCENT OF EXAM

DOMAIN	% OF EXAMINATION
1.0 I–Net Basics	10%
2.0 I–Net Clients	20%
3.0 Development	20%
4.0 Networking	25%
5.0 Net Security	15%
6.0 Business Concepts	10%

Domain 1.0: i-Net Basics

1.1. Describe a URL, its functions and components, different types of URLs, and use of the appropriate type of URL to access a given type of server. Content may include the following:

- Protocol
- Address
- Port

1.2. Identify the issues that affect Internet site functionality (e.g., performance, security and reliability). Content may include the following:

- Bandwidth
- Internet connection points
- Audience access
- Internet Service Provider (ISP)
- Connection types
- Corrupt files
- Files taking too long to load
- Inability to open files
- Resolution of graphics

1.3. Describe the concept of caching and its implications. Content may include the following:

- Server caching
- Client caching
- Proxy caching
- Cleaning out client-side cache
- Server may cache information as well
- Web page update settings in browsers

1.4. Describe different types of search indexes — static index/site map, keyword index, full text index. Examples could include the following:

- Searching your site
- Searching content
- Indexing your site for a search

Domain 2.0: i–Net Clients

2.1. Describe the infrastructure needed to support an Internet client. Content could include the following:

- TCP/IP stack
- Operating system
- Network connection
- Web browser
- E-mail
- Hardware platform (PC, handheld device, WebTV, Internet phone)

2.2. Describe the use of Web browsers and various clients (e.g., FTP clients, Telnet clients, email clients, all-in-one clients/universal clients) within a given context of use. Examples of context could include the following:

- When you would use each
- The basic commands you would use (e.g., put and get) with each client (e.g., FTP, Telnet)

2.3. Explain the issues to consider when configuring the desktop. Content could include the following:

- TCP/IP configuration (NetBIOS name server such as WINS), DNS, default gateway, subnet mask
- Host file configuration
- DHCP versus static IP
- Configuring browser (proxy configuration, client-side caching)

2.4. Describe MIME types and their components. Content could include the following:

o Whether a client can understand various email types (MIME, HTML, uuencode)

o The need to define MIME file types for special download procedures such as unusual documents or graphic formats

2.5. Identify problems related to legacy clients (e.g., TCP/IP sockets and their implication on the operating system). Content could include the following:

o Checking revision date, manufacturer/vendor

o Troubleshooting and performance issues

o Compatibility issues

o Version of the Web browser

2.6. Explain the function of patches and updates to client software and associated problems. Content could include the following:

o Desktop security

o Virus protection

o Encryption levels

o Web browsers

o E-mail clients

2.7. Describe the advantages and disadvantages of using a cookie and how to set cookies. Content could include the following:

o Setting a cookie without the knowledge of the user

o Automatically accepting cookies versus query

o Remembering everything the user has done

o Security and privacy implications

Domain 3.0: Development

3.1. Define programming-related terms as they relate to Internet applications development. Content could include the following:

- API
- CGI
- SQL
- SAPI
- DLL — dynamic linking and static linking
- Client and server-side scripting

3.2. Describe the differences between popular client-side and server-side programming languages. Examples could include the following:

- Java
- JavaScript
- Perl
- C
- C++
- Visual Basic
- VBScript
- Jscript
- XML
- VRML
- ASP

Content could include the following:

- When to use the languages
- When they are executed

3.3. Describe the differences between a relational database and a non-relational database.

3.4. Identify when to integrate a database with a Web site and the technologies used to connect the two.

3.5. Demonstrate the ability to create HTML pages. Content could include the following:

- HTML document structure
- Coding simple tables, headings, forms
- Compatibility between different browsers
- Difference between text editors and GUI editors
- Importance of creating cross-browser coding in your HTML

3.6. Identify popular multimedia extensions or plug-ins. Examples could include the following:

- QTVR (quick time)
- Flash
- Shockwave
- RealPlayer
- Windows Media Player

3.8. Describe the uses and benefits of various multimedia file formats. Examples could include the following:

- GIF
- GIF89a
- JPEG
- PNG
- PDF
- RTF
- TIFF
- PostScript

- EPS
- BMP
- MOV
- MPEG
- AVI
- Streaming media
- Non-streaming media

3.8. Describe the process of pre-launch site/application functionality testing. Content could including the following:

- Checking hot links
- Testing different browsers
- Testing to ensure it does not corrupt your e-commerce site
- Load testing
- Access to the site
- Testing with various speed connections

Domain 4.0: Networking and Infrastructure

4.1. Describe the core components of the current Internet infrastructure and how they relate to each other. Content may include the following:

- Network access points
- Backbone

4.2. Identify problems with Internet connectivity from source to destination for various types of servers. Examples could include the following:

- E-mail
- Slow server
- Website

4.3. Describe Internet domain names and DNS. Content could include the following:

- DNS entry types
- Hierarchical structure
- Role of root domain server
- Top level or original domains — edu, com, mil, net, gov, org
- Country level domains —.UK

4.4. Describe the nature, purpose, and operational essentials of TCP/IP. Content could include the following:

- What addresses are and their classifications (A, B, C, D)
- Determining which ones are valid and which ones are not (subnet masks)
- Public versus private IP addresses

4.5. Describe the purpose of remote access protocols. Content could include the following:

- SLIP
- PPP
- PPTP
- Point-to-point/multipoint

4.6. Describe how various protocols or services apply to the function of a mail system, Web system, and file transfer system. Content could include the following:

- POP3
- SMTP
- HTTP
- FTP
- NNTP (news servers)
- TCP/IP
- LDAP

- LPR
- Telnet
- Gopher

4.7. Describe when to use various diagnostic tools for identifying and resolving Internet problems. Content could include the following:

- Ping
- WinIPCfg
- IPC Config
- ARP
- Trace Routing Utility
- Network Analyzer
- Netstat

4.8. Describe hardware and software connection devices and their uses. Content could include the following:

- Network interface card
- Various types of modems including analog, ISDN, DSL, and cable
- Modem setup and commands
- Adapter
- Bridge
- Internet-in-a-box
- Cache-in-a-box
- Hub
- Router
- Switch
- Gateway
- NOS
- Firewall

4.9. Describe various types of Internet bandwidth technologies (link types). Content could include the following:

- T1/E1
- T3/E3
- Frame relay
- X.25
- ATM
- DSL

4.10. Describe the purpose of various servers—what they are, their functionality, and features. Content could include the following:

- Proxy
- Mail
- Mirrored
- Cache
- List
- Web (HTTP)
- News
- Certificate
- Directory (LDAP)
- E-commerce
- Telnet
- FTP

Domain 5.0: I-Net Security

5.1. Define the following Internet security concepts: access control, encryption, auditing and authentication, and provide appropriate types of technologies currently available for each. Examples could include the following:

- Access control—access control list, firewall, packet filters, proxy

- Authentication — certificates, digital signatures, non-repudiation
- Encryption — public and private keys, secure socket layers (SSL), S/MIME, digital signatures, global versus country-specific encryption standards
- Auditing — intrusion detection utilities, log files, auditing logs
- SET (Secure Electronic Transactions)

5.2. Describe VPN and what it does. Content could include the following:

- VPN is encrypted communications
- Connecting two different company sites via an Internet VPN (extranet)
- Connecting a remote user to a site

5.3. Describe various types of suspicious activities. Examples could include the following:

- Multiple login failures
- Denial of service attacks
- Mail flooding/spam
- Ping floods
- Syn floods

5.4. Describe access security features for an Internet server (e.g., email server, Web server). Examples could include the following:

- User name and password
- File level
- Certificate
- File-level access: read, write, no access

5.5. Describe the purpose of anti-virus software and when to use it. Content could include the following:

- Browser/client
- Server

5.6. Describe the differences between the following as they relate to security requirements:

- Intranet
- Extranet
- Internet

Domain 6.0: Business Concepts

6.1. Explain the issues involved in copyrighting, trademarking, and licensing. Content could include the following:

- How to license copyright materials
- Scope of your copyright
- How to copyright your material anywhere
- Consequences of not being aware of copyright issues, not following copyright restrictions

6.2. Identify the issues related to working in a global environment. Content could include the following:

- Working in a multi-vendor environment with different currencies, etc.
- International issues — shipping, supply chain
- Multi-lingual or multi-character issues (Unicode)
- Legal and regulatory issues

6.3. Define the following Web-related mechanisms for audience development (i.e., attracting and retaining an audience):

- Push technology
- Pull technology

6.4. Describe the differences between the following from a business standpoint:

- Intranet
- Extranet
- Internet

6.5. Define e-commerce terms and concepts. Content could include the following:

- EDI
- Business to Business
- Business to Consumer
- Internet commerce
- Merchant systems
- Online Cataloging
- Relationship management
- Customer self-service
- Internet marketing

Answers to Instant Assessment Questions

CHAPTER ONE: AN INTRODUCTION TO THE INTERNET

1. What two methods are used to connect computers together on the Internet?

   Wires and Satellite

2. What term is used when describing two or more computers connected for the purpose of sharing information?

   A Data Network

3. What type of company do most people subscribe to in order to access the Internet?

   An Internet Service Provider or ISP

4. What two methods are most commonly used when connecting to the Internet?

   Analog/Dial-up and Digital (often directly connected)

5. Most Internet services require two computers to communicate. One computer fills requests made to it by another. What term is used to describe this type of computer relationship?

   Client/Server

6. What is the primary protocol, or "common language" of the Internet?

   TCP/IP

7. What protocol is used to copy files between computers?

File Transfer Protocol or FTP

8. What protocol is used between servers to transport e-mail messages?

Simple Mail Transport Protocol or SMTP

9. How many classification states are there in the RFC process?

Five

10. What type of organized storage method do many businesses use to maintain their information which increasingly is required to be accessible on the Internet?

A database

CHAPTER TWO: COMPONENTS OF THE INTERNET

1. A high-speed backbone of the Internet is connected throughout the United States at four primary locations. Select two of the cities connected by this backbone.

A. Chicago

C. San Francisco

D. Washington, D.C.

2. Companies that offer Internet services to business and individuals are called

C. Internet Service Providers (ISP)

3. What device is required to access the Internet over analog telephone lines?

B. Modem

4. All devices on the Internet have unique numeric addresses called

A. An Internet Protocol number

5. Internet addresses are composed of specific components. The first of these identifies

D. The Service Protocol Type

6. The prefix `http://` refers to this type of Internet Service:

D. A World Wide Web site

7. The Top Level Domain name used by *most* service providers is

   B. .net

8. When typing an Internet Address into a browser, all letters must be in uppercase.

   B. False

9. Domain Names can have a maximum of _____ characters including the Top Level Domain identifier.

   A. 26

10. Internet subscribers must follow standards issued and maintained by what organization?

    C. None, adherence is strictly voluntary

11. New Internet Standards are submitted by means of

    A. Request for Comments

12. Connecting to the Internet using Windows 95/98, what service makes defining the connection easy?

    B. Dial-Up Networking

13. Where do you test a modem's proper configuration in Windows 95/98?

    D. Start ➪ Control Panel ➪ Modems ➪ Properties ➪ More Info

14. Which two tool bar buttons are common to both Internet Explorer and Navigator?

    D. Forward and Home

15. The Refresh/Restart buttons

    D. Fetch a new copy of a Web page from the Web site

CHAPTER THREE: INTERNET PERFORMANCE AND INDEXING

1. The fastest upload speed possible from a dial-up modem is

   B. 33Kbps

2. The specification of 56K modems is

   A. V.90

3. Which of these connection types is generally the fastest?

   D. OC3

4. Running multiple protocols on a LAN, such as TCP/IP, IPX, and NetBEUI, can increase overall performance because applications don't need to worry about what protocol to use; the network will provide this function.

   B. False

5. Cache technology can be implemented

   A. In the browser

   C. By a special appliance connected to the network

6. Caching technology works best when

   D. Placed between the LAN and the Internet for all users

7. Cached files in Internet Explorer are called

   B. Temporary Files

8. When cost is more of a factor than performance gains, which proxy type is the best selection for a LAN with less than 20 computers?

   B. A dedicated "black box" proxy that bonds multiple dial-up lines

9. Indexing your site for publication on the World Wide Web should contain

   A. Keywords that help search engines such as Yahoo properly categorize your site

   D. A keyword mechanism that searches on words and/or complete phrases

10. Placing predefined keywords in an HTML page is done by the use of

   B. Meta tags

CHAPTER FOUR: THE BUILDING BLOCKS

1. An IP datagram contains which two of these components?

   B. User data

   C. Source address

2. According to the TCP/IP protocol, Internet hosts are

    D. Any device connected to the Internet

3. Which of these IP Addresses are valid host numbers?

    A. 191.162.100.20

    D. 101.1.101.1

4. Subnet masks are only included when they differ from the default value for the IP class being used.

    B. False

5. Which of these connection types can be used to connect two routers?

    A. ISDN

    B. Serial analog

    D. "T" channel

6. The service used to automatically assign IP addresses is

    D. Dynamic Host Core Protocol

7. Which of these are valid Top-Level Domains?

    C. MIL – Military Sites

    D. NET – Internet Service Providers

8. The "Central Server" in the DNS tree is known as what server?

    A. Root

9. What utilities show the TCP/IP settings configured on Windows-based computers?

    B. WinIPcfg

    D. ipconfig

10. What three commands are valid when using FTP?

    A. send

    C. recv

    D. get

Chapter Five: Client Side Troubleshooting and Security Issues

1. DOS-based applications are not well suited for browsing because

   C. DOS-based browsers can't display most Web graphic formats

2. Which statements are true regarding the WINSOCK.DLL?

   A. Winsock is an interface between Windows applications and the TCP/IP stack.

   D. The WINSOCK.DLL file can be modified by a Windows programmer.

3. A software service pack usually

   C. Fixes bugs and may add features to existing applications

   D. Should only be applied after understanding its implications

4. Service packs should be applied when security holes are identified in the application.

   A. True

5. Viruses can be transmitted

   A. In an e-mail attachment

   C. From a program downloaded from an FTP site

   D. By a VBA macro file

6. A major consideration when choosing an antivirus solution is

   D. It should provide easy assess to signature updates

7. The best technology currently available to ensure privacy of data is

   C. Data encryption

8. Public-key data encryption can be useful for data

   B. Transmitted across a private network

   C. Transmitted across the Public network (Internet)

9. Digital Certificates are issued by

   D. Trusted third-party corporations

10. A negative side effect of allowing cookies from the web is

    A. Companies can track your online habits

CHAPTER SIX: COMPONENTS OF THE WEB PAGE

1. An API is

C. An interface that provides simple access to common programming routines.

2. The proper syntax to center a line of text in bold type on a web page is

B. `<CENTER><B>`This is sample text`</CENTER></B>`

3. Predefined colors can be set for which web page elements?

A. All of the text on the page

B. Links that have already been clicked

C. Links that have not been clicked

D. Solid backgrounds

4. Hyperlinks can be defined on which two elements of a web page?

C. Any text

D. A graphic image

5. The `WIDTH` attribute of the `HTML TABLE` tag contains

A. A percentage of the viewable page to display the table

C. A fixed integer defining a non-resizable area for the table

6. Two attributes for formatting objects within a cell are

B. CELLSPACING

C. CELLPADDING

7. The two HTML tags used to create cells within a table are

A. TD

D. TR

8. To format an object in the exact center of a cell, which two attributes are used?

B. <ALIGN=CENTER>

D. <VALIGN=CENTER>

CHAPTER SEVEN: ADVANCED WEB TECHNIQUES

1. Data collected from a form can be sent to

    A. The site visitor via e-mail

    B. A corporate database

    C. The webmaster of the site via e-mail

    D. A custom-written program for further processing

2. The `FORM` tag requires which two additional attributes?

    D. An `ACTION` and `METHOD` directive

3. Which tag(s) must be included to send the data collected in an HTML form?

    A. `<INPUT TYPE=SUBMIT>`

4. SQL is

    A. A specialty language to manipulate data in a relational database

5. Which of the following are primary elements of JavaScripts?

    A. Operators

    D. Expressions

6. A PerlScript can be properly used in any web browser of version 4 or higher.

    B. False

7. C is a high-level programming language written as a series of

    C. Functions

8. A relational database links common database items by means of

    B. Unique values called keys

9. Which of the following image formats are supported on all browser platforms?

    C. JPEG

    D. GIF

CHAPTER EIGHT: CORE COMPONENTS OF THE INTERNET INFRASTRUCTURE

1. WebTV is most useful for

   C. Less technical people who want simple Internet services with little fuss

2. Internet "telephone" calls can be made providing

   B. At least one user has a multimedia system including a sound card and speakers

   C. You are willing to accept less than clear communications

3. When a company provides linked text computer communications to employees that are not connected to the Internet, it has implemented a:

   D. An intranet

4. When two separate companies want to link their computer systems but ensure that private data remains secure, they can implement

   B. An extranet

5. By default, Web Servers respond to requests on TCP/IP port

   C. 80

6. The Multipurpose Internet Mail Extensions, or MIME, is used to

   A. Specify how messages must be formatted in order to be exchanged between different systems

7. TCP/IP ports 110 and 25 are used by what two protocols?

   B. SMTP uses 25

   D. POP3 uses 110

8. MX records define the username in a fully qualified domain name (FQDM).

   B. False

9. Certificate servers are useful in preventing

   A. One person from impersonating another

10. Newsgroup servers use which protocol?

    A. Network News Transfer Protocol (NNTP)

CHAPTER NINE: NETWORKING HARDWARE AND SOFTWARE COMPONENTS

1. The collection of the cable system and a common protocol is called the network

   C. Topology

2. The PCI technology provides

   B. Plug-and-play capability

3. Routing takes place between

   B. Two MAC addresses

4. Category 5 cable consists of

   D. 4 wire pairs

5. Advantages of fiber optic cable include

   A. Protection from radiation and electrical pulses

   C. Line taps are easily detectable

   D. Light weight

6. Network switches provide

   C. Dedicated bandwidth between 2 devices

   D. The ability to route data between 2 ports

7. Routers require _____ to be included in the data packet.

   A. Routing information

8. The Routing Information Protocol performs route discovery based on available bandwidth.

   B. False

9. A CSU/DSU connecting a T1 line to a router is used to

   B. Separate channels for voice and data

10. Common connection types from the slowest to fastest are

    B. ISDN, DSL, T1, E1

CHAPTER TEN: NETWORK TROUBLESHOOTING AND SECURITY

1. A part of the first step to systematically approaching the diagnostic process is to create a

   C. Problem resolution document

2. Server degradation issues caused by a NIC flooding the cable system is commonly called

   B. A broadcast storm

3. What two things can be done to increase a Web server's performance?

   A. Defragment the hard drive

   D. Place Web pages and graphic files on a RAM disk

4. What utility could you use to determine the TCP/IP settings of an NT computer?

   D. ipconfig

5. Which utility is useful in identifying where routing bottlenecks are occurring?

   A. tracert

6. What type of firewall technology is most useful for preventing incoming FTP requests?

   C. Protocol screening

7. A security protocol created by Visa and MasterCard for secure credit card transactions across the Internet is

   A. SET

8. Global encryption standards are based on 128-bit algorithms.

   B. False

9. To minimize administration time while still maintaining the integrity of critical data, antivirus software could be implemented

   C. On the servers

10. What two technologies are used to facilitate the sharing of organized information between two businesses?

B. Intranets

D. Extranets

CHAPTER ELEVEN: THE ROLE OF E-COMMERCE WITHIN A BUSINESS STRATEGY

1. Because of its business advantage, the EDI process is sometimes called

B. Paperless trading

2. According to the i-Net+ definition, a Merchant System consists of these features:

A. Secured Web page

C. A credit authorization account

3. Advantages to payment gateways are

A. They provide unattended, real-time credit card authorization

D. They eliminate the need for advanced firewalls

4. Two advantages to using dynamic HTML catalog pages are

C. Price changes can be maintained quickly

D. Inventory levels can be adjusted in real-time

5. Search engines differ from directories because?

A. Search engines will automatically locate changes in Web pages

6. Banner ads are normally

B. 468 × 60 pixel graphics

7. Original material is considered protected by copyright only when

C. Tangibly committed to real media

8. Material used for non-profit results can be copied under the fair use exclusion.

B. False

9. Web pages can be created in multiple languages by

  A. Using the Unicode standards

10. What objectives must be defined when doing e-commerce internationally?

  A. Consideration of available shipping methods

  C. Ability to accept payments in different currencies

Exam Preparation Tips

This appendix contains some useful tips and pointers to help you prepare for the i-Net+ Certification exam. Read these pages carefully before you schedule your exam, and review this appendix again just before you take the test. Pay special attention to the exam blueprint and make sure you understand all of the objectives covered on the exam.

CompTIA and IT industry leaders researched and developed a vendor-neutral, entry-level Internet certification program that will test baseline technical knowledge of Internet, intranet, and extranet topics, independent of specific Internet-related career roles. Learning objectives and domains examined include Internet basics, Internet clients, development, networking, security, and business concepts.

The exam is designed to test Internet technicians responsible for implementing and maintaining Internet, intranet, and extranet infrastructure and services as well as development of related applications.

HOW THE I-NET+ EXAM WAS DEVELOPED

In order to develop the exam objectives and formalize the final version of the exam, CompTIA leveraged relationships with many of the industry's leading vendors. They also recruited industry professionals, both from inside and outside of the organization, to develop the objectives and formalize the final exam. And many vendors offering their own certification programs have stated that they will likely wave their base test requirement for applicants who are i-Net+ certified. The following phases were part of the i-Net+ program development:

1. Identifying subject matter experts (SMEs) to develop test objectives

2. Conducting a blueprint survey to determine the number of test items needed for each objective

3. Writing exam questions

4. Reviewing the exam for technical accuracy, congruence, psychometrics, and grammar

5. Performing a beta test and analyzing it

6. Conducting a cut-score survey to determine the pass/fail rate

7. Completing a final review of the items

Exam Items and Scoring

The i-Net+ Certification exam questions are derived from an industry-wide job task analysis. At the time this book was published, CompTIA had stated that there would be approximately 75 questions on the exam. These 75 questions are randomly selected from a much larger pool of questions, so if you take the test more than once, it is not likely that you will receive duplicate items. Each question and each section is given a weighted value (see Table A-1 in Appendix A for the weight value chart). While the exact passing score has not yet been established, tests of this nature typically require you to answer 80 to 85 percent correctly in order to pass. If you do fail the exam, you are allowed to retake it as many times as necessary. However, if you study diligently, and take the practice exams presented in this book, you should be able to pass the first time.

The exam questions are a mix of multiple-score, multiple-choice, and (some) true/false. Multiple-score questions have more than one correct answer to a question. Multiple-choice, on the other hand, have a single correct answer. The test is administered through the Sylvan Prometric Authorized Test Centers. You can schedule your test by calling Sylvan in the United States at 1-888-895-6116. When you call, please have the following available:

1. Your Social Security number. (If you do not have it on hand, or do not wish to use your Social Security number, Sylvan Prometric will provide an ID number.)

2. Your mailing address and telephone number.

3. Your employer or organization (optional).

4. The date(s) you wish to take the test. Depending on where you live, you may not be able to schedule the exam on your preferred date, so be prepared to provide a few alternate dates. The further in advance that you can schedule, the better chance you have of getting your first choice of times.

5. A method of payment (credit card or check). The final exam price has not yet been published, but it will probably be about $175.

Test-Taking Tips

Here are some tips that may be helpful as you prepare to take the i-Net+ Certification exam.

Before the Exam

Review the Exam Preparation Summary pages at the end of each chapter in this book. Answer the questions at the end of each chapter and on the Beachfront Quizzer CD supplied with this book. If you have trouble with questions, review the sections pertaining to the areas that you are not clear on. Pay special attention to the exam preparation pointers scattered throughout this book, because they will help you focus on important exam-related topics. If you have access to a computer lab either at school or in your office, try duplicating the problems discussed and install some equipment to see firsthand how the hardware interacts. The IRS allows you to deduct certain expenses for continuing education pertaining to your employment. If you can, purchase a few PCs and some basic networking components and build a small network at home. You don't need the latest and greatest equipment, just about anything that runs will do. Remember: the exam measures real-world skills that you will not obtain simply by reading about them. Follow the sidebar guidelines in Chapter 11 to put your own server on the Internet and see exactly what steps are involved.

Don't study the entire night before the test. A good night's sleep is often better preparation than extra studying. Besides, if you prepare properly, you won't learn anything new by cramming the night before.

Try to schedule your exam during your own *peak* time. In other words, if you're a morning person, avoid scheduling the exam at 3:00 p.m. Take the exam preparation process seriously. Remember, this exam is not designed to be easy — it is intended to recognize and certify *professionals* with specific skill sets.

On Exam Day

Arrive 10 to 15 minutes early and don't forget your picture ID. Dress comfortably. The more comfortable you are, the more you are able to focus on the exam. If you carry a pager and/or a cellular telephone, leave them at home, or in your car. You will be asked to remove them before the test, and you don't want to accidentally leave them behind when you leave. Don't bring a note pad or other note-taking materials with you. The testing center provides you with such materials. Books, notes, and other such items are not permitted in the test area. Don't drink a lot of coffee or other beverages before the exam. The test is timed, and you don't want to waste precious time going back and forth to the restroom.

During the Exam

Answer the questions that you know first. Once you have these questions out of the way, go back to the beginning and answer the ones you're reasonably sure of. Mark any questions that you'd like to spend more time on. You will be able to return to these later. Remember that there are no *trick* questions. The correct answer is always among the choices listed. Don't try to read too much into the question; take the information as it is presented. Eliminate the most obvious incorrect answers first. Answer all of the questions before you end the exam. Unanswered questions are counted as incorrect. Read the questions carefully. At first glance, you may think you know the answer right away, but there may be a subtle shift in the way the question is phrased. Approaching the question from one viewpoint may lead you to the incorrect answer. Once you have completed the exam, you will receive immediate, online notification of your pass or fail status.

After the Exam

Take a deep breath.

Make sure the testing administrator certifies your exam report, and take the report with you. Although the report is sent to CompTIA, you want to be sure you have it should you ever need to prove your results.

If you don't pass, use the report to see where your weak points are. The exam report shows the percentage correct for each area. Go back to this book and spend a good deal of time reviewing these areas. Remember that you probably won't have the exact same questions on your next exam, but you will be tested in the same categories.

If you did pass, congratulations! Job well done. CompTIA will send you your confirmation and certificate within a few weeks. Don't stop learning now, though. Remember that this industry changes quickly. Your next certification test may be only months away.

What's on the CD-ROM

The CD-ROM that accompanies this book features BeachFront Quizzer's interactive testing software, along with many useful Internet applications mentioned in this book. This appendix will tell you how to install and use each of the items on the CD.

The CD-ROM includes the following programs:

- BeachFront Quizzer text engine
- Microsoft Internet Explorer 5.0 Web browser
- Netscape Communicator 4.7 Web browser
- HTML Notes, a text-based HTML editor
- Web Express, a WYSIWIG HTML editor
- SERV-U, an FTP server
- MDaemon, an e-mail server
- WinGate, a proxy server
- JWeb, a Web server
- Xitami, a Web server
- Simple DNS, a DNS server
- United States copyright forms in PDF format

BEACHFRONT QUIZZER

The version of the BeachFront Quizzer software included on the CD-ROM gives you the opportunity to test your knowledge with simulated exam questions. The features of the BeachFront Quizzer product include

- Study sessions, standard exams, and adaptive exams

o New exam every time

o Historical analysis

If you want more exam questions, you can purchase the full retail version of the BeachFront Quizzer software directly from them. See the BeachFront Quizzer ad in the back of this book.

To install BeachFront Quizzer, follow these steps:

1. Open My Computer. Double-click your CD-ROM drive (usually D:). Double-click the BFQuiz folder. Double-click setupbfq.exe. The BeachFront Quizzer setup program will start.

2. On the Welcome screen, click Next to continue to the license agreement screen. Read the agreement, and click I Agree to continue.

3. On the Choose Destination Location screen, click Next to accept the default file location (C:\Quizzer). If you want to install the files to a different location, click Browse and select the file location. After you click Next, the installation begins.

4. After the installation, you will be asked to install Adobe Acrobat Reader. You'll need Acrobat Reader to enhance the BeachFront Quizzer product. The test questions are mapped to the contents of the book, which you access with the Acrobat (PDF) files. Click the check box marked "Install Adobe Acrobat Reader," and click Next.

5. The Acrobat Reader installation program starts. The Acrobat Reader Welcome screen appears first. Click Next to continue. The License agreement screen appears next. Read the agreement, and click I Accept to continue.

6. The Choose Destination Location screen appears. If you want to choose a different location, click Browse and select the destination to install the files to. To accept the default, click Next to continue.

7. The Acrobat Reader installation program runs. After the installer is finished, a dialog box will appear that reads "Thank you for choosing Acrobat Reader." Click OK to finish.

8. You're returned to the BeachFront Quizzer installation process. The next screen gives you the option to install the online books. These are the Acrobat (PDF) files that contain the text of the book and are linked to the questions.

You should install these to get the most benefit out of BeachFront Quizzer. Check the "Install supplied online books" check box, and click Next.

9. The online books install. When they're done, click Finish to complete the installation. You have the option of starting the BeachFront Quizzer engine now, or later.

To use BeachFront Quizzer, follow these steps:

1. Start BeachFront Quizzer by selecting Start ⇨ Programs ⇨ BeachFront Quizzer. The select Exam Screen appears.

2. Select the exam you want to practice for and click OK. A legal warning window appears. Click OK to continue.

3. You will be asked for the CD key. The CD key can be found in a file named Password.txt within the BFQuiz folder. Enter the CD key and click OK.

4. The BeachFront Quizzer test engine starts. Select the category you wish to study, and the study mode you want to use, and click Start.

MICROSOFT INTERNET EXPLORER

A complete copy of Microsoft Internet Explorer version 5.0 is included on the CD-ROM. You can use Internet Explorer to browse the Internet if you have an Internet connection.

To install and run Microsoft Internet Explorer, follow these steps:

1. Start Windows Explorer (if you're using Windows 95/98) or Windows NT Explorer (if you're using Windows NT), and then open the Internet Explorer 5 folder on the CD-ROM.

2. In the Internet Explorer 5 folder, double-click ie.exe and follow the instructions presented onscreen for installing Microsoft Internet Explorer.

3. To run Microsoft Internet Explorer, double-click the Internet Explorer icon on the desktop.

Netscape Communicator

The Netscape Communicator Web browser suite is included on the CD. To install and run Netscape Communicator, follow these steps:

1. Start Windows Explorer (if you're using Windows 95/98) or Windows NT Explorer (if you're using Windows NT), and then open the `Netscape Communicator 4.7` folder on the CD-ROM.

2. In the `Netscape Communicator 4.7` folder, double-click `cc32e47.exe` and follow the instructions presented onscreen for installing Netscape Communicator.

3. To run Netscape Communicator, double-click the Netscape icon on the desktop.

HTML Notes

This is a simple HTML editor with very configurable toolbars and interface. This program isn't flashy, but it's fully functional and absolutely free.

Install HTML Notes by running the single installation program `html-notes.exe` located on the CD in the `\HTML Notes` directory. During the installation process, you will be asked to select a directory on your computer to place the programs and related files into. (The full installation requires about 2.5MB of hard drive space.) Once the install program finishes, run the program by choosing Start ⇨ Program Files ⇨ HTML Notes ⇨ Html notes v1.19. Complete user documentation is provided from the HELP option within the program.

WebExpress WYSIWYG Editor

WebExpress is the easiest and most powerful Web Site designer available. Whether you are an Internet newbie or a seasoned web wonk, WebExpress's visual design environment is the perfect tool for creating sophisticated Web Sites. WebExpress is as easy to use as any word processor, and as powerful as any HTML editor.

Install WebExpress by running the single installation program `wbx32.exe` located on the CD in the `\WebExpress` directory. During the installation process, you will be asked to select a directory on your computer to place the programs and related files into. (The full installation requires about 5MB of hard drive space.) Once the install program finishes, run the program by choosing Start ⇨ Program Files ⇨ MicroVision Applications ⇨ WebExpress. Please refer to the online documentation for a detailed user guide.

SERV-U FTP SERVER

FTP Serv-U from Deerfield.com is a full-featured FTP server that allows you to turn almost any MS Windows (95/98, NT, Win3.1) computer into an Internet FTP Server. Ranked as one of the most popular FTP servers in the industry, Serv-U has won a host of awards as a best of breed FTP server

Serv-U comes in a zip-file which in turn contains a self-extracting executable which is a deluxe install program guiding you through the installation.

1. Unzip the zip-file in a temporary directory

2. Run the setup program (`setup.exe`)

The same single setup program contains both the 16- and 32-bit version of Serv-U and depending on your operating system the right one will be installed.

After starting the setup program follow the interactive dialog and it will do the hard work for you. The setup program also installs a start menu group and un-installer program. Once you are done you can delete the temporary directory with the original zip-file and the extracted files. Note that the same downloaded Serv-U executable will work on any Windows machine (3.1, 95, NT, etc.).

MDAEMON E-MAIL SERVER

MDaemon Server brings SMTP/POP3 and MIME mail services commonplace on UNIX hosts and the Internet to a Windows-based 486 or Pentium class micro-computer. MDaemon is designed to manage the e-mail needs of any number of individual users and comes complete with a powerful set of integrated tools for managing mail accounts and message formats.

MDaemon Server installs on any Microsoft Windows 95 or Windows NT computer system. The CD contains a separate version for both platforms. Please be sure you use the program appropriate for your system. SMTP and POP3 services require a Winsock compliant TCP/IP stack such as that which ships with Microsoft Windows as well as a valid Internet hookup with an ISP service.

To install using Windows 95 or Windows NT 4.0, select Add/Remove Programs from the control panel. The installation process will prompt you for some basic information such as a registration name and a root directory where MDaemon files should be created. The installation process also provides a step-by-step configuration wizard which can be used to guide you through the most common configuration scenarios.

If this is a first-time setup and you elect not to use the installer's configuration guide you will be prompted to enter your domain settings and a default set of account templates once the server is started for the first time.

A detailed installation and user guide in PDF and Word formats for both operating systems is included in the `Deerfield\MDaemon\` directory named: `MDaemon.pdf` and `MDaemon.doc`.

WINGATE PROXY SERVER

WinGate is a proxy server firewall that allows the sharing of an Internet connection with a computer network. A network is a group of computers connected together via Ethernet, phone networking adapters, cabling, or other media to facilitate resource sharing. Traditionally the type of product reserved for network specialists, WinGate 3 represents the latest innovations in Internet sharing solutions and is so simple anyone can use it.

The WinGate 3 Server component runs as a *service* on your WG Server computer, meaning that it will start when Windows starts. This is convenient since no user has to be logged in for WinGate to run, and it won't shut down when a user logs off. It operates behind the scenes without interfering with the usability of your computer.

Installation is a simple process since you use the same file to install WinGate to the WG Server, as is used to install the WinGate Internet Client (WGIC) to the WG Client(s). It is very important that you install the WG Server prior to attempting installation on the WG Client(s).

The following steps are performed on the computer with the Internet connection, which will act as the WG Server.

Locate the file on the CD in the `Deerfield\Wingate` directory. There are two versions beneath that directory depending on your operating system. The

Win9x directory contains the install file `wg3059x.exe` for Windows 95/98, and the WinNT directory contains the file `wg3059nt.exe` for Windows NT. Double-click the appropriate file to begin the installation process.

Follow the onscreen prompts to continue the installation. If the installation process detects an operational WinGate 3 Server on the network, it will default this installation to a WG Client installation. You can override this setting by clicking the WG Server installation radio button and selecting Next.

Enter the details of your trial WinGate license when prompted. Please note that

1. The "License Name" is the name under which you will or have registered WinGate

2. If you register your copy, the "License Key" is the 24-character key that was provided with your purchase of WinGateor was e-mailed to you

Easy-to-follow prompts will guide you through the installation. By default, WinGate will be installed to the directory `C:\Program Files\WinGate\` on your hard drive. You may change this to a preferred location on your hard drive, if you wish.

When the installation routine is complete, the WinGate Engine will be started automatically. Choose Start ⇨ Program Files ⇨ WinGate, and you will find that program icons are available to start and stop the service.

JWEB WEB SERVER

JWeb is a very small, yet effective Web Server. JWeb is copyrighted software, but no fee is charged for its usage. JWeb supports HTTP, directory browsing, CGI-BIN and can be configured through the web. JWeb uses highly efficient Multi-Threaded code for maximum performance.

Installation and Configuration is a snap. There is one single executable file for JWeb (which is under a megabyte). JWeb installs to a single directory and makes no relevant changes to your computer beyond this directory. That means it's very transportable. You could run a web server from a 3.5-inch disk if you desired to. This makes JWeb ideal for companies not wanting to deal with all of the configuration issues and costs associated with more complex Web server software. JWeb can be run in the background on nearly any computer.

Xitami Web server

Xitami is a high-quality portable free web server. It is distributed with source code according to a liberal License Agreement.

The installation Wizard will prompt you for an installation directory and will build a program group and icons to run Xitami. To run the installation Wizard without the iMatix logo display, pass in `-nologo` on the command line.

When you have installed Xitami, run it, then connect with any web browser. You should see the "Welcome To Xitami" test page. If Xitami cannot run on its normal port (80), it shows an error message: this can happen if another server is using port 80. You can use an alternative HTTP port such as 5080. You then connect using the URL `http://localhost:5080/`.

If you use Windows 95, be aware that the earlier versions of this OS can get into serious problems when heavily loaded with TCP/IP connections. While Windows 95 is adequate for testing and for small sites, we cannot really recommend it for serious sites—use NT or Linux. If you find that your Win95 system shows the classic Blue Screen of Death when the server is heavily loaded, consider installing the various patches and upgrades that are supplied on the Microsoft site.

Simple DNS Domain Name Server

Thanks to DNS servers we use easy-to-remember names such as `www.jhsoft.com` when surfing the Internet. DNS servers translate these domain names into IP addresses needed to locate the requested Web server. With Simple DNS Plus you can hosts your own domain name, or simply speed up Internet access by running your own DNS server. Simple DNS Plus is also a DHCP server; it comes with a DNS Look Up tool and many other features.

Install Simple DNS by running the single installation program *sdnsplus.exe* located on the CD in the `\SimpleDNS directory`. During the installation process, you will be asked to select a directory on your computer to place the programs and related files into. (The full installation requires less than 1MB of hard drive space.) Once the install program finishes, run the program by choosing Start ⇨ Program Files ⇨ Simple DNS Plus ⇨ Simple DNS Plus. Please refer to the online documentation for a detailed user guide, and to the Web site at `http://www.jhsoft.com` for additional support options.

Glossary

ActiveX A Microsoft concept for merging technologies by using an enhanced object linking and embedding (OLE) interface. ActiveX-enabled pages can feature powerful yet easy-to-use interfaces that merge virtual reality, 360-degree control over video, real-time audio, and even games into Web pages.

Advanced Research Projects Agency Network (ARPANET) The Internet's grandaddy, ARPANET was born in the late 1960s by the Defense Department. The government wanted to develop a wide –area network that could survive a nuclear war. The project started small but has developed into the Internet we know today.

Alias A short and quick nickname to refer to something else with a longer name. For example, to e-mail Danielle, if I have created an alias for Danielle's e-mail address, I just type Danielle instead of `Danielle@IDGBooks.com`. The same would apply for a system resource or application to which you assign an alias.

Anonymous FTP Logging on to a server anonymously allows you to access and download files in the public domain. If you are logging on to an FTP site from your web browser, chances are you will be logged on as anonymous automatically. Most FTP sites support anonymous access.

Application A computer program that fulfils a specific task. Applications are also called apps or simply programs. Some common Internet applications include FTP, e-mail, and Telnet. Netscape Navigator and Microsoft's Internet Explorer are also common Web applications.

Authentication The process of entering your username and password. You prove, or authenticate, that you are who you say you are when you enter your password.

Bandwidth A reference to how much data or how many independent lines of data can be carried through a communication line simultaneously.

Baud rate The number of signal events per second occurring on a communications channel. Although not technically accurate, baud rate is commonly used to mean bit rate.

Bit The basic binary unit for storing and transferring data.

bps The speed of data transmission of bits. Used as a measure of modem speeds.

Browser A software program used for viewing Web pages, a process known as *browsing*.

Browsing Moving from Web site to Web site, also known as *surfing*.

Byte A unit of measure equal to 8 bits, which can store one character of data.

Cache The area of memory on your computer where most browsers store files of Web pages that you have viewed recently. This speeds up your viewing time, but takes up space on your hard drive.

Client The computer that requests services from another computer. When you access a service, the other computer is referred to as the *server* and yours is the *client*.

Common Gateway Interface (CGI) The protocol that allows a Web page to run a program on a Web server. Forms, counters, and guest books are common examples of CGI programs.

Connect time The length of time a user is connected to the Internet, usually via a dial-up connection. Many home users pay for Internet service based on their connect time.

Cookie A text file placed on your hard drive by some Web pages that you visit. The cookie allows the Webmaster to track your visits to that Web site as well as correlate that information with other information such as the previous page you visited, your operating system, your browser plus any information that you volunteer via a form. When you return to that Web site the site will retrieve your cookie file from your hard drive and use whatever information is stored to target content and advertising to both your stated preferences (where asked) and the behavior that you exhibited. It is this technology that allows you to store items in an electronic shopping basket and remember other useful pieces of information such as passwords.

Counter A means of checking the number of visitors your page gets. Available free from many sites on the net, some of these programs also let you check the platform and browser visitors use.

daemon (Pronounced *demon*.) In UNIX environments, a program that runs in the background as a type of application on the server, such as a mail daemon.

Data Encryption Standard (DES) A standard encryption scheme approved for use within the United States by the National Security Agency.

Decryption Decoding data encrypted (often for security purposes) to its original.

Domain name The registered site name used as part of the address for an organization on the Internet.

Domain Name Service (DNS) A server service that translates the human-readable domain name of a computer connected to the Internet into a numeric IP address.

Downloading Transferring documents or programs from the Internet onto a computer.

Driver A program that controls a piece of hardware, such as a printer, modem, speaker, or terminal.

E-mail Short for electronic mail, probably the most-used aspect of the Internet. With e-mail, you can send a text message to any e-mail address on the Internet, usually instantaneously. E-mail messages can also include images, documents, programs, and more as *attachments*.

Encryption A means of encoding data, such as e-mail or credit card information, to prevent unauthorized access.

Extranet Two or more intranets connected together usually to exchange transactions between businesses.

FAQ (Frequently Asked Questions) Documents found on many Web sites that answer the most common questions visitors have about the site.

File Transfer Protocol (FTP) A protocol for uploading or downloading files between the Internet and your local system.

Firewall A program that partially or totally blocks access from the Internet to a local network. It can also refer to a method of filtering or monitoring incoming packets.

Freeware Software that is distributed free of charge, but often without customer service or much documentation.

Gateway A machine that is connected directly to the Internet backbone, also called an *IP router*. The connection is over a "dedicated" communications line capable of high-speed transfers, and the machine must remain online at all times. A gateway is often the connection point between a LAN and the Internet.

GIF (Graphics Interchange Format) A standard color image format commonly encountered on the Internet. Other common formats are TIFF, PICT, and JPEG.

Gopher A menu-based system for organizing and distributing information on the Internet that allows users to browse or download files and directories. Simpler to use but similar in functionality to FTP.

Graphical User Interface (GUI) A point-and-click user interface, where a mouse is used to position a cursor over objects displayed on the monitor and selections are made by clicking. The Macintosh operating system, Microsoft Windows, and the UNIX X Window system are examples of such an interface.

Guest When you connect to or log onto a remote computer on which you do not have your own account, you are referred to as a guest or visitor. The other computer is the host.

Hacker Originally, this term referred to skilled programmers and computer experts and connoted respect. Though this meaning is still in use, this word is now also used (especially by the media) to refer to people who deliberately try to penetrate the security of other computers. The computer user community prefers to call these people *crackers*.

Header Information at the beginning of IP Packets that describes the packet's contents and routing data.

Home page The first page of a site, a one-page site, or a company/personal page within a multi-paged site. Also used to refer to the first page displayed when you start a browser, which can be set by the user.

Hypertext A new concept for organizing information made possible by computers, where keywords or phrases can be used not only to reference additional resources but also serve as links to these resources. When viewing an HTML document with a browser, hypertext *anchors* are displayed as underlined text. Clicking on this text immediately establishes a network connection to another file (or another place in the same file), and causes the browser to display this information. The other file can be anywhere on the Internet, and may contain almost anything, including text, images, movies, or sounds.

Hypertext Markup Language (HTML) The language used for publishing content on the World Wide Web. HTML is independent of platform and browser type.

Hypertext Transfer Protocol (HTTP) A system for transferring HTML data between computers.

Internet A collection of many computer networks that communicate across dedicated high-speed phone lines using a single protocol family called TCP/IP. It consists of a backbone connected via gateways to many smaller networks such as LANs and WANs.

Internet Service Provider (ISP) A company that provides private users or companies with access to the Internet, for a fee.

InterNIC The Internet Network Information Center. The original center to set up domain names and proper gateways on the Internet backbone. They also maintain the WHOIS database.

Intranet A private network that is owned by a specific organization and uses the technology and formats of the larger Internet. An intranet resembles the Internet but is only accessible to specific users.

IP address A 32-bit binary number identifying the unique position of a computer on the Internet. Users do not normally use IP addresses for navigation because they are difficult to remember. DNS converts easy-to-remember URLs into IP addresses.

ISDN (Integrated Services Digital Network) A voice and data telephone network that can carry a greater amount of data than copper telephone wires.

JPEG (Joint Photographic Experts Group) A standard (compressed) format for color images, common on the Internet. JPEGs tend to be smaller files than GIFs.

Keywords A selection of words used with META tags or placed on Search Engines to make it easy for people to find your site.

Links A means of moving from one location to another within an HTML file. Links can be used from one part of a page to another part of the same page (internal links), from one part of a site to another part of the same site (on-site links), and from one site to another site (off-site links).

Linux A freeware implementation of the UNIX operating system for use with PCs.

LISTSERV A program for the management of electronic mailing lists that allows the user to join lists, quit lists, and send messages to mailing lists.

Local Area Network (LAN) A network local to a building, company, institute, etc. that usually has only a single point of access to the Internet.

Mailing list A mechanism for the simultaneous distribution of e-mail messages to a group of subscribed e-mail users. Mailing lists often function as electronic newsletters or magazines.

META tag Tags placed at the beginning of an HTML fileincluding the title, keywords, and short description of content, to be read by Search Engine spiders or robots, which makes your page easier to search.

MIME (Multipurpose Internet Mail Extensions) A way to encapsulate binary file attachments (such as images and sounds) into e-mail messages.

Mirror site A secondary or backup site where files are made available for download, if the original site has too much traffic.

Modem A hardware device that enables your computer to communicate with other computers over phone lines.

MPEG A format for a series of compressed images, to be played as a movie.

Multimedia A term for any file involving several different media such as graphics, animation, and sound.

Netnews A collection of electronic bulletin boards on a huge variety of topics, available on the Internet. Also, the information available from these bulletin boards.

Newsgroup A UseNet discussion group or bulletin board. See *netnews*.

NIC Also Network Interface Card. A device used in computers to connect them to a network.

Operating System (OS) Low-level software that performs a variety of basic functions such as copying, deleting, and renaming files; creating, deleting, and listing directories; memory management; connecting to networks; etc., that must be run before any application software can be used.

Packet When data is transmitted through networks, it is often broken up into small packets rather than being sent as a continuous byte stream. This allows multiple transmissions to share the same line, and also facilitates error detection.

Page A set of text and images saved at one URL address. This material may be longer than one printed page but is referred to as a single page.

Pixel One dot on a computer screen. Most computer monitors typically range from either 640 pixels wide by 480 pixels high to 1600 by 1200.

Plug-ins Software program additions that allow you to take advantage of new technologies and capabilities from your browser. You can frequently download plug-ins from the author's Website with their permission for free.

Point of Presence (POP) Connections to your ISP through which you connect to the Internet. Choosing an ISP with a POP near you can reduce connection costs.

Point-to-Point Protocol (PPP) The protocol used to transmit data across a LAN.

Post Office Protocol version 3 (POP3) The most common method of e-mail transfer.

Postmaster An individual or group responsible for ensuring the delivery of e-mail at a specific domain. If you have a problem with e-mail, or can't find a user's address by other means, you can send e-mail to ~~postmaster@host~~, where *host* is the domain you're trying to send mail to.

Protocol A standardized set of rules defining how two machines will communicate with one another via their local software over a network. Often includes error detection/correction schemes.

Request for Comments (RFC) The working notes of the committees that develop the protocols and standards of the Internet, including proposed changes. These documents contain a great deal of information about the Internet standards, and are maintained by the Internet Activities Board (IAB).

Search Engine A program enabling Internet users to find specific sites or subjects on the Internet, instead of requiring users to know the specific URL that contains the information they want.

Server A high-end computer used to provide network services to workstation computers. See *client*.

Service The programs, protocols, etc. that are made available to users by their service provider. These may include e-mail and standard utilities like FTP, Web, telnet, and e-mail.

Shareware Software that is distributed for a small fee on the honor system. There is a large shareware community that is philosophically opposed to selling software for profit.

Site A location where a company's Web pages and other Internet services can be accessed, usually through a single IP address.

Spam Mass unsolicited e-mailing by companies or individuals wanting to sell their services, sites, or products.

Syntax The way in which words are put together to form valid computer commands. Typically a command will be followed by a list of arguments, with the arguments separated by spaces, commas, or some other delimiter.

TCP/IP Transmission Control Protocol/Internet Protocol. A widely used family of protocols that has been the official standard for the Internet since 1983. This family includes protocols for handling data transport, routing, addresses, user services, gateways, and other services.

telnet A standard utility for logging onto a remote computer.

Text file A file containing text characters (usually ASCII) that can be viewed with any standard text editor. Most mail utilities can only handle text files.

Uniform Resource Locator (URL) The address of a particular page, image, or sound on the World Wide Web. URLs are converted to IP addresses with DNS.

UNIX A popular operating system with many variants, which supports multiple users and multi-tasking. The philosophy behind UNIX is to provide a large number of simple and efficient utility routines for specific tasks that can then be chained together to solve more complex problems.

Uploading Sending work from the publisher's computers to the Internet to be available worldwide.

UseNet Short for Users' Network. A text-based mechanism which supports discussion groups, called *newsgroups*, that allow users from anywhere on the Internet to participate. Though a service rather than a network, it is one of the more popular Internet services.

User Someone who uses a computer, network, or piece of software.

Utility An application or subroutine designed with a very particular task in mind, like converting between two formats.

uuencode Short for Unix-to-Unix encoding. A UNIX utility for converting binary files to ASCII for transmission via e-mail between UNIX machines. On the receiving end, uudecode is used to convert back to binary.

Wide Area Network (WAN) Large-scale networks that encompass more than one physical building, and are often connected to the Internet.

Web page A hypertext page on the World Wide Web.

Web site An Internet location comprising one or more Web pages.

WHOIS A program and accompanying database maintained by the InterNIC for obtaining e-mail adresses and other information about other Internet users. It is meant to be a database of all Internet users, but is far from complete.

World Wide Web (WWW) Also called "the Web." A system which allows users to graphically browse through documents on sites throughout the Internet and follow pointers (called links or hyperlinks) to other documents that can be anywhere. These documents can contain text, graphics, sounds, and even movies. The original idea was developed at CERN (the European Laboratory for Particle Physics) between 1989 and 1992.

Index

Symbols and Numbers

/ (forward slash), 170
(comment symbol), 116
<! (comment tag), 170
<>. *See* tags, HTML; *specific tags*
~ (tilde), 219
3Com corporation, 243
6bone, 371–372

A

<A> tag, 174
access, Internet. *See also* connecting to
    the Internet
  handheld devices, 243–244
  Internet Phone, 245–246
  WebTV, 244–245
access control lists, 325
ACTION parameter, 196
Active Server Pages, 248
ActiveX, 167, 219
Address Resolution Protocol (ARP),
    317–318
Adobe Acrobat, 230
ADSL (Asymmetric Digital Subscriber
    Line), 296
Advanced Research Projects Agency
    (ARPA), 14
advertising. *See* marketing, Internet
Aldus, 229
ALIGN attribute, cell, 181
Amazon.com
  auctions, 354
  cookies, 158

value-added services, 353–354
America Online (AOL)
  Instant Messenger, 134–135
  oversubscription of service by, 32
analog dial-up connection, 8, 9
anchor tag (<A>), 174
animation, GIF file, 229
antivirus software, 150–151
  signature files, 338–339
  updating, 338–339
  where to deploy scanning, 337–338
AOL. *See* America Online (AOL)
Apache Software Foundation (ASF), 248
Apache Web server, 248
API. *See* Application Program Interface
    (API)
application gateway, 288
Application Program Interface (API), 167,
    203, 217
ARP (Address Resolution Protocol),
    317–318
ARPA (Advanced Research Projects
    Agency), 14
assembly language, 221
Asymmetric Digital Subscriber Line
    (ADSL), 296
Asynchronous Transfer Mode (ATM), 295
Atrium Software, 267
auction, online, 354
auditing, 331
authentication, user, 326–329
authorizations, credit card, 355–356
AVI (Audio video Interleaved), 231
Axent, 330

Continued

Continued

The Xitami Web Server on the companion CD-ROM is not covered by this IDG Books Worldwide, Inc. End-User License Agreement, but by the license agreement included on the CD-ROM together with the Xitami Web Server.

IDG BOOKS WORLDWIDE, INC. END-USER LICENSE AGREEMENT

subscriber system or bulletin-board system, or (iii) modify, adapt, or create derivative works based on the Software.

(b) You may not reverse engineer, decompile, or disassemble the Software. You may transfer the Software and user documentation on a permanent basis, provided that the transferee agrees to accept the terms and conditions of this Agreement and you retain no copies. If the Software is an update or has been updated, any transfer must include the most recent update and all prior versions.

4. <u>Restrictions on Use of Individual Programs.</u> You must follow the individual requirements and restrictions detailed for each individual program in Appendix D of this Book. These limitations are also contained in the individual license agreements recorded on the Software Media. These limitations may include a requirement that after using the program for a specified period of time, the user must pay a registration fee or discontinue use. By opening the Software packet(s), you will be agreeing to abide by the licenses and restrictions for these individual programs that are detailed in Appendix D and on the Software Media. None of the material on this Software Media or listed in this Book may ever be redistributed, in original or modified form, for commercial purposes.

5. <u>Limited Warranty.</u>

(a) IDGB warrants that the Software and Software Media are free from defects in materials and workmanship under normal use for a period of sixty (60) days from the date of purchase of this Book. If IDGB receives notification within the warranty period of defects in materials or workmanship, IDGB will replace the defective Software Media.

(b) IDGB AND THE AUTHOR OF THE BOOK DISCLAIM ALL OTHER WARRANTIES, EXPRESS OR IMPLIED, INCLUDING WITHOUT LIMITATION IMPLIED WARRANTIES OF MERCHANTABILITY AND FITNESS FOR A PARTICULAR PURPOSE, WITH RESPECT TO THE SOFTWARE, THE PROGRAMS, THE SOURCE CODE CONTAINED THEREIN, AND/OR THE TECHNIQUES DESCRIBED IN THIS BOOK. IDGB DOES NOT WARRANT THAT THE FUNCTIONS CONTAINED IN THE SOFTWARE WILL MEET YOUR REQUIREMENTS OR THAT THE OPERATION OF THE SOFTWARE WILL BE ERROR FREE.

(c) This limited warranty gives you specific legal rights, and you may have other rights that vary from jurisdiction to jurisdiction.

6. Remedies.

(a) IDGB's entire liability and your exclusive remedy for defects in materials and workmanship shall be limited to replacement of the Software Media, which may be returned to IDGB with a copy of your receipt at the following address: Software Media Fulfillment Department, Attn.: *i-Net+ Certification Study System*, IDG Books Worldwide, Inc., 10475 Crosspoint Blvd., Indianapolis, IN 46256, or call 1-800-762-2974. Please allow three to four weeks for delivery. This Limited Warranty is void if failure of the Software Media has resulted from accident, abuse, or misapplication. Any replacement Software Media will be warranted for the remainder of the original warranty period or thirty (30) days, whichever is longer.

(b) In no event shall IDGB or the author be liable for any damages whatsoever (including without limitation damages for loss of business profits, business interruption, loss of business information, or any other pecuniary loss) arising from the use of or inability to use the Book or the Software, even if IDGB has been advised of the possibility of such damages.

(c) Because some jurisdictions do not allow the exclusion or limitation of liability for consequential or incidental damages, the above limitation or exclusion may not apply to you.

7. U.S. Government Restricted Rights.
Use, duplication, or disclosure of the Software by the U.S. Government is subject to restrictions stated in paragraph (c)(1)(ii) of the Rights in Technical Data and Computer Software clause of DFARS 252.227-7013, and in subparagraphs (a) through (d) of the Commercial Computer — Restricted Rights clause at FAR 52.227-19, and in similar clauses in the NASA FAR supplement, when applicable.

8. General.
This Agreement constitutes the entire understanding of the parties and revokes and supersedes all prior agreements, oral or written, between them and may not be modified or amended except in a writing signed by both parties hereto that specifically refers to this Agreement. This Agreement shall take precedence over any other documents that may be in conflict herewith. If any one or more provisions contained in this

Agreement are held by any court or tribunal to be invalid, illegal, or otherwise unenforceable, each and every other provision shall remain in full force and effect.

my2cents.idgbooks.com

Register This Book — And Win!

Visit **http://my2cents.idgbooks.com** to register this book and we'll automatically enter you in our fantastic monthly prize giveaway. It's also your opportunity to give us feedback: let us know what you thought of this book and how you would like to see other topics covered.

Discover IDG Books Online!

The IDG Books Online Web site is your online resource for tackling technology — at home and at the office. Frequently updated, the IDG Books Online Web site features exclusive software, insider information, online books, and live events!

10 Productive & Career-Enhancing Things You Can Do at www.idgbooks.com

- Nab source code for your own programming projects.

- Download software.

- Read Web exclusives: special articles and book excerpts by IDG Books Worldwide authors.

- Take advantage of resources to help you advance your career as a Novell or Microsoft professional.

- Buy IDG Books Worldwide titles or find a convenient bookstore that carries them.

- Register your book and win a prize.

- Chat live online with authors.

- Sign up for regular e-mail updates about our latest books.

- Suggest a book you'd like to read or write.

- Give us your 2¢ about our books and about our Web site.

You say you're not on the Web yet? It's easy to get started with IDG Books' *Discover the Internet*, available at local retailers everywhere.

INSTALLATION INSTRUCTIONS

Each software item on the *i-Net+ Certification Study System* CD-ROM is located in its own folder. To install a particular piece of software, open its folder with My Computer or Internet Explorer. What you do next depends on what you find in the software's folder:

1. First, look for a ReadMe.txt file or a .doc or .htm document. If this is present, it should contain installation instructions and other useful information.

2. If the folder contains an executable (.exe) file, this is usually an installation program. Often it will be called Setup.exe or Install.exe, but in some cases the filename reflects an abbreviated version of the software's name and version number. Run the .exe file to start the installation process.

3. In the case of some simple software, the .exe file probably is the software—no real installation step is required. You can run the software from the CD to try it out. If you like it, copy it to your hard disk and create a Start menu shortcut for it.

The ReadMe.txt file in the CD-ROM's root directory may contain additional installation information, so be sure to check it.

For a listing of the software on the CD-ROM, see Appendix D.